PALESTINE STORIES

Mansor visited Ramallah in September, 1999 and
twenty years later wrote this novel, set in 1915-1936,
before the first Arab Revolt...

Mansor
bin Puteh

26 25 24 23 22 21   9 8 7 6 5 4 3 2 1

PALESTINE STORIES

Copyright ©2021 Mansor bin Puteh

Published by Emergent Press USA
Tulsa, OK

* * * * * *

The Prophet Mohammad (Peace and blessings
of Allah be upon him) said:
'Whoever among you sees an evil action, let him change
it with his hand (by taking action); if he cannot, then
with his tongue (by speaking out); and if he cannot, then
with his heart (by at least hating it and believing that it
is wrong), and that is the weakest of faith.'
(Narrated by Muslim in his 'Saheeh'.)

* * * * * **

'The most excellent Jihad is that for the conquest of self.'
(Narrated by Bukhari.)
'Allah will not give mercy to anyone, except those who
give mercy to other creatures.'
(Narrated by Abdullah b. Amr: Abu
Dawud and Tirmidhi.)

* * * * * *

CONTENTS

1

Prologue: Off to Ramallah In September, 1999

September, 1999.:

I wrote an email to the Khalil Sakakini Cultural Center (KSCC) in Ramallah, on the West Bank in Palestine, and I immediately received a reply from them inviting me to come over to show some of my film and other works at their center, which then would allow me, to have special permission from the Malaysian government to make the trip to Palestine (or Israel) since visas had to be applied for at the Israeli Embassy in Jordan, Amman.

It was exactly a year after my father, Puteh bin Sulong died on 15 September, 1998, aged eighty-eight years.

The officer at the Prime Minister's Department, then in Kuala Lumpur, approved my application and off I went to Amman in Jordon, flying on Pakistan International Airlines (PIA) with a long stopover at Karachi Airport. I was forced to purchase a business class return ticket from Kuala Lumpur International Airport (KLIA), that allowed me to go to the special room to rest and stretch out and enjoy some refreshments before taking the connecting flight to Amman.

And what I was not expecting to happen, did happen on the flight out of KLIA to Karachi, when I found out that there were many vacant seats in the economy class, but I was not allowed to purchase a ticket for this class because the ticketing agent in Kuala Lumpur said all economy tickets had been sold and I had to get one in the business class which I found out when I was on the plane, not to be true. In the business class there was just another passenger, a Japanese. So, the in-flight staff did not have much to do other than to try and force us to eat food they were serving at two a.m., Malaysian time, when I would be fast asleep, if not for the flight that had kept me awake.

And at that time security was not tight inside the cabins and I was able to go to the cockpit with its door unlocked and I could see the captains sitting there.

At Karachi, transit passengers, were given a night's stay in their transit hotel called the Midway Hotel which is not very far from the airport. I took my luggage out of the airport and an elderly Pakistani man quickly grabbed it and carried it to the small bus that was taking the transit passengers to the Hotel and demanded to be paid. I wanted to argue with him but a fellow passenger I had met at the airport in Kuala Lumpur, also a Pakistani, like him, but who worked in Malaysia, immediately pulled out a Five-Malaysian ringgit note and handed it to him because he did not want me to create a stir and to shoot the old Pakistani man. The Pakistani felt embarrassed that I had to experience this because I could easily have carried my own luggage to the bus which was no more than twenty feet away from the exit door of the arrival hall of the airport to the bus that was already waiting for the transit passengers.

The next day, I got a cab and asked the driver to take me around the city of Karachi without getting out of the cab for most of the time, and took photos with my old analogue camera, before bringing me back to the hotel for me to go to the airport for the next flight to Amman, Jordan, which is what I normally do when I am in a new city I had not been to before, and there was no time to spend there. I would get a cab for five hours to go anywhere the driver takes me, after I told him what I would like to see in their city, which is usually, the old section and the bazaars.

I had not been to Jordan before or Israel, but had been to Karachi when I flew on PIA to return to New York City from Malaysia in 1980 to resume classes at Columbia University in the city, after taking a three-month break in Malaysia. The one-year break I got from school as 'medical leave' following the two surgeries I had at the St. Luke's Hospital and the Memorial Sloan-Kettering Cancer Center, both in Manhattan forced me to walk with the aid of two crutches for many years. But for this trip I did not use them because I was able to walk on my own two feet unaided, for ambulation, which also allowed me to carry luggage on my own. It was also good to know that Malaysians were not required to have a visa to visit Jordan. It is also good that the Malaysian passport is good to use to visit more than one hundred and fifty countries.

It would not have been possible for me to visit Ramallah in Palestine if not for the invitation that came from KSCC. And traveling from Amman in Jordan to Ramallah was not easy. The organizers asked for my particulars allowing them to apply for a visa to enter 'Israel' which I gave, however, after landing at the Queen Alian International Airport (QAIA) outside of Amman, where I could see some disabled Iraqi Airways Boeing planes sitting on the tarmac. I got a cab to go to the border thinking that I could pass through immigration and then take another cab to go to Ramallah.

I got there close to midnight when I got to at Allenby Bridge (Named after British General Edmund Allenby), also known as the King Hussein Bridge which is located at the West Bank-Israeli border and was told I could not pass through immigration by the Israeli officers because there was no visa for me that was left with them. I had no choice but to take another cab back to Amman around midnight and had to go to a bus station which was packed with local passengers. They turned to look at the entrance and saw me and I quickly greeted them with 'Asalamulaikum' (Peace be with you) and all of a sudden all of those passengers who were inside the station replied the greeting with 'Mulaikum salam' (Peace be with you too) which sounded as a roar to my ears.

The bridge crosses the Jordan River near the city of Jericho which was the only point between Jordan and Palestine where the locals from the two countries and visitors from abroad could cross to get into either of the two countries. It has a long history because it was first built in 1918, and rebuilt in 1968 and completed in 1994, or five years before I arrived there for the first time. It was built over the remnants of the old bridge by a British General Edmund Allenby, hence it was renamed after him.

I busied myself or distracted myself from reading about the history of this bridge as a way to not get annoyed because I was not able to pass the immigration at the bridge to go to Ramallah, and had to turn around to return to Amman and see if there was a way for me to get a visa that would allow me to go to Ramallah later, or if I might have to remain in Amman and Jordan for the whole period and to fly back to Malaysia later without ever going to Ramallah in the West Bank of Palestine.

The trip in the cab from the station to Amman took a while, and in total darkness for most of the trip, and I did not know where the driver was taking me. I tried to remain calm and did not want ugly thoughts entering my head. The cab-driver and his friend sitting beside me asked me to recite some verses from the Noble Qu'ran to ensure that I was a Muslim; once I had done that they were happy and relieved to know that I was.

I did not look Arabic or even Melayu, but Japanese, (That's what many say, and even when I am in Japan, the locals there also thought so!) so when I told them earlier I was a Muslim they did not fully think so, and hence they thought there was a need for me to show my affirmation to the religion, which I did. I asked them to send me to a hotel in the city and they sent me to one which is near the Coliseum, a simple hotel called Al-Hajal Hotel where I hoped to stay for the few days I was stuck in the city with no prospect of ever crossing into Palestine to get to Ramallah. More expensive hotels are located elsewhere and not in the city center where the historical sites are especially the Roman Coliseum, where there are many souvenir stores and restaurants where I can easily grab a bite if and when I want to, because the small hotel I was staying at did not have any restaurant in it.

At the same time, I sent a fax to KSCC to inform them on my whereabouts in case if they thought they could get somebody to come and see me and help me to get a visa to go there.

Earlier I had contacted the Malaysian Embassy in Amman when I was still in Malaysia and they did not see me at the airport and I did not think of them. But they surprised me by coming to the hotel the next morning and took me to the embassy and told me that they could help me get a visa so the official and his local staff who drove the car could join me to go to Palestine although they would leave me at the hotel in Ramallah or 'Ramle' so they could proceed to Baitullaham or 'Bethlehem' for the night.

I did not tell them where I was staying, at which hotel in the city, and still they managed to locate me two days after I arrived at Amman, and not knowing if I would ever make it to Ramallah for the function that was starting without me. They appeared at the counter on the ground floor of the small hotel and someone called me to come down to meet them. I asked how did they know where I was staying and they said they got the information on my whereabouts from the local authorities who they told me were informed by hotels of foreigners who had come to stay at their hotel. I thought it was a marvelous system so that foreigners, once they entered the country and registered to stay at any hotel, big or small, expensive or cheap ones, are registered with those authorities too. And I thought, Malaysia, too, should have similar system to determine where the foreign tourists in Malaysia stay and if they are not engaged in unlawful activities. And if they overstay, they can be easily apprehended.

They then took me to the house of the official to wait for a while before going to the Israeli Embassy which is located in the middle of a residential area for the wealthy; but the entire building of the embassy sits in vacant land around it and there was a queue of Palestinians lining up to get their visas or permits to return to Palestine. I waited outside of the embassy and far away near some stores while the two persons from the Malaysian embassy entered it to apply for visas for the three of us. This took a while to get done.

I was told the Palestinians had to queue in the hot weather in summer and in the cold of winter for hours before they could even get to the door of the Israeli embassy.

Once we were done, we drove all the way to the border called the Jordan River Border Control where we were subjected to through inspection and our car was also given a though inspection with the final ritual when it was driven by an Israeli staff into a room which turned out to be an x-ray area where they looked into the car for hidden objects.

In the end we were at the border control for two hours, before being allowed to move on to drive towards Ramallah where KSCC had booked a room for me to stay for the night. The trip took me along areas I was not familiar with, passing through a vast and wide desert, which quite resembled Saudi Arabia which I had been to in January, 1981, when I took the bus from Jeddah to Madinnah and from Madinnah to Makkeh to perform Umrah or Minor Hajj.

I spent the first day in Amman touring the historical site, the Roman Coliseum which is just across the street from the hotel where I was staying, where a large photo of King Abdullah is hung with tourists hanging around the Coliseum to take photos and buy souvenirs at the stores nearby. There is even a broken statue of what looks like a Roman gladiator with his head and legs severed. How could they just put it at the side of the wall in the Coliseum like that, like it has no historical value or financial worth, especially to thieves? I only took some photos of it and of the Coliseum and walked away.

I then walked further to go to the other sites, to pass my time in Amman away before my return flight to KLIA, and thinking that the trip I had made to Ramallah to attend the function would end here in Amman.

But the visit by the two officers from the Malaysian Embassy changed all that and they gave me the opportunity to really make the trip to Ramallah, even though by the time I would arrive the two-day function at the cultural center would be over with the forum with me not happening.

The trip in the car owned by the official of the Malaysian Embassy ran through vast and empty desert most of the way, passing some isolated villages and small towns, one of which we stopped at for refueling. I got some yellow dates from them and ate one or two. They were not yet fully ripe so they had a bit of bitter taste, which I took to be the taste of young dates. I saw a small group of Palestinian kids across the street far away from the petrol station and waved at them. I did not see any of their faces. But I could guess that they were in the mid-teens. They waved back. I held some of the dates to indicate that I wanted them to have some. And when our car was moving I quickly put some of the dates on a bench for them to come and take them to eat.

It was late evening when we got to Ramallah and the driver of the car sent me to the hotel where a room had been booked for me by the cultural center and I was told by the hotel staff that the center is not so far away from it and I could go there tomorrow morning after breakfast. The two officers from the embassy drove off to go to Baitullaham where the driver has his parents' house to stay in for the night with the Malaysian officer, and they would return to the hotel tomorrow afternoon to pick me up to drive back to Amman. And we were due to drive to Baitulmukaddis or Jerusalem.

I was in Ramallah, Palestine and not in Israel although I was given a visa from the Israeli Embassy in Amman and got through the Israeli immigration checkpoint but I do not want to think I am in Israel but Palestine and in the City of Ramallah.

I had not seen any Israeli Jews the whole time I was here except for the officers at the checkpoint, and once at a petrol station I had gone to the toilet to relieve myself when an Israeli man around forty years appeared and I greeted him with 'Shalom' to test if he would respond. He did with the same word.

I also noticed some Japanese tourists by the roadside but they looked very confident and that made me wonder if they were tourists or long-time residents of Israel.

It was also at the time when the two-state solution was said to happen in a couple of months, but in the end the plan could not happen and war broke up between Israel and Palestine which caused the plan to be totally forgotten. Maybe the Israeli aggression on the West Bank was made to look like the plan had failed. Indeed, it was and till now, in October, 2019, the situation in Palestine's Gaza Strip and West Bank had shrunk even more than it was then in September, 1999, or twenty years ago.

The few Palestinian kids who were sitting across the street from the petrol station along the long desert road from Amman to Ramallah, to who I had offered some young yellow dates must be in their late thirties or forties by now and who amongst them had been killed and become martyrs of the Cause of Palestine? I have seen reports in the newspapers and on television in Malaysia on some Palestinians men who had been bombed to smithereens or kidnapped and tortured through most of the years since 1999 till now, in an endless war which is clearly one-sided that left the Palestinians with no way of standing up to their aggressors who knew not how to defend themselves, only to launch attacks on the flimsiest excuse often more vicious than whatever attacks that might have been launched by some Palestinians using stones and others by IDF infiltrators themselves.

It is twenty years now since I first went to Palestine and the situation there is worse today than it was then, from the press reports that anyone can see on the internet and newspapers with more Palestinian lands being seized turning the Gaza Strip and West Bank into nothing more than tiny areas for the Palestinians surrounded by settler compounds where even roads are not connecting the small patches of land and whose total population, especially the young children and men and women having been detained, with their houses and buildings razed. Even their olive groves were burnt, just before the harvest season by the settlers and it is done under the watchful eyes of the IDF who looked elsewhere.

The two-state solution is dead!

Turkish President Tayyip Erdogan brought into the United Nations (UN) General Assembly meeting in New York City, a series of maps of Palestine that showed how it looked like in 1948 when the state of Israel was first established to the recent ones that show how Palestine lands had been seized leaving with nothing more than tiny areas in the Gaza Strip and West Bank that would soon be seized, to complete the land-grabbing exercises conducted by Israel, over more than seven decades! Yet, Erdogan, continued to add, Israel, when it was admitted into the UN as a member, never revealed to the international organization its borders!

I was driven through the West Bank to Ramallah and all around me was empty desert which looked pristine then in 1999, or twenty years ago. The lights were low and the intensity became less harsh as we approached Ramallah which was close to sunset.

I lay on the bed in my room in the small hotel in Ramallah and across the street at the left of the hotel is a church and beside it is the KSCC where I would be going to tomorrow morning to see the official at the Center to see what else that I could do there, now that my program to show my few works had taken place before I got to Ramallah and the forum that was scheduled to happen had passed. I would be there merely as a visitor, to look at the Center.

And the next morning after breakfast I walked to the Center and met a woman who took me around the Center and even showed me the desk where a prominent Palestinian poet, Mohammad Darwish worked.

After the visit to the Center, my two friends from the Malaysian Embassy in Amman who had taken me to the hotel in Ramallah returned to the hotel and picked me up; they would be sending me back to the airport in Amman for my flight back to Malaysia. But we would be stopping briefly at Baitulmukaddis or Jerusalem for a visit where I hoped to visit the Dome of the Rock or 'Qubbat As-Sakhrah' and Masjid Al-Aqsa which were known by the Arabs as 'Al Haram Al Sharif'. This would make my trip to Ramallah, although not as planned, with the screening of my works held without my presence and the forum not held, to be eventful. It was not easy for Malaysians then to be able to visit Baitulmukaddis and not many had gone there by then. After all, for Muslims the Masjid Al-Aqsa is the third most sacred 'mosque' or masjid in Islam after the Majidil Haram in Makkah and Masjid Nabawi in Madinnah in Saudi Arabia. And it was at the Dome of the Rock where Nabi Muhammad, Peace be upon Him (P.b.u.h.) or 'Sallah alaihi wasallam' or (s.a.w.) ascended to Heaven on the Night Journey or Flight flying on the Buraq. And Nabi Muhammad, (s.a.w.) was reported by Tharmizi to have remarked, 'I met Nabi Ibrahim, a.s. on the night journey (through the Heavens) and he said to me, 'O, Muhammad, (s.a.w.), give me my salaam to your Ummah and tell them that Jannah (Heaven) is a wide plain with pure oil and sweet water. And the plants grow there by saying, 'Subhan Allah, Alhamdulillah, laa ilaaha il Allah, ALlahu Akhbar.'

Driving from Ramallah to Baitulmukaddis took two hours and once we were there, we walked in the Old Quarter, in the Arab Section. Because I did not have at that time any digital recording device such as a digital camera and camcorder, I could not record video or take many photos because the analogue camera I still used had limitations; I also did not have with me that many rolls of film. So I shot photos with the Nikon I had bought at the store in Boston, sparingly. I would not know when I could return to Baitulmukaddis or Palestine again. It would be good if such an opportunity could avail itself so I can be sure to record a lot of video footages and thousands of photos using digital cameras I would be bringing with me.

A Malaysian friend of mine said he spent about two weeks traveling in Palestine and Israel and even went to as far as Haifa and Tel Aviv. I was stunned because I thought Malaysians are forbidden by the government to go beyond Baitulmukaddis; so I was intrigued when he casually told me how he and some of his friends had gone to those places. They rented a van and traveled everywhere in Israel.

From Baitulmukaddis we drove to the airport outside of Amman and I was close to boarding time when we got there; and during the entire time we were driving from Baitulmukaddis I was worried if would get to the airport in time without missing the flight.

I made it there in time and dutifully checked in at the business class counter of PIA, which unfortunately was also opened to economy class passengers and because of that I had to wait in line with them. I tried to complain with the PIA counter staff who immediately removed the sign which said 'business class'. And not only that, he also removed my luggage tag to send my luggage to KLIA and replaced it with another tag to send it to 'Lahore' in Pakistan! In the end when I got to KLIA my luggage was not on the turnstile; and I had to lodge a report for the loss of the luggage. It was returned to me after the PIA staff in Pakistan managed to locate it in Lahore, and twelve days after I returned from Amman.

I was not worried about the contents inside the luggage which were mostly clothes, but of the rolls of film I had mistakenly left in it which had all the photos I had taken on the trip to Jordan, Palestine and Israel. There were about two hundred photos which I later printed to remind me of the trip.

There were only two passengers in the business class; me and another Japanese. And the in-flight staff of PIA was not so particular and allowed passengers, mostly Pakistanis, in the economy class to grab vacant seats in the business class so in the end the two business class passengers including me, were given economy class service throughout the flight from Amman to Karachi in Pakistan which took about seven hours, with food not offered on china ware but in packages. "Why are you sitting here"? I asked the old Pakistani man who was now sitting in the vacant seat beside me, that I thought I could use to put my sling bag where my note book and a camera are. He did not say a word; he did not want to look guilty. But did he know that stealing anything, including a seat in a plane of a higher class was not good, wrong and punishment for theft in Islam is harsh? He did not care.

I could have taken action on PIA then for giving shabby treatment to their business class passengers by allowing passengers from the economy class to invade their space thus spoiling our flight. But I did not, as I was happy and relieved to be handed my luggage with the film in it.

There was some respite at the Karachi Airport when I was allowed to wait during transit to catch the connecting flight to KLIA, and sit in the business class lounge where snacks were offered. I was able to stretch my legs for an hour or so before the next flight took off.

And what did I get out of the trip to Palestine? Plenty! This novel is influenced from that trip I had taken twenty years ago, which also allowed me to come up with a novel to write and complete soon after the trip; and this one I am writing...

OCTOBER, 2019.:

I got an idea, which was to write a novel set in Palestine before or during the British Palestine Mandate of 28 July, 1922, which was about a Palestinian family doing about their business that did not touch on any religious or racial issues or matters; they just spend their time with each other and were not fully aware of what was happening in their village or country or the world.

After so many years, I decided to not wait further and start to write and write, and after a while I noticed that the plot had changed course, and this, to me, was for the better, because I felt like the characters were taking me deeper into their lives. I could not guess what that was, because I had not lived anywhere in Palestine for an extended period of time and had only been there to stay for the night in a hotel in Ramallah in September, 1999, and that was twenty years ago. Palestine and the whole of the Middle East had seen tremendous changes from the Palestine and Middle East of twenty years before.

And with no written notes or names of Palestinians I had met and the villages they came from and lived all their lives, I could not depend on my memory to guide me along, and I was forced to invent names for most of the time and decided not to give some characters names, their villages and towns, or cities where they lived. Worse, I had also jumbled the names of some of the characters for which I am not going to make the necessary corrections. And I am not going to feel guilty about it by being exact in this way, and let these names be written, although they may be of different persons in the story and novel, so that in the end this will look and read like a novel which is totally different than the others I had written. Some can compare to see the differences and hopefully appreciate and understand why this novel is written in this fashion and style, that some can see it as one which tries to uphold Islamic values in literature and not one that tries to compete with the many styles writers in the west have chosen to use as it was the styles that they had copied and improved upon that were introduced in the past using their social, cultural and religious or non-religious values to guide them alone.

I am happy with the style I am trying to show in this novel and am not making any excuses as to why it is this way, and does not resemble the styles that they were familiar with.

2

Ahmed and I

I never actually met Munir in person. I never knew what he looked like when he was alive. I met or saw his shadows lying in the desert, long before he was gone…when his son was relating about him and his exploits. He was killed when he was approaching forty years, after having married two women, one after the other and getting five children from each of his wives. His eldest son Ahmed related the story of his father one fine day when I found myself sitting in a restaurant in a small town along the way from Amman to Ramallah. We had stopped just to stretch our legs, to have some snacks, check out what they were serving, and the local delicacies, some of which I had eaten in Amman at the restaurant where they sold them. But Ahmed was quick to say and admit that his late father was not a hero; there are many others whose deeds were recorded and duly acknowledged by the Palestinians. Munir was a local hero.

But this novel is not about what he had done when he was alive and in his adulthood before he was killed by the Israeli Defense Force (IDF) soldiers. It is about the time when he was a small boy living in a small village in Palestine, before any Jew had come to seek help and support from the local population after they were thrown out of some countries in Europe, especially Germany, Poland, and the former Soviet Union or USSR for Union of Soviet Socialist Republics. Munir was a young boy, no more than ten years. I got his first son to relate to me his story, briefly, but with some imagination I managed to piece in those that Ahmed could not express in his halting English and the limited vocabulary he had. Fortunately, I managed to understand what he was saying in English in the thick Arabic accent that he had. It added color and brought me closer to the character of his father, Munir, the local hero of Palestine who grew up in a small village even his son had difficulty in remembering. I was not concerned with that; I only wanted to know what life was like for him in Palestine – in 1936! That was eleven years before the Partition of Palestine and twelve years before the 'Al-Nakbah' or 'Dispossession' or 'Displacement' or at its most apt, 'Catastrophe.'

Ahmed, is also not his real name. And Munir is also not the real name of his father. I made them up because for convenience because I had to give the characters in this novel real Palestinian names. But they are real characters, like all those that are in this novel who I will reveal one by one in due course, when the plot reaches them.

I also do not know how Munir looked like, how tall he was, etc. I could imagine by looking at Ahmed, if he might resemble his late father. He said, no! Ahmed said, he took the features, or was given the features of his mother, Asma, who is now in her late eighties and not feeling well and might not be the person for me or anyone to probe into her past. She was Munir's second wife; his first one died, at a young age, in 1966, she was not yet thirty, with the name of Maimunah. All of Munir's children have gotten married and many are living in countries around Palestine mostly in Amman, Jordan, with Ahmed the only son still living in Palestine and in a village of his late mother, Maimunah. So, no wonder why he did not know where his late father's village was; and even if it still existed chances are it might have been taken over by the Zionists to house the new settlers who had come from America and Europe.

Ahmed said he had a photo of his late father, which he kept in his wallet but it was confiscated by the IDF soldiers one day as he was busy tending to his farm, and when the wallet was returned, everything inside of it was missing. He did not care so much for the few American dollar notes and some Israeli shekels he had in the wallet; he was stunned when the photo in black-and-white was missing. He had it with him since he was young and about to get married when he said he found it in one of the drawers of his parents' house and asked his father and mother if he

14

could keep it. They allowed him to keep it as he was their eldest son and the photo is also a family heirloom, for him to keep as it also belonged to him, their eldest son.

Ahmed was stunned for a long while because he had just wanted to take the photo to the photo store in one of the small cities where there was one, to get the photographer to make a duplicate of the photo and in a larger size so he could then later put it in a frame. But it was a few days before his wallet were seized together with the photo.

One thing that Ahmed had told me which I remembered the most was how totally different it was in Palestine during his father's time and now, in 1999 or fifty-one years after Al-Nakbah. Munir had a close friend, not a close relative, but a friend who also lived in his village and they got to know and like each other when they first met when they were learning how to read the Noble Qu'ran from a Sheikh who would come on a camel to a neighbor's house where other children waited to start their class. The two of them were five years old. Munir grew fond of Ali because they had similar values except that Ali's father was the owner of a farm that had scores of goats and camels where Munir's father, too, worked. Munir's father's name was Saleem. So his full name was Munir bin Saleem.

There was a river, not wide but where clear and clean water flowed, which extended to the River Jordan, and this river passed through Munir's village. It is an isolated village but it is now gone from the map. Ahmed had tried to locate it when he was much younger but couldn't find it and his relatives from his father's side, too, could not help much because they were already too old and had not lived there for decades when the IDF forces came one night to expel all of them and soon, the entire village was empty for the Zionists to do whatever they wanted to it, to turn it into a new settlement for the new settlers who had flown in airplanes from America and Europe and sent there where new houses had been built for them to live in which had all the modern amenities.

I could fully understand how he might not be willing to talk a lot on his father and their family's experience living in Palestine now with many of their members in exile in Amman and some who might also get to go to America and some other countries in Europe for a new future for themselves and mostly, for their children.

There was a lot of trauma that he had experienced personally at the death of his close family members and other Palestinians some who were his close friends. There was a funeral service at the masjid in his village and the others he had to attend for them, which happened every few weeks and sometimes, every week. There were times funerals for his friends and relatives happened every week.

I sat there in the restaurant in the small town in the West Bank frozen on my seat, a wooden stool that had seen better days and staring at the advertisements of American cigarette brands on the walls of the restaurant which was packed and with cigarette smoke emitted from the noses of some of the Palestinian men who smoke to forget the traumas they were experiencing. I had a tough time trying not to inhale some of the secondary cigarette smoke which was starting to choke me.

I had to stand up. Ahmed looked at me; he thought I had wanted to go to the restroom. No, I am not going to go there. I wanted to go to the front of the restaurant to sit there in the open. He guessed it and was right. He followed me to sit on two vacant wooden stools in the front of the restaurant which was the walkway in front of the building which extends to two hundred meters to the left where there are more stores selling many things and also two other restaurants where there were more men sitting and smoking and not talking or saying a word. Each of them was in their own private thoughts which they did not find good enough to share as they are the same as those that their friends around them were also thinking.

Ahmed was good enough to share some of his private thoughts with me, a total stranger. He was probably excited to do some talking to release his emotions and pent-up feelings to me, a total stranger, who shares the same religion as his. I felt guilty for prodding him on to tell me his story and especially that of his late father, the unknown Palestinian hero who would never be mentioned in any book or report.

There was a silence; a long one. I was relieved because I could now inhale some fresh air from the surroundings and Ahmed was sitting beside me at the same small round table. He chose not to smoke earlier because I had declined to accept his offer of one when we first sat at the table inside the restaurant where he thought there would be some silence and peace. There was a bit of a noise from the television which was showing a local news program, a word of which I could not understand as it was in Arabic. But I could see how some IDF soldiers were entering Masjid Al-Aqsa.

Once in a while some local men walk into the restaurant and when they recognized Ahmed they would touch his shoulder and moved inside it to sit with their friends. Some others who did not know him well, would greet him with 'Asalamulaikum' for which he and I, too, would reply accordingly with 'Mulaikum salam', although I did not know them.

One man called his name (not Ahmed; the name I have since forgotten what it was.) because he was called by his close friends and relatives by this name. He would stop Ahmed to talk a bit in Arabic, of course, a word I did not know of and Ahmed would introduce him to me and said, 'Syed' is from Malaysia for which his friend, Kamil would acknowledge with glee baring the two front teeth that were cut in half. I learnt later that they were hit by the back of an IDF soldier's rifle. And he did not want to fix it because he wanted to let his two half-teeth to show as a sign of pride at being hit by a Zionist soldier.

Kamil told his friend, Ahmed, that he had a friend whose friend who had been to Malaysia or Malasie, as he would say it, for a brief visit and found the country to be peaceful and there are many people of different races who could live with each other. Ahmed was impressed by what his friend had said; he did not have any friend who had gone anywhere outside of Palestine other than to Jordan, but certainly not so far away to Malaysia. The chances of him going to Malaysia seemed bleak.

Kamil too said he would never go anywhere other than to Amman in Jordan as he had his wife and children there and he was back in Palestine for a chore for his family and had come to the restaurant to check on it to see if he could meet with some of his friends. He was delighted to meet Ahmed again after more than one year.

Ahmed and I sat at our table in front of the restaurant for a while without saying anything. The traffic in front of the restaurant and on the road had become busier than it was earlier that choked at the end of it when few buses suddenly appeared to turn at different directions that cause the traffic to halt. A local policeman quickly went to the junction to direct traffic.

Then I noticed how a building at the junction to the right was badly burnt with the front part completely demolished. Ahmed noticed me staring at it and he immediately told me the story of how some IDF imposters and impersonators had gone there in a group of three, all wearing Arabic robes and headgear, looking like other Arab men in such gear and when they saw someone standing in front of the store, they immediately fired at him with such vehemence and hatred that the man who was standing and trying to check some notes in front of him got so severely wounded that he was barely recognizable and the bullets also hit the front of the building which was later destroyed when one of the impersonators threw a small mortar bomb to ensure that the Arab man died. He was already dead before they threw the mortar, which was later revealed to be nothing but a ploy to distract everybody there to rush to the building with them immediately rushing away.

When Ahmed explained to me what happened I was stunned. I thought this small town in the West Bank which was Arab-majority area was peaceful, but it wasn't. He said there is no place in all of Palestine which can be said to be peaceful. He added to say that he was in the vicinity of this area when the bomb exploded.

Ah, the smell of shawarma, falafel, kebab and other local delicacies affected my nose; I wanted to take a bit of it but, I had to leave. My two friends had started to move from the table where they were sitting near me. They did not care with what I was doing with Ahmed; they did not know what I was talking with him about.

The Arab staff of the embassy turned to look at me and then came over to inquire to see if I was good, which I was. He spoke in Arabic to Ahmed and the two of them started to smile a bit and then laugh a bit. I hoped they were not laughing about me. No, Ahmed told him he had not spoken in English with anyone in a very long time and he was worried if he thought he sounded funny to me. I told him that he spoke okay.

The three of us left in the car to go elsewhere towards Baitulmukaddis. It was going to be a journey that would take another one and a half hours. I sat beside the driver who was at the left of the car. The Malaysian Embassy official sat at the back and seemed to be tough. I turned to look at him and did not want to disturb him.

I then started to look ahead on the road in front of us which was empty and despite it sitting in a desert, the road was clean and not dusty as one would have guessed.

Then my mind started to wander, at what Ahmed had told me, about his late father, Munir. I had specifically wanted to know what life was for him when he was a small boy in his village in 1936.

3

Munir and Ali, 1936

'Munir, Munir!'

Munir was only ten years and Palestine at that time was the land of the Palestinians, peaceful and whatever happened in his village was uneventful. He had just finished learning the Nobel Qu'ran from an elderly Sheikh; everybody who learnt to recite the Noble Qu'ran just called him Sheikh; none bothered to know what his name was, as it was not proper for the young boys to enquire and call him by his name.

Munir heard his name being called and he turned around and saw his best friend, Ali who was the same age as his. Both were in the class with ten other students with Sheikh earlier and all had left the house where the class was held, to return home. 'Anything?' asked Munir, as he waited for Ali to walk towards him, holding a copy of the Noble Qu'ran with him, as did Munir who also had a copy for himself. Sometimes after class, Munir would sit below a date tree to read the Noble Qu'ran by himself. He dared not read it aloud as he was not confident that he would sound right or good and he did not want to create a spectacle of himself as he knew the other boys in the same class as he was, were able to read it better in the right intonation and grace; he did not have any of that. Even Ali could read it better without trying.

'Where are you going?' Ali asked when he was close to Munir. The other students were already far away from the two, most were walking towards their own homes, with a few wealthier ones being carried in horse-driven carts by their helpers. Munir walked as always because his house was not far away from the house in the village where the class was held, which belonged to a relative of the Sheikh himself who offered it to him for his students in the village to study the Noble Qu'ran from him. He thought the sounds of the students and their teacher reading the Noble Qu'ran would bring blessings to his entire family.

It was late evening and on a weekend, so the whole village was quiet with most of the parents of the students having done their chores in the fields to tend to what they were growing. Date trees were cluttered at an area that provided shade to some camels who had had enough for the day and further away is the river that linked to River Jordan. It is not wide nor is it deep and it was here where Munir would stop to read the Noble Qu'ran himself and later on when he thought he was done, he would take a dip in it and later on pick some dates to eat to replenish himself before he returned home to eat whatever his mother had cooked.

Munir always reminded himself of his age, ten years old! Not old enough to make any decision for his family; and the only decision he could make at that time was if he wanted to continue reading the Noble Qu'ran himself under the date trees and taking a dip later, and as long as he did not get into any harm his way was done, by sitting at his parents' feet to listen to radio – Radio Palestine which often plays Arabic songs mostly by singers from Egypt, whose names he did not bother to remember; all that he was interested in was the songs they sang.

'Yes, Ali,' Munir asked his friend. 'Anything's the matter? I thought you were going somewhere...'

'Not today, tomorrow.'

'Oh! What happened?'

'My parents had a change of plans.'

Ali then kept quiet and Munir knew what he had in mind; he wanted to take a dip in the river. 'You want to swim?'

Ali nodded and they started to remove their shirts and jumped into the river which was at that time, in low tide. But it was refreshing; they enjoyed dipping themselves in the river and could not dive inside it to hide themselves. Some birds which had stood on the date trees flew off and knocked off some over-ripped dates that fell to the ground on the banks of the river or stream. At that time, it did not resemble even a narrow river but a stream. Both Munir and Ali did not care less what it was as long as there was water in it that they can wet their bodies in and to stay there for a while, before they started to shiver, as the day was getting along with the temperature dipping very quickly, as it was toward the end of summer, when the evenings are cool and the nights can often be cold, if not chilly.

When both of them then had had enough of soaking themselves in the stream; they went to the bank, reached for some of the dates that had fallen, and ate them with glee. The birds they had caused to fly off in haste had saved them a bit of time which they would otherwise have had to spend to shake the dates from the trees which were too tall for either of them to reach with their bare hands.

Some of the birds which had flown off earlier turned around at the far distance to return to the trees where Munir and Ali were taking shade to go back to the nests they had made for themselves. They knew the day was getting along and soon it would be dark as at that time the sun quickly dipped into the horizons and there was no need for them to be flying everywhere again as they had saved amply supply of food to last them for a few days. Munir looked up and Ali followed suit to look at the birds sitting on the tree, hoping that some of them would kick down more dates for them to eat. None dropped.

Munir sat in the living room of his parents' house and listened to the radio which was playing some songs by singers from Egypt who were the craze at that time. His parents were there with him, sitting on the floor with their three daughters sitting on the thick carpet and one of them, Jameelah was sewing her shirt that had got torn at the sleeves and her elder sister, Saleha just sat there not really listening to the songs. The English officers called it Egypt but the Palestinian Arabs prefer to call it Mesir.

But the singers are not those that often hog the limelight, the top singers of Egypt, but the lesser known ones who also have nice and melodic voice that they like; it is soothing to their ears and lulls their minds. Their village is at peace and they crave to experience more of it in their own home, with Saleem at the helm and his wife Sameerah, sitting beside him with a large pot of hot tea or 'chai', as they called it, and small cups sitting on a bronze tray at the ready that she had prepared, and ready for her husband and children to consume. But none of them had as yet bothered to think of tea at that time; they are too engrossed with the songs sang by Salima, who often duets with her husband, Samad, but for this song they are listening so intensely, she is performing solo.

Hashim, who is Munir's younger brother, was not around; he had gone to the town on errands for his mother to buy some provisions but had not returned home. He would normally sit in the restaurant with his friends sipping tea and listening to the radio that they had there for the customers. Sometimes they would listen to the news programs on the British officers and what they were doing in Baitulmukaddis, a city he had never been to. It is not so near to his village so he'd suppose it would be a long while before he could ever get to go there and his father, Saleem, too was not too willing to take him when he goes there every now and then because he did not have the time to show his son around and had to rush to return to his house after he had done what he was supposed to do there, so that he was not held back by some of his friends who operated some stores who were always happy to see him dropping by and talk endlessly over tea and sometimes kebab, too, that their wives cooked; not forgetting some shawarma.

Father Saleem was stern who would not brook any dissent but this was a quality that he had inherited from his father who also inherited it from his own father, Munir's grand-father; so in a way the trait ran in the family and Munir too realized that he would also adopt similar traits as he grew to adulthood, especially when he was finally married, a time when his parents felt he was ready enough to carry the responsibility as a husband. The two of them had not yet determined which of the girls in the village and the nearby ones who would be good for them to be their daughter-in-law; they did want to rush but wait until Munir or any of his sons and daughters were old enough before they could tell who would be good matches for them. Saleem's children are 'a good buy' for most of the elder men and women in the village and those nearby because Saleem and his wife, Sameerah seemed to hold high esteem amongst them.

Few songs have passed and Saleem suddenly felt his throat getting dry; he reached for the cup of tea that had been poured by his wife and took a few small sips. He glanced at Munir and Munir knew what his father was saying with the glance, which is: Have some tea, too!

Munir pushed himself over the carpet to the tray of tea and poured himself some tea in an empty cup and pushed himself back to the side of the room where he was leaning earlier. He took a few sips and put the half-full cup of tea on the low table near him and continued to listen to more songs by Salima who is now singing with her husband, Samad who is not more than five years older than her. They had met when they were students at a music school and soon they were paired to sing songs for the classes they were taking, which also included reading the Noble Qu'ran, in Cairo or Kahirah.

After they performed in public for the first time, they were noticed by some recording company producers who offered them contracts to record songs for their label which they initially declined because their parents did not approve of them, to do that, since they were still at school. They would only agree once they had graduated from their music school and after they were married, which would not be too long afterwards. When their first record was produced with some four songs, all composed for them, it went on the charts very quickly, thrusting them into the limelight.

Unfortunately, after Salima's first baby was born, her voice started to become weak and she did not have the guts to force herself to sing in public or to cut another record. So the songs that are often played on the radio in Palestine and also many other Arab countries are those that are on her debut album. Only her husband, Samad, continued to sing, solo, and later on for his fourth album, the recording company paired him another budding singer, Fatima, whose relationship with Samad, who was ten years older than her, created rifts between Samad and his wife, so in the end they decided to divorce.

So this was what Munir was thinking the whole time he was listening to the songs sang by Salima, and also her husband, Samad, who he despised because Munir thought Samad had been negligent and surrendered his lust for a younger woman, when he should have been more careful and taken better care and control of his lusts and emotions to be with his wife even after she had lost her voice.

Ahmed only listened to Salima's songs for her melodious voice; he did not know anything about the scandals between her and her husband and another young singer.

The call of the adhan coming from the nearby masjid broke the silence in the house where Saleem and his family were listening to modern songs, and he immediately looked at Munir who knew what the glance meant, which was for him to quickly switch off the radio to allow the call of the adhan to continue until it ended, after which all of the men and women in the house would perform their Maghrib prayers (salah) together in the same room as they were earlier.

Saleem did not say in words, but Munir and his mother and sisters knew what he wanted to say or ask, which is: Where is Hashim? They were all supposed to be at home by this time, to pray after which they would eat dinner together, also in the same room as they were, and wait until it is time to perform the Isyak prayers together.

But Hashim is nowhere to be seen. 'Where is he?' Saleem asked.

His wife, Sameerah had to quickly give the answer since no other persons in her family knew where Hashim was at that time. She had asked him to go for an errand in the town and he had taken a bicycle to go there which can delay his return. ''I have sent him on an errand,' said Sameerah.

No wonder, Saleem, thought he did not see his bicycle outside the house earlier when he got out to check on the chicken in the coop, behind the house. But why didn't Munir go instead of Hashim, who was barely eight years old? He didn't ask that question to his wife and kept it to himself.

Saleem nodded a bit, stood up to go to the back of the house to have his ablution followed by Munir who also did likewise, before they returned to the room and lined in rows, with the men at the left and the women at the right. Saleem motioned to Munir to lead the prayers as Imam after the women had all covered themselves in prayer garbs white in color that covered their entire bodies, baring only their face and palms. Their everyday clothes were mostly black in color, and even when they were in their house they would cover themselves up.

Meanwhile at Ali's house not far away from where Munir's family house was, the ritual they were practicing was identical to that which was being practiced in the Saleem household as in all the households in the whole of Palestine. In fact, in all of the households of the Arabs in other countries, too, they did the same, as a common ritual that they practiced as Muslims like their forefathers before them.

The only difference is that the house where Ali was staying was much larger. It was made of bricks and not mud like the house Saleem had inherited from his father who had also inherited it from his father. In fact, his house had been standing at the same spot in the village for about one hundred years and had seen marginal or insignificant renovations or additions. However, the house where Ali's family lived was relatively new and not yet thirty years, made of bricks by artisans who were brought to the village from the city by Ali's grand-father who drew the design of the house with a stick and with his bare-hands drew it for the construction workers to build the house for him for a lot of 'Junyah Filastini' or Palestinian Pounds. His grandfather was a landowner who had more goats and camels then anyone in the village and his son, who was Ali's father, took over from him his properties upon his untimely death when he fell off a camel that went wild with rage upon seeing a strange apparition although it was not the first time such an incident had happened and his grand-father, Abdul Malek had got help from a religious elder who came to ward off the evil spirits he said were lurking on his properties.

Ironically, everything went well immediately after the death of Abdul Malek, and the whole house was peaceful and the villagers who lived around his property, were relieved. Some of them had guessed that Abdul Malek himself had bad intentions and the wealth he had acquired might not be proper. But none of them dared to say aloud what they thought of him because some of them or their children were working for him in the farm, too.

Ali prayed for Maghrib, dutifully like a filial son, standing behind his father who acted as Imam, who recited the verses for the prayers in a style that only he could do, which some said was enticing. But he dared and had never braved himself to become Imam in other congregations except for the one comprising his close family members only.

It had happened a few times when Ali was much younger, around six years, he started to be the Imam for the prayers in his own house, but not anywhere else, even when he had become older and was capable of doing so. He wanted the older men to play the role and he also wanted to hear them recite the supplications or 'dua' after the prayers, which he thought he was too young to offer because he had as yet not come to realize a lot of things that were happening in his own village, much less in other parts of Palestine. News that he had heard on the radio was sketchy and he did not quite comprehend what the British Mandate of Palestine was, or what it meant to him and his family and people. Munir would know more, he thought, but he never got to discuss the matter with Munir. Maybe he should ask Munir about the British in Palestine and why they were there in his country.

His village was in the West Bank and very far away from Baitulmukaddis which the British had called Jerusalem after the name given by the Jews, and Ali had never met any Jewish boys in his village as there was no Jew who had lived in it since he was born, although he had heard of a family who had lived at the edge of the village long ago and before he was even born. But they had left the village to go to the north of the country. Yes, the Jews spoke Arabic like the other Arabs in the village, and were kind and liked to mix with the Arabs.

Ali only had heard of them from a stranger who had loitered near his parents' house to enquire if he knew where the Jews had lived. Ali did not know any of them and could not be of any help to the stranger who, to him, also looked like a Jew. He was in the forties and was wearing Jewish traditional clothes with some hair dropping at the sides of his head called 'payot' or 'payos' in line with the Biblical injunction banning the shaving the 'corners of one's head' and wore clothes that were black with his head covered by a black hat.

Ali and his parents and bothers and sisters sat in the living room on carpet which was thick and lush and in glorious colors that his father had bought from a trader who wandered to his village one day; he said he was on his way to Baitullaham, but lost the direction and ended up in the village and because it was late, he thought he would find a place to stay there for the night before riding his horse-cart along to go to Baitullaham which was still a very long way from there.

Ali's father offered the trader a place to sleep for the night and in between the Maghrib and Isyak prayers, they sat in front of the house where the horse-cart with the horse were, the trader showed Ali's father some of the carpets he had for sale, and Ali's father got interested in one, for its pattern and paid for it. So, he immediately replaced the carpet in the living room of his house that had been there for decades until the colors had faded. He wanted to roll it and give it to the masjid in the village. So Ali's father was grateful for the sudden and unannounced visit by the carpet trader who he welcomed as an Arab and a Muslim who saw it as his own responsibility to look after strangers and wanderers and such like if and at any time they might appear, as it was what the Noble Qu'ran and the Sayings or Sunnah of the Holy Nabi Muhammad, (s.a.w.) (Peace be upon Him) had taught him to do, and it also did not cost him too much to entertain the stranger but nevertheless, a brother in Islam, who was in dire need as there was no hotel or caravanserai in the village or the whole area. The trader had escaped a boarding house in a small town earlier before he got to this village and to return to it, would take a lot of time and it was also not a good option he had since it was already going dark with the lights in the sky dimming, with the coming of Maghrib, which he had to perform by the side of his horse-cart on the road before he could proceed with his journey, into darkness. And he knew he was in no-man's land and there was no one living near him since he could not hear the cry of adhan for Maghrib, that said that there was no masjid near him.

The trader too was happy to have found a fellow man who gave him a place to stay, but also some business that he did not expect to get at such an hour and in the village where he had never been to in his entire life. He told Saleem, he might have passed by the village few times before but it was in the day and he did not have to put up anywhere along the way, until now when his horse got cramps and he had to stop to tend to him until he got better and was able to move on carrying him and the goods comprised of more carpets which are heavy and other things to trade in Baitulmukaddis.

'So both of us are indeed lucky,' remarked Saleem as he sat on the carpet he had just purchased for a good price, half from the original price that the trader offered him, out of his gratitude to him for showing understanding and giving protection and hospitality to him, a total stranger to Saleem. 'We have been blessed by Allah the Almighty tonight. And do drop by when you are on your way back from Baitullaham,' added Saleem.

'It has been indeed my pleasure, sir; and I surely will, if God wills... But I might proceed to other cities and towns from Baitullaham.'

'You are always welcome here, with open arms.'

Just then Saleem's wife alighted from the kitchen carrying some snacks and drinks for the two men to take before the Trader could respond to Saleem's kind offer. She too marveled at the beauty of the carpet that her husband had just bought and agreed to let him to take the old one to give to their village masjid, as it would be a sin to discard or throw such a nice carpet that they had used for many years, which was still in good condition. She sniffed the sweet smell that came from the new carpet that was not there before. 'I will give it a bit of dusting and washing, tomorrow,' she added.

'I can help you with that, Sister,' added the trader. 'I can take it to the nearby stream and dip it in the water for a while before cleaning it with soap and some detergent that I have which are good for washing carpets.'

'You need special detergents to wash carpets with?' asked Saleem.

The Trader nodded with replying in words. He knew how to wash carpets, as it was his business for many years, to not only sell carpets, but also to wash them, for some clients who did not want to replace their worn carpets which had a lot of sentimental value to them, that they still wanted to keep even though they still bought a new one from the Trader out of courtesy or to put at another place in their house.

'We can do that in the morning,' added the Trader. 'In the meantime just put it there.'

There was silence and they thought some angels were present and they had to stop talking.

'Maybe I can take a look at the other carpets you have in your cart, tomorrow,' said Saleem, to break the impasse. He did not know quite why he said that and waited for his wife to comment on his statement.' She did not say a word. She thought her husband would know better if they needed another carpet to buy from the Trader, whose name Saleem and his wife or anyone in the house did not bother to ask.

'By the way, my name is Omar.'

Only then did Saleem and his wife, Sameerah know his name, Omar. And only then did they also realize that he seemed to be a fine young man, in his mid-twenties; but they did not want to probe into his personal matters to enquire if he was married or how many children he had. But he was grateful for the Trader for telling them his name.

'And where do you plan to put the carpet?' Sameerah asked her husband who did not answer immediately because he also did not know where he wanted to put it, or why he wanted to get another piece from Omar, now that he knows his name.

'That's okay if you do not want to buy it, sir,' remarked Omar, the Trader – the Carpet Trader, who came into their world out of the blue one fine evening when it was already almost dark who they could not ask to go away as it was a Traveler; and in Islam any Traveler needed to be given protection and support until the time he had to leave. But Omar was not a common traveler without a cause; he is a carpet trader and who just so happened to enter their lives because his horse had become too tired to continue to pull Omar's cart. And Saleem had known a few traders who traveled with their wares and products to sell, including carpets and other things who also passed by his village and sold some items to the neighbors. They are fine people, he thought, who followed in the ways of the Prophet who encouraged Muslims to trade as much as possible.

That night Omar slept in the living room alone, which is also the guest room and prayer room, on the new carpet he had just sold to Saleem. He was given a pillow and a blanket to sleep, but sleep was difficult to get; he tried to sleep but he could not do it. His mind was racing. It took him back to the time barely a few days ago when his father, asked him to pack up and take as much as possible, mostly the new carpets and other items from his house to go to Baitullaham, where he could try to sell the carpets that they did not need anymore and to share some with his relatives who are there. His father, was anxious to get him to flee from his village as soon as possible.

Omar looked at the clock on the wall; it showed one o'clock in the morning. The window at the left of the room on the ground floor of the house where he was, was slightly ajar so he could get the cool winds from outside to blow into it to make him feel fine. He had a shower earlier before he went to bed, after having dinner with Saleem and his sons, Ahmed and also Hashim, who had just returned from the town where he was sent by his mother to get something. They were all sleeping in other rooms on the first floor of the two-storey building that is made of bricks and clay with the top of the building which is a flat surface where the family would go to sit and relax when the weather is fine.

Outside, the moon was not shining brightly as usual because it was hidden partially by some dark clouds. Omar took it as some sort of an omen, a bad one. He kept hearing the voice of his father in his head, reminding him to go to Baitullaham. Stay there until it is safe for you to return, he advised Omar again and again.

Suddenly Omar felt guilty because he did not tell Saleem the truth on why he had come by; he only said he was going to Baitullaham, which is a fact, but the truth, the real truth was something he had not dared to tell Saleem – yet. He promised himself that he would explain to Saleem why he was there and why he was heading for Baitullaham. He hoped Allah did not punish him for hiding the truth from Saleem, now that he was convinced that Saleem was a good man, a pious man, in the morning before he leaves the house to take the horse-cart and go to on to Baitullaham, a trip that could easily take a few hours, or even half a day to reach, with the horse not very fit to undertake the task. He also felt sorry for the horse for being forced to pull the cart with the carpets and other things and Omar.

It is three o'clock and Omar is still wide awake. He still could not sleep. He could only close his eyes and try to think about sleep, but each time he tried to do that, he was taken back to his father, whose image appeared in his head staring at him, not in anger, but feeling sorry that he had to push his son to undertake the trip. Although it was not the first trip for Omar to go to Baitullaham, but in the past he went there either with his father or uncles; but this time Omar was going there all by himself and leaving the house late so he could not get to his destination during the day and had to spend the night anywhere along the route. Latif was worried for his son because the route he would take was not very hospitable; and most of the time it is deserted. If he had left the house early in the morning, chances are he could get to Baitullaham before nightfall. But he left the house around noon. He did not know where his son was now; he imagined Omar sleeping in the cart beside a road, deserted and quiet in the middle of the desert. Latif could not do the trip on his own if he had to start off at noon. His son, Omar was just twenty-five and fortunately, his wife and two children, who were very young had left for Baitullaham two weeks earlier to visit their grandparents there, and this was where Omar too would head for, which he did not, or had not told Saleem about. And he felt guilty when he realized that he had actually told Saleem a lie about why he was going to Baitullaham and why he was stuck in his village and was desperately looking for shelter to spend the night.

He felt comfortable and safe sleeping in the living room of Saleem's house, alone, and not in anyway related to Saleem or his family but who was still welcome by them, like he was a family member or at least a close friend. Omar tried to ask himself if he or his father had given similar treatment to any stranger or straggler who had the misfortune to find himself in his own village and who was alone and in desperate need to find temporary accommodation. There was none that he could remember. But then his village had some places where strangers or travelers could go to stay for the night or for any period of time. So they did not need to seek the charity from strangers in his village who wouldn't mind offering some assistance from anyone when necessary. And there is also a masjid in the village where some strangers had gone to sleep over for the night and pray.

The clock struck four o'clock and Omar heard, or swore he heard a cock crow in the back. True, Saleem had some chickens in the barn. Then he felled asleep, but it was not very long afterwards when he was awoken by the melodious sound of someone whose voice he had not heard of before, reciting verses from the Noble Qu'ran that came to his mind, reading it by heart and to himself with both eyes closed.

* * * * * * *

"Show forgiveness, enjoin what is good, and turn away from the ignorant." – *The Holy Quran 7:199*

"And speak to him with gentle speech that perhaps he may be reminded or fear [Allah]." – *The Holy Quran 20:44*

"O you who have believed, let not a people ridicule [another] people; perhaps they may be better than them; nor let women ridicule [other] women; perhaps they may be better than them. And do not insult one another and do not call each other by [offensive] nicknames. Wretched is the name of disobedience after [one's] faith. And whoever does not repent – then it is those who are the wrongdoers." – *The Holy Quran 49:11*

"Say not to them [so much as], "uff," and do not repel them but speak to them a noble word" – *The Holy Quran 17:23*

"And when it is said to them, 'Follow what Allah has revealed,' they say, 'Rather, we will follow that which we found our fathers doing.' Even though their fathers understood nothing, nor were they guided?" – *The Holy Quran 2:170*

"And if someone is in hardship, then [let there be] postponement until [a time of] ease. But if you give [from your right as] charity, then it is better for you, if you only knew." – *The Holy Quran 2:280*

* * * * * * *

He instinctively decided to wake up as he thought it was not respectful for him to stay asleep when someone was reading verses from the Noble Qu'ran. But he could not tell where the voice was coming from. He turned to look at the windows which were still slightly ajar and stood up to look outside and he saw someone sitting under a date tree and holding a copy of the Noble Qu'ran in his hands and reading it. It was Saleem. And it was close to the sunrise, to indicate that it was dawn time for the first prayer of the day. He needed to get out and have an ablution to wait for the sound of the adhan for the Maghrib prayers.

Ahmed knocked on the door and Omar turned to look at it and even before he walked towards it to open it, Ahmed was already starting to open the door. Omar decided to wait and see who the person behind the door might be. It was Ahmed, as it was not possible for any woman to open it, including Saleem's wife.

'Is uncle ready to pray?' asked Ahmed.

Omar looked at Ahmed's face and saw the glittering of a thin layer of water on his face; this showed that Ahmed had had his ablution and was ready to perform his prayers. And today they were going to pray outside near where Saleem was reading the Noble Qu'ran as he would on almost every morning before dawn, while the women in the house; there were three of them – Saleem's wife, Saleha and their two daughters. But where was Hashim, Omar suddenly remembered him, but he dared not ask about his whereabouts. He knew Hashim would be somewhere; for he could not be anywhere but at the prayer service too. And Omar was sure Saleem, as the eldest amongst the men would lead the prayers as their Imam.

For each morning Saleem would read from a Surah or Verse in the Noble Qu'ran, and continued to read it until it was done, before he started to read it from the first Surah, and all the way to the end.

At times there were also birds sitting perched on the branches of the trees nearby would stand still to listen to him reciting the verses like they too were engrossed in them, to also know what they mean. They chirped when he was done.

Saleem picked the Noble Qu'ran which was sitting on the low table and opened a page where he had left; it was the Surah Al Buruj of Chapter Eighty-five.

* * * * * *

AL BURUJ (MANSIONS OF THE
STARS CONSTELLATION.)
In the name of Allah, the Gracious,
the Merciful.
I swear by the mansions of the stars,
And the promised day,
And the bearer of witness and those against
whom the witness is borne.
Cursed be the makers of the pit,
Of the fire (kept burning) with fuel,
When they sat by it,
And they were witnesses of what they did
with the believers.
And they did not take vengeance on them
for aught except that they believed in Allah, the
Mighty, the Praised,
Whose is the kingdom of the heavens
and the earth; and Allah is a Witness of all things.
Surely (as for) those who persecute the
believing men and the believing women, then
do not repent, they shall have the chastisement
of hell, and they shall have the chastisement
of burning.
Surely (as for) those who believe and

do good, they shall have gardens beneath which
rivers flow, that is the great achievement.
Surely the might of your Lord is great.
Surely He it is Who originates and
reproduces,
And He is the Forgiving, the Loving,
Lord of the Arsh, the Glorious,
The great doer of what He will.
Has not there come to you the story
of the hosts,
of Firon and Samood?
Nay! those who disbelieve are in
(the act of) giving the lie to the truth.
And Allah encompasses them on
every side.
Nay! it is a glorious Qu'ran,
In a guarded tablet.

* * * * * *

He started to read it from beginning to the end in the short surah
and stopped after he was done, and just then he heard the adhan being
called from the masjid. And Omar quickly followed Ahmed to go out
of the house to a pond where he performed his ablution. The water was
cold and a bit frigid because it was exposed to the weather the whole
night when it was cold outside, as it was also inside the living room where
Omar was sleeping earlier, even though he did not have so much as a
sleep, but was awaken by the reading of the Noble Qu'ran by Saleem.

Saleem put aside the copy of the Noble Qu'ran aside and started to
lay down some prayer carpets outside of the house on sand and stood on
his carpet which was in front of the others. Hashim alighted from the
house and was ready to start praying with them while Omar was wiping
excess water from his face, to also give it a massage to make it feel warm.
He then went to Saleem and stood on another prayer carpet and waited

for Saleem to start the prayer service. Hashim and Ahmed were already at their places standing on two other carpets, which looked worn with wear.

The sun started to peep from the horizons which was slightly hidden by a low hill; but otherwise, the whole village, still engulfed in semi-darkness was also starting to be light, to show Omar what beauty that would soon be created before his eyes, that he had not seen before, because he had first arrived at the village when it was almost dark, after Maghrib, which quickly became dark, pitch dark, until he felt like he was at a place that was not seen but still he could feel the warmth emitted by Saleem's friendship and that of his children, despite not having met them previously. He knew it was God who had made the moment happen and it was for a good reason but he could not yet guess as to what it might be.

Saleem then started to pray and the small congregation behind him followed suit and in unison followed every move he made to create the first rakaat, and then the next to complete the whole cycle for the morning or dawn or fajar prayers. And after the prayers were done, all sat, and Saleem turned slightly to the back and started to recite a supplication and this time he had a new one, which was to seek Allah's blessings for Omar who had appeared in his household to bring much luck and happiness, so that his journey to Baitullaham would be uneventful, safe, and fruitful, to his desired intention. Once it was done, the congregation of Saleem's two children and Omar, said, 'Amin...' and they shook each other's hand.

Ahmed and Hashim went to school with their parents at a school which was not so far away from the house and they rode a motorcycle, made in England with the brand name of Norton whose engine sound was big to suit the size of the engine, with three of them on the motorcycle. Saleem's two daughters had already gone to another school or madrasah for women, walking together with the schoolbags because the school was not so far away from their house.

The sound could be heard even after it was so far away because it bounced on the low hills that Omar had seen earlier when he peeped out of the windows, just before dawn. Saleem had asked him to wait for him to return before he could excuse himself to go on his journey to

Baitullaham. Saleem did not want him to just go without sending him off with enough food that his wife had cooked for breakfast and more to ensure that Omar was well-fed throughout the journey that could take many hours, with no town along the way that had coffee shops for him to stop and eat or drink. Omar said he had enough food to last till he got to Baitullaham, but Saleem did not care; he asked his wife the night before to cook extra food for their family and to pack some for Omar to take.

The sounds of the engine of the Norton died when Omar, not knowing what to do, laid down in the living room, after he had had a shower in the outdoor bathroom where there was a large pond with fresh water that came down from the hill which he thought was good and clean enough for him to even drink it, and he did have some and it tasted fresh and clean, to add to the tea he had with his breakfast with Saleem and his two young boys. Omar opened the sling bag made of leather and pulled out his own copy of the Noble Qu'ran, which his father had given him when he was small and started to read it but quietly, although he could read it by heart; but he insisted on having the Noble Qu'ran with him when he recited verses from it, often with his eyes shut, so he said he could be closer to what he was reading and to understate the meaning of the verses more that way. He was at peace with himself when he did that, alone but not feeling it, because he knew and felt that he was being looked after well by the Almighty.

Then he heard a voice from behind the doors; it was the voice of Saleem's wife, Sameera, who did not dare to knock on it, much less to open it to peep inside at Omar. It was not their nature to do such things and women and men in Palestine as in all Arab countries too never did that. Omar stopped reading the Noble Qu'ran to respond to Sameerah who asked if he had taken a shower. 'Yes, Auntie, I have had it,' replied Omar, still sitting on the carpet and lying his back on the wall, with his hand holding the book. 'I had it before prayers, at the outdoor bathroom.'

'I see,' said Sameera. 'Did Saleem ask you to wait for him to return from sending the children to school?'

'Yes, he did, Auntie.'

'Very well…and is there anything that you need…tea?'

'No, Auntie, I have had enough to eat for breakfast for which I want to thank you for cooking it just like my own mother would have done it. It was delicious.'

'And I have packed some food for you to take on your journey.'

'Shukran… (Thank you.) I appreciate that.'

'Very well…'

Sameerah then walked away and Omar could hear her footsteps as she walked towards the kitchen, until the sound was heard no more and Omar was back with his own private thoughts. He did not know what he was thinking; he was not thinking of anyone or anything, not even of his forthcoming journey to Baitulkaddis or his father or mother in his village he had left and driven on the horse-cart for some six hours before reaching this village whose name he still did not know and he did not want to ask what it was from anyone including from Saleem.

Omar then decided to go out of the house to check on his horse that was tied to a tree; and he felt relieved to see that it was alive and well and not tired like it was yesterday, for most of the journey from his village when he noticed that it was limping and not running as fast as before. He pitied the horse for having to be given the burden to pull the cart with carpets and other goods and him.

He gave the horse some hay to eat and then later, water he had taken from the pond, where he had used some to bathe and drink a bit, too; so he thought if it was good for him to drink, it should also be good for his horse to take some of it. It neighed a few times, to indicate that it appreciated what Omar was giving him, food and water to drink. It was like mineral water that flowed in the low hills to the pond which was closed all around by planks for the privacy of Saleem and his family to go inside to bathe especially. But the women of the household did not have their baths there; they do it inside the house which was more proper and decent.

The sounds of the Norton motorcycle started to be heard and Omar felt the vibration hitting his chest because the sound boomed a bit and it got louder and louder until he could catch sight of it with Saleem on it, and he was riding it slowly towards Omar. Saleem stopped and immediately greeted him with, 'Asalamulaikum' for which Omar replied by saying, 'Mulaikum salam'. Saleem switched off the engine of the Norton and shook Omar's hand while the horse continued to eat the hay and feel contented. Saleem knew he had arrived a bit later than usual because he had stopped to talk to some of his friends who were also sending their children to school and who were the same ages as his own two sons, Ahmed and Hashim.

'It must be a good day to ride a motorcycle like that,' remarked Omar.

Saleem nodded and said, 'I hope it will be like this the whole day so you can ride all the way to Baitulmukaddis in this fine weather. But it was not like this yesterday or the last few days.'

'I should be off anytime soon now, Mister Saleem,' said Omar. 'And I want to thank you, your wife, and children for extending such wonderful hospitality to me, a mere stranger...'

Saleem cut short the speech Omar was going to give by saying, 'You are not a stranger to me and my family; you are part of my family too.'

Omar was taken aback by the remarks and he froze and tried to think on what he could say. There were no words that he could think of; he knew as fellow Muslims, it was Saleem's and his family's duty to look after, not only him, but any stranger or traveler who might come their way. And living in such an isolated village as Saleem's, he must have been visited by many of them, especially those who were traveling along the side or minor roads to go to Baitulmukaddis such as him. But Omar surely did not want to take advantage of the hospitality that had been offered to him by Saleem, and wanted to leave as soon as possible. 'I need to leave soon,' he added, after worrying how his presence in Saleem's life might have disrupted it a bit because he would surely be doing a lot for his family and might even need not have to rush back from sending his two boys to school and could stay on with his friends to sit in a coffee shop and talk. But Omar felt his presence had forced Saleem to rush back so he could be at his house and be with him. For once, Omar started to feel guilty.

'Stay on and you can leave after lunch,' said Saleem.

Omar almost froze when he heard the offer from Saleem. 'Er...er...' Omar was lost for words; he did not know what else to say.

'It won't be long; it will be just a while more and we can have lunch together in the olive grove over there.'

Omar turned to look at the left and further up, he saw some olive trees, which reminded him of the olive garden or plot that his father too had in his village that he had left yesterday where he also liked to go to sit under some of them especially when it was hot and in summer, to take shade and often he would also put a mat or carpet on the ground to lie on it. What could he say to the offer, he asked himself? He knew it would not be polite to decline it; and at the same time he also knew it would be rude if he forced Saleem to extend his hospitality from what he had shown yesterday, by allowing him to sleep in their living room and providing him with food, too.

Saleem did not have a horse but a Norton motorcycle that seemed to confuse Omar's horse a bit, to think that it might also be a horse of some type, one which is made of metal, smaller in size than it is, but which could also run like him, a horse. Saleem looked at his Norton and the horse and wondered what the two might be saying. He then said, 'Your horse too needs to have more rest.'

This made Omar feel guilty because he knew he had caused his horse to suffer yesterday until it almost collapsed in sheer exhaustion, that also forced him to not want to force it to run like a horse, but to gallop and to take its own time, until it was almost on the verge of exhaustion and collapse, and forced it to limp and with Omar getting off the cart to walk with it, to lessen the burden the horse had to bear, until they arrived near Saleem's house where they were now. He was pleased to see the horse looking healthy and fresh after getting a good rest and nap the whole night. Only then did Omar realized that the horse had not neighed, the whole night and even till now.

'What do you say? Your horse too needs a good rest, still,' said Saleem.

Omar nodded politely. And only now the horse started to neigh.

'But you won't be able to see Ahmed and Hashim back from school, because they return later in the afternoon around one o'clock when I pick them on the old and trusted Norton again. Or, unless, if you want to wait for them to return first so they can bid you farewell, you will be more than welcome to wait either in the house or here, sitting under this date tree, or there in the olive grove where it is cooler.'

'I would like it if I can see your two sons, Ahmed and Hashim again before I take my leave, Mr. Saleem.'

'Then just stay here until I bring the two back here,' Saleem chipped which forced Omar to stop completing his sentence when he wanted to say, how he still had to leave…

Lunch was ready and Saleem's wife took a tray full of food to them and put them on a low table that had been left near the tree outside the house with the horse standing on the spot where he was tied to the tree. Omar had loosened the rope that tied it to the tree so it could run around playfully running slowly or galloping around the date trees and into the olive grove to let the leaves from the trees rub his body with.

'Doesn't your horse too need a bit of a wash?' asked Saleem. 'There is a pond further up that you can dip him into and let him sit there until he feels good with himself.'

Omar agreed and walked to the horse to take it to the pond and got it to go in it and the horse sat in the water until only his head was seen.

'You can later give him a good scrub,' said Saleem. He then turned to his wife, Sameerah and asked, 'Where did you put the scrub I used to scrub my Norton, Sameera?'

'I took it inside the house; I will bring it out,' she said. She then removed the food in different plates from the tray and put them on the low table. Saleem was already sitting on a low chair and he motion Omar to sit on another in front of him while Sameerah returned to the house and not long afterwards alighted from it carrying the scrub brush. She put it near her husband and left him and Omar to have their lunch, and to return to the house.

'You'll have a brand new horse, after it is done dipping itself in the pond and given a scrub. And if you want to wash your clothes, just leave them there and my wife can wash them together with our own.'

'That's alright, Mr. Saleem.'

They then start to eat, using bare hands to cut the pita bread that Saleem's wife had made early this morning so they felt and tasted fresh. 'My wife has packed some food for you to take on your journey.'

'You and your wife and children are extremely kind; and I will not be able to repay your kind deeds.'

'Oh, this is nothing. Everybody in my family is happy that you have allowed us to keep you company while you are here. It was Allah that had caused you to be here in our village and it is for us to keep you safe and fed.'

They continued to eat and Omar seemed to be full. 'I am done; the food is extremely good and very tasty. And the gravy is something I had not tasted before. It must be a local recipe...'

'Precisely. It was a local delicacy, but the recipe my wife used was handed down from her mother to her and from her grand-mother to her own mother. I knew her late mother before I married her daughter, but not her grand-mother who died when I was still an infant, not yet five months. We do not have photos of them, but my relatives and even my father said my wife's grand-mother looked like my wife's mother, so I could imagine how she might look like, like my wife, too, who looks like her own mother. But my two daughters, do not look like their mother, because they took their looks from me just like my two sons, as you can see.'

'Yes, Mr. Saleem; and I am sure your two sons, Ahmed and Hisham will grow up into fine men like you are.'

Saleem had to finish chewing the bread and swallow it down his throat after dipping it into the gravy before he could respond to Omar's remarks. 'But today's youth may not necessarily take the style and ways of their parents. Palestine is changing; it has started to change since 1928...'

Omar chipped in; he was not quite sure why Saleem mentioned the year, 1928. He was not familiar with the history of Palestine, but was aware that he was born before the British came to their country. 'And why, from 1928, Mr. Saleem?'

'The British started to change everything in Palestine ever since 1928. I was two years when that happened; but it was not prevalent here since our village is isolated. It is worse in the bigger towns and city and mostly in Baitumukaddis and maybe a bit in Baitullaham, where you will be going to later today.'

Omar was taken aback by what Saleem had said; it came as a shock and he was not prepared to hear of it from Saleem especially when they were having breakfast out in the open in the cool morning with a breeze blowing into their faces. He immediately turned to look at his horse which was still in the pond with its head showing above the water. The Norton was sitting near the tree. It will roar again when Saleem start its engine to go to the school where his two sons were studying to bring them back. Omar thought it was good for him to be able to see them again before he moves on. But he reminded to himself to give his horse a good scrub after lunch and when Saleem was gone to the school. It should not take too long to scrub the horse, he opined, because he had done that many times in his village where there was also a pond like the one in Saleem's compound. No wonder, the horse felt it was still back in Omar's village and not anywhere else since Saleem's village was not any different than Omar's village like most of the isolated villages in Palestine.

Saleem had just left on his Norton to go to the school to collect his two sons; and at Omar took the opportunity to go to his horse in the pond to give it a good scrubbing on his body where a thick layer of dirt had gotten stuck to it and he had to pour more water on its' body to loosen the sand which was forced to slip off from the horse' body. The horse seemed to appreciate what Omar was doing and showed its appreciation by neighing a few times. Sameerah who was in the kitchen could see Omar and the horse in the pond and smiled; she especially liked to see the bonding between a man and his horse who seemed to be at peace with each other and who knew what to expect from each other. She thought Omar must have had the horse since it was small and to be able to fully understand what it was saying in its' gestures and moves and occasional neighing.

Omar was happy to see his horse enjoying the scrubbing after allowing it to dip and lay in the pond submerged until only its' head could be seen and he felt guilty for going to him to give the scrub to also indicate that it was close to the time for the two of them to move on; and ahead was a journey full of uncertainties and it might be very long around four to five hours during which time, they could stop by the side of a road where there might be shade from some date trees or olive trees and perhaps some people to bump into that were like Saleem.

Omar brought the horse that he refused to give a name to, but a nickname of Strong meaning 'Qawiun', to dry land. He remembered when it was still a foal born early one morning when he and his family were asleep. There was no noise and when dawn came, and when he and his parents and brothers and sisters woke up, his father noticed silence from the barn where he kept his few horses. It aroused his suspicion and he immediately put on his leather sandals and went to it only to find a new member of his family of horses, a male one which was lying on the thick layer of hay that he had put in the barn because he knew the female horse was expecting to deliver a foal anytime and it was the night when the moon was missing from the sky, at the end of the month five years ago, when Omar was twenty years old and had finished school and was going to take over from his father what ever business he was doing at that time which was trading.

Omar gave the horse some massaging while drying its body which now had a shine that it did not have before because it was covered by a lot of dust and sand that had got to the skin when they were traveling along the road from his village to where they were now. Qawiun seemed to enjoy the massage and felt fresh from the bathing and dipping in the pond.

Saleem's Norton's sound started to be heard faintly in the background and it caused Omar to become alert; he did not want Saleem and his sons to see him cleaning his horse and wanted them to see the horse in its new appearance, clean and tidy.

The sounds of the engine of the Norton became louder and louder until Omar could see it with Saleem and his two sons riding together on it. It then stopped by the date tree and all three of them got off the motorcycle to greet Omar and the horse. 'He looks very good,' remarked Saleem as he patted Strong's back. Ahmed and Hashim were excited to see the horse in the day; they did not get to see it that well the first time it came over as the light of the day was dimming and Hashim only returned home after dusk and did not see it at all and did not know there was such a horse, except when he was told by his mother who said there was one that came with their guest by the name of Omar.

It was one o'clock and Omar had lunch earlier with Saleem under the shade of the date tree and was now ready to move on. He did not wish to bother Saleem and his family any longer with his presence as it was not a nice thing for him to do, so he thought. Nevertheless, he enjoyed the hospitality given to him by them and did not know what else that he could do to repay them for what they had given. He put the horse to the cart and went to the back of the cart and pulled another carpet while Saleem and his two sons looked. His wife, Sameerah too looked from the window of the kitchen.

'This is a present from me, Mr. Saleem,' said Omar as he trusted the carpet which was rolled tidily. 'It is something that my family's workers made.'

Saleem did not say a word; he wanted not to accept the offer as his two children watch. 'Here take it,' insisted Omar.

'How much does it cost?' asked Saleem. 'I'll pay for it.'

'That won't be necessary,' said Omar. 'It is a special present from me.'

'But you are in the business of selling carpets and I have bought one from you and I can pay for another one, which I can put in a room in the house.'

'No, just take it. I will be very happy if you take it.'

Omar then took Ahmed and then Hashim on a ride with him on Qawiun to gallop slowly around the compound of the house and in between the olive trees, which thrilled them because they had never rode any horse before other than riding on their father's Norton which to them also felt like riding a horse.

4

Omar and Qawiun the Horse.

Omar rode his horse-cart pulled by Strong or 'Qawiun' in Arabic along a deserted road, in the middle of a wide desert and in the middle of nowhere. He was happy to be able to convince Saleem to accept his gift, a new carpet as a token of appreciation for his gratitude to him, his four children, and his wife, Sameera. He looked at Qawiun who galloped along the dusty road in stride, after being treated like a king by Omar who fed him well and also cleaned him with fresh water from the pond that had come from the low hills so he felt appreciated and wanted to show his own gratitude to his master and to take him to his final destination which was Baitullaham.

It was already two in the afternoon. Omar looked at his watch and then the sun above him. Fortunately, the day was not hot or humid so he did not sweat. He hoped Qawiun could go on for another hour before they stopped for a break and to have a snack by the side of the road. Thus far, after leaving Saleem's village, one and a half hours ago, he did not have a break because he felt fresh and managed to travel for about twenty miles. He worried if Qawiun could go on. Then he noticed a tall tree by the side of the road in front of him and wanted to go there to stop for a break. He felt excited with the sight of the tree that tall and with a lot of leaves and nice shade underneath. He thought he could have a short nap there too and allow Qawiun some rest before they would go on.

The tree was about two hundred meters ahead of him. But it did not seem to be closer the more he traveled towards it; it seemed to be moving further away and after more than ten minutes, he realized that he was not going to reach it. It was a mirage that he had seen in his mind's eye and it was not a real tree. In the desert, his father, had often reminded him before he started on the journey, one can see many things which are not in real life; they only exist in one's mind. And this was one tree that popped in his mind's eye, just like what his father had reminded me a few times.

Omar felt disappointed because there was no tree where h could go to and have a rest, and the sun was also getting to be brighter than it was earlier after it had escaped the clouds that were hanging underneath it, causing the desert too to become bright.

He looked at Qawiun in front of him; he pitied his horse and wanted to stop anywhere where it was hospitable for them to do so.

And till now they had not seen anyone traveling on either side of the road. Did he get on the right junction earlier to get here? Omar began to feel worried if he might have taken the wrong junction to be where he was now and not on the road that could lead him to Baitullaham. But there was no way for him to stop and turn around to go back to the junction and there was no way for him to find direction with anyone there. He hoped there would be some strangers who would pass by from the other direction that he could stop to ask for direction. But chances of that happening were bleak. He had seen some local Arabs on their horses galloping on the other side of the road earlier before he reached the junction, the only junction he had seen, to come here. And only now he began to realize that the road where he was at now seemed to be narrower than the one he had traveled along before he got to the junction. Saleem said, or asked him to be certain and not miss the first junction he reached which was about one hour after leaving the house. So he was now thirty minutes from the first junction. There was no signboard for him to see where he was and which road he ought to take to go to Baitullaham. He felt lost. Qawiun galloped along and not knowing what Omar was thinking or worrying about.

Then he saw another tree; ah, it was not a real tree, he said to himself; it was a fake tree that he had implanted in his mind, he said to himself so he did not want his horse to rush towards it. It was two hundred meters from where they were. And the tree was not as tall and it had more leaves than the tree that was a mirage he saw earlier. Omar got closer to the tree but the tree did not run away from him. Then he realized that it might be a real tree and not one he was thinking in his mind. He felt a great relief when he felt that it was indeed a real tree and not one that had formed in his mind's eye.

Omar got the cart closer to the tree which was on the left side of the road, and on the other side of the road from where he was riding the cart and when he got closer to the tree, he knew it was a real one. He then maneuvered Qawiun to go to the tree to rest under it. And when he got there he stopped and got off and looked around. It was bare; the desert was vast and he and Qawiun were the only two creatures who were there in the middle of nowhere.

Omar got some snacks and ate and drank from a large bottle of water Saleem's wife had packed and gave him. He gave some water to Qawiun who then partook some grass on the ground; it was tall and quite fresh.

Where am I, Omar asked himself. I am in the middle of nowhere. God help us! He then recited some supplication or 'dua' prayers his father had asked him to do, if he thought he was faced with some difficulties. He closed his eyes as he was doing that. He tried to calm himself down and did not want to worry for nothing. He said it might be a good place and time for him and the horse to take a break, wherever they were. But this time they were not as lucky as before when they got to a small village which had a few houses and families living in them and Saleem and his family who were so kind to accept him and Qawiun to stay for the night with them.

Omar found a spot under the tree and lay on it to take a rest for no more than thirty minutes, he said. Thirty minutes only. Few birds flew above them and within some seconds they were gone to the other side of the desert. He pulled a copy of the Noble Qu'ran he had in his leather sling bag and opened a page in it where he had left off after reading it the last time just before he left his father's house, and found Chapter One Hundred called Surah Al Adiyat and read it to himself without raising his voice. He could recite it by heart but he still needed the book to hold for greater satisfaction. And once in a while he would let out a sound that startled his horse, Qawiun who turned to look at him as he continued to read.

* * * * * * *

AL ADIYAT (THE COURSER, THE CHARGERS)

In the name of Allah, the Gracious,
the Merciful.
I swear by the runners breathing
pantingly,
Then those that produce fire striking,
Then those that make raids at morn,
Then thereby raise dust,
Then rush thereby upon an assembly:
Most surely man is ungrateful to his Lord.
And most surely he is a witness of that.
And most surely he is tenacious in the
love of wealth.
Does he not then know when what
is in the graves is raised,
And what is in the breasts is made
apparent?
Most surely their Lord that day shall be
fully aware of them.

* * * * * * *

Qawiun often felt at peace when he heard Omar or anyone reading passages or surah from the Noble Qu'ran like he knew what they meant. The sounds made by the reciters was soothing not only to all Arab-Muslims but also to animals. Even birds too were known to stand perched on the branches of olive and date trees when sounds of anyone reciting verses from the Noble Qu'ran was heard and more so when they were blared from speakers at many masjids everywhere in any village, towns and cities throughout Palestine. None of them would dare to move until the recital was over. Even babies would keep quiet to listen with full concentration when they heard anyone reciting verses from the Noble Qu'ran, too. And many Arab parents would pacify their young babies who were hardly few months old by reading any passage from the Noble Qu'ran if they could not stop crying and giving them milk in bottles or pacifiers did not work.

Omar had finished reading the chapter from the Noble Qu'ran and he closed the book and put it back into his sling bag. Qawiun waited to see what he wanted to do next; to move on or to continue resting until he was fully rested and was ready to go.

Omar seemed to be unduly worried; Saleem had mentioned about the Year 1928 which was the year when he was only two years old and then continued to talk about the British Mandate over Palestine which he did not know much of since he was too young then. Saleem told him his village had never been visited by any British officers; but those who lived in the larger cities and towns especially Baitulmukaddis and even Baitullaham where he was heading for had seen some of them.

What could he expect to see and get when he was in Baitullaham, he asked himself. He did not know the answer. His father did not say what he could expect to do there except for him to sell off the carpets and other things he had packed in the cart he was not taking there. He had relatives to meet and to whom he wanted to give some of the carpets; but for the rest, he wanted to sell them to get cash which might be handy in times of need compared to carpets. He then started to worry for his father who had left behind if he would be okay; if his mother and other brothers and sisters too would be okay. Their village was not very far from Baitulmukaddis. And if what Saleem had said to him was true, then whatever happened to Palestine could have a direct impact on his village and his family and those who also live in it.

Suddenly Omar felt his hands were sweating. He rubbed them on his robe to dry them. Qawiun neighed, this time quite loud. What was it trying to say? And suddenly the horse started to twist and turn like he was possessed. Omar sprung to his feet and grabbed Qawiun by the head and asked it to stay calm. Did he see something that Omar could not see? Omar did not believe in ghosts; it was haram of forbidden for him or any Muslim to believe in them. In God's Earth, they did not exist, he pacified himself with such thought. His Ustaz or Religious Teacher who went by the name of Ustaz, often told him and the other students to never believe in such things, although they had also been taught to believe in Ghosts that existed and some of them were Good Ghosts and others Bad Ghosts. Most or all Ghosts were caged during the fasting month of Ramadan to be released after the month was done.

Qawiun neighed another time and this time it was accompanied by his body twisting even more than it was earlier; which caused Omar to feel even more worried. He then decided to leave the place while there was still light around them, which would soon dim to make way for evening and the Magic Hour to break few minutes before sunset or Maghrib. Then Omar realized that it was time for Zohor and he called out the adhan and then started to pray. He laid a prayer carpet on the ground and prayed with Qawiun watching. It was over in less than two minutes for him to complete all the rakaat and a short supplication, this time he prayed for his and his horse's safety, because he now knew he was lost in the desert and the light from the sun was dimming very fast.

Omar was back on the cart with Qawiun pulling it along by the side of the road, at the right; and there was no other direction that they could take other than to just ride on and on ahead, until Omar thought he could find another junction to force himself to choose which to take. There was no one there and also no road signs to tell him the direction to Baitullaham. He just wanted to move on, regardless of where he might have to stop, which was when it had become too dark for him to continue to ride when he had to stop to rest for the night. He knew the whole of Palestine was safe for anyone. But he was not sure if there might be wild wolves or dogs that could make his life miserable and put him in some danger.

Suddenly, out of the blue, a stray camel came rushing in the opposite direction with no one riding it. There was a saddle on its back so Omar thought that the camel had managed to escape from its master or was facing some danger. Camels normally did not rush away like that, he thought; they knew how to look after the well-being of their owners if they had kept them well and gave them shelter and food.

Omar stopped his horse to wait and see if there might be anyone coming to rush after the camel. There was also no way for him to catch it because it was running at a fast speed and in the other direction and by the time he could guess what was happening, the camel had gone far past him. He could only watch it from his cart which was not static. He waited for ten minutes and no one was seen to try and rush after the camel. What happened, he asked the horse. It didn't answer but just gave a slight neigh.

It was time for them to move on. The light around them was now dim. It was three o'clock and sunset would come at five-thirty, for Maghrib; for Omar to pray again, but he was not sure if he was also going to pray outside by the side of the road like he just did for Zohor earlier. He reached for a bottle and took a few gulps and then poured a bit on his right palm and threw the water in it on the back of the horse which welcomed it.

Omar then remember the advice given to him by Saleem, who said, once you see the first junction, make sure to take the one at the right and from there just ride on and on until you get to a village where you can find shelter. They have some stores where you can buy provisions and food and drinks, too.

Omar blamed himself for not taking the advice properly; he realized that he had taken the wrong junction; and instead of going to the right one, he took the left one that caused him to be where he was, in the middle of nowhere and with no village in sight. Remember, the right road at the junction, reminded Saleem. However, if you had made a mistake and take the road at the right after the junction, you can still ride on and on, but there is no village or small town and you need to gallop fast to get to the next one for two and a half hours, and by that time it would be sunset for the Maghrib prayers. In any case, do not unduly worry because this whole area is safe, reminded Saleem, except for some lone wolf or dog that might sniff your presence or that of your horse, Qawiun. Just ignore it if it comes by. Throw some food for it to eat and go away.

But Omar was not assuaged by the advice and encouragement; he began to worry for his personal safety and that of his horse, who did not know any better than to ride as ordered by Omar who now started to stare at the horizon of the sun dipping into it taking with it the last rays of light of the day; and the Magic Hour was truly magnificent; it manage to distract him of his worries and uncertainties. There was no sound of the call of the adhan for Maghrib and he had to call it himself as he was riding the cart along.

He decided to find a place to rest and pray, but there was no place that was hospitable enough for him to do that. Everywhere him it was the same.

Omar had his Maghrib prayers and was now resting by the side of the road; he had untied Qawiun and tied him to cart to stop him from running off. He was reminded of the stray camel he had seen running the other direction with no one on it. He then started to fear if Qawiun too would do the same to him to escape being bonded to him when he could be on its own to live in the desert as a true horse with no master.

The night came very quickly and Omar had just performed the Isyak prayers, alone. The horse was lying on the ground and was well-fed with food and drink. The full moon was shining over the vast desert and Omar could not sleep. He was worried about how his father back in his village who might by now knew he had not arrived in Baitullaham. He must have called them by phone to check on him, to see if he had arrived there.

Omar hoped the night would go on uneventful and he could somehow get some sleep. He lied on the cart and felt safe there instead of lying on the ground beside it where there could be insects. But he could not go to sleep. He had had a lot to eat and drink after the final prayers for the day. And it was now ten at night. He needed to get some sleep, he told himself. He checked Qawiun and found that he had fallen asleep; he pitied the horse for having to bear with him. But what had happened along the way, was nothing he could imagine or expect to happen, but it did through no fault of anyone. The God must have some plans for him and the horse, he thought with the delay in arriving at Baitullaham. But he thought he was blessed when he bumped into Saleem and his family who were especially kind to him.

He felt comfortable lying on the cart and being protected by the rolls of carpet beside him one of which he used as a pillow, and was well hidden near some rocks he had purposely chosen to spend the night at, for added protection. He had never had to spend the night in such a condition before.

Then the camel that had ran away from his master he saw in the day, running in the opposite direction, ran again and in the direction he was heading, and still with no one on the saddle. Omar trusted his head to look at the camel as it ran away not knowing what it might be experiencing and if he was returning to his master who he had left earlier in the day. What was it up to? It had been more than one and a half hours since he last saw the camel and now it was back but running in the opposite direction. Did he suddenly realize that he had left his master behind and now wanted to go back to him? Some camels and even horses were known to have done that, thought Omar and this one smart camel could be one of them smart ones!

He did not want to think about them too much. All that he wanted to do was to get some sleep so that he could resume his journey tomorrow morning after the Maghrib prayers and having breakfast of the food that Saleem's wife had packed for him. He was certain he could get to his final destination before noon tomorrow traveling in the day all the way there, into safety but still an uncertain future. He did not actually know what his father had wanted him to do there; all that he wanted Omar to do was to sell the carpets, as many as he could, and the remainder give to their relatives. But how long did he want Omar to remain there with his family, he did not know. And for the first time he felt like his own father had wanted to disown him. He did not like to think negatively what his father did and wanted to think that he was doing it for Omar's own good.

Omar did fall asleep and when he woke up it was before the sun started to rise, as it was normal for him to wake up at such time, to allow him to prepare for the Dawn prayers, a practice he had been taught by his parents since he was small. He looked around and could only see the whole area still hidden in shadows, with the hills in the foreground all around him. His horse, Qawiun was still sleeping on the ground beside the cart below him. It was cold the whole night as it would be in the desert, and Omar had enough carpets to cover his body with; he pitied his horse which did not have any covering over his body. He then went down with a thick blanket made of wool and covered its body. He then thought he heard the faint call of the Adhan for the Dawn prayers; he must be imagining because he knew there was no masjid around in the whole area as far as he could see and if there was one nearby, or in the far distance, he would have known about it because calls for Adhan would have been made few times in the day ending with the last one for the Isyak or the late night prayers. He heard none of it. So he thought he must be dreaming, when he thought he had heard the call for Adhan at such an hour. Besides, the first break of dawn had not happened because the sky was still not lit by any light from the sun which was still hidden in the horizon. He looked at the East for it; but it was not yet there. So the Adhan that he thought he had heard was just in his head.

Qawiun, felt better with a thick woolen blanket now covering his entire body.

Then a few minutes later Omar saw the first light of the sun lighting up the sky over the horizon and just a bit of the sun was peeping; he knew now for certain that dawn of the new day had appeared. And he called out the Adhan to himself, and not too loud because he did not want to attract undue attention of strangers who might be in his vicinity, and who might be of a certain type. He did not want to say they were thieves but people of some shady character. He blamed himself for having such negative thoughts; he knew in the whole of Palestine, all Arabs, be they those who professed the Muslim faith or Christianity were good people; they were People of the Book who believed in their religion and who would never inflict any harm or pain onto anyone else. But he still called out the Adhan in a muted way, to himself, before he performed the Dawn prayer, all by himself and beside his cart. Qawiun was still sleeping and was not about to wake up, even after Omar had finished with his prayers, before which he had to perform his ablution using dusts he collected from the sand to cleanse his body called 'tayamum' which he was allowed to do in the absence of water, which he had a bit, but which he wanted to save for drinking purposes for him and his horse.

Qawiun woke up with a neigh feeling fresh; and Omar noticed that the horse was up and about when he immediately sprang onto his four feet, as he would do everyday when he woke up. It made Omar very happy to see his horse looking hale and healthy. He went to it and gave it a pat on the back with a massage. 'Good horse, Qawiun,' he said as he continued to pat and massage it.

Omar took the blanket and folded it and put it back on the cart. He gave Qawiun some food to eat and water to drink and said to it, 'We'll be back on the road, Qawiun.'

Omar and Qawiun were back on the road, heading towards Baitullaham, which was still a distance away; and it was early morning when they left the spot where they had spent the night to sleep and rest. They had not seen anyone since leaving Saleem's village, other than the stray camel that rushed in the opposite direction yesterday afternoon and later in the evening when it ran again in the direction they were heading now. Omar was sure and hoped he could see it again along the way, and better still, with the camel and its master. His watch showed it was nine in the morning of the new day, and two days after he left his village with his father, mother and brothers and sisters and some other close relatives and friends in the village waving him goodbye and after his father had recited a supplication to seek Allah's divine help to ensure that his son's journey to Baitullaham would be uneventful and safe.

So far Omar was relieved that he and his horse were safe other than the two nights when they had to sleep in a stranger's house and last night beside a road in the vast and empty desert. Omar believed it was Allah's will that had put him in the situation and it was for a very good reason. In his village, he led a pampered live because his father was considered to be someone of wealth and he had never had to suffer, and was treated nicely by everybody in the whole village who also knew his father's reputation; being kind and helpful who would often give them alms and food when they needed it. Often he would also become the Imam of the masjid where he took the opportunity to give friendly advice to his fellow congregation comprising mostly of the villagers, many of who might not be as lucky as he was.

What was his father's idea for sending him in a horse-cart with Qawiun pulling to go to Baitullaham, Omar asked himself?

Ahmed...er...was it Ali, the son of Saleem who he had given a ride on Qawiun. Omar could not remember which was which. He asked Qawiun, 'Do you what is the name of Mister Saleem's first son? Is it Ahmed or Ali?' He suddenly remembered the name, Ali. The horse was smart to be able to understand the question. 'Ahmed?' Qawiun shook his head to the right and left. 'No? Not Ahmed?' Qawiun shook his head to the right and left again as it galloped briskly ahead. 'Are you sure?' Qawiun nodded.

Omar paused and tried to remember, which was which – Ahmed or Ali. 'Hmmm...I guess you are right, Qawiun. Ali, is his name, not Ahmed. I must have got it confused with another person. And what's the name of Mister Saleem's wife? Sameera?'

Qawiun nodded his head.

'You are smarter than me.'

Qawiun gave a loud neigh and moved ahead running along the dusty road ahead which did not look like they were heading anywhere as the scenery was the same all the time they were moving. There was not a single soul in sight; even the birds were missing. Except for some breeze that blew in their faces, it was difficult for them to feel comfortable in the heat that was suddenly appearing as the sun started to rise above them which soon would be directly above them, when it was noon and when it was also the time for Zohor prayers.

Omar was relieved that he had got Saleem's sons' name correctly; they were Ali and Hashim, aged ten and nine. Both did not have familiar facial features but who looked pleasant; they took after their mother's features while their two elder sisters took those of their father.

It was now noon and Omar had stopped by the side of the road with food in his hands; it was the same food that Sameerah had packed for them that could last for a few more meals. By then he hoped to be able to get to Baitullaham, where he promised Qawiun that he would give him a long and good rest for a long time before he would even consider taking him for another ride. Besides, in Baitullaham, there was no place for them to go to as it was their destination and it would be where he would be given further instructions from his uncle on what he ought to do. That was what his father, had called his younger brother to tell him to do. He took the lunch after performing the Zohor prayers which came just before noon. Qawiun too had some food and water to take him to their next stop, where Omar hoped he could find the second junction from where he should be able to get to Baitullaham, where they would be small villages and people he could meet. And there would be road signs at proper Macadamized or turf roads that he could take to go directly to Baitullaham with comfort and safety.

Omar decided to give Qawiun some exercise by loosing him from the cart and riding it around it and further away to some low hills to give his horse some new moves to take instead of forcing it to ride along roads in straight lines and not being able to use his other muscles which might have become weak. The horse seemed to enjoy taking Omar on the ride in great strides and sometimes when instructed by Omar, he would speed ahead in great joy, like he owned the whole place. There were no horses or camels and there were also no birds for as far as Omar could see. It also gave Omar some respite from his trivial and mundane life as a traveler in his own country like he was running away from something, or who was forced to lead such a life by his own father for something else which he could not as yet guess what it was. The answer would await him when he got to his uncle's house in Baitullaham where he would go to before he could ever go to his own house where his wife and children and their grand-parents were waiting. Did they know that he was coming over soon? His uncle might have told them that.

Take your time! Take your time! His father would remind him before he drove off on his horse-cart with Qawiun, after he had read a supplication or short prayer outside of their house. And this was what Omar had suddenly remembered his father advising him to do, which was not to rush to get to Baitullaham. And with this he felt at peace with himself and started to enjoy the journey he had made thus far and in the company of his horse. In all Omar thought he had spent a good half hour riding the horse going around the area in the vast desert and to one of the low hills from where he managed to see a valley below and might even have seen some small and isolated villages, one of which might be where Saleem lived. He offered his gratitude to Allah for the sight that beheld before him and all around him which to him looked pristine and how he would like it to remain like this forever and ever...

Palestine is as good as it was when the Arabs lived here many years ago, said Omar to himself, and it should not be a pawn to any foreign political power to change its course in history. He did not want to mention the British; but he did not want to remind himself that they were 'Kafir' or 'Al-Kafiroun', who had come to Palestine to cause trouble and to create dissent, albeit an unnecessary one that could cause the breaking up of their vast country.

The sky above him was clear blue and there were clean, white clouds hanging there motionlessly. What a sight! Omar remarked. He imagined and guessed Baitullaham would be at the right, so he turned around a bit with the help of his horse and wondered if it might be there, further away from where he was now. And Baitulmukaddis would be at the right to it but much further away from Baitullaham, beyond the horizons, where the Tomb of the Rock and Masjid Al-Aqsa were and also The Old City, also known as The Walled City where people from the three religions, the People of the Book lived in complete understanding and full appreciation of each other's religious, cultural and social backgrounds with one part in The Old City having three lanes that merged and blocked by the walls of a Masjid, church and synagogue. Of course, Omar had not seen the three houses of worship or been to The Old City but he had heard stories about them from those who had been there including from his father who said he would have to go to one there.

Omar did not know that the horse he was riding which he wanted to take him to Baitullaham, was a horse that was given by his father's good friend who lived in The Old City in Baitulmukaddis, who was a Jew and good friend of his, but who had a piece of land outside of the city where he reared horses and camels. And that was how Gawiun came to be in his family and now belonged to Omar. His father did not have the opportunity to relate to him how he had met his Jewish friend because there was no reason for him to raise the matter to him or to his family. He forgot to mention it when he asked Omar to take it to Baitullaham. So no wonder the horse looked different that those that his father had in his village which were taller and bigger while Qawiun was shorter and smaller yet agile and strong, so no wonder, too he called it 'Qawiun' which means 'Strong' in Arabic.

Then suddenly, Omar felt fear in his head; he now wanted to delay arriving in Baitullaham, where uncertainties awaited him. He thought it was now good for him to have delayed arriving at his destination because now he knew exactly why his father had ordered him to go there. But he had no clue as to what he was worried of. He just did not feel good with the whole thing. Qawiun kept on galloping ahead. Omar wanted to ask him to slow down; there was now no rush for him to get to Baitullaham. He wanted to stop somewhere to take another rest. It was now four o'clock and the day was still bright and sunny and cool. There was no one he had seen and no birds flying in the sky and no camel running astray anymore.

Omar sat beside the cart with his horse running loose; he had loosened the rope around him for the first time because he did not care if the horse would leave him to go anywhere to free himself of the bondage. But Qawiun did not have any intention of deserting his master who had treated him well, and provided him with shelter, food, and drink. And now Qawiun seemed to think that Omar was even allowing him to experience more freedom, by letting himself loose by removing the noose around it neck so he could run anywhere and even go away without ever returning to him.

Qawiun ran around but not furiously; the speed he had chosen was fast because he had not gotten the opportunity to run this fast before, and he was only required to gallop at a constant speed. Now he wanted to run as fast as he could to shake some of his muscles from lethargy. It then stopped and turned around and looked at Omar in the distance; Omar was not looking at the horse; he was almost closing his eyes and in deep thought. In his hand is the copy of the Noble Qu'ran which was not opened. He was just holding it in his hands. He might be reciting a verse in the book he had memorized by heart.

* * * * * * *

"And do not consume one another's wealth unjustly or send it (in bribery) to the rulers in order that (they might aid) you (to) consume a portion of the wealth of the people in sin, while you know (it is unlawful)." – *The Holy Quran 2:188*

"Righteousness is not that you turn your faces toward the east or the west, but (true) righteousness is (in) one who believes in Allah , the Last Day, the angels, the Book, and the prophets and gives wealth, in spite of love for it, to relatives, orphans, the needy, the traveler, those who ask (for help), and for freeing slaves; (and who) establishes prayer and gives zakah; (those who) fulfill their promise when they promise; and (those who) are patient in poverty and hardship and during battle. Those are the ones who have been true, and it is those who are the righteous." – *The Holy Quran 2:177*

"O you who have believed, be persistently standing firm in justice, witnesses for Allah, even if it be against yourselves or parents and relatives. Whether one is rich or poor, Allah is more worthy of both. So follow not (personal) inclination, lest you not be just. And if you distort (your testimony) or refuse (to give it), then indeed Allah is ever, with what you do, Acquainted." – *The Holy Quran 4:135*

"And for women is a share of what the parents and close relatives leave, be it little or much – an obligatory share." – *The Holy Quran 4:7*

"To this world and the Hereafter. And they ask you about orphans. Say, "Improvement for them is best. And if you mix your affairs with theirs – they are your brothers. And Allah knows the corrupter from the amender. And if Allah had willed, He could have put you in difficulty. Indeed, Allah is Exalted in Might and Wise." – *The Holy Quran 2:220*

* * * * * *

Qawiun then started to walk slowly towards Omar and sat beside him. This woke up Omar. He turned to look at it and rested his body on the horse's body to keep each other warm but by just a bit. Qawiun felt good with it and allowed Omar to continue resting on its body.

We'll be okay, Qawiun, said Omar to the horse; he also said it to remind himself that it would be okay. There was a slight tinge of fear in the way he had said it. We'll be okay... Omar blamed himself for not asking his father what the real intention was for him to go force him to go to Baitullaham; and he now knew for certain that it was not for him to get rid of carpets and to sell some if he could, one he had done to Saleem on the way here. He then began to feel guilty when he thought that he might have told Saleem a lie when he said he was going to Baitullaham to trade and to meet with his relatives there. He hoped Saleem could forgive him.

* * * * * *

AL QARI'AH (Revealed before Hijrah)
In the name of Allah, the Gracious, the Merciful.
The great Calamity! At is the great Calamity is?
And what should make thee know what the great

Calamity is?
The day when mankind will be like scattered moths,
And the mountains will be like carded wool.

63

Then, as for him whose scales are heavy,
He will have a pleasant life.
But as for him whose scales are light,
Hell will be his nursing mother.
And what should make thee know what that is?
It is a burning Fire.

* * * * * *

Omar then opened the Noble Qu'ran at the page where he had left off and saw Surah 101 – Al Adiqat, and found it to be what the Surah was, was exactly what he feeling then. And he started to read the Surah; and this time, he read it quite loudly which startled Qawiun but who enjoyed hearing the sound of the text and his voice, until he was done not long after he started to read which was not very long. And he was done. He closed the Noble Qu'ran and put it back in his sling bag and rose to his feet. Qawiun too rose afterwards to get ready to move along.

The light of the day had started to dim a bit but Omar was not in any hurry to arrive at his destination and this time he wanted to delay it further and if possible, he wouldn't mind taking any night out in the open like what he had done the night before, sleeping with his horse in the middle of nowhere in the desert with no one in sight. He read a supplication by heart and when it was over he wiped his face with both his hands. He asked for Allah's guidance for the real journey that he was embarking for which he knew not of; and he wanted to be certain that his horse, Qawiun would be safe and 'strong' so that whatever goals his father had for him to achieve were achievable. He also prayed for his parents and brothers and sisters and mostly for his wife and his two children who were in Baitullaham and who he had not seen in a while. They were staying with her parents there.

Amin.

5

Hajji Othman, 1915

Omar was traveling along the dusty road not very far from the junction where he was supposed to take a right to get to Baitullaham. He was relieved that it was still bright and he could get to his destination before dusk. He felt very emotional earlier because he forgot to give gratitude to his Grandfather, Hajji Othman when he was offering supplications to his family, before continuing on with his journey.

Haji Othman is his grandfather, who is the father of his father, Munir, who died at an advanced age of eighty-five in 1915 or twenty-one years ago. Omar remembered the funeral of his grandfather Hajji Othman, which was well-attended by the members of his family and almost everybody in his village. He died in his sleep. Omar was four years old and was especially close to him, and who was Hajji Othman's first grandchild, a boy, who was born a year after his father, Munir got married by him to a woman he and his wife had chosen who was the daughter of his best friend, Hajji Khalid who had gone to Makkah to perform the Hajj with their wives together, which was the last of the Five Pillars of Islam – To testify to Allah's oneness; To pray five times a day; Pay zakat or alms; Fast or 'sawm' throughout the Holy Month of Ramadan, and finally: Perform Hajj, for a Muslim if he or she is physically, mentally, and financially capable.

They took the land route to get there and spent a week on the road before they got to Makkah early one morning, feeling elated and relieved that they had finally managed to arrive there in good health, after traveling for so long. They were in a caravan together with about ten other horse-driven carts carrying other Arabs from Palestine who were performing Hajj together.

Omar could not remember which month it was when his grandfather and grandmother, Muneerah left their village. And it took them four months before they returned after performing the Hajj. Fortunately, all those who went there in the same caravan of ten horse-driven carts managed to return, safely, except for one, who suffered some disease and had to receive medical attention in Jeddah for a few days before he was allowed to rejoin his group. And almost every year there would be some from his village and the neighboring ones who would group together to go on the pilgrimage to Makkah. The women would cook food along the way where they decided to camp for the night and pray together in the open facing Makkah, which was their direction before sleeping and waking up early the next morning to do the same ritual which was to perform the Maghrib prayers and continuing their travel.

But Omar could remember it was a few days after he had his circumcision, which had to be delayed for a year, because his parents, grandparents, and granduncles wanted him to wait for his younger brother and a few other cousins who were of the ripe age to have it together so they could have a grander celebration in their village. And because of this he was not able to see his grandfather and grandmother, and the others in the village were paraded outside to send them off on their pilgrimage. His grandparents and two others rode in the same horse-cart that Omar was using later, because he was given it as a present which thrilled him, only because of the cart, which his father did not want to use because he had a bigger one. But Omar was not happy to receive the cart as a present, barely two years after his grandfather, now Hajji Othman had died.

Omar could only peeped outside of the window of his parents' house to see the future Hajjis and Hajjjahs being paraded in the village and fortunately, he had a room on the first floor of the house that allowed him to have a wider and a bird's-eye view of the whole activity where a few hundred of the other villagers had gathered to see the group of fifteen sitting in their horse-driven carts and moving slowly with the beat of the drums by the village music group perform songs that sounded like supplications to entertain them and to give them further encouragement so they would have an enjoyable and uneventful journey that would take a few weeks to get to Makkah, after a full supplication had already been given by the Imam of the village masjid, who himself had performed the Hajj at least two times, or maybe even three times, depending on how to count it. And some of the villagers who had also performed the Hajj earlier were there to give encouragement and advice. Some of them were much younger than Omar's grandparents who had decided long before that they should go to Makkah for the Hajj, while Omar's grandfather was slow in doing that and only managed to perform his Hajj very late in his life. And because of that Omar's own parents were not able to go there, as it was not proper for them to go there to perform their Hajj before their parents did.

And there was also the 'dabka' dance performed by the young boys and girls, which was strenuous which Omar had not yet gotten to do as it involved a lot of kicking and jumping, which some older men and women in the village and in some others thought it was too vulgar. So, no wonder Omar and his brothers and sisters, too were not encouraged to do the dance by their parents and grandparents. But they didn't mind them watching the dance as long as it was performed less wildly.

Omar's parents would go to Makkah two years later in 1917. But by this time some of the wealthier Arabs were able to go to Makkah not on horse-driven carts but in cars that were imported from England which were reliable. But many who had gone in such vehicles said they were not comfortable sitting in such vehicles because they were small; so the others who decided to go to Makkah later, preferred to take their carts to go there, where they did not have to also worry about the vehicles breaking down, or when there was no fuel to run them. And in the end some of them needed some horses to pull them until their owners could get mechanics to fix the problems with the engine which often became hot and died along the way; or when they could top up on petrol to continue to drive them on.

Omar's parents' trip to Makkah would take up a whole episode to describe as it happened at a later time when things were different and when there were more Muslim pilgrims from other countries outside of the Arab World were starting to join the pilgrims to perform their Hajj together that his grandparents could not see.

No one took photos as it was not their priority to do so on such a trip; but Omar's grandfather, did write in his book of his experience traveling with the group to and from Makkah for their pilgrimage and Omar was happy that the book of notes was handed to him by his father who did not want to keep it and trusted Omar to keep it safe. The book was not with him but he had left it in his wife's house. So he would certainly want to take another look at it the moment he returned to the house probably in one and a half hours' time; or two at the most, but still before dusk. Again he reminded himself not to rush; and if he had to stay for the night somewhere along the way, he would do it gladly; and this time he did not want to worry and enjoy the time he would be spending there, wherever it might be, in the middle of the desert again, or near a stream where he could dip himself in the water for hours with Qawiun, and lay there until the two of them were fully satisfied; or, better still, in an oasis, where there were dates and other fruits and surely, some people living in it since it was a hospitable place for them to live with some who might even have lived there for ages.

Omar remembered how his grandfather reminded his father to take good care of him, whilst he was not around in the village to keep an eye on him or to teach him to read the Noble Qu'ran. But why did they choose a date so close to them going off to Makkah? Omar did not wonder about this issue then as it was just four years, and who did not know why dates for such important events in the entire village was chosen. Later on when he reflected on it, he thought it was not right. Why didn't they have the circumcision ceremony for the boys at an earlier date so by the time the parade for the future Hajj pilgrims happened, they were healthy enough to walk on both feet and wearing their clothes properly without being held hostage inside their own homes and lying like they were sick people? And from where he was he could see many boys his age who were there in the crowd; obviously, their parents had given them circumcision earlier when they were two or three years old and not four years like Omar. Some of them had their circumcision when they were even one-year-old, or less. Omar looked at them wearing normal clothes and running around and some mimicking the dabka dance they were seeing at the side amongst them, using the music that was being played. They were good with their steps because they had seen the dance many times before unlike Omar and his brothers and sisters who did not. And they had grown to become frigid in their movements and feel shy because they were not physically expressive, and that also took a toll when they started to learn how to read the Noble Qu'ran, when they could not trust their voices loud enough for even the Ustaz to hear. The others were confident and were able to recite all the verses or Surah properly.

What Omar's grandfather had written in his note books on his journey to Makkah was revealing; he not only wrote about his observations on the trip and where they were but also on the antics of his fellow pilgrims and those who they met along the way, the help they got from strangers wherever they were. And the note books were kept in a secret compartment in the cart that no one knew, not even his father, Munir, so when Omar was handed the cart without the horse, which had since died, he found the books. He was shocked when he read them because his grandfather was a person with a few words, or who hardly spoke, but when he wrote, he knew what to say. There were even passages on Omar himself on when he was born and how he behaved when he arrived in the world, etc. Yes, Omar cried a lot and very loudly even at night when he would wake up to demand to be given milk that his own mother did not have in large volumes so that his father had to give some he had taken from the camels, the few that he had, to pacify his first son.

Omar laughed to himself when he first read about him as described by his grandfather. But he and his father and grandmother and mother did not have any bad words for him; they all knew he was their first son or grandson so they thought he was very precious, a gift from God. More so, when he came into their family earlier than the nine months that was required. He was in a hurry to see all of us, his grandfather would remark. This made Omar smile to himself and some moments afterwards he would feel emotional because he felt like both his grandparents were still there to offer them their love, by carrying them everywhere in the village and his grandfather would also take him on rides on his horse-cart around the village and to the neighboring ones, to show his grandson, Omar to his close friends.

Why didn't he go to Makkah for Umrah or the Minor Hajj? His grandfather had mentioned it in his notebook and what he had written startled Omar; he didn't realize that for so long his grandfather never went to Makkah before he went to perform his Hajj. The reasons that were given by his grandfather were quite amusing at times; this made Omar feel confused if his grandfather was joking. But he was never a joker and had never cracked a joke that he knew of. As far as Omar knew his grandfather, as well as his own father were stern people and he would be like them had he not mixed with more boys his age and some who were younger and older then him, until he got married at the age of twenty.

Omar's grandfather, was busy raising his family as he was not a wealthy person, even though he had camels, goats, horses, and a large plot of land where there were date and olive trees which grew abundant fruits that he could sell to provide for his family. But it was a plot of land that he got from a larger piece which was divided equally between his siblings upon the death of their father, Hajji Manna, who was quite wealthy and who also had a few wives and many children. And the properties especially the large piece of land he had was divided and this left Hajji Othman a smaller piece but which was large enough for him to use to raise the animals and build his own house using his own bare hands using materials he could get in his properties, such as clay and stones, to create a house which looked like no other. And because of that, he missed going for Umrah and Hajji until much later. And so it also did not dawn upon his son, Hajji Othman to follow suit until he became old before he could make the trip to go there, finally, much to the relief of his own children.

The notebooks were in good condition because they were not touched by bare hands or exposed to the elements. Omar wondered if he could get hold of them if his grandfather had handed them to his father to keep, because chances were the notebooks could be lost or at least spoilt because they were not going to be kept properly. And now with them hidden in a secret compartment in the horse-cart, he assumed they, too, belonged to him as did some old coins which were printed by the Palestine government and some British pounds that could still be good to buy. The total value of all the coins was worth a bit. But why did his grandfather leave them in the secret compartment? Omar guessed it was for safety, since he was traveling far from his village to Makkah he had to keep his money and even notebooks in a special place he did not disclose to anyone, even to his own wife, Omar's grandmother, who never said anything about them until she died, when Omar was already in the possession of the cart.

Omar thought he would have to finally tell his father and uncles about the loot; they might want to have a share of it, but he doubted it if they would care so much for the notebooks which were all written in perfect Arabic and in a spelling that could leave the calligraphers in Baitulmukaddis in awe. Did he think he had stolen the properties? No. He did not think he has stolen the notebooks or coins; he was given them when he was given the horse-cart that had them. The only thing that he thought he needed to do or ought to do as was his religion of Islam had told him to do, was to declare the find to his father who had been bequeathed the cart from his father who died. And if his father agreed to allow him to continue to keep the items that had come together with the cart, so be it; or he could just give them to him to decide what to do with them. There was some worth in the coins to them but not necessarily the notebooks that was the diary his grandfather had written which aroused his attention and mostly emotion because what he had written were matters that he did not live to experience but who learnt a lot from being able to read the notes and other jottings to appreciate the life his grandfather and for that matter, his grandmother and whoever that was mentioned in them. And in this way he felt he was still alive then when the incidents as described happened, even though he was not born to the world and to the family yet.

Omar was stunned when he read the first page that contained so much information on his grandfather and his relatives when he was alive; and he could see which part of them and their qualities matched those he also truly appreciated and believed in. All of them had strong faith in Islam, the religion of his ancestors since so many generations past, and of him, too, and all of his children and their children to come.

Did he want to cry? He also wanted to smile; and mostly, he wanted to laugh, especially in the other pages where his grandfather wrote about an incident when he was traveling in the middle of a desert and not knowing where he and the others in the caravan were; the only thing that they could see was the sun and moon to guide them towards their destination which was Makkah. The incident that he described in detail was when a camel ran passed by them on the other direction, with no one on the saddle.

What was that? Omar tried to remember what made him feel anxious and quite confused. He tried to remember a similar incident that happened to someone he knew or if it was related to him by Saleem or Ahmed, or Hisham or Ali. He could not tell who had told him such an incident that sounded similar with the one as written by his grandfather.

No, none of them had told him that incident. He looked at his horse, Qawiun and immediately remembered the incident that happened when the two of them were riding slowly in the middle of nowhere after they had left Saleem's village when Omar saw a stray camel rushing very quickly on the other side of the road, at the left and on the opposite direction. That was it, he remarked to himself! How could it be?! He could not believe his eyes when he read the notes written by his grandfather in 1915, when he was going to Makkah and when Omar was four years, that a camel had ran astray and not long earlier the same incident happened to him when another stray camel with an empty saddle on its back had done the same, although it did not happen anywhere near Makkah but in Palestine!

Of course, I was astounded; of course I was stunned, remarked Omar to his friend, when he mentioned it to him when they met in a coffee shop near his village. The two of them were in the same classes from the time they first went to school until they finished it. They were around twenty years old and his friend had just got married and Omar was soon to be married and had been engaged for less than a year, and he bumped into his friend who he invited to his wedding. His friend, of course, thought it was an incident that was related by his father or grandfather to Omar, or one he had read in a magazine or newspaper or book somewhere. No, he did not; said Omar. It was an incident my grandfather had related. To you? No, not to me personally but in the notes he wrote when he was going to perform his Hajj in 1915, just after the First World War broke on 28 July, 1914, which finally ended on 11 November, 1918 with Ramadan which started end of July, to end of August, 1915. Omar's father and his friends went to Makkah in early October of that year. It was not very cold in the day, just nice; except that at night it could be very chilly especially if there were strong winds. Last year, it even snowed, so those who had gone to perform their Hajj then said they were tested by Allah the Almighty. But they were all prepared because they knew the weather in Palestine and the varying temperatures and also in Makkah where it could even flood if there was heavy downpour. It could still be difficult if they had to camp out in the open desert with no trees or boulders to hide themselves; all they had were the horse-driven carts to sleep in and sometimes under, with their horses too, giving cover.

He did not explain to Omar why he thought the incident was not an unusual one because it happened all the time; and he might have heard the same story few times before. It was, to him, 'a desert story', which was quite funny depending on how it was said or related and at which place and at what time. So he assumed it was not an issue, if he did not prod Omar to extend the tale any further.

There was also a sketch of the route they had taken in October which showed it starting from his village to Makkah, which amazingly looked very good and in great details, all written in free hand, like he knew the exact direction and the map of the few countries they had to go through to get to their final destination taking some side roads which were dusty and through the vast and empty deserts and sometime even managed to arrive in oases and isolated villages that allowed them to spend the night, or even two or three days, to enjoy the stream and fruits that grew in abundance on the trees, all courtesy of the local villages who welcomed them with open arms; because to them, greeting and looking after the well-being of strangers especially those who were on their way to Makkah to perform their Hajj was a blessing. They thought the men and women could have taken other routes but they chose to take the ones that led them to their villages. If there were masjid they would stop there to rest and sleep, or they would just camp under the date or olive trees.

Omar was lucky no one bothered to look under the seat of the cart where the secret compartment was, and it was here where he found the notebooks and some coins. In fact, no one in his family including his father, had taken the cart for a ride because they had their own carts which were new and had better features and were also larger. So no wonder none of them including his uncles and aunties wanted to take over the cart which was left in a barn behind the house for so many years before Omar noticed it after he removed some bales and other objects, to find it hidden underneath them. And for someone then who did not have a cart, he was excited with the prospect of having and owning one for himself, to use with a horse he had that he often rode everywhere. And with the cart he was able to do more and carry more things and sometimes took some friends on a joy ride to the neighboring villages and on a few occasions, they spent a few days on their own and camping wherever they found a nice and safe place to put the night, before moving on. They enjoyed seeing the sights of their country, Palestine, despite it being a British Mandate, but from where they were, where they had not seen any British officials, and it did not matter if their country was under the British occupation or of any other country. They bumped into a few Jewish men and women, along the way but they never got the chance to sit with them to discuss things or to ask what they were doing there. They did not live in the villages where they were seen but elsewhere.

Omar's friend, Rahman, who was a year younger than him said those Jewish people did not speak Arabic or Hebrew or 'Ibrani' because they were new to the area and had just come from elsewhere, very far – from Europe.

'Europe?' remarked Omar. 'How could they be here from so far away?'

Rahman and Sulaiman who were there with Omar in the restaurant sat silent; he was shocked to see Omar's reaction to the presence of the Jews they had bumped into. 'What are they doing here?' he asked.

There was silence. It was obvious Omar was not aware of what was going on in Palestine with the arrival of Jews from Europe who had come to live here and working on their own and slowly creating a presence in some of the towns and cities. Omar had not been out of his village in a long while so he did not notice what was happening.

'My 'Jady' and 'Jadaty',' said Omar, to his friend, in reference to his grandfather and grandmother, which startled his friends even more. 'Not 'Walidaya' or 'Ummi',' he added in reference to his Father and Mother. 'And it is also good all their 'abnay' (sons) and 'abnatay' (daughters), their 'tafali' (children) have grown up to become good 'tafali', he added, almost speaking to himself. 'Ours is a good 'eayilati' (family) and I can say to that. And most of our family members – distant and close ones, have become good Muslims and able to fend for ourselves and not many have become 'fellah' (peasant/farmers) although I have nothing against them. After all there are good 'fellah' and bad 'fellah', too as in all villages. But whatever it is, it is prudent for all of use to look at the 'Faranj' (Foreigners) who have come here to sow discord amongst us, and lest we forget about their hidden agendas and intentions, we will find ourselves fighting and hating each other in due course, even when we do not realize that we are hating each other.' He used the word 'Faranj' and not 'Ajam' or 'Ajnabi' or 'Mujahir' which were less derogatory because he was referring to the invaders and who else that wanted to break up Palestine, bit by bit and if the situation was not curtailed and stopped, the whole of Palestine could become another person's territory with the Palestinians living in prison.

What's that got to do with the conversation, they were having, his friends wondered amongst themselves. But they did not want to interrupt his train of thought and allowed him to say everything he wanted as long as he was able to release some of his pent up energies and not trap them inside his mind which could later on destroy his own body and soul. They just nodded, took a sip of tea or coffee and cut a piece of the bread on the wide tray before them, on the table and dipped it in gravy and chewed it.

His friends knew Omar was in another world and in another time, that of his grandfather, grandmother…and also mother and father. He then followed suit and had held the cup of coffee in front of him which was now cold and took a sip as it was thick with no sugar; and he then put the cup down to pick a piece of pita bread and chewed it without dipping it into gravy to eat. 'In the old days, people would eat pita bread without gravy,' he said. 'That was what my grandfather said in the notes he wrote on his trip to Makkah.

His friends, Rahman and Sulaiman sat frozen in their seats; they noticed Omar was still with his grandfather and grandmother who were on their way to Makkah in October, 1915, after Eidul Fitri and before Eidul Adha, for their pilgrimage to perform Hajj, not that they did not enjoy listening to anyone who were relating their personal experiences going to Makkah, that must be very tiring and long and sometimes dangerous too as there were cases when some had been attacked by wild wolves who appeared from nowhere.

'I sometimes take bread without gravy, too,' said Rahman, nonchalantly. His intention was to get Omar to stop, before he got worse and said more personal things. But what startled them was how he talked about the Foreigners, meaning the British and Jews who had suddenly started to appear in groups from out of nowhere to come to Palestine and live amongst themselves with some of them being wealthy who could afford to purchase properties, such as houses and large tracts of land. They did not mix with the local Arabs and stuck to themselves, even with the local Jews who had lived in Palestine for ages, and many of them could also speak good Arabic like the Arabs. Many had local

Arab names, but not the Faranj who had strange ones, which were alien to their culture and existence. But they did not mind their presence as long as they did not inflict any harm on others, who they thought were lower to them in dignity, they were mostly the local fellah, who would oftentimes go to them to seek employment, to do menial jobs that the did not want to do themselves.

Rahman looked at Sulaiman and they then turned to look at Omar who was now suddenly in deep thought. What might he be thinking of now, they asked themselves quietly.

'Have a bite, Omar,' said Sulaiman.

Omar nodded but did not take any more food. He remained silent sitting on the wooden chair in the restaurant which was not crowded. There were some Egyptian songs being played over the radio and by the singer who was a favorite for many in Palestine, including himself. Rahman and Sulaiman then thought Omar was engrossed by it and let him continue to listen to the song until it ended, before a new one began, that did not seem to attract his attention; it was sung by an unknown male singer, not a female one who sang earlier.

Omar then reached for a piece of bread and ate it. Suddenly, he almost shrieked, 'Ma Sha Allah' (My goodness), 'I'm running late; I'd better get going.' He then sprung on his feet and rushed to pay for the food and drinks the three of them had taken and wanted to leave the restaurant when the waiter called out. He had seen the coins Omar had given and they were old ones. 'Hey, Omar! Omar! Come back here!'

Omar heard him and wondered why was the matter; he walked to the waiter and did not say a word.

'You have given me old coins.'

Omar took the coins back from the waiter and tried to find some new ones in his pocket but they were all like the ones he had given the waiter. 'Can I pay you later? I only have the same coins with me.'

'That's okay; pay up the next time you come by.'

'Shukran' (Thank you.)

Rahman finished up his drink and went to the waiter and asked, 'What's the matter, Mohammad?'

'He gave me coins that were old and not in use anymore.'

'How old?'

'Very old.' He pulled some coins from his pants pocket and handed them to Mohammed. 'Here, take these. Are they enough?'

Mohammed took the coins and nodded.

Sulaiman joined them and then walked out of the restaurant with Rahman.

'How old is he?' asked Rahman to his friend as they walked along the sidewalks in front of other stores selling a host of things.

'Four,' said Sulaiman, 'like me, too. I'm four. How old are you?'

'I was four last year.'

'So you are now five?'

'Did you have to say that?'

'No, those were not old coins, Omar had given Mohammed.'

'No?'

'They were coins from other countries. His grandfather or father must have got them when they went there and brought some back and gave them to him.'

'But they are still good to use, aren't they?'

'Yes, but not in Palestine. Maybe if you want to go to those countries where they are good, then you can take them.'

'I had never seen him behave like this, like an old man. It would not have been bad if he was thirty or forty or fifty...'

'My father often does the same thing to strangers who do not know him well enough to realize what he is experiencing...'

'Your father?'

'Haji Hamza, that's his name. And may Allah bless his soul. He is a good father who has been fair too all of us, his children and who also helped his nephews and nieces by paying for their tuition and clothes to wear for school; because he said the money he spent on them was from the properties he bequeathed from the properties owned by his late father, my grandfather; so he did not want to think that it was entirely his own money but theirs too. The land he got was not so many 'dunnams', but large enough for him to grow 'zaytun' (olives) which he got some local women to grind using large stones. He even named one of his daughters, Zaytun.'

'He has a very kind heart, Sulaiman – your father and also mother for allowing him to do that.'

'My cousins are also his own children, he often said, when there were times when my mother asked why he was spending so much money on my cousins. We are family, like all Palestinians are one big family too.'

'I'm worried…Omar is so young and he is starting to sound like an old man,' remarked Rahman, to change the subject back to Omar, who had by now disappeared from the scene, after he got on a bicycle to cycle off into the distance and hidden by other buildings and vehicles, horses and carts. I do not want him to sink like the ship that sank in the Atlantic Ocean, he said to himself. He was referring to the 'Titanic' that sank in the ocean on 14 or 15 April, 1912 that he had heard about when he was in Jerusalem and met some men there who talked about it and how three years earlier, it was reported in the newspapers about the sinking of the ship, which was claimed to be the safest ship in the world, yet, it could sink. Omar felt like the ship could be his son, who despite having been given all the right religious education and financial support to allow him to become his own man with his new family and some children of his own, with his wife, both his parents and her parents had agreed to match them, because their religious upbringing and backgrounds that matched, could also suffer, if it was not his luck to continue living the way his father and mother had wanted him to experience for himself. In more than one way, he did not want Omar to be like the ship – the Titanic that sank despite it being touted as the safest ship in the world. On 14 or 15 April, 1912, it still sank and even now no one knew exactly what happened to it and where its carcass might be now. Many in the ship perished, but a few survived.

6

Munir goes to Makkah for Hajj.

Omar's father, Munir went to Makkah to perform Hajj early 1935, and he like a loyal husband also brought his wife. He hoped he did not have to wait too long to perform their Hajj unlike his father who only went there so late in his life, and fortunately, he was blessed with a long and healthy life so he was able to go there without bothering anyone unlike some others who were younger than he was who had to be carried to perform the rites, to ambulate around the Holy Kaabah, seven times. If he did not bring long his wife, there was no way for her to go there on her own or with her other close relatives or friends.

That was nineteen years after the Battle of Makkah which occurred in June and July of 1916, when Munir was still a young man and had seen how his own father had gone on his pilgrimage a year earlier before the Battle that he was not aware was brewing then, as he was so busy with his Hajj rituals and did not know what might happen there after he had left Makkah and Arabia. He had heard some rumors of what was happening but he did not care to know more about them, because he said he was not an Arabian but a Palestinian.

It was on 10 June of 1916 when the Sharif of Makkah, by the name of Hussein bin Ali, who was then the leader of the Banu Hashim clan who started a revolt against the Uthmaniyah (or Ottoman, as the British said it) Caliphate and it later became part of the Arab Revolt of the First World War. Fortunately, Munir and the people in his group of pilgrims who had come from all the way from their village in Palestine were spared the confusion that ensued in the Holy City of Makkah, barely months after they left Arabia after performing their Hajj, to return to Palestine. And what happened in the end was that this battle marked the beginning of the end of the Uthmaniyah Caliphate or the Ottoman Empire, and it also sparked the beginning of a Hashemite Kingdom with Makkah as their chosen capital.

It was around October, 1935 when Munir and his wife and some friends in the village and a few more from the neighboring ones who he had known since childhood embarked on the journey with the same rituals of being sent off by their whole village to start on their journey that would take two weeks before they could get to Makkah, to start their pilgrimage. In all there were five horse-driven carts in their caravan led by Munir. And he and his friends had charted out their route which was almost the same as that taken by his father, Hajji Othman.

But this time, Munir's parents had long died; his father died few years upon returning from Makkah and in a few more years, his mother followed suit. Both were buried beside each other in the cemetery in the village, where he would go to offer his blessings, and to put some flowers. Sometimes he would bring along Omar and his other children.

And when Munir and his wife and the others were being paraded and after the village Imam had read a supplication or 'dua', and they started move in their respective horse-driven carts, Munir suddenly felt a strong pang of emotion; he felt like it was a scene that had happened way back in 1915 when his own parents were paraded until they had left the sight of everybody in the village, to proceed on their long and arduous journey to Makkah which at this time was not so dangerous because the roads where they were to travel on to get there had been paved; but it was not the same during his parents' time when some of the stretches of road they had to travel on were not yet paved and were dusty village roads. Now there were more villages and small towns along the way and facilities such as coffee shops and even places where they could put up the night at, before continuing with their journey the next morning or when they felt like. Nevertheless, Munir and the others, still anxious with the journey they were undertaking.

Omar, at this time was twenty-four years old and had been married and with two children so it was for him now to watch his parents leave their village to perform their Hajj; and when the time came, he too would get to experience what his grandparents got in 1915, and now his own parents in 1935 were getting. In 1915, he only could watch his grandparents being paraded from the first storey of their house because he had just been circumcised and was immobile for a few weeks, before he was able wear normal clothes and move about freely; and this time he was with the crowd on the ground near the same house as it was in 1915 when he was staring down on the future pilgrims as they were being bid farewell by their relatives and close friends.

He was four years ago in 1915 and twenty-four in 1935, a difference of a period of twenty years. If this was the trend that had happened for Omar's relatives to perform their Hajj, he wondered if it would also take another twenty years before it became his turn to do so, when he would be forty-four years! But he would not be that old to go on the pilgrimage compared to what age his grandfather was – eighty-five and his father, who was not yet fifty years old! So his father did not wait till he was older to go to Makkah; he was only forty-eight years old! And he did not look like his age, but much younger, and healthy.

Omar's grandfather had his own colorful history that caused him to also marry at an age that was considered to be 'old' by Palestinian standards, when even his younger brothers, had got married many years earlier and both of them had got two children of their own, who were Omar's cousins. And despite being cousins of parents who were his younger uncles, they were older than him. It seemed to be a rare case and they often had to explain to older men and women in their villages who often like to wonder why Omar was younger than children of his younger uncles.

Omar's grandfather, Hajji Othman was playful; he liked to enjoy life and pretended that he was an artistically inclined person who liked to write and do sketches, and mostly to travel to the countries around Palestine and beyond; he even got to Egypt or Mesir, all by himself by hitch-hiking, or getting rides from anyone who was willing to take him on their horse-driven carts and sometimes on camels that did not have riders. And he would be away from his family and village for months on end. But the strange part was he had also been to Makkah but never made the pilgrimage because he was there not during the Hajj season and could only perform the Umrah or Minor Hajj. He said he had performed it more than a dozen times, so he could be said to have performed the Hajj as it was assumed that any Muslim who had performed the Umrah for seven times, could be said to have performed the Hajj, too. But he did not feel like it so in his later years, he finally managed to go to Makkah to perform Hajj, and with his wife, who was probably the main reason why he wanted to do it, despite having been to Makkah many times before and who was said to have also performed the Hajj, by default for having done Umrah many times. His wife, Muneerah, was thrilled when told that Hajji Othman wanted to go to Makkah and take her with him. But he did not tell his wife or anyone that he suddenly realized that he was going on with age, then eighty-four years and might not be able to travel long distances at such an advanced age, so he decided to perform the Hajj the next year with his wife and some others from his village and those from the neighboring ones who were all much younger than him and his wife, who was thirty years younger than Hajji Othman so much so that many guessed if she could very well be his second or even third wife. No one dared to ask him or his wife on this matter as it was not proper for any of them to do so, especially when they were much younger than the two.

Omar did not know anything about his grandfather's interests in the arts especially writing and sketching, so it intrigued him when he was first told of it and more so when he found, much later, some notebooks he had written on his pilgrimage to Makkah in 1915, that were hidden in a secret compartment in the horse-cart he was later given. Omar's father, was told in case if he did not want the cart, if he had his own, then he should give it to Omar, Hajji Othman's first grandson, as tradition would have it. So that was how Omar got the horse-cart which was still in good condition, and the notebooks. And much later, he also discovered a photo album with photos of his grandfather and grandmother and their friends who went to Makkah, hidden in another secret compartment in the cart that he did not know existed; he was happy to find the notebooks which were in mint condition. The photos were all in black-and-white and processed and printed in some photo studios in Makkah, because there were none in his area where his grandfather could send the negatives to process and print.

Omar was excited to see thirty photos showing how happy and excited his grandparents and their friends were; with a photo of them resting in an oasis along the way and it was bright and sunny and all of them were enjoying some dates that the notes in the book had also described. Omar pulled out all the photos carefully and cleaned some of the dusts that had got stuck on them and looked at the back of each of the photos where there were some notes to describe the incidents that were recorded in the photos. One of the horses they took on the trip tripped and fell and broke his right-hind leg; it could not be healed soon enough and they had to give it away to one of the villagers in a village along the way who promised to look after it. Because of that, his grandfather had to buy another horse to replace the one he had given to the villager. He gave the villager some money for the medication and food. He felt sorry for not being able to take good care of the horse and to let it run on its own, so he thought it could stretch out its muscles, and have some fun at the same time, together with the other horses which were lucky that they did not suffer the same fate and the horse which was now limping around and too weak to pull any cart. The villager said the horse needed a week to ten days before the fracture to its right-hind leg could heal. It was too long for Hajji Othman, who was not yet a Hajji then, to wait, because they had to move on. He also said if he and his group did not return after their Hajj, because they might take another route to return to their village in Palestine, the villager could keep the horse.

Haji Othman blamed himself for the calamity even though he thought it was destined to happen. 'But you meant well,' said his wife, Muneerah. 'Trust Shahid to look after the horse.'

'Shahid? Who is that?'

'The man who is looking after the horse.'

'You know him? How did you know his name?'

'I was with his wife, in the kitchen of their house...'

Haji Othman smiled.

'His wife said this was the second time someone stopped over when his own horse got one of its leg fractured, but in the left-front leg.'

'Was it okay afterwards?'

'Shahid looked after it and it was good afterwards. So don't worry about your horse. Just worry about the journey we still have to take, to get to the House of Allah.'

'In Sha Allah, we'll get there in ten days or less, depending on the weather.'

Haji Othman slipped out of his tent to let his wife sleep by herself, and got outside to a night which was bright with the rays from the full moon shining the whole village leaving the houses that were scattered in it and the date and olive and other trees hidden in silhouette. He went to sit on a wooden bench under one of the trees to marvel at the sight. The horses that were pulling the carts and carriages were all tied to them, and they were all resting in peace and sleeping. Hajji Othman looked at the right and caught sight of Shahid who was approaching him and carrying a large 'dallah' or pot with hot coffee or 'qahwa' inside and two cups. It was chilly outside and Hajji Othman had a coat over his robe to keep him warm. But he wanted to enjoy the cold winds blowing into his face; it made it freeze a bit and he rubbed it a few times to warm his face as well as his palms, by also reciting some verses from the Noble Qur'an, and feeling happy with the thought that he was approaching the House of God. He also heard one of his friends, reading some passages from the Noble Qur'an, in a melodious voice. He could not tell who the person was from the voice that had changed so much from his normal voice. It was spoilt when his concentration was disturbed by the sounds of Shahid's feet as he approached him.

He greeted Hajji Othman with 'Asalamulaikum!' Hajji Othman replied accordingly with, 'Mulaikum salam.' He moved aside a bit to allow Shahih to sit beside him on the wooden bench which was just enough for two persons. But since it now had the 'dallah', they had to sit closer to each other.

Shahid poured some tea in the two cups and handed one of them to Hajji Othman who took it. 'Shukaran,' he said, and took a sip. It was hot. But it would soon be cool because of the weather outside which was cool.

'How's the horse?' asked Hajji Othman after taking two sips of tea.

'He's resting and should be up by tomorrow evening and I will take him for a short walk to test his fractured leg to see if it is good, before I take him on a gallop later.'

'We won't be able to wait until he is good to run, Shahid.'

Shahid was surprised that Hajji Othman mentioned him by his name. He wanted to ask him how he knew it, but didn't because it was a small matter.

'We have to take our leave after lunch tomorrow. And you and your wife, Salmah, too, can join us, if you want to.'

Salmah? How did he also know my wife's name, Shahid asked himself? And before he could ask Hajji Othman about it, Hajji Othman revealed that his wife, Muneerah had told him about it and also his name.

'How's Auntie, Muneerah?'

'She's fine and resting in the tent over there.'

There were around eight tents where married couples slept in and two larger ones where the young men who did not bring his wife, or those who had their wives with them, but who chose to sleep with other women, were sleeping. Some of the tents were lit in the inside with the others not, as it was already late at night and it would soon past midnight.

'Are you from this village?' asked Hajji Othman. 'I mean, did your ancestors live here before you?'

Shahid nodded and did not answer him in words because he was just sipping tea, when he heard the question. Hajji Othman waited.

'Yes, Uncle,' said Shahid. 'My ancestors had lived here for hundreds of years and there are some olive trees my great-great-great-great grand-uncle had grown which are still alive. Some are over there, at the left and the older ones are those at the right.'

Haji Othman looked at the left and right and saw the olive trees which were thick and definitely looked very old. 'They are definitely much, much older than me!' he remarked, and trying to make it sound like a joke. But Shahid did not laugh at it; he just smiled and sipped some more tea. He did not like to think remarks on a person's – any person's age to be a joke. He took what Hajji Othman had said as seriously as he could pretend. He knew Hajji Othman was also much older than his late father, Hajji Karim, who died in his sleep two years ago, and he, Shahid himself, was half Hajji Othman's age. He did not want to ask for Hajji Othman's age as he thought it was not proper, unless if Hajji Othman told it himself. 'I am only eighty-five.'

'You don't look like it, Uncle.'

'I thought you were in the seventies…mid-seventies.'

'That's because I am a very active person. That's also because I like to think like a young person. My eldest son is close to fifty years.'

'He is slightly older than I am, Uncle.'

Then there was silence. The two of them, suddenly felt awkward talking about names, ages and soon, they would start to talk about children, grandchildren, grandparents and so on. Shahid had already mentioned about his great-great-great-grandparents earlier…

One of the horses neighed very loud; it shook the two men from being frozen in their own private thoughts.

'It's probably time for me to return to my tent,' said Hajji Othman. He put the cup down on the bench and started to walk after greeting Shahid again, 'Asalamulaikum.'

Shahid stood and replied, 'Mulaikum salam' and watched Hajji Othman walked towards his tent and entered it. He then saw the light from the lamp in the tent shut.

* * * * * *

During that time, Omar had seen other parades of people in his own village who were going to Makkah but the feeling he felt was not the same, compared to that he felt in 1915 and 1935; but each of the parade and occasion that caused it to happen was not the same as the other.

He was in a different age, and with different attitudes and emotions, and who was able to look at each of them differently than the others. The scenes may look similar as those parades and gatherings to send off groups of pilgrims to Makkah were the same for as long as he could remember.

Few days before his parents' departure for Makkah, he and his wife and other relatives were busy helping them to prepare, to choose what clothes to pack up to wear on the trip and food to eat along the journey. They were helped by most of the women and men in the whole village who took it upon themselves to do their part in the preparations, especially cooking. Some of them who had already gone to Makkah for the Hajj now felt it was their duty to help those who were going to perform theirs next.

He wondered when it was time for him and his wife to go on the pilgrimage to Makkah, then his two children would be given the task of helping him and his wife to do help out, except may, by then when they were already older and maybe also in their forties or fifties, the mode of transportation would not be the same as that used by his grandparents and now parents, who still had to ride in horse-driven carts. Most likely, with the introduction of more modern modes of transportation, they could travel by taking a train or at least, a bus which would be very convenient and mostly, comfortable with traveling time cut from two weeks to a few days.

7

Moath goes to Makkah in 1935.

Moath, arrived in Makkah with his wife and the whole group from Palestine during the Hajj season in November of 1935. Their journey from their village in Palestine to Makkah took two weeks with no untoward events happening along the way except that there was a change of weather that had caused some of them to feel sick, but they managed to get by takings some medicines and drinks that their wives had made for them which were bitter, but which helped to ease their pain and the sprains they had on their legs and various parts of the body.

He was a soft-spoken man, an elderly man who lived in the same village as Munir, except that he belonged to Munir's father's generation, now in his early eighties, who knew Munir's father very well despite their age difference, and it was Moath who always went to the pharmacy in the town to get medications for Munir's father, so the two of them became very close and often visited Munir when he was a boy and not yet married. So naturally, Munir was excited that finally Moath decided to make the pilgrimage to Makkah, for another time. He had gone there the first time long ago when he was a young man, at the age Munir was at now. He also took the land route traveling in a caravan with some friends and relatives but he did not remember much of it. And it was also his later father's orders for Munir to take care of Moath when he grew older, which Munir did as told, sometimes treating 'The Old Man' as his own 'Old Man' as he would often describe his special relationship with Moath who he sometimes also called 'Uncle Moath'. It was not a difficult task for Munir to undertake because Moath had been very independent and was also able; he was strong and maybe much stronger than many men who were much younger than he was. He liked to joke that he was as strong or even stronger than his own horse.

So the whole village came out to send him and his entourage off on their pilgrimage to Makkah, for the first time, but for Moath it was the second time, and this time he was taking with him his wife, Fatimah, who was twenty-five years younger than he was.

There was a bit of snow on the top of some of the hills they passed by along the way. And the closer they got to Makkah they found that the strangers and locals they met seemed to be cold; not because of the weather but because all of them were in a hurry and were busy with the chores they were doing, especially those who had come there to perform their Hajj and were there for the first time. There were also many people who were not Arabs like them, who spoke in various types of languages, the words of which Moath and his friends could not understand. But they had the good intentions in their hearts, being Muslims, like them, who also had to traveled by land for longer distances and over different types of terrains and for longer periods. One group they met when they were at the edge of the city of Makkah said they were from Tajikistan, the name of a country they had not heard of; the men were taller and sturdier and they and their women had Asian features with small eyes. They spoke in Farsi which had some Arabic words they could understand. But their leader, also at Tajik, as they are called, spoke good Arabic because he had lived and studied the language in Makkah itself. So from him they were able to understand and fully appreciate what the Tajiks and the others from the countries in Central Asia who had come to perform their Hajj. They also met a smaller group of pilgrims from the Xingjian district in China. They had set up their camps near each other in Makkah, which they preferred more than staying in rental homes or hotels.

Moath had met many people who were not Arabs before, when he was traveling around the region; but he had not met people of so many diverse racial backgrounds who have different features, heights, and appearances; but one thing he liked to see was how all of the men especially were wearing their 'ihram' clothes for pilgrims to wear when performing rituals for the Hajj, which are in two pieces and both are white in color so no one could tell their financial status as it was not of anyone's concern when they were there to perform Hajj, that they had to forget, and be just like any other pilgrim, so one can be someone who was not so wealthy yet, he can mix with those who were better off than him.

Here they met many pilgrims from other parts of Palestine and the Arab countries who had gathered here with the sole intention of performing their Hajj, together so they could return to their respective villages, as 'newborn', to face their future ahead. Some of the older pilgrims, however, did not make it because they died along the way to Makkah or in Makkah itself and were buried where they had died.

All of them were tired when they got to Makkah traveling by land but as soon as they caught sight of the Holy Kaabah, they felt rejuvenated and wanted to go straight into the rituals that would lead them to be Hajjis and Hajjjahs. Some of the feet of the men were swollen.

There were some men who almost fainted upon arriving at Masjidil Haram (The Grand Masjid) where the Holy Kaabah (The Cube) was, and the only reason why they were said to have experienced such a phenomenon was, that they had done some misdeeds on others and when they got there their body systems and mind could not accept the fact that they were confronting the truth they had succeeded in hiding from everyone, that they simply collapsed. The medical staff could only ask them to take a good rest in their respective tents and not to force themselves to perform the rituals that require a lot of physical effort to achieve especially for the ritual where they were to walk briskly from the hills of Safa and Marwa for seven times, and to circle around the Holy Kaabah, also for seven times. The third and last ritual all pilgrims should perform could only be done during the Hajj season which was to go to Mount Arafat to cast stones seven times which was where Nabi Muhammad, (s.a.w.) gave His final sermon and all pilgrims had to go there for the day.

Makkah is strategically located, about seventy kilometers inland from the Red Sea coast in a narrow valley in the Hijaz or 'backbone' region called the Sarat Mountain range where there are volcanic peaks and depressions which were deep in some areas. It was once an oasis that was connected by caravan trade routes where traders would stop to have a meal break or to spend the nights in caravanserais before they would move on in their caravans and carts, and on mules, camels, and horses to go to Jeddah which was a port city to send off their goods or to acquire new ones from foreign traders who stopped there, who had come from the Mediterranean, South Asia, East Africa, and South Arabia, with some all the way from Gujerat on the west coast of India. The road linking Makkah to Jeddah was not wide and at times there were traffic snarls and jams along the way, so going there often took a long time, and more during the Hajj season when there was an influx of pilgrims from all over Arabia and the world converging to it, for one to two or even three months, before the situation became less congested after the foreign pilgrims started to return to Jeddah to return to their own countries.

Hundreds of thousands from all over the world had converged on Makkah and Mount Arafat and went to Madinnah to perform their Hajj. No wonder Moath felt lost in the sea of pilgrims and other local Arabs, and was not sure where he was the first time he stepped foot in the Holy City, and staring unblinkingly at the sight of the Grand Masjid or Masjidil Haram standing before him. What was he thinking? What was he wondering? He did not want to seek answers to these questions. He wanted to feel that he was indeed here in the Holy City and staring at the Grand Masjid, for the first time in his life. But he did not want to feel guilty for being able to be here, to fulfill the last commands in the Five Pillars of Islam, which was to perform his Hajj, knowing how old he was. He looked around but did not notice any other pilgrims who was as old as he. Most of the others were half his age. There were some who were being carried on the backs of their children or pushed in small carts by them.

Worse, there were some who were said to have gone crazy.

Moath marveled at the sight of the Holy Kaabah and he sat cross-legged each time after performing his prayers there, and reading a different supplication afterwards, to just stare at the Holy Kaabah that sat in front of him, in the center of the square in The Grand Masjid that he had only before seen in his eyes, in his sleep, in his dreams and in illustrations or photos, some of which he hung in his house, to remind him of the time when he would be there to see it with his own eyes. He sat there motionless and tried to remember the history and physical features it had that he had learnt by heart; the Holy Kaabah was the most sacred building for all Muslims in the world; it is also the most sacred spot them, where they would turn to face it from wherever they were, from all over the world, to pray; and in death, their bodies would be laid in their graves so their eyes face it. And all masjid built anywhere in the world, too face the direction of the Holy Kaabah. It is fifteen meters in height and ten by fourteen meters at its base, so that it is not really a square block that many had assumed it to be with each side of it roughly corresponding to the four sides of the compass; he was also a bit surprised when he first learnt of it. It is made of grey stone and marble and the whole of it was wrapped by a piece of thick carpet-like clothing or brocade called the 'Kiswah' that was sewed throughout the year by artisans in a specially built factory, which was only made for the Kiswah which is embossed with verses from the Noble Qur'an. And at the eastern corner of the Holy Kaabah, is Black Stone called 'Hajar Al Aswad'. And legend has it that the stone was given to Nabi Adam, a.s. when he was expelled from Heaven. And it is only after the end of the Hajj season, 'Dhul-Hijjah', is over that the Hajjal Aswad is removed for the ceremonial washing of the Holy Kaabah and the covering is cut into pieces and given as presents to important local and foreign dignitaries. But what Moath remembered most about the Holy Kaabah was when in 630 CE, after Nabi Muhammad, (s.a.w.) finally captured the city of Makkah, He ordered his followers to enter the Holy Kaabah to destroy all the statues of the deities of the Pagans.

Moath was also worried because he had received the call from Allah, very late to perform his Hajj and he feared if his presence there was not welcomed. He made sure he read the Noble Qur'an everyday and also offered prayers to the departed from his family such his parents and grandparents and other relatives and close friends, and sought not to speak with any strangers, save for his wife who was with other women in other tents and close friends, who came to Makkah with him in the carts from their villages. To him performing Hajj for the first time was not an enjoyable affair; it was more like a responsibility that he had to do; and how he wished he had gone to Makkah much earlier when he was much younger, say, twenty or thirty years ago, when he was sixty or fifty years old and stronger and could perform the rituals again and again to satisfy himself. But all that he had managed to do was to walk briskly from the Hills of Safa and Marwa seven times and to circle the Holy Kaabah seven times and not more. His wife, who was much younger than him was able to do the two rituals twice with her friends, who were wives of the men from their village who were half the age of Moath. Even then when he circled the Holy Kaabah he made sure to do it very early in the morning around two in the morning when the circle of pilgrims was small and he could finish the ritual in minutes. He noticed that those who waited till the day was bright had to spend twenty minutes just to circle the Holy Kaabah which was then full of people. He did not want to pay anyone to carry him on a stretcher because he did not think he needed to have such a service; he wanted to walk on his two feet to walk to perform the two rituals at the Masjidil Haram. And he managed to do it.

One night, Moath sat by himself in his tent; his friends had gone out and had not returned. He did not ask them what they wanted to do at breakfast and after the Maghrib prayers. And they, too, did not want to ask him to join them because they thought Moath had plans for himself. Besides, they knew he was the type of person who liked to be left alone with his thoughts. While they were in Makkah, he would meet with his wife later in the afternoon, before she would return to the group of women to perform prayers together in their tents and to eat and to drink zam-zam, the holy water that could only be found in Makkah and at no other place in the world.

He felt light. He felt his burden of skipping Hajj for so long and not thinking about it for so long towards the end of his life to be a new type of burden he now had to carry through all his remaining life. He did not know how many more years he had left. He remembered his father, had died at the ripe age of ninety-one years old. Moath was now eighty-five years or six years younger than his father when he died. There were no one his age who was performing Hajj. He did not see anyone who looked old like him; all of the men were much younger than him. And he felt guilty each time he saw a young boy, performing Hajj with his parents. He hoped his eldest son would not wait too long to perform his Hajj. He was not yet fifty; he should come here to Makkah, next year, he thought. And he wanted to advise him to take his wife to come here next year.

He wanted to cry. And he did. A bit of tears started to flow down his eyes to his cheeks, but he did not want to wipe them; he just let them flow down until some slipped off his cheeks. He then took up his left hand and held the end of the sleeve with the right one and used it to wipe the tears. He did not want to feel bad for crying. He did not want to think that he was indeed crying without a reason; he knew it had to happen. He had not cried like that before in his life; and at his age, he shouldn't have any tear left to release from his eyes. They should all have been used in the course of his life, now in its ninth decade of existence. He had indeed tried to suppress emotions that he had had before, and even when his parents died some twenty years ago, he did not cry as it was forbidden by his religion; his religious teachers, the Ustaz had told him never to do that. And he and his brothers and sisters and all their relatives did not cry even a tear. When they felt sad and emotional at their demise, they prayed and prayed until they received guidance from the Almighty that made them feel stronger than they were before. His parents died when the two of them were in their eighties. Moath was now in his mid-eighties, and at the age when his parents died, twenty years ago.

His mind suddenly turned to a more mundane matter. Why did it suddenly appear in his head now, he asked himself; when he was just being brought back to the time of his parents' death, twenty years ago, in 1916? He remembered holding his first grandson, Omar, who was five years old, who probably did not know what death was and what it meant to him and the family. He had known his great-grand-parents since he was born one night in 1911, and it was also his grandmother who had cared for him since he was born to the time when she suddenly became weak and lost much of her memory and did not remember Omar, her great-grandson, though he had cared for her for four years or more.

They had 'tahlil' for three nights after the death of Moath's parents attended by relatives and friends in their village. They did not care for the World War that had just broken up somewhere in Europe; it was their war, he remarked, the war that broke up amongst countries and supporters of the Crusaders, he like to say when asked about it. The death of his parents was more serious calamity to him than the death that happened in Europe in the World War which many were to remark or think of as the First World War. It was not a 'world war' he liked to remind those who would later bring up the matter to him; it was an 'European War', a war amongst the Europeans, he would say; or to be more exact, the 'First Crusaders' War' – a war amongst the Crusaders, the 'Faranjis'.

Not a historian of international or European history, yet, Moath could talk a lot more on it than the others in his village; he was barely in his sixties, so he could garner interest and respect because of that, because in his village as in the whole of Palestine and also the Arab World, age counted more than intellect; and he also had some intellect and knowledge or world affairs, because he was one of the few Palestinians who had left his village to go abroad to live in other Arab countries and a long while in Mesir or Egypt where he got the information on Europe and the Crusaders that those around him in his village had scant knowledge of. But at his age now, in the eighties, he did not want to argue over them anymore.

Moath invited scorn with his views on the Crusaders' War, but also managed to convince some others who believed in his version of the history of Europe, when they also admitted that it was not the First World War as it did not spread beyond Europe.

Moath stopped crying; he looked around and saw no one outside of his tent. Where could everybody be at that time? He had put aside the episodes on the death of his parents and the Crusaders' War. He decided to stand up and go out of his tent. He went to his wife's tent but it was quiet as were the others around it. He turned his gaze around but there was no one. Was he dreaming, he thought to himself. He was not; he knew he was not. He recited a short prayer without saying it loudly; only his lips moved, but they looked like he was trembling. Suddenly he felt cold. He then returned to his tent and took out a coat and wore it over his robe. He had performed the two rituals for Hajj and he and the others had to go to Mount Arafat to spend a day there for the final one which was the stoning of the devil, before he could complete all the three rituals and become a full-fledged Hajji. He hoped his pilgrimage and those of his wife and everybody in his group and the others, could be rewarded with 'Haji Mabrur'.

Moath walked around in between the tents and said to himself, 'Haji Mabrur...Haji Mabrur...Haji Mabrur...' repeatedly like he was going crazy. He didn't know what he was saying or where he was going. He also did not care who was looking at him; there was no one there. There was silence. And in the far distance in front of him was the Masjidil Haram, where the Holy Kaabah was and his feet were taking him there; and he just let them do that as it was already 'Zohor' or noon-time to pray.

He prayed at the back since there were already so many other pilgrims and locals who had gathered in the masjid earlier. But he did not care because he knew he could perform his prayer anywhere like the many others he could see praying on rooftops, in the streets, on the sidewalks, and everywhere where there was space for them to lay down their prayer mats, where they could face, bend, and bow towards the Holy Kaabah. And once he was done, to perform the number of 'rakaats' necessary for the zohor prayers – four in all, he remained seated with his feet crossed and started to recite a prayer to himself. He felt like crying; but he tried to stop any tear from rolling down his cheeks. It was not unusual for any pilgrim to not feel sad and overwhelmed especially when he is staring at the Holy Kaabah; many of them do, and openly without any shame. What is there to be ashamed of, to cry before the House of God? Most of them who went on the pilgrimage cried because they were happy to be here in Makkah and in the compound of the Masjidil Haram, and performing their Hajj, most probably for the first time, and chances were most of them could not return to perform the next time as it was not easy or cheap for them to do so especially for those who had come from so far away such as Tanah Melayu, Jawa, Sumatera, India, and even China! They could not go to Makkah by traveling in carts like Moath and the many others from Palestine, but had to go there by boats that took two weeks to arrive at Jeddah, and it was months before they were able to return to their own villages and countries, very much a changed person, with some 'Nur' or 'Light' beaming from their faces, that was a mark of a person's piety and obedience to the teachings and values of Islam, and hopefully, also a sign that they had achieved 'Haji Mabrur.' One of the Melayu pilgrims in their group, however, he died before he could complete his Hajj; and he was rewarded by being buried in a cemetery in Makkah. There was one other pilgrim who had also sailed on the same ship with them, who died, and he was buried in the sea with his remains dropped into the ocean after it was given the last rites.

Moath, was done reciting the short prayer or 'doa' and he stood up to walk back to his tent which is about half a mile from the masjid. What was he thinking now, he asked himself; he wanted to know what was in his mind, now that he had performed the zohor prayer, together with the scores of the thousands of others from all over the world who had converged in the masjid and also outside of it. Most of the locals had returned to their stores and houses near the masjid to resume work. So they knew what they ought to do next. But not Moath who was still groggy, walking along back to his tent. He did not go to the Holy Kaabah this time to kiss the Black Stone raja Aswad as he was wont to do because there was a sizeable crowd of people there who had converged around it to kiss the Stone for blessing. He had kissed it a few times before when he first got here and later after prayers at this masjid; so he did not want to create a larger crowd, and let those who were already there to get their opportunity to kiss it; it could be their first time to do it, too, from the looks of it since most of those who were near the Stone looked Asian. True, they were some Melayu from Tanah Melayu and Jawa and also Chinese-Muslims from China and the others from India who looked taller.

Moath sat in his tent, alone. Where is everybody? He wandered quietly but did not manage to find any answer, however hard he tried to. No one told him where they were going to this morning. Ah, he now remembered telling one of his friends, last night that he was too tired and did not want to be disturbed; he wanted to rest alone with his thoughts. They understood him, because they knew he was not as young as the others and who might be overwhelmed too, like them, but because of his age, and because he had spent most of the night outside of the tent to do his own thing, he came back looking frail and sickly and dead tired. Fortunately, his disheveled hair was not shown as it was hidden in his piece of headscarf of 'kaffiyeh' together with the robe he was wearing.

He was also wearing the same robe and headscarf now. And with no one present, he removed the scarf to reveal his disheveled hair. He looked at it in the mirror and immediately pushed it with his hand to make it look more pleasant. He then pulled a book from his bag that was lying on the ground. It was a religious book that he had not fully read even after buying it at the store in Amman many years ago. He checked the chapters and found one on 'Haji Mabrur', which was on how to achieve the perfect Hajj, whose deeds are accepted by God, so that their pilgrimage was not turned to waste, as did some who went to Makkah for Hajj few times, but whose deeds were not accepted by God, but worse, who also became mad and sick afterwards and died a miserable death. They were still Hajjis or Hajjjahs, but they were useless ones, because they had performed their pilgrimage for other reasons that only they knew; one of which was to free themselves of the sins that they had made in their early lives, mostly for cheating and for crimes, including murder, that were not known by anyone because it happened in isolated places and away from the long hands of the law. They shall go down into their graves, taking with them their deeds and misdeeds and if their misdeeds overwhelmed their deeds, however much faith in Islam they had exhibited in their behavior and clothing or charity, would not be of any use. Moath knew this and he also felt sorry for a few of the men he knew who had done some grave misdeeds, for which they did not repent or didn't know correctly how to repent. They were afraid to confront the law or any Ustaz to admit to their past crimes, so they force themselves to overdo deeds in anyway they could by offering lots of 'Fitrah' and 'Zakat' to the needy and any masjid they could fine.

Moath prayed for them and their souls especially those who had passed on, and the few others who were still very much alive some, who were as old as he was, yet who did not bother to go to Makkah to perform their Hajj, sending only their wife or few wives instead. That often left others in their villages to wonder why they, men of immense wealth had not bothered to go to Makkah. And no wonder, too, their faces looked unusually dark which made them look like the evil men that they were, but who often like to cover them with wide headscarves of different colors and designs that indicated from where in Palestine, and also from which other Arab country, they came from which were made of fine cotton from their trips to other cities such as Amman, Kaherah, or Cairo.

Moath pitied them. But mostly, he pitied himself as he felt now that he was also not a man of fine character although his close relatives and friends who were with him on the pilgrimage and those who he had left behind in his village thought he was a person with impeccable character, which he was in many ways but not entirely. He knew from his heart that he had evil thoughts, that forced him to delay his pilgrimage and this was suddenly making him feel sick, very sick and almost on the verge of mental breakdown, that only his praying and 'doa' could manage to free himself of his negative thoughts that he had of himself. But for the others, he only had nice thoughts. He tried to shake off the thoughts on the time he was enjoying himself watching the belly dancing in clubs in Kaherah, especially at those clubs in the notorious Haret el Wasser Street, here horse and mule carts travel along with trams plying the street carrying passengers and goods; where there were many clubs where belly dancing shows which the Arabs called, 'Raqs sharqi', which literally means "oriental dancing" were available; and he would often go there with his friends, when they were younger and when they couldn't care less about themselves and who would quite often take to the bottle to taste some fine liquor, wine, and beer, which he was not quite sure then was 'haram' or forbidden because all his friends his age, all of whom were Egyptians couldn't care less what they were drinking with some falling down on the sidewalks outside of the bar with one or two being knocked down by vehicles while they were crossing the streets. One even fell into the River Nile and drowned and made front-page news the next day in the local newspapers especially the Al Ahram Al Arabiya and all the others, because it was an incident that was not a rare one that needed to be splashed on the front pages of the newspapers to encourage greater care amongst those who wanted to take rides on the boats. There were some foreign tourists, too, who had drowned in the river.

You can't tell, looking at the Egyptian men from what they wear; some wear flowing robes and yet, they can be seen any of the brothel houses, while those who wear modern, British-style clothes, in jackets and pants and sometimes a hat, but who just walked along the street to do their business and going to work in their offices. But during the day there are hardly any women in the streets; the good ones stay at home and only the 'wild' ones would venture to go out, but they are often driven to their 'place of work' by their handlers, Moath was told by some of his friends. So a person's piety is not in the way he dresses. You look decent to me and to yourself when you look in the mirror in your flat, but to the others who do not know you, they might think you have some negative thoughts lurking in your heads somewhere that caused you to be out in the streets, at night and even in the day in search for some worldly pleasures!

Moath had not met people who spoke like this and using language he considered to be harsh in his life; in his village and the whole of Palestine, they did not have such nocturnal activities to tempt their men and also women to do things they considered to be 'haram' or 'forbidden'. He got nervous when one of his friends, tried to pull him by his arm to enter one of the brothel houses – and in bright daylight. No, no...I am not entering it; you can go ahead and I will wait for you in the sidewalk café over there, he would say. His friend's attempt to initiate him to living in the city such as Cairo, failed; and even after a few attempts at doing so, he still failed. His friend secretly tried to think of using another way to persuade him to do what he wanted to do, when he was less attentive and was in need of companionship. He had tried some other ways before on some of his friends from his villages, but they were from Egypt like him and not some other Arabs from other neighboring countries, and definitely, not from Palestine. Maybe Palestine was where the Masjid Al-Aqsa and Baitulmukaddis were, and this might be the reason why Palestinian men like Moath were not inclined to enjoy life the way some Egyptian men living in Cairo would do.

And it was also here where in April, 1915, many Australian soldiers and officers forming the Allied Forces had come to find pleasure and entertainment and booze to drink, before or after they were sent for the Gallipoli campaign which started in 25 April, 1915 till 9 January, 1916 that the Allied Forces thought they could create as a second war front to Turkey and to stop the First World War; but it turned out to be a tragic mistake when 187,959 men from the Allied Forces were killed including those from England, France, and Scotland. Armed personnel from New Zealand, forming the Anzac troops, too came here for the same reasons as did those from Australia and oftentimes there were fist-fighting amongst themselves. Their rude behavior was attributed to 'culture shock' that those men who were very young and who had been sent to Cairo and in an Arab country without being prepared for what to expect and when they were let loose, they became unpredictable in their behavior. Fortunately, not many of the locals understood what they were saying amongst themselves and mostly about the locals that were not nice for them to say; if the locals knew what they were saying of them, surely, they would not like it. Many ended up on Haret el Wasser Street, and enjoyed their time here too much which might have been one of the many reasons why the Gallipoli Campaign failed miserably. Even before the men from the different countries were sent to the battlefields in Turkey, they were already fighting with each other here in Haret El Wasser Street, that they conveniently called Wozzer, and the fighting they created was described as the 'Battle of the Wazzir' that started on 2 April, 1915 which involved 2,500 men from the Allied Forces were at loggerheads with some locals who disdained what the foreigners were doing and misbehaving themselves in public and in such crude manner and all sorts of complaints the soldiers had on the brothels themselves and the quality of the liquor served, with attempts made by their officers to break up the fracas failed leading to an all-out 'battle' that saw many from both sides dying or seriously injured. The 'Second Battle of Wazzir' broke up not long afterwards, also for the same reasons. But mostly the young men in the Armed Forces of Australia and New Zealand did not have any good reason to fight anyone, much less to want to kill any Turk. So their bodies ended up being buried in the Commonwealth War Graves.

At that time Moath was new to Cairo and Egypt and did not know many people to to go out with and those he knew then were mostly people who grew up in the city and who did not know of other ways of living, especially for their nocturnal activities and were attracted to see such shows they considered to be mild. But they soon became less rigid with their religious practices and they finally embraced the 'western-style' of living that their British colonial masters had introduced into their society and lives of the ordinary folks especially those who were born in the larger cities especially Cairo. But he tried to distance himself with his friends and tried to go to the masjid to mix with a different type of people who looked differently and also behaved differently, but he found them to be cold but they could not embrace him, because they found him to be an 'agam' or foreigner and who did not fit into their styles of doing things. Moath became frustrated when his attempts at trying to join the crowd of people with stronger religious values failed. Belly dancing provided him with the diversion. He befriended some 'Awalem', the slang for 'dancers' and got to know one of them better, who said she had come from a remote village in Egypt and was in Cairo in search of a better life, but drifted to becoming a belly dancer herself. She wanted to use Moath to get out of the life she did not favor but he, too, was not a person with exceptional character or one the others could call, 'a religious' person. So in the end, he drifted from her and their relationship broke off, when she was taken to another club in Alexandria, so the dance company thought she would be able to live a better life living in a smaller city. They had other plans for her which they did not disclose. And the most that they could offer was a 'call girl'.

Most of the belly dancers were young and who were from families which could not provide for them, and they left their villages far from Kaherah to work in the clubs to entertain their guests, with some even marrying their patrons to end their career as belly dancers and working in such clubs; and ironically, soon after became pious and started to wear the 'chador', or black robes for women.

Moath had his fair share of accidents. One such accident happened as he was walking out of the night club and in a state of drunkenness and he fell down with his forehead hitting the pavement that caused him to have some stitches at the local clinic, so even at his old age the scar could still be seen, except now it could be hidden by the headgear or headscarf he often wore these days, partly to hide it from anyone. Those who noticed it earlier when he was much younger and not wearing the headscarf were given all sorts of excuses to hide the truth behind it, on how it got to his forehead. He often liked to tell them he had had it since he was a baby when he fell from his cot. All of them were too young to know the truth behind it and they also could not verify with anyone on the veracity of what Moath had said to him. He did not like it when he had to lie to anyone concerning the scar. But there was no way for him to admit to them or anyone on how he had got it. It had become faint over the years but on some occasions it appeared to look like a fresh cut and it often made him feel worried to go out, lest anyone would notice it.

Moath had gone to Cairo and Egypt at the time of uncertainty that the whole country was heading for; it was called The Kingdom of Egypt, (Al-Mamlaka Al-Misreyya) was the de jure independent Egyptian state established under the dynasty headed by Muhammad Ali, a few years before he first arrived in the new country which was established in 1922 following the Unilateral Declaration of Egyptian Independence by the United Kingdom. The legal status of this new country had been highly convoluted, due to its de facto breakaway from the Ottoman Empire in 1805 and its occupation by Britain in 1882, and its transformation into a sultanate and British protectorate in 1914. On 15 March 1922, Fuad issued a decree changing his title from Sultan of Egypt to King of Egypt, which in line with the change in status from a sultanate to a kingdom, the Sultan of Egypt, Fuad I, suddenly saw his official title changed to King which Egypt never had before in its entire history and Sovereign of Nubia, Kordofan, and Dharfur, succeeding his elder brother, Sultan Hussein Kamel, and having ten ministers in his cabinet, two wives, and seven children.   Earlier in 1913, King Fuad had the audacity to try and secure the throne of Albania for himself, which had obtained its independence from the Ottoman Empire a year earlier, because the chances of him ever to become sultan of his own country was remote. At the time, Egypt and Sudan were ruled by his nephew, Abbas II; also because he thought that the Muhammad Ali dynasty was of Albanian descent, he encouraged King Fuad to seek the Albanian throne, but was surpassed and the throne was handed to a Christian ruler, instead. He was not successful in his effort.

Moath did not know of this sudden change before he left his village in Palestine to come to Cairo and Egypt; he assumed that being another Arab country that he had heard of since he was very small and in school, going there to live, would not be too difficult because their people spoke in the same language and practiced the same way of life and most of all, they also shared similar religion, of Islam! He did not realize that because of the British who controlled much of Egypt, the country was formally united with another Arab country in Africa, which was Sudan, and the British also controlled them, which in turned severely limited the country's sovereignty and the daily life of the Egyptians, too, and whose army continued to control the whole country, and started to follow the style of the British or non-Muslims which he realized when he first started to watch the belly dancing openly. But he was happy to be in Cairo and Egypt where he also managed to travel through the length and breath of the country and stayed briefly in Alexandria and visited the Valley of the Kings where the mausoleum of King Tutankhamen or known or referred to simply as King Tut, who ruled between 1342 B.C.E to 1325 BCE was discovered by a British explorer by the name of Howard Carter by chance in 1922 and funded by Lord Carnavarvon, whose tomb which was nearly intact. King Tut was just a small boy, aged eight or nine years when he became Pharaoh and whose reign was also short, about nine years before he died in an accident or war when he fell off his chariot.

During the reign of King Fuad the First, the monarchy had to struggle with the broadly-based nationalist party, the Wafd Party, which openly and strongly opposed the British domination of the country which they claimed was fraught with danger and cheating, and with even the British themselves, who had eyes on the Suez Canal that they wanted in order to control the free flow of ships, mostly commercial ones. Other political forces also started to emerge in this period included the Communist Party which appeared in 1925, and the Muslim Brotherhood or Ikhwan Muslimin in 1928, which eventually became a potent political and religious force in the country because of their strong Islamic religious character.

This was not the Cairo and Egypt that Moath thought he was going to when he decided to take the trip from his village in Palestine to there.

Moath almost laughed when he found out that the traditional dance of the Palestinians that he had seen and danced with the groups in his village was not of Palestinian origin, but here in Egypt. He also didn't know what he was seeing in Cairo and Egypt because he had seen and experienced a lot in his first year and had even got to know King Fuad I and then King Tut, who ruled over Egypt, at different eras in the country's history. He knew his father had not sent him to go there to see these things; and he later learnt that his father had wanted to send him to study at one of the madrassahs in Cairo and later on, to try and study for a degree at the University of Al-Azhar, which was reputed to be one of the most influential and prestigious universities not only in Egypt and also the Arab World, a center of higher of education where not even the wealthy in Egypt and other Arab countries could send their sons to study even when they could afford it.

Unfortunately, Moath was distracted by what he saw and with the friends he had made, that caused his father's real intention to see him become a scholar of Islam fail, much to his chagrin, so that when he visited his son two years after he got there all that he could see was a 'spoilt brat', who did not have any higher education but whose future was waiting for him back in his village to look after his father's land and later on, take over his properties, in the advent of his death.

But at least Moath had become someone of culture having briefly met with or had an unofficial audience with King Fuad I when he visited the Cairo Museum to inspect the items found in the tomb of King Tut, when he bumped into the King who had gone there unannounced, and not looking regal or royal so much so that Moath thought he was meeting with an ordinary citizen of Egypt, who was also keen and interested in the history of King Tut. They spoke briefly and with the King also was interested in Moath from the accent he had when he spoke in Arabic and in the Palestinian accent which the King was not familiar with. "Are you from Jordan?", he would ask. Palestine, replied Moath.

You have come such a long way from 'Filasteen', remarked King Fuad I.

Indeed, said Moath, but it has been worth it.

Moath did not care to find out who the man he was speaking in the museum earlier and walked out of it later on after viewing the exhibits, only to be scoffed at by one of the senior palace officials who chided him for not showing the King any respect and who treated him like an ordinary person, he was not.

But why are you angry with me, sir?, asked Moath.

He is His Majesty King Fuad, in case if you are not aware.

Moath was shocked and tried to apologize profusely to the senior official, when King Fuad appeared from inside the museum, and noticed him there, and immediately greeted him with, 'Asalamulaikum, Othman.'

All the ten or so palace officials stood stiff near their King as he spoke with Moath in a casual manner. I hope you enjoy your stay in Kaherah and Mesir, he said.

Yes, Your Majesty, said Moath.

King Fuad then extended his hand and Moath took it and then kissed it, now that he knew who he was, not an ordinary Egyptian, but their King. The King then walked to a waiting car with an encourage with many other vehicles and police escorts with the senior officials scampering to wait until their King had entered the royal vehicle to take him back to the royal palace. But King Fuad suddenly stopped just before he entered the car, and turned around and called Moath. Can you come over, for a minute, Othman? Moath rushed to the car and waited in front of King Fuad, not knowing what to do next or expect from the king, who suddenly removed his watch and gave it to him. It was made in England. King Fuad then entered his car and was driven off, with Moath staring at him and his entourage until they disappeared from his eyesight, hidden behind buildings and with a small crowd of locals waving at him. Moath stood with the watch in his hand, frozen in front of the Cairo Museum located in Downtown Cairo and in Maidan Tahrir, where there were also many restaurants selling shawarma, kebab, falafel, and other local delicacies. Moath did not know what else that he could do and he was starting to feel uneasy when the crowd of locals who had waited to see their king at the museum continued to stare at him; they realized that he was not a local from his features, but none bothered or dared to go closer to him to check with him why their King was so friendly to him. Maybe he was the King's close relatives, they thought. He was not. He then walked away and sat in front of a restaurant and ordered some food to eat for a snack, with his hand still holding the watch that King Fuad had just given him. He realized that it was 'Made in England' and also of gold, and could be very expensive.

Ah, England, he exclaimed, England, he almost said it to himself when he looked at the inscription on the back of the watch. It must be very expensive; the watch looked like it was made in a gold cast, with few small diamonds on the face, and the leather strap, too, looked very exquisite and expensive. He wondered if the Palestinian passport he held was able to allow it to be used to enter the country. He thought he could travel by land, the same way he did when he came to Cairo; and now he could try and do the same, by traveling by land to cross to Europe, the Crusader region and arrive in England, where he thought he could learn how to speak in English better based on what he had learnt of it so far, that he hardly ever used it with anyone in his village who preferred to speak in Arabic. And since arriving in Cairo, he only had a few opportunities to speak in English with the few English tourists, scholars and other visitors he bumped in the streets, or when he was sitting on the sidewalk cafes and they would sit with him at the same table when the others were all taken up.

England. London. Nottingham. Cambridge, Oxford, he said to himself as he tried to wear the watch given by King Fuad the First, barely two hours earlier and he had by now eaten the snacks he had ordered and most of the tea in the cup whose remainder was now cold. He asked for another cup of tea. He had not been to England but he could remember the names of some of the cities and universities from reading about them in the newspapers and magazines.

The waiter brought the new cup of hot tea and put it on the table in front of Moath who showed the watch to him. The waiter instinctively knew it was a very expensive watch. 'King Fuad gave it to me,' said Moath. The waiter was not surprised; he did not show any reaction. 'Here touch it,' said Moath. 'You didn't believe me when I said it was given to me just now by King Fuad himself, outside of the Cairo Museum.'

The waiter touched the watch and didn't say a word. He then turned around and went to a local customer who had just sat at a table with his friend. There were also some English men and women sitting at the table not so far away from Moath. The men were wearing their army uniforms and the women were their wives. They spoke in English with such rapidity that Moath found it difficult to understand what they were saying, except for a few words. England, here I come, he said to himself and smiled. But he knew if he ever got to go to England and tried to speak with the locals in their thick British accent, chances were he might not be able to understand a word of what they were saying; or if he were to speak with him in his own style of speaking in English, the locals, too, would find it difficult to know what he was saying. He remembered the few Palestinians who had gone to live for some years in England, who spoke very good English and with their European looks and clothes they were wearing, all of them could pass for Englishmen. No, I do not want to be like them, Moath said to himself; I want to be as Arab as I can.

And from the sidewalk café, he decided to take a ride on the tram to go to the beach to look at the River Nile that spread before his eyes. It was now dusk and the streetlights had been lit and the night would soon to come. In the river were small boats and some larger ones plying on it with many foreign tourists who looked like they were from England. The locals could not afford to take such rides, which cost a lot; the locals could only take the rides in the smaller boats that did not serve food or drinks.

He had never been on any of the small boats; and he said to himself that he would soon take a ride in one to look at the city from the River Nile. And later on go by bus to Giza where the Pyramids and Sphinx were, to marvel at them, to wonder at their sizes and to imagine what might have actually caused them to be built, in the way that they were built from the photos of them that he had seen before. Now he wanted to see them with his own eyes. The whole of the three major Pyramids in the Giza were flooded once in 1927; no one expected it to happen with them sitting in the middle of a desert that did not see much or any rain falling at all; and even so, it was never heavy and if it did fall the water seeped into the ground in seconds. The locals thought amongst themselves if this was some kind of an omen, and it was not a good one, for such a natural calamity to happen at such a place in such a manner? It had even flooded around the Holy Kaabah, someone added.

He did not want to disappoint his father who kept sending him money to spend for his education but he had not yet tried to find a good university to study at. And he did not want to have to write to his father to say that he had not started school even after five months arriving in Cairo.

He stared at the flickering lights on the surface of the River Nile and once in a while stared at his new watch he had got from King Fuad the First.

'Haji Mabrur…Haji Mabrur…Haji Mabrur…' he asked if he could achieve this, on his first and most likely, last pilgrimage to Makkah. He had not felt like he could achieve it. He had only one ritual to perform before he became a full-fledged Hajji, which was to wait for the right day to go with the others to Mount Arafat in Arafat Valley with all the pilgrims from all over the world to cast stones seven times at the Jabal Ar-Rahmah. He wanted to do it diligently, to cast off the devils, and especially those that had inhibited in his body and soul, he reminded himself.

He opened the chapter on 'Haji Mabrur' and read it by himself so he knew what it meant fully and how to achieve it since he thought he could still do it, if he followed all the rules while he was still here in Makkah and about to complete all the three rituals. The first thing that he learnt was that it was 'Haj that was accepted – by God – Allah! He feared that Allah might not accept his pilgrimage because Allah would know why he was there in the first place and why he decided to perform his Hajj at an age which was too advanced for anyone to do it. Then he felt guilty and did not think his Hajj would be accepted. And the next item that he saw was on how the pilgrimage was not tainted by sins that one might have committed while performing the Hajj. Did he commit any sin since he left his village till now? One ought to have strong faith in wanting to go on Hajj and one should not be boastful in wanting to do it. One who leaves his house to go on the pilgrimage is said to be carrying two flags in his hand; one which flies the flag of Satan and the other the flag of the angels. And any expenses spent on the pilgrimage must be gotten from proper means. He almost choked when he read this because he did not know if whatever he possessed and the money he had spent to come to Makkah was not ill-gotten, he could never know. He tried to assuage himself by saying: How would anyone know this, if what he now possessed was not by ill-gotten means, and if so, whatever Fitrah and Zakat that he had given to anyone and any masjid, too, could not be accepted by them and if they did he would have sinned even more because he had given the money willingly and knowing that it was not got by ill-gotten means.

Moath almost collapsed. His heart was beating very fast in his chest and he was sweating until a bit of his sweat dampened his robe. But there was no one there in the tent so he was able to lie down on the carpet that had been laid on the ground for them to sit and sleep on. He tried to inhale briskly so that he did not faint. He thought it was good for him if he started to not think of where he was at this time, but elsewhere. He didn't realize that performing the Hajj could be a traumatic experience as he had discovered.

Moath was woken by the cries of the Adhan for Maghrib prayers. He woke up and looked at the lights outside which had dampened, because it was already sundown. He poured some water for a cistern and performed his ablution and walked out of the tent to go to the Masjidil Haram where he again had to perform his evening prayers at the back because a crowd of pilgrims and locals had converged there to pray. He was not disappointed as he could pray wherever he liked.

After the prayers were over he returned to his tent and sat there, again alone by himself. By then the sun had disappeared into the horizon, which was hidden by the buildings that were built around the masjid. The sky had a faint glow or golden lights, which began to dim very fast, to welcome the night, where stars started to appear, and then Isyak prayers would happen, for the last prayers for the day. Moath was ready for it; and this time he did not have to perform his ablution because he had just done it for the earlier, Maghrib prayers. He still wondered where everybody was. It was also time for dinner which would be served after the Isyak prayers.

There were hundreds of thousands of people, many from outside of the country, who looked totally different then he was, yet, Moath felt alone, sitting in the tent and not knowing what was happening and where were the others in his group, including his wife.

It was only after the Isyak prayers after Moath had returned from that his wife and the others returned; they all looked tired and exhausted like they had gone very far to see something. But where did they go to, and what did they see there? His wife, Fatimah, had a lot of explaining to do, he thought when she got back. First was: Why was he left alone in the tent? Second: Where did all go to and what did they do that he, too, could go and see? The two questions were simple ones; not loaded, except that he didn't realize that she and his friends had explained to him the night before they retired to go to sleep that they had plans to go to a village outside of Makkah, and took some hours to get there and some hours to get back to Makkah, but Moath said he was not into it; there was nothing interesting there for him to see. What was it that they wanted to see there? A small village of Jews! No wonder Moath declined to go there with everybody, because he had plans to take them to Baitulmukaddis after their pilgrimage to spend a few days there where they could visit The Old City where there were some, no; many Jews and also Christians living there in peaceful harmony. And he also wanted to take them to his friend, Moshe's store to sit and see if they would like to buy anything he sold.

So that was how Moath learnt that he had totally forgotten about the plans the others had the whole day, and they started to worry for him, because some of the more educated men, felt that Moath was slowly losing his ability to remember well, because of his advanced age. His wife, Fatimah, also felt the same but she did not dare to ask her husband if he was alright. She only asked if he had lunch and dinner and if he had gone to the Masjidil Haram to perform his prayers there, for which he just nodded without saying a word, which the others took to mean another sign of his failing mental health. Otherwise, he was okay and able to move about on his own two feet, when they learnt that he had gone to the Masjid to pray there, twice earlier in the day, and had not skipped eating lunch and dinner, so he could still be trusted with his faculties. But they feared what might happen to him in the next few days, with his wife swearing to herself that she would not leave him alone in his tent and would not go anywhere else even if her husband allowed her to do so like what he did earlier when she finally agreed to visit the Jewish village outside of Makkah that afternoon. The only reason why they wanted to visit their Jewish friends there was because they had heard of their plans to leave Arabia; they were starting to feel the heat; they did not fear the local Arabs around them who were Muslims, but the situation in the whole region, especially in Palestine where they feared many Jews had gone to live and had started to displace the local Arab population, and soon the Arabs would be overwhelmed and this could pose serious problems to Jews like them whose ancestors had lived peacefully amongst the Arabs there and everywhere in all the Arab countries, and they did not want to see themselves suffer as a direct result of the encroachment of Jews who they described as 'foreign Jews' who were not original Jews, but converts to the religion. Not only Arabia would change, the whole of Palestine as they knew it, too, would change, and change for the worse; definitely not for the better.

They were able to communicate with the small Jewish community there in perfect Arabic, as did all the other Jews in small communities that could still be found around Madinnah and few other cities in Arabia, whose numbers, too, had shrunk considerably over the last decade or so.

There was nothing special there in the village except that one of those men from Palestine knew him when they were small and he promised to visit him when he was in Makkah; and now the occasion had availed itself and he did not want to miss the opportunity to meet his childhood friend again. Both were in the forties and married with five children each. And they also got to watch the Jews performing their prayers inside their house as there was no Jewish Synagogue or Temple, standing quietly at the side of the room which was adorned with Jewish pray paraphernalia that they had not seen before, with the sermon given by the Rabbi in 'Ibrani' or Hebrew a word they did not understand, except for 'Shalom' which means 'Peace' or 'Salam' in Arabic, that they exchanged and greeted each other a lot earlier when they first met. There were some but that was many years ago, his Jewish friend explained, but as their numbers began to shrink, the synagogues were closed as there were also no Rabbis who could lead their congregations.

In the past, there were many Jewish clans or families such as, Baju Al Fageer, Banu Awf, Banu Harith or Bnei Chorath, Banu Jusham, Banu Qad'a, Banu Shutayba, Banu Nadir, Banu Qainuga, Banu Qurayza, and so on, with some in Madinnah and Hejaz whose ancestors had arrived there in from the Second Century, but most of them had left Arabia to go to Israel or other Arab countries that they said were more modern with some others fleeing to go to the Crusader states of Europe. But all of them were forbidden from entering Makkah, much less to visit the Masjidil Haram. They all knew the laws banning them from entering the holy city and none of them had ever breached the law because those found to breach it would be severely punished. Moath, like the other Arabs, did not know exactly why non-Muslims were not allowed to enter Makkah; they could guess why, but the answer they could think of was not the exact reason, and none of them bothered to enquire about it and took it for granted, as did the non-Muslims who too, would come to Jeddah and other cities near Makkah but who never went any further than those places, lest they would be punished. Moath, told himself to check on this matter when he was back in his village to see if there was anyone there who had it. He forgot to ask about it when he was in Makkah recently because the matter did not crop in his head; besides he was too busy observing his prayer rituals throughout the whole time he was in Makkah and also Madinnah Mukarammah, until now when it was brought to his attention with the presence of the Jewish community in the village away from Makkah that his wife and friend had visited. He supposed, the Jews would know of the answer, because it concerned them more than the Arab-Muslims like him.

He later found out from reading the Noble Qur'an, that the reason why non-Muslims were banned from going to Makkah was because they were described to be 'unclean' and therefore not allowed to go there. 'Oh you who believe! Truly the idolaters are unclean; so let them not, after this year, approach the Sacred Mosque. ...' (9:28). However, upon inspection he realized that this verse specifically referred to the Masjidil Haram in Makkah, and not to the entire city of Makkah; whereas there were some Islamic religious leaders or Ustaz or Ulamak who decreed that some provisions were allowed for them to go to Makkah, mostly for the purpose of trading, and for people who wanted to go there, provided they were under some supervision from the authorities. He was relieved to learn of this because even though it was a minor issue, since there would be no non-Muslim who would want to go there and had made any attempts to go there, coming from outside of Arabia, and especially those who were living in the country, it finally gave him some sort of closure on the matter, a minor but a significant one, so in case if anyone were to bring it out for a casual discussion on it, he was sure to have the answer to him, a convincing one and the only answer he would have. The other reason he learnt was to not allow non-Muslims to enter Makkah which was always crowded at any given time, so additional visitors who just wanted to be there, without any intention of performing Islamic rituals and act like tourists, would further aggravate the situation and congest it even more with the thousands or people and roads that were congested with traffic and trading at stalls offering good and other things.

On the way back to Makkah, after visiting the Jews, everybody in the group was silent; they were in deep thought; and what they had seen of the Jews and the way they practiced their religion of Judaism, was new to them. Some of them felt sorry for having met them to see how they were living in fear of being persecuted; and why not, some of their relatives and close friends, too, had left the country to go elsewhere including to Palestine, where they congregate in cities there that had large groups of Jews like them, some of who had lived all their lives in other Arab countries but most of the others were from Europe, or the Crusader countries there.

Moath slept well with the men in their tents while his wife slept with the women in another tent, laying on the thick carpet and two layers of blankets made of wool his wife had given him to ensure that he felt warm, from the cold night, and beside his friends who slept three abreast with the few others lying at the other side of the tent which was large enough to take six of them with the others sleeping in other tents nearby. There was someone in the far distance who was reading the Noble Qur'an, with his melodious voice sounding faint; but everybody was entranced by the verses that he was reading, the sound that never failed to cool them, with no one daring to speak amongst themselves until the reading was done and there was silence, when some of the men remarked how they were happy to see Moath was sleeping and looking so peacefully.

She had ensured her husband was given some hot tea to drink and put more in a tumbler for him to drink later at night when he woke up.

But he never did and the tea in the tumbler soon became cold and tasted a bit stale; and it was not good to drink less it could cause constipation. So that was what she thought and reminded him not to take it once the tea had become cold.

Moath had no reason to wake up from his sleep; he was happy to meet his wife and the others again and had even managed to not worry about achieving 'Haji Mabrur' or 'Haji Wada' after reading about it and he thought it would not be good if he continued to worry about his Hajj that would soon end, with their trip to Arafat Valley that would happen in a few days' time. For now, he wanted to look ahead and not to the past; he could shape his future, but not his past, which was long gone. He told his wife and friends, it would have been a lot better if he had joined them to go to the village to meet the Jewish community there, all of whom spoke very good Arabic much like them, and also Hebrew or 'Ibrani'. They must be descendants of the Jewish people who had lived there for hundreds of years, with some stretching to the time of Nabi Muhammad, (s.a.w.) when there were many Jews living there as did in Madinnah Mukarammah, that they had visited earlier; where the Mausoleum of Nabi Muhammad, (s.a.w.) was. And what made him especially happy was that he had finally made it to the three most important Masjid in the three most important cities in Islam, namely: Makkah, Madinnah, and Baitulmukaddis the Jews called Jerusalem. And this was where he planned to take his group – Baitulmukaddis a.k.a. Jerusalem for a few days on their way back to their village in Palestine, where he wanted to meet with his Jewish friend who went by the name of Moshe. He could have followed the others to go to the village outside of Makkah to meet with Moshe if not because he was tired and exhausted; and his wife too, advised him not to come along and forced him to stay behind so he could rest and be by himself, because she knew her husband better than anyone else and being alone often helped to rejuvenate his mind, body and soul that he badly needed to experience especially after traveling from their village to Makkah that took longer than expected because he wanted to not rush to get here as there was still time for them to join the other pilgrims from all over the world.

Moath and the others then left for Arafat Valley where they were scheduled to stay for two days, to perform the stoning of the devils, which was the last of the three rituals they had to do for the pilgrimage after which they were done. And they were not in any rush to return to their village in Palestine; Moath wanted to take them to Baitulmukaddis for a few days there to see the place especially The Old City and to meet some of his friends there, who were Arabs like them and Jews, too, and other Arab who were Christians.

Hundreds of thousands of pilgrims, possible more than half a million had gathered in the Valley of Arafat, and they stayed in tents that had been erected throughout the valley and beyond to the horizons. Moath's wife, was relieved that her husband was hale and hearty when they were still in their horse-cart traveling for a few hours from Makkah, where they made a brief stop along the way to eat lunch and to relieve themselves, and also to perform the Noon or Zohor prayers, this time together on the ground with Moath acting as their Imam, where later read an extra long supplication or 'doa' when he took the opportunity to remind the small congregation of about twenty, and also to himself how everybody ought to keep remind themselves that performing their Hajj was not everything, but a start of the new phase or era in their personal existence and the challenges to their faith or 'Iman' would far greater now then it was before. He almost broke down when he said that because he was saying it from his heart and had not prepared the supplication, and decided to point out this matter, lest they did not know of their duty to help and support each other and everybody else in their village who might be in need of some assistance and, maybe, money, too. He reminded the congregation that he said that as an older man, who looked at the others like his own sons and daughters. Finally, he thanked all of them for supporting and accompanying him to perform his Hajj together with his wife, despite his advanced age when he said, he would have done it a few decades before.

'Amin,' everybody said when Moath finally ended reading the supplication.

While his wife and friends and their wives were excited to be able to visit the few Jews that were still left in Makkah, and to know them, Moath was more interested in the history of the Crusades, now that he was going to Baitulmukaddis, which they called Jerusalem, where the main focus of the Crusaders were. They thought the Jews there did not look or behave like some of those they could see in Palestine especially in the larger cities especially Haifa and Tel Aviv, who hardly mix with the local Arabs; they preferred to be by themselves. The reason being that there were many of them in these two cities so they could stick with each other and did not have any need to mix with anyone else, especially those who did not look like them. But the older ones were nice; and the younger ones, were not so nice.

He had heard of Sallahuddin Al Ayubi which those in the west and Crusaders called 'Saladin', and had read about him in books and newspaper articles that he could get his hands on and more, so when he was in Kaherah (Cairo) where there was a lot of literature on him and other aspects of him and the Crusades that he did not know of. He bought some of the books to read and gave few to his friends, so they, too, would know more who Sallehuddin al Ayubi was, and especially how he could even get the respect of the Crusaders and those in the west themselves, despite having trounced them earlier so Baitulmukaddis finally fell in the hands of the Arabs and Muslims. He made sure he read all the literature he had bought and kept them as souvenirs or for future references to read again when he was back in his village in Palestine where he was certain there would not be any book store there that had them on their shelves for anyone there to buy.

8

Off to Baitulmukaddis a.k.a Jerusalem

Moath and his wife, Fatimah and the others from their village looked cheerful and happy, and also relieved that all of them had performed their Hajj, to their satisfaction, with nothing untoward happening along the way to Makkah, and now they were returning back to their village in Palestine as Hajjis and Hajjjahs. They had started to call each other Hajji or Hajjah, for having performed their pilgrimage, like the others, and with the men who now sported short hair that they had trimmed after performing The Stoning of the Devils at the Valley of Arafat a few days earlier. And all of them seemed to be behaving different now that they had performed their Hajj; and they seemed to talk less and in deep thoughts when they were resting during their breaks for their meals and prayers, in the open desert, and did not exhibit too much emotions, other than to feel relieved that they had managed to come this far and in a few days' time they would be back to their village in Palestine where Moath had arranged to give all of them a feast together with their relatives and friends there, to show their gratitude to them for supporting them and to send them off to Makkah two months ago. They also did not seem to realize that they had looked much older than they were earlier and surely those in their villages could see it when they meet them again in a few days. That to them, should be a mark of piety and maturity and their rejection of worldly possession and the time for greater reflection on who they were and why they were there on this earth and where they were going, to the unknown entity, hoping that it would be 'Jannah' or

Heaven. Some of the men who were said to have a youthful demeanor, too, had suddenly looked sullen and less cheerful; they were more thoughtful and less talkative than they were before. Their trip to Makkah to perform their Hajj together was a blessing and the changes that they had experienced upon completion of the pilgrimage had become a life-changing experience for all. But they never thought they had changed so much; only those who knew them before they embarked on their journey of a life time would be able to see the differences in them and they, too, would surely be delighted to see all of them in their new style and attitudes – behaving and acting like men and women of piety and greater subservience to Allah the Almighty.

Moath, now a full-fledged Hajji, too, had seen tremendous differences in his thinking and he was still grappling with the negative thoughts that had suddenly entered his consciousness; and no matter how hard he tried to dispel them, they continued to stick in his head. After a while trying to clear his mind of them, he then decided not to get rid of those negative thoughts and used them to recover his lost senses and of values and attitudes and also, and mostly, some sins that he might have committed unknowingly, when he was much, much younger and who did not care too much to look after his behavior, and only now when he was in Makkah performing his Hajj, he was reminded of them. He said to himself that he should strive to make amends for all the sins that he had committed and henceforth become a better person. He then realized that his gait, too had become a bit weak and he feared if his physical body had started to become any weaker chances were he might have to walk with a stick for easy ambulation. So far he thought he was okay; but trying to stand up after performing the prostration each time while praying had suddenly become a slight burden and he started to feel his own weight pulling him down. He had to touch his knees with both hands to push his body upwards.

He also noticed his eyesight getting blurry and he was not able to read the newspapers that much unless if the text was written in bigger sizes. There was nothing interesting in the news and most of what was written was on the past Hajj season that had just ended and a bit on the Crusaders' War, which he preferred to describe it as and not the so-called First World War, because the war was not happening in the world but in Europe only. It would not spread to the Arab World as there was no indication of that happening, as what he could see when he was performing Hajj.

The Crusaders' War started on 28 July, 1914, more than a year ago. He, or no one knew how long it would last and how severe it has been. The newspaper reports he had seen the whole time he was performing Hajj did not say exactly who was winning and who was loosing; but as far as he could tell, in any war, there were no real winners – all were losers. The photos published in the reports looked bleak with many buildings torn down by bombs that were dropped from airplanes. And the number of casualties were many because the war was fought using modern weapons and not conventional ones, that were used during the time of the Crusades, when even their leaders fought and took the front lines; but in the First Crusaders' War, the leaders were nowhere to be seen; they only knew how to give orders while hiding themselves in bunkers that were hidden deep in the ground. In the end most who were killed were soldiers and privates who risked their lives by going to the front line and the pilots whose planes were shot down and, mostly, the ordinary citizens who happened to be at the wrong place at the wrong time when the buildings they were in were attacked.

Couldn't the war have been stopped, before it even started? He asked himself. He did not want to hazard an answer because he did not have the facts on why it broke up in the first place. He and his friends were still in their village in Palestine when it broke out on 28 July, 1914. But news of it started to appear in the newspapers he would read a few days later.

The photos of all the major cities in Europe were defaced and with many completely destroyed. It would take Europe many years to clear the mess they had created and more years to rebuild them.

Moath prayed such wars would not come anywhere near Palestine or any Arab country; they had had enough of them with the last Crusade which fortunately was trounced by Sallehuddin Al Ayubi, who the Crusaders and Europeans called 'Saladin' who managed to repel them and wrest control of Baitulmukaddis from them, so now the Palestinians like him were able to go there whenever they wanted to, and this was why he was there with his friends, to stop for a few days before they moved on to return to the village they had originated from, as their final destination.

It had been this long that they had been away, and everyday, they had spent away from their village, they felt they had come closer to Allah, by performing more supplementary or 'Sunnat' prayers and saying long supplications. One of the men and his wife in the group decided to fast a few days, so when everybody else were having their meals, they would sit elsewhere; and they would eat at sunset, together without everybody else, because it was not the time for them to have their dinner together which they would do only after the last prayers for the day called the 'Isyak' prayers.

And the two days of traveling from Makkah to Baitulmukaddis was also eventful and an interesting one. They decided not to take the main road, but the subsidiary ones, that passed through small and isolated villages and small towns that none of them had passed or been to before. They stopped at a few places to have their meals and a long break and to also pray, before moving on, to spend the night in an open desert with no one around. They liked the cool winds blowing everywhere and hitting their faces and to stare at the moon hanging in the clear sky at night, and to read the Noble Qur'an whenever they can, even when they were riding on their horse-driven carts to get to Baitulmukaddis. But they also missed being in the crowd of pilgrims in Madinnah, Makkah, and the Valley of Arafat, so they suddenly felt alone, walking in a sea of hundreds of thousand of pilgrims like him, with many who were local Arabs and also those non-Arab Muslims from all over the world; and suddenly, he missed all of them, the sight of the men and women wearing in their proper clothing called 'ehram', in two pieces of white covering their waist and the rest of the body with the women in white praying attire. Suddenly, he felt alone. He knew the others were also making their way back to where they had come from to be greeted by their family members and those from their community who would now look up to them for religious guidance on many matters, as and when they arose, because they were now their elders who had performed Hajj, an achievement that everybody who had not done so, would feel privileged to know.

He was now casting his sights on Baitulmukaddis, which was their next destination, a place where they wanted to stay at for a few days before continuing on with their journey. They saw more camels, horses, and mules along the roads to Baitulmukaddis than they had seen before because the roads were wider and better paved and there were many, like him, who wanted to go there for different reasons, some for trading. Moath looked outside of his cart to look at the crowds of people traveling along the same route as he was with their horses and mules galloping along to take them to their different destinations in the city or elsewhere. He saw road signs for 'Jericho', 'Nablus', 'Hebron', 'Haifa', 'Tel Aviv' and also 'Amman', and so on along the way. They were the major cities in Palestine, some of which Moath had visited or been to before for various reasons or purposes, when he was much younger and was in need for new adventure, before he braved himself by going beyond these cities to go to those in the neighboring countries to as far as Kaherah in Mesir where he lived and worked for some years, and started to speak Arabic in the local accent. He did not dare to venture further than Kaherah, to go to Tripoli in Libya, that some of his Egyptian friends had invited him to with them.

Why not? He asked himself many times, before deciding that it was not a good idea at all. He felt he had gone too far already, to be in Kaherah where not many of his friends in his village had dared to go to; they did not have any reason or purpose to go there. So most of the boys grew up to be men who hardly went out of the villages, never mind, their country, Palestine, died and were buried in the same village where they were born. Sometimes Moath pitied them; but mostly as he grew up and thought he had become wiser, he realized that it was folly on his part to depart from his village to go elsewhere, because his village was everything to them, so why was there any need to go anywhere else? Unless, of course, if they wanted to go to Arabia to perform their Hajj or Ummrah, which was fine as it was prescribed by Islam that all Muslims, like them, ought to go there at least once in their lifetime. Some went there earlier in their lives but Moath only went there when he was already very old. He did not have any good or reasonable excuse to give to anyone who wondered why he took so long to perform Hajj; most thought he had gone earlier when they found him missing from their village for many years. No, he had not gone to Makkah. They were shocked with the revelation and did not probe into the issue and whatever that might have caused him to delay going there, until he was so old. To all of them, it was Fate; and one could do so much, and the rest was up to Allah to decide. They needed to get the necessary and also right inspiration to go to Makkah which could only come from Allah who decides everything for them. It was not about money, because he had more than enough to spend on the pilgrimage if he had wanted to go there earlier. He knew he did not have the urge and sense of urgent to undertake such a task then. He marveled at the sight of the pilgrims from India, China, and also Tanah Melayu, and Jawa who had come from so very away in boats that sailed in the oceans whose waters were rough, to go to Makkah to perform their Hajj and praying in Arabic, an alien language to them, but they pursued. He was told by some of the Melayu men how there were also some Arabs who had come to Tanah Melayu to trade with some of them marrying local women and a few had decided to call Tanah Melayu their home where they had children to rear, and in time, they too, began to look and behave like Melayu men, like them. Some got to be very wealthy dealing in all sorts of business.

Are they from Palestine? Moath asked them in Arabic which they understood. No. Most are from Yemen and other Arab countries. They were the Aljuned, Alsaggof, Barakhbah and so on. He was impressed with the Melayu from Tanah Melayu and Jawa who could speak Arabic well, except that their accent was a bit different, because they did not speak in the language all the time, but sparingly; yet, when they read the Noble Qur'an, they sounded very, very good. They bought a lot of 'tasbih' – prayer beads, 'sejadah' or prayer mats and also robes to give to their relatives when they returned home after their Hajj.

Ma sha Alah, he remarked. They must be very, very brave to leave their countries to go to your country, he added. But he was happier when told that the Arab men in Tanah Melayu were still Arabs and staunch Muslims. This was what mattered to him, more than the wealth they had managed to acquire. And how they had followed in the footsteps of The Prophet – Nabi Muhammad, (s.a.w.) who also did trading and a lot of traveling and it is also what Islam preached for Muslims to venture out, and to go even to as far as 'to China'!

Moath said he would not have minded to go there if he was much, much younger; but now it was too late. And he also did not want to encourage his son or grandson to do it, to embark on such an arduous trip to Tanah Melayu or Jawa at that time when the situation in Palestine was fluid. He remembered the Jews who had been coming in droves to live in the larger cities where there were already many of them and feared that if things did not happen to stop the inflow of such people, Palestine could easily turn upside down.

There were many small villages and towns which he could see along the way, with so many people like him, Arabs and Palestinians but there were also quite a few of those Jews that he had not seen there before living in their own enclaves they had created. They lived peacefully being surrounded by Arabs and that was how it had been for so long since their ancestors' time, hundreds of years ago, with them not knowing how else they could live, other than in the village. Of course, there had been a few of the Jewish men and also women who had opted to marry out of their communities to Arabs from the same village and others, and some of them had also left the village to follow the spouses to live elsewhere, as it was fated that it had to happen to them, and they would return to their village during Eidul Adha or Eidul Fitri or the Jewish festivals, to celebrate together taking their children along who had their parents' features, not so Arabic and not so Jewish, but a mixture of both.

How did they get there? Where did they come from? Many of them did not look like they had been here for so long because they did not have features of other Jews that he knew, and they also did not speak Arabic like most of the Jews he knew. Moath was happy that he could see with his own eyes those villages and towns and the many Arabs and now, more Jews that he did not see before, with his eyes still good, and before they failed him.

Suddenly, he began to feel emotional; he was worried that God wanted him to lose his eyesight, for a good reason, that only He knew what it was; so that he (Moath) was not be able to look at Palestine, the Arabs and the more and more Jews that were coming in droves from everywhere the he had heard when he was in Arabia performing Hajj, that would make him very sad and angry. He wanted to cry, but he forced himself not to, as his cart moved along ahead towards Baitulmukaddis which he had not been to in a long while. He did not mind crying if he was alone, but there was his wife in the cart with him and who was also lying beside him, being carried on the cart along the roads which were at times bumpy that bounced their bodies upward and sideward, that didn't worry them a bit; on the contrary they felt like they were being lulled by the movements of their bodies with each swaying of the cart. Her eyes were closed. It would not be long when they were scheduled to make another brief stop anywhere where they would be, for a break to eat, perform their prayers and to stretch out and look at the views around them. It was still bright outside in the desert, but the road they were traveling on had many vehicles of all kinds, some old types, like horse and mule-carts, and the others, buses and cars and also motorcycles. There were train services in Palestine but none that connected Makkah to Baitulmukaddis yet. He did not know if such a service would be introduced and if there was one, it should make life much easier for them to go to Makkah not only for Hajj but also for Ummrah and to trade so they could bring more things and goods to Palestine for the stores to sell, and in the process encouraged the growth of the trading class.

'Sallahuddin Al Ayubi! Sallehuddin Al Ayubi! Sallehuddin Al Ayubi!!' Moath cried in his afternoon nap when they stopped for a break somewhere along the route to Baitulmukaddis. He realized that he was fast approaching the city and his thoughts started to race towards it, and he felt he could 'see' the city, but only in his mind and The Old City he had imagined it to be like the last time he was there. He had been there many times but from a different route, from the West Bank and mostly from his village where his father had taken him there when he was small; so he did not remember much or anything at all about it or what it looked like until the second time his father took him there and this time he was much older and was aware of what was going on and what he was seeing, The Old City and the Four Quarter that separate people of the different faiths, but who were able to live peacefully with each other and with each other's styles and ways and beliefs. And the Temple Mount and Masjid Al Aqsa, he did not remember well but managed to see photos of them that he had kept.

His wife, Fatimah was with the wives of the other pilgrims outside their carts and they were preparing for their next meal while the men, were praying on the ground, without Moath, who was sleeping earlier and they did not want to stir him up; he could do the 'Asar' prayers when he woke up. He had told them not to disturb him because his wife, too, had reminded the men and their wives not to create too much commotion or noise or to wake him up, because he was not quite well. None of them ever said he was already 'an old man' as it was not nice to say so, like he was close to death; because they could not tell who amongst them would 'go first' or die as anyone at any age and in any physical condition could be called to meet with his Creator at any time. They all knew what Fate was. None of them knew that his eyesight had started to fail, except for his wife who did not want to tell them. And she had also started to notice that her husband had also started to become weaker and easily tire himself, so that was why she did not want anyone to disturb him while he took a nab, lying in the cart and on some thick carpets that they had bought in Makkah, as a valuable souvenir from the Holy City even though it was not made there, but elsewhere, in Iran! So he also thought, he had a souvenir from Makkah and also from Iran – or Isfahan, to be exact, a place so far away from his village that he could not imagine how it might look like. Many Iranians told him it was a beautiful place with some ancient palaces.

The men had finished their 'Asar' prayers and rolled their prayer mats or carpets and put them in their own carts. Fatimah signaled to them to come over where she and the other women had lain on mats, food for them to eat. It was a snack, but loaded with some dishes meant for dinner, that they allowed the men to take some and a lot more at dinner, when it would be dark and they might be in another area where there were caravanserai to put up the night at, or if they so wished, they could move on until they got to Baitulmukaddis where they could either camp out or find lodging to sleep in.

The men sat cross-legged on the mat and started to tear the bread and dip it into some gravy. A large 'dallah' made of bronze that Fatimah had bought in Madinnah, had been filled with hot tea, and on the mat were cups made of bronze, too, had been filled with some of it, waiting to be sipped. There was emptiness around them with a road further away, because they made sure they did not stop to park by the roadside where there was a lot of traffic and people. They were almost perched on a low hill overlooking the road where they could see many vehicles of all types and some modern ones, with mules and camels, goats and even other strange creatures they could not guess well what they were. They also did not want to be eating and resting in full view of the public.

They were then distracted by the sound of someone calling out the name which was familiar to all of them, 'Sallehuddin Al Ayubi! Sallehuddin Al Ayubi!' being called a few times. They turned to Moath's cart and saw him sitting at the back with his legs dangling over it. His wife immediately called out, 'Are you alright?'

'I had a dream,' he said.

The men and the women were surprised, but his wife was not. Fatimah wanted to stand up to go to her husband, but he immediately jumped down from the cart onto his feet and walked towards them. His wife waited.

'I had a dream,' said Moath. 'I dreamt of Sallehuddin Al Ayubi who came to me and told me to go to Baitulmukaddis where something was waiting for me.'

'Something?' asked Imran. 'Like what, Uncle?'

Moath sat on the mat with the men while his wife was at the other side with the women. She reached out for a plate to give to her husband,

and a cup she put in front of him into which she then poured hot tea. 'Have something to eat. We'll be traveling a bit more towards Baitulmukaddis,' she said.

Moath reached for a piece of bread and tore a piece of it with both hands, dipped it into a gravy and chewed it while the others waited impatiently on what else he would tell them of his dream, other than that their Arab hero of an earlier time, the time of the Crusaders, Sallehuddin Al Ayubi had given him some instructions through a dream.

'What is that something, Uncle,' chipped Idris.

Moath did not hear him and continued to eat. His wife who was near him was starting to feel anxious, because she did not want Idris and the other men and women to find out that her husband was hard on hearing and also eyesight. 'Let's just eat,' she added, to change the topic and to cover for her husband weaknesses. She felt sorry for the men and women and mostly for her husband. 'Don't forget to perform your Asar prayers,' she reminded her husband who did not look at her or acknowledged her reminder. 'Once you have done it, and we can start to pack up and leave this place. It is indeed a nice place to take a short break and to have a snack.'

Her husband chewed a bit more of the bread which had been dipped in gravy, and not looking at his wife and the others near him, said, 'Sallehuddin Al Ayubi, was my hero when I was a small boy. And I grew to like and appreciate what he had done to us, Arabs, even more when I grew up and read about his exploits in magazines and books that I was given by my father and uncles, which I still have kept somewhere.' He grabbed another piece of bread and this time did not dip it in gravy, until he was done. 'He destroyed the Crusaders, yet, he could become a hero in the Crusade countries,' he added. 'And this is not what was marvelous about him. Sallehuddin Al Ayubi freed Baitulmukaddis. Some of the leaders of the Crusaders even called him a 'sultan'. That was how they admired him, how they hailed him.

He then continued on with his rendition on the history and exploits of Sallehuddin Al Ayubi, in his own style by talking almost to himself and not looking at anyone. He said, 'Saladin ended the Crusaders' reign over Baitulmukaddis or Jerusalem over eighty-eight years, and by the time he died in 1193 CE he managed to create an Emirate which stretched from Tunisia to Iran destroying all the countries along the way, and all the while exhibited positive traits and humanity and humility to those he had vanquished without torturing and further reducing their stature as humans. So no wonder even those who he had destroyed amongst the Crusaders themselves had high respects for him for the merciful character he had shown to them that they themselves and their predecessors had not shown. For he was generous in triumph with high sense of 'Adab' or chivalry, as any Arab and Muslim should show. And no wonder he later became heroes in many Victorian novels of the romantic sorts although by then he was called by them not by his original Arabic name, but by the name they had given him, which was Saladin, which was not tinged with any negative remarks or connotation but simply by virtue of the fact that their tongue found it difficult to pronounce his original name like any Arab would.

Saladin or Sallebuddin Al Ayubi was unlike the leaders of the Crusaders who enjoyed in killing the people of countries and places they had captured, and they even defiled the Masjid Al-Aqsa, using it to keep their horses as stables, after capturing it, but Saladin, on the other hand spared the lives of anyone who did not manage to escape when his forces came to them and even ensured that their holy places in Baitulmukaddis be preserved especially the Church of the Holy Sepulchre and Hospital of the Order of St. John, which we will be seeing when we get to The Old City soon, either this evening or tomorrow morning.' Moath then paused while the men and women waited. His wife was especially anxious and worried, because she had not seen her husband behave like this before talking almost to himself. She wanted to stop him but feared this act might make it even worse for him. So far what he had said made a lot of sense and some of which they had not heard of before; with many who had not even read the book on Sallahuddin Al Ayubi and who they only knew by name and not much else.

Moath then stood up and said, 'Let me pray Asar, so we can all leave here,' leaving everybody especially his wife frozen in their seats, after being told almost the entire history of Sallehuddin Al Ayubi the Twelfth Century Arab warrior and hero. But he did not touch on the Crusades launched by the Crusaders of Europe. That, he thought was another story, that needed another time and place for him to relate the little he thought he knew of. But for him, talking and remembering Sallahuddin Al Ayubi was more interesting and important to him than the Crusaders.

The Crusaders received the blessings from the Roman Church to embark on a series of wars against the Arabs who were then occupying Baitulmukaddis, and the more significant wars were those that happened in the Eleventh, Twelfth and Thirteenth Centuries that were chiefly fought in the eastern Mediterranean region, whose sole purpose was for the Christians to recover the Holy Land from the Arabs and Muslims. So over time the term or word 'Crusade', was even applied to other activities sanctioned by the Church including other non-religious campaigns and acts. The word actually was derived from the French word for 'cross' which is 'crux'. And the Arabs called them 'Salib' also for the same word. The call for the launching of the First Crusade then happened in 1095 at the Council of Clemount, which aroused the passion and anger of the Christians and leaders in few Crusader countries in Europe which attracted a lot of volunteers from amongst their brethren and supporters who willingly and gladly took public vow of support and sacrifice, with some of them hoping they would find a safe route to Heaven or at least their sins were reduced or wiped away completely, while some others quietly prayed to gain some measure of notoriety and financial gain from their exploits.

The Christian angst over the loss of their Holy Land in Jerusalem came to a pinnacle when Pope Urban II openly called for the Roman Emperor Alexious I who was in desperate need for military reinforcements for their conflict with the Turks who had advanced to Anatolia, because Pope Urban II wanted to guarantee the Christian's access to their holy sites in the eastern Mediterranean, such as in the County of Edessa, the Principality of Antioch, the Kingdom of Jerusalem and the County of Tripoli.

The First Crusade was unsuccessful while the second only allowed them the capture of Lisbon in Portugal, and the Third Crusade which was planned to recapture Jerusalem, but their efforts to achieve this goal turned out to be a dismal failure. And because of that, the church leaders and elders got their men to embark on another campaign for their Fourth Crusade to sack Constantinople in Turkey, while the Fifth Crusade saw their forces suffering defeat in Egypt.

However, their Sixth Crusade was met with tremendous success when they managed to regain Jerusalem, but not with the use of force, but by negotiations.

The Seventh Crusade was a huge blow to the Crusaders when they were defeated in Egypt with the following Eighth Crusade was met with failure in Tunis. The Eighth and Ninth Crusades could be considered to linked together, but they were not seriously considered as part of the overall plan of the Crusaders and their actual leaders in the Catholic Papacy in Rome, which was directing all the crusades, with the exception that in these two crusades, the main significance that could be seen was in the presence of Prince Edward of England who would later become the king of the country. In the end the crusades that were first launched in 1095 all failed to recover the Holy Land of the Christians, after the last crusade that was launched in 1291.

Moath had a book specifically on the Crusades, but he had yet to read it again before he could remember and relate to his friends what they were and why they failed to gain control of Jerusalem which they claimed to be the Holy Land of the Christians, as much as the Arabs, too, wanted to claim it as their own, one of the most important centers of Islam. He knew he had the time to read the book on the way to Baitulmukaddis which he thought was the right place for him to talk about the Crusades of the Christians that failed.

The other men and women and Moath's wife, Fatimah, looked at him as he walked to the side of his cart; he then rubbed his hand with some fine sand from the ground and did his ablution using it called 'tayamum'. He then pulled a prayer mat from his cart and laid it on the ground and started to perform his prayers (salah). Ghassan, suddenly had to say it: 'He may be advanced in age, but his mind is still racing like a fox. And don't be surprised if he jumps all over to do the 'dabke' when we return to our village in a few days' time.'

The others wanted to think that Ghassan was saying it as a joke, especially the part on the 'dabke' but did not to think so when they realized that his wife was there with their wives, who might not like the insinuation. And Moath's wife, Fatimah was quick to chip in by saying, 'He was good with it, when he was much younger.'

'Oh, yes, he surely was; and I had seen him doing it many times then,' said Ghassan, who was surprised when Fatimah said it. They had not been married then, but even after they got married he still did some 'dabke' but in strides that did not match his age, with his legs kicking very high and with him jumping all over to do the dance like a young man.

'We'll see if he will still do it,' Fatimah added. She suddenly felt a shock when she looked at her husband who had just finished performing his prayers and had rolled up the prayer mat and put it back in the cart started to walk to the side of the cart, when he suddenly tripped and wanted to fall. He however, managed to grab the side of the cart and fell on the horse that was lying beside it, or he might have hurt himself if he had fallen onto the ground where there were some large stones.

'Ma Sha Allah!' she shrieked. The others around her turned to look at her. 'What happened?' someone asked her? But Fatimah ignored her and shouted at her husband, 'Be careful. Are you alright?'

The others turned to look at Moath and a few of them sprang onto their feet to rush to his aid. 'Are you alright, Uncle Othman?' asked Ghassan.

Moath stood up and wiped the dust and sand on his palms and robe and said, 'I'm okay; I'm okay. I just felt groggy a bit with the dust and especially road which was not even.'

'Do you want to see a doctor?' someone called.

'No, that won't be necessary. I'm okay. See…' He then tried to make some moves of the 'dabke'. The others, including his wife wanted to laugh but they refrained from doing that. 'You don't want to break your legs,' she remarked.

'No, I won't. I will surely do a bit of it when we get to our village soon.' He then stopped dancing and turned to look at Ghassan and not seeing him, asked, 'Ghassan, where are you?'

'Here, Uncle!'

Moath turned to look at him and said, 'What time do we want to move on, or are we camping here for the night?'

There was no answer; everybody thought the only person who could decide on it was he, Moath, himself; but they were surprised that he was the one now who was asking such a question. Ghassan then broke the silence and said, 'Uncle normally decides on this matter...'

'If it is still bright now, we can move and since we already had our snacks and a long break with praying done, why don't we just move on and when it is dark, before we get to Baitulmukaddis, we will camp again, wherever we will be.'

'Dabka, or Dabke...is pronounced in slightly different accents and intonations by the Arabs, depending on which country they are from,' said Moath, as he was being led in a horse-cart, which was not his own. His wife, Fatimah was sitting in their cart with some women and her husband decided to spend a bit of time with the men in their carts because he felt sorry for not spending too much or enough time with them while they were on the road, from the time they left their village close to two months ago; and now he decide to sit with them in one of their carts, and with Ghassan too. He was in the mood to talk about 'Dhabke'. He wanted to remember the times when he was much younger, and even younger than any of the four men in the cart he was in, as it moves ahead being bumped left and right and upwards and downwards with the cart swaying like they were sitting on the back of a camel as it galloped on the desert dunes and uneven ground.

'I have seen all of you do the dabke,' said Moath. 'And all of you were good, nay, very, very good, with a lot of energy and feelings and emotions; and these are the two qualities that not many men and even women, or young boys and girls could not exhibit when they jump,

135

stamp their feet to do the dancing because they were doing it without passion, without any real purpose other than to want to be entertained or to enjoy. This is not the right or real purpose on why we dance the dabke. It is to show solidarity with each other, to tell everybody we are proud Arabs.

'In some countries, Arab countries, I mean, it is called 'Dubki', 'Dabkeh'...depending on where they are at or in which country they are in. But mostly, on what type of food they eat...' He tried to crack a joke but it fell flat, because none of the men would take anything he said to be a joke even when he had meant to crack one or two, to entertain them. They still could not laugh or smile even when he said, 'It is a joke! Don't be serious!' And only then, they would smile, but not widely.

'On stage, the dabke is often done in a line style but in the villages or square it is normally done in the circle style with the dancers standing in a circle.

But why did we have to stamp our feet to the ground, I'm not certain. I have not investigated the matter.' He then remembered something on it and said, 'But from what I had read and heard, the dance started long ago, when the Arabs of Lubnan which the English call 'Lebanon' because of their stiff tongue and frozen brain...who wanted to build their houses made of mud, straw and wood; and for that reason they had to get some people to stamp the mud and clay so it is compact to be made walls and floors of their houses. This communal help brought everybody in the village together to build one house after the other, and the event or cooperation was later described as 'ta'awon' which later a word was created which is 'awneh' for 'help' which in turned helped to form the song called 'Ala Dalouna' which roughly translated to mean, 'Let's go and help', which blended together work and fun, that finally turned into a traditional or folk dance of the Arabs which later spread to the other Arab countries including to our own, Palestine! And amongst us, here in Palestine, there are also two common types of dabke: The 'shamaliyya' and 'sha'rawiyya', 'karaadiyya', for men to dance only, and the 'dabkeniswaniyyah', which is for the women.'

The horse in front of their cart neighed, and there was silence in the cart; Moath had told the men everything he knew of the dance and they were happy to learn of it, so they know could perform it better and for the right and real reasons and not just to be merry and have fun. And someone, a man, started to play the 'Oud' or 'lute' in his cart. And no one could tell who might be the person who was playing it with the sounds from the 'oud' bouncing off the hills and the original source of the lilting music boomed as they echoed off them. Moath just wanted to say something to the men in the cart he was in, to ask them not to feel and look serious; they were all Hajjis now but they can still enjoy life a bit, but not too much. He then said, 'And whoever is playing the 'oud' must be very good. Any idea who might the person be?'

There was no answer. Moath turned to Ghassan, 'Know him?'

'I saw at least two persons carrying the instrument; and the one who is playing it now could be anyone of them and I do not know the person might be.'

Then someone in another cart started to hit the 'tablah', to create a more complete music. This surprised Moath and the others in his cart. And then someone else started to join in by playing the 'Daff' also known as 'Riq', so the music was thus expanded even more. Ghassan then decided to pull his 'Arghoul' instrument and joined in the merriment to add yet another line of music in the piece called 'Dal Ouna' followed by the 'Al Jafra' and 'Al Dahiyya' as their carts and caravans in a row of moved ahead as the lights of the day started to dim, when the Magic Hour appeared to show streaks of bright reddish-orange light in all its splendor, in the sky that would soon turn dark, as the call of the 'adhan' for Maghrib would be heard from all the masjid in the area where they would be traveling it. And it was also the time for the musicians in the carts and caravans to stop, for the music to end, much to their delight, at being to arrive at this period of time in their lives, and in this fashion and mood, which they took to be a good omen especially as they were already getting close to arriving at the edges of the city of Baitulmukaddis. So they also figured they did not need to stop by the side of the road to spend the night. They would have to find a place in the city to camp.

They did not want to find a rooming house or caravanserai to sleep. They preferred to stay outside so that they could marvel at the sight around them and feel the cool Baitulmukaddis air hitting their bodies, just like what Sallehuddin Al Ayubi and his warriors experienced more than seven hundred years ago, as they approached the city to recapture it from the Crusaders.

Ghassan then disclosed how he was given the 'arghoul' instrument when they were in Makkah but he did not want to play it there as it was not the right place to be merry besides, they were performing Hajj. But as they approached Baitulmukaddis he felt compelled to take it out to play along with his friends, as a way to celebrate their success in having done their Hajj together, and also, or mostly, to react the feelings and emotions he thought Sallehuddin Al Ayubi and his warriors and soldiers might have felt when they started to see The Old City and Baitulmukaddis to recapture it from the Crusaders and to free The Temple Mount and Masjid Al-Aqsa. He felt emotional and wanted to cry but forced himself from doing so.

Moath and the men and their wives knew that playing musical instruments, singing, and even dancing was allowed by the religion of Islam, except that they could only do it with moderation; for it was not 'haram' or 'forbidden' entirely, or 'halal' or 'permitted' or allowed entirely; the 'hukum' or law that was stated that it was that it was 'sama'ah' that is something that is allowed but done in moderation and within the limits of the laws of Islam; they were the devotional songs called 'nasheed.' So no wonder they did not overdo their acts in playing the musical instruments, except when the men and women did the 'dabke' they tended to overdo it, but it was because the dance was normally done in the open space for everybody to watch.

Everybody in Palestine and the other Arab countries knew what form of entertainment which was allowed by their religion of Islam and also knew which law in Islam that allowed them to seek any form of entertainment or to use to entertain others and the term of 'sama'ah', but often-times, some of them tended to overdo what was supposed to be mild forms of entertainment into something which was way beyond the limits that were imposed on them, and their elders often had to come in to tone everybody done and to not overdo what they were doing that seemed to have transgressed their religious and also cultural and social values. And it was people like Moath and some others who were as old as he and also some village Ustaz who had to explain again what 'sama'ah' meant with Moath relating the story or a 'Saying' or 'Hadith' by a close companion of the Prophet, Nabi Muhammad, (s.a.w.) who bore witness to a small group of Arabs who were entertaining themselves to some good music and songs and he asked the Prophet what he thought about what the others were doing, if it was 'halal' or if it was 'haram'. The Prophet did not utter any word of advice or comment and stood still that the companion was quick to take as a way for the Prophet to make his wise decision on the matter which he interpreted to mean that the form of entertainment that he was also witnessing was neither 'halal' nor was it 'haram'. It was a 'sama'ah,' meaning that it was neither allowed nor not allowed; but it was just acceptable for as long as the performers and entertainers did not go any further and make more noises or used other forms or musical equipments other than that was made by simple musical equipments that they were using.

Moath readily admitted to all that he was not a very religious person, (because he did not want to think too highly of himself and only wanted to be truthful) and he was also not an Ustaz or religious teacher, and everybody in the crowd knew that too; who only studied Islam from the village Ustaz, and he could recite the Noble Qur'an like everybody else. The only thing that he had learnt when he was a small boy was on the law concerning entertainment called 'sama'ah' that he had explained earlier, which should be very clear to all and he also hoped they could keep that in mind and if the occasions called for it, they, too, like he had just done, give similar advice to those who were seeking entertainment, so they did not go beyond what was permissable in Islam. He closed his 'lecture' or sermon as some described it with the question, 'Did I make myself clear?'

Everybody nodded; none felt guilty because they too knew they had not transgressed beyond the limits set forth by their religion, but still they considered the advice from Moath who all of them knew, to be valuable and acceptable as a constant reminder. 'Tafahum!' they said, some in clear voices and others in their hearts. They knew and accepted the fact that as an elderly person, Moath only needed to tell them to stop playing loud music or singing loudly and boisterously, and everybody would take heed, but he did not want to exert his authority by virtue of the fact that he was an old man in the village who everybody knew and respected because of his age, but also his knowledge in religion, so he did not do that; instead, he brought out the tale of how the Prophet had made his decision on music and singing and dancing, based on the 'Hadith' as related by one of his companions. And the reason why there was an edict on the forms of entertainment that Muslims could participate in or enjoy, was not deemed as 'haram' or 'halal' was because, God did not want to put a damper on the believers to not have some, so that was why the edict was called 'sama'ah'. That was what he thought the issue was and he welcomed any other views on the matter from those who were there, if they had any. He scanned the faces of everybody there, but none wanted to scoff at what he had said or to offer any differing views on the matter.

'Close your mouth with a cover,' said Fatimah to her husband when she started to see dust flying from the distance which appeared to be coming their way with the strong wind that started to appear from nowhere taking with it sand and dusts, and dried leaves were blown with them. Moath and the others quickly covered their faces with the headscarves, which also acted as their eyeshades. And soon, the whole area was covered in a thick layer of dust and sand particles which flew everywhere in all directions. The land had not experienced any rain in the last few months and the ground had become very dry and sand and dust flew very easily with the slight blowing of the wind and even with the vibrations created by the many horse, mule, camel carts and caravans and modern vehicles such as motorcars and motorcycles, being driven by the people who moved from one city to the other and on the roads where Moath and his friends were traveling to.

They hoped the wind would go away to take all the sand particles and dusts with it, but it did not go away very quickly and hovered above them swirling in the hot day that was going to be darkened by the fading sunlight from the sun which was now partially hidden in the dust. Nobody liked to be stuck in any sandstorm, not even the local Arabs who were familiar with it, so after a while, all of them decided to stop and pull their carts and caravans and vehicles to the side of the road, lest they would bang into each other as their vision had been greatly hindered.

Sounds of carts and vehicles banging into each other could be heard with shouts of 'Beware! Be careful! Ma Sha Allah, Ya, Rabbi!'

No one blamed each other for the accidents, which were mild because all of them were not traveling at fast speeds; there was no way that anyone of them could travel as such a speed in the roads that were already clogged with all modes of transportation and animals and objects that were lying on the roads and more dropping onto them. Everybody treated everybody else in the most cordial and civilized manner, that the Arabs had been known to do in such a situation. They were being tried, they thought; that God...Allah was trying them! Many recited verses from the Noble Qur'an and said supplications to seek God's help to ensure that all of them would be safe from any harm as the wind continue to blow and starting to become less furious.

Moath peeled open the covering over his eyes and looked at his friends and asked, 'Are you alright?'

They nodded.

'Just take it easy, Allah is with us, as always....as long as we do not stray from the path of Islam, our holy religion and that of our forefathers and all our descendants.' He sounded like he was offering a supplication because it sounded like one except that he did not begin it with the right phrases, so no one said 'Amin' at the end of each of the sentence he had said or recited. Many others in the whole area that were affected by the sandstorm, also recited supplications amongst themselves with one even reading the Noble Qur'an loudly that he could be heard by almost everybody around him. No one could see who he was because he, like the others were almost hidden in the sand and dust that were flying around them.

Then suddenly there was stillness; the rays from the sun started to show and the sand particles and dusts started to thin so everybody who was there was able to see where they were and what was happening and also the man who was reading the Noble Qur'an earlier, who had now stopped when he saw the change in the climate. Now they could see the hundreds of carts pulled by horses, camels, mules and donkeys all stuck in the same area on the only road leading to Baitulmukaddis and beside it.

Then suddenly, the sun reappeared and the whole area was bathed with bright light and almost everybody there exclaimed, and almost shouting, 'Allahukhbar! Allahuakhbar!' for 'Allah is Great! Allah is Great!'

The others too shouted loudly until the whole area boomed with the words that bounced off some low hills. And they were more surprised when they realized that they had arrived at a small town called Quba, which was also very close to the coast of the Red Sea, at their left whose waters were blue and the sky above was clear, with hardly no clouds hanging in it. Moath immediately called to his friends and said, 'Listen, this is the place we spend the night, at this glorious place, I believe in Quba we passed two months or so earlier on our way from our village to Madinnah Mukarammah. What do you all think?'

There was silence. Everybody agreed. 'And we can have a dip in the Al Bahr Al'Ahmar (Red Sea), before Maghrib that will soon fall, in this glorious day. And we set up tents over there, near those people who I believe are also like us, pilgrims from our country and also Jordan and elsewhere. Bless them, too. We all have been blessed; the sandstorm was a blessing in disguise indeed.'

They traveled over two and a half days to get to Makkah from their village in Palestine and now they were going back in the opposite direction whose distance is 1,500 kilometers, each way, but they were not in any hurry to get to Madinnah and Makkah earlier and now back to their own village in Palestine.

Some of the men brought out to discuss amongst themselves the adventures of Ibn Battuta and even Marco Polo, the Arab adventurer and explorer from Morocco and Italy, respectively, who they said had to endure greater pains and uncertainties at earlier times when the conditions where they were and situations they had found themselves in, were more enormous than what they had experienced so far. With this they made each other felt better. They did not know the adventures of the two in greater details, except for the fact that they had traveled for many years and to scores of countries, with books written on them and their adventures, that they knew a bit of.

So the men quickly set up tents while the women started to prepare food for dinner. The light in the sky was still bright and there was ample time for all the men to dip themselves in the Red Sea, while some others later brought some water in pails for their wives to wash themselves in shades that they had erected between their carts, to hide themselves from the public. There were many such groups of recent pilgrims who had erected them before Moath's group appeared there with some of the pilgrims who looked like they had been there few days earlier where they wanted to camp out for a few days more before moving on. Ghassan made friends with some of them in Madinnah and approached them to ask how they were doing. 'In sha Allah,' they said. 'And how about you, brother?' they asked. 'In sha Allah, too,' my brother. None of them dared to set up their camps on the beach because they were warned not to do so because the tide could rise very quickly and suddenly, that could flood their tents and take them into the sea. So they made sure they set up their tents further inland where it was safe, at a distance the level of the water in the Red Sea never rose to before. He remembered the few pilgrims from Tanah Melayu he had met in Madinnah and again in Makkah and who were now back on their ships sailing to their country, and they might be on one of the ships that was plying in the Red Sea, where the waters were calmer, and heading away from it to enter the Gulf of Arabia where the waters were rougher. He hoped and prayed they would be fine. He remembered giving them some robes and 'tasbih' that were made in Palestine to bring back to their families and friends as souvenirs for them to add to the many bottles of the zam-zam holy water that they had taken with them.

Everybody felt fresh after taking the long dip in the sea and were ready to welcome the sounds of the adhan for Maghrib which came from many directions, where there were groups of pilgrims who had set up their own camps where there was someone who also called out the adhan almost simultaneously.

They then decided to pray together with someone acting as Imam, who later on gave a long supplication to thank Allah for putting them here together at the same time, and with most who happened to be fellow pilgrims who had just performed their duty to Allah and who were not Hajjis and Hajjjahs, and who were on their way back to their respective villages in their respective countries; and how they had been away from their villages for two months. He then hoped Allah would further guide them to their final destination which was their village, so they could rejoin their families and friends they had left behind for so long.

'Amin!' cried everybody in unison, to note their ascent or approval to what the Imam had just recited.

Then the Magic Hour appeared for a few minutes putting all of them and their tents and horses, mules, donkeys, and tents in silhouette, that lasted not very long before darkness engulfed all of them and their things. The men then broke up in groups with the women from the different groups forming their own groups, to talk amongst themselves, but mostly, to wait for the Isyak prayers to start, so they could pray again together; and afterwards all of them could then have their dinner. And suddenly kerosene lamps were lit at all the tents that changed the whole scene, like there was a festival of lights, in an area near the Red Sea that would normally be dark at that hour. But at the main road at the side of it there were activities of carts moving and horses, mules and donkeys and occasionally, of buses, cars and motorcycles, taking passengers and goods with them, that broke the silence of the night. They had all come to a complete stop earlier when Maghrib prayers were done with those in the vehicles stopping to perform their prayers by the sides of the roads, with some who were close to the groups of men from Makkah, joining in the impromptu congregation to pray together although all of them were complete strangers to each other; who were only united by their common faith in Islam. There were also some merchant ships plying in the Red Sea with some having crossed the Suez Canal in Egypt that was constructed from 1859 that took ten years to complete; and many other pilgrims had taken boats and ships to travel from where they were in the Mediterranean to get to the port city of Jeddah to perform Hajj, while those from the East too had arrived in Jeddah for the Hajj.

'We had indeed traveled very long,' remarked Amin, who was sitting with some of his friends and the other men from the other groups. 'It was 1,500 kilometers from the village where we came from to Makkah. But we did not feel like it was that long, traveling over two weeks, riding slowly, at our own sweet time to enjoy the nature that was presented before us. There was no need for any of us to rush to get to Madinnah and then Makkah to perform our Hajj, because they are there waiting for us, whenever, we arrived, we would be welcome.'

Some two or three persons called out, 'Amin!' and 'Praise be to God!' And one of them from the other group, added, 'We also take it as our good luck to be here and at the same time as all of you. We are from Amman in Jordan, with a few others from Baghdad in Iraq, Turkey, and also Gaza and other countries. And it was the first time all of us in our group of twenty who had performed our Hajj and we weren't getting any younger, so we decide to do it now when we could afford it using the financial resources that we had and how physically healthy we were to be able to withstand the trip both ways. But there is still some more distance that we have to make to finally get back to Amman in one piece.'

'All of you will be okay, brother; Allah will guide you and whoever desires to do good deed,' said Ghassan.

'Amin! Amin! Ya Rabbal Alimin...'

The women, led informally by Fatimah, who was Moath's wife, did not say anything as she was wont to do; she preferred to keep quiet and listened to the other women including those who were in her group, and the new ones they had just got to know who were from others, not because she was not Hajji, but because it was her trait, her nature, that the women who just met her did not know. Her female friends from her group too chose not to talk too much, but because they thought they had just performed their Hajj and it was proper for all of them to not talk too much but must show a lot of fortitude and care in what they say or do, to not show too much emotions or feelings. And the other women, too, were behaving in-like manner befitting the 'new Hajjjahs' that they all were. Many other Arab women, younger in age, would be boisterous and also loud at times, if they struck up a conversation with even strangers once they had found a common topic to talk and dwell, as the women who were in the camps would do when they were much younger and not married, and when they met some old friends who they had not seen in years, or even decades because many in their village often moved to other villages to be with their husband upon their marriages.

But their conversation, like those of the other Arab women, centered on their families and children. One of the women, Aisyah, said her daughter was expecting a baby, and if she was lucky she could be at her side when she delivered it. It was going to be her fifth grandchild.

'I hope your daughter and her daughter, would be well,' said Fatimah.

'In sha Allah,' was all the woman could say, which was also said by the others in the camp they had set earlier.

Some of the men including Moath chose to sleep in the open; they laid carpets and mats on the ground and laid their bodies. They had done their Isyak prayers together and had dinner together sharing food they had with them. Above them was the moon, not full but which gave enough glow to lighten the whole area with the Red Sea not too far away from them where some ships were sailing slowly from both sides. Some of the tents had their lights switched off as it was already very late at night and the men and women in them had gone to sleep. Some of them would continue to move on after breakfast tomorrow but there were other who still preferred to remain there for a while more. Moath and his men had decided to leave after breakfast to go to Baitulmukaddis, and they wanted to arrive there before Zohor so they could perform their prayers at Masjid Al Aqsa together.

And because of that Moath could not sleep; he thought of the masjid and Sallehuddin Al Ayubi again like he did each time he remembered the Masjid, The Old City and the Muslim Quarter or 'Ḥārat al-Muslimīn' in Arabic and in Hebrew it is 'Ha-Rovah ha-Muslemi'. His mind was brought back to Cairo – Kaherah and the Haret El Wasser, in the city where he had lived in when he was young and not married. He did not know what he would be like if he had gone to study at the university in Cairo his father had wanted him to, and he felt guilty, even scared when he decided to return to his village in Palestine, with achieving what he was set out to be. He had mixed with the wrong crowd most of the time he was in Cairo, but at least he did not end up like some of the people he knew there, drowned in the River Nile or being knocked down by fast vehicles when they crossed the busy street when they were drunk, like the Australian and New Zealand soldiers in April of 1915.

He looked at his friends lying near him and saw all of them were fast asleep. He could never guess what they were thinking the whole time they were together on the trip. He then looked at the watch he got from King Fuad and stared at it and wore it on his right wrist, until he, too, fell asleep, as some ships continue to sail in the Red Sea carrying passengers and cargo heading to their respective destinations, some pilgrims who had just performed their Hajj, and were being sent back to their countries in Africa, India, and also Tanah Melayu and Jawa who had come in droves to Makkah three months before. And sure enough there was a ship that was moving southwards one of which was carrying the former pilgrims from Melayu Land, who were going back to where they had come from; one of them was Mahmud. He was leaning on the railings on the deck with a few others, and all of them were looking at the banks of the sea to wonder at the wonders of nature and wondering if he would ever get the next opportunity to take the same ship or another to come back to Makkah to perform his Hajj, for the second time. It was a feat for him to be able to make it this time, but it was at the cost of having to save money all his life to ensure that he could get a spot on the boat to come to Makkah. That alone took more than twenty years of working for the government as minor staff and keeping it under the mattress in his bedroom, and even at times tightening his stomach so that he could feed his family continuously with him at times having to make do with what they had left behind in the kitchen, before his wife cleaned the plates and utensils. He wanted to cry, but if he did, that would be because he was happy to be able to make the return trip back to Melaka, where the ship would berth at Port Swettenham near Kelang Town, and further a bit, the capital of Kuala Lumpur from where he and his friends and other pilgrims had boarded the same ship to come to Makkah. It is interesting, said Moath, when Mahmud also mentioned to him that there were some Arabs living in Melaka and some were married to local Melayu women and who spoke in good Bahasa Melayu or the Melayu Language, and raising their children like Melayu, too. Do you also have Arabic blood in you? Moath asked Mahmud. 'Lek' (No), he replied, in Arabic; But I do have a bit of Indian blood. No wonder, you look taller than the other Melayu men I see here. Moath remembered the repartee he had had with Mahmud with a smile. And he was sure he would remember it for a long while. But he forgot to ask Mahmud how the Arab men found themselves in Melaka and not returning to their countries, such as Yemen and others. Were they sailors or traders? But it was also from the few Arab men he knew who taught him how to speak Arabic.

Moath saw the ship and the others near it, but he could not tell if it was the one that was carrying pilgrims, or former pilgrims with his friend, Mahmud back to their own country, because all ships looked the same; they were of the same size and type and they looked similar especially when the light was shining from the East and almost obliterating their images. And Mahmud, too, did not notice his friend, Moath, standing on the beach and looking at his and the other ships that were plying along the Red Sea.

But what surprised or shocked Moath the most when he met the Melayu from the Melayu Land was what they had told him about 'Malaya' the name of their country that the British had given to it, which was also a British colony, and he feared that Palestine, too, would become like Malaya, if the Palestinians were not careful. Hmmm...how could the British Crusaders go so far to the East from their country of England, to invade, it and not only Malaya, but many other countries along the way especially India which had a population of three hundred million, compared to the whole of England. Moath just could not believe how evil the English or British were being pushed by their evil intentions to break up people wherever they went and to steal natural resources and to export their religion and language to the natives. Worse than that he was more shocked when told by the fellow Melayu pilgrims that the English had started to bring in Indian laborers and Chinese coolies to their country, with the view of displacing the local Melayu population who were all Muslims! 'Ma Sha Allah!' he exclaimed. 'Ya, Allah! How could those people have come from so far, to perform their Hajj and pay homage to Allah and had to travel very long distances to prove that they were worthy to be called Muslims; unlike many of us here in Palestine who hardly ever left our country, other than to come to Makkah? Yet, they had embraced Islam for a much shorter period of them than us, from, I was told 1400 of the Common Era when the Sultan of Melaka reverted to Islam, causing the whole of Melaka to follow suit and turning Melaka into an important center for the spread of Islam! And it happened through trading that the people in the region called Southeast Asia or the Melayu World, and not by using force and arms to entice the natives and other locals to revert to the religion too!?' And that should be in 802 Hijrah of the Islamic calendar. Nabi Muhammad, (s.a.w.) was born in Makkah in 570 and lived in the city till 622 Hijrah when He fled to Madinnah only to return to Makkah seven years later in 629 to conquer it. And Islam came to Melaka in 1400 C.E. or 802 Hijrah, or 173 years after Nabi Muhammad, (s.a.w.) conquered Makkah!?

Moath found it so amazing about the Melayu pilgrims he had met, the few who were in Makkah and Madinnah who related to him the story. 'Ma Sha Allah! Ya, Rabbi! And Islam came to Melaka when Muslim traders from Gujerat in East India to trade who took along their beliefs and attracted the attention of the first Ruler of Melaka, a Hindu man called Parameswara to want to revert to Islam?'

'Ma Sha Allah! Ya, Rabbi!' Moath was not sure if what he had heard from the Melayu pilgrims were true; to him it was too good to be true!

One of the elderly Melayu men by the name of Mahmud who had a penchant for history and who was eager to tell anyone on the history of the state in Melayu Land he came from. He told Moath about how Islam came to Melaka and in 1414 C.E., caused their ruler who was then a Hindu queen consort from Palembang in Sumatera, who was called Parameswara reverted to Islam at the age of seventy-two or seventy-four years. He then changed his name to Megat Iskandar Shah, and was said to be a descendant of Alexander the Great or Iskandar Zulkarnain as the Arabs called him. And because of that, the whole of Melaka followed suit so, instead of being a Hindu kingdom that he had founded fourteen years earlier in 1400 C.E. it became a Muslim Sultanate of Melaka, and in time it also became the center for the spread of Islam in the whole region known as the World of the Melayu or 'Nusantara Melayu.' Megat Iskandar Shah died ten years later at the age of eighty-two or eighty-four, he added and was succeeded by his son who went by the name of Sultan Iskandar Shah.

Moath was stunned when he heard the story as related by Mahmud, a man who was younger than he was and who was still in good health, and pious from his looks and who was excited to be able to come to Makkah to perform his Hajj for the first time, and coming all the way from the Melayu Land and sailing in a ship together with a few hundred other pilgrims. He thought how nice it would be if he could take the long trip on a ship to go to the place where his new-found friend, Mahmud, from the Melayu Land had come, to see how beautiful it must be; especially where there are so much green around and no desert land and everywhere there are trees, tall, and especially how the Melaka tree looks like, which according to Mahmud, was the tree where Parameswara had sat under its shade and then founded his new state and named it after the name of the tree. How interesting, he thought. Here, we have so few trees, said Moath, and those that we have are mostly olive trees, that we harvest the seeds and turn them into olive oil or 'zaytun' oil that we put in bottles. Mahmud said, he had bought some bottles of olive oil to take back to his country to give as presents to his female relatives who had sent him and his friends to Makkah few months ago, and for them to wear, apart from the zam-zam holy water that he and his friends had kept in some drums to also take back to share with everybody in his village, other than the 'jubah' or robes and 'tasbih' prayer beads and 'sejadah', prayer mats, and also eyeliners, he said many Melayu women liked to wear over their eyes. He and his friends from Melaka, were also very excited when they got to an olive plantation where they saw olive trees for the first time, after having heard about them and using its oil for so long. They did not have such trees in Melaka and the whole of the Melayu Land; they had other equally more exotic trees and plants that we did not have here in Palestine, or the Middle East, by God's Grave! So we may share what God had given each of us, something different and something special, he said. And Moath couldn't agree more.

Moath said he was excited with the news about the abundant trees in the Melayu Land that his friend from there had described him and also on the amount of rain that fell there where it often resulted in flooding so much so that the people there built their houses on stilts so that they are above the water level when there was flooding. And there were no seasons, only night and day and, maybe, the fruit seasons when different types of fruits would grow at different times of the year. Ma Sha Allah, he said again and again. In your country, it is green everywhere, said Moath, and rain falling all the time. But here, it's all brown with sand… and desert everywhere with rain hardly falling except for a few days in the year, but it hardly created flooding, with the water disappearing as soon as it fell. Just like on the beaches in Melaka, added Mahmud, where rain seeped into the ground as soon as it fell.

Moath tried to listen to what Mahmud and his fellow pilgrims from Melaka were saying, in a language he had not understood because it was totally different; but he still managed to catch the few words that sounded familiar to him, because they were in Arabic. How so, he asked Mahmud. When we reverted to Islam, we started to accept many words from Arabic into our own Melayu language, Mister Moath. Oh, I see… In fact, some of them organized the trip for us to come to Makkah,

Mahmud added. It takes two weeks to sixteen days from there to Jeddah with stops at few ports. Really? Amazing. Ma Sha Allah, remarked Moath. Truly, Amazing indeed. 'Ya Rabbi!' (Oh, my God!) And what's worse, was when the Suez Canal was opened on 17 November, 1869, said Mahmud; This allowed and encouraged the British to come all the way to Southeast Asia to invade the countries there, as did the Dutch and Spanish who got the idea that there was land there for them to steal and destroy whatever history and culture the people there had and steal their land that they had developed over thousands years, to call their own and to replace them with their own, including their Crusader religions. Moath was stunned by the revelation that he had not heard of before being said in such a way, very dramatic and real like he could see with his own eyes the invasion of those countries in East Asia and Southeast Asia by the three Crusader Countries, as Mahmud described them. You think so? asked Moath. Mahmud nodded and said, if there was no Suez Canal the three Crusader Countries would need to spend too long at sea to get to our countries and they had to be contented in grabbing lands in Africa and South America only; just like us from Melayu Land who could only come to Makkah to perform our Hajj by sailing in ships, because there is no way for us to come here by land as it would take too long a time to travel each way, from our villages to here and from here back to our villages.

Moath was speechless; and all that he could do was to shake his head and exclaimed, 'Allahukhbar! 'Ya, Rabbi!

And with the Suez Canal, too, added Mahmud, the British and the other two Crusader Countries were able to loot our resources and valuables and bring all of them back to their countries, because it was easy sailing through the Red Sea and the Suez Canal back to their own countries. And when was the Suez Canal built? asked Moath. Its construction started in 1859 and lasted for ten years and was officially opened on 17 November 1869.

Moath looked at the Red Sea at the many ships plying it on both ways, with some heading towards the Suez Canal in the north and the others sailing southwards to enter the Gulf of Persia. There are so many of them, he said to himself. But he didn't realize that one of them was the ship that was taking Mahmud and his friends back to Melayu Land. There must be a reason for all that to happen, he said. He then started to shiver when he realized how the future of his own country might be worse than what the present had shown when everybody would be forced to do things that they did not like simply because the economic growth would create a vicious circle when everybody would be trapped in it until they survive purely to serve the major companies and corporations when trading became a global undertaking and more and more people started to move around the globe in a maddening speed until they finally lost their self-worth and dignity, and maybe, their cultural, social and religious beliefs, too. We don't look at the time according to the height of the sun anymore, he said, but on the face of some small machines they called, 'watches'. And we have started to travel not on the backs of camels, horses, donkeys or mules, but on the backs of man-made machines they called 'motorcars' and bicycles all made in England with the brand name of Raleigh. It sure made traveling faster, but we would lose our self-worth and be totally dependent on machines and not on our own strength and ingenuity anymore like our ancestors since the time of our Noble Prophet Muhammad, Peace be upon Him! 'Ma Sha Allah! Ma Sha Allah!' (Oh, my God! Oh, my God!), he almost shrieked.

He then pulled something from his pocket; they are two pieces of currency notes, which were not Egyptian or Palestinian pounds, but the British Malaya currency notes with the portrait of King Edward on the front of it which showed that it was a Ten-British Malaya note, and the other a Five-British Malaya note, that Mahmud had given him as a souvenir. He had leftover Egyptian and Palestinian pound notes with him that he wanted to show to some of his friends in Melayu Land, so I gave him some three small bottles of eyeliners for the women to wear; and in his language, he said they were called 'celak'. He also bought a lot of religious books especially many copies of the Noble Qur'an, which he said were written in more ornate ways than those that he could find in his own country, and novels as well as newspapers to bring back to his country as souvenirs. And not forgetting the string of Christian prayer beads or rosaries, he bought for his good Christian friends, comprising of the Chinese and Indians, and a few Melaka-Portuguese where they would sit in some restaurants along Pengkalan Rama Tengah Road, talking about everyday things. And sometimes the priests from the St. Peter's Church near by would also join them. They often went to the nearby restaurant serving 'halal' food to eat and talk and sometimes they were joined by some Taoist and Buddhist priests from their temples further down the Bunga Raya Road in the city center. Most of them had studied at the St. Francis' Institution (S.F.I.) or Banda Hilir English School at Banda Hilir Road, since Standard One to Form Five before they went their separate ways only to return later to Melaka as leaders of their respective religions. But that was a long ago, before I was even born, and I only enrolled at the S.F.I. in 1960 for Form One when all of them had long died.

At the end of the road along Pengkaan Rama Tengah Road, and at the junction to Durian Daun Road at the right and ahead along Mata Kuching Road, was a masjid, the Pengkalan Rama Tengah Masjid was where I would go to for the Friday or 'Jumaah' prayers, and at the side were some food stalls and after the prayers were over, I would go to one of the stalls and had 'rojak' a condiment of vegetables and spicy peanut sauce for a few cents a plate, and took it all before walking back to my parents' house at the middle of Pengkalan Rama Tengah Road, before it was renamed Taming Sari Road, more than twenty years ago. And from my parents' house I could hear the call of the azan five times a day and also the ringing from the masjid and of the church bell at the hour. And every morning I could also hear the singing of the national anthem or 'Negara Ku' (My Nation) coming from the Chinese-medium schools sung by the students during the assembly before class started.

Every time I drove back to Melaka from Kuala Lumpur and passed by the Masjid I would try and see the food stall beside it where I had my fair share of 'rojak', but it was not there as did the small Chinese village which had been flattened and on its site was now a car park for the congregation to park to go to the Masjid. And the small boy who almost never went to school who helped to clean plates and cups and glasses I heard had become a very successful businessman in the Capital City of Kuala Lumpur and a philanthropist who did not want to be known as such who disdained publicity and self-promotion, choosing to live by himself. Even his children chose to drive old cars themselves with his father still going to the stall he first opened there which had sprung to a few throughout the city which gave employment to people like him who did not have the advantage of getting proper formal education who needed support and encouragement to live their lives who would otherwise be begging in the streets and sleeping anywhere they could lay their heads. I met him once before by chance; and it was he who called me to remind me that he had seen me come to the stall beside the masjid and we talked. I told him what I was doing only when he asked. I knew he was a very successful man, so I did not wish to dwell on his past or what he was doing now, which was evidently clear. I heard and read somewhere that you had gone to study in America, he said. I nodded. You look like someone who had gone abroad, he added. I can tell it from looking at the faces of anyone who had gone to study abroad. And you have also come from very far, I told him. He seemed startled with such a statement. You had come to Malaysia from Tamil Nadu in India. And I am sure if you return to your village in India, everybody there, too, can tell that you had lived abroad.

In Malaysia, a person tends to talk a lot and loudly the less educated they are; and those who are educated seemed to be less talkative and who preferred to keep their minds to themselves. No wonder most who entered politics were those who did not care what they said because they could entertain many with their empty speech and get elected to high office in the process.

Was your country ever under the British, Moath asked Mahmud. Yes, in fact, we are still under the British right now. And in fact, we were under the Portuguese, then the Dutch, then the British, the Japanese, and the British again since 1976 till today, as we speak, said Mahmud. Moath was shocked; how any country could be under so many foreign colonial domination and still remain strict to its own ideals, culture and most importantly, religion, he thought. And when are you going to get rid of the British from your country? asked Moath. I'm not sure; I can't tell for how long they will be in our country; but whatever it is, they have to pack up and leave, like what is happening in India right now. They sent some of our boys to study at their prestigious universities such as Cambridge or Oxford, and they received first-class education there and they will use it against them, the British. Ma sha Allah, Moath almost shrieked.

Mahmud went on to tell Moath about a Japanese 'yakuza' spy who was called Tani Yutaka who came to Malaysia and even converted to Islam and assumed a Muslim name of Muhammad Ali bin Abdullah and who even wore Melayu clothes but he was there to spy for the British, like many other Japanese spies before the Second World War who came to Melayu Land, mostly to open photo stores where they take photos of the locals during weddings and other festivals and on the side, which was the main reason for them to be there in the first place, was to also take photos of the area and buildings that they would send to their headquarters in Tokyo, for their military officers to draft out a plan of attack on Melayu Land which they finally did with so much ease just after midnight on 8 December, 1941, and before they attacked Pearl Harbor in Hawaii, by landing on the northeast part of the Melayu Peninsula and rode their bicycles south and all the way to Singapore without meeting with any aggression from the British Military of Malaya then. He was known as 'Harimau' or 'Tiger' because he was supposed to be merciless despite his demeanor.

What happened to him afterwards? asked Moath. He was shot by the British and died in 1947 and was buried in Singapore at the age of thirty-six.

Moath was speechless when Mahmud described the strategy used by the Japanese Imperial Army then to invade Melayu Peninsula with so much ease and at the same time launched a surprise attack on Pearl Harbor that even caught the American Army and Navy by complete surprise.

Moath said also remembered the Britain's Salt Act in India that was first introduced in India way back in 1880 which banned Indians from collecting and selling salt, which the British colonial government wanted to monopolize but Mahatma Gandhi, the freedom fighter of the Indians began a march from Sabarmati Ashram to Dandi on the Arabian Sea coast on 12 March, 1930 a distance of 241 miles which eventually led to the colonial government to repeal the Act. Somehow Moath remembered about this particular incident and mentioned it to some of the Indian-Muslim pilgrims, who skipped the issue and instead said they were hopeful that Gandhi could achieve Independence for their country, but the road to achieve it was long and winding; they hoped it did not cause untold hardship to its citizens, for which Moath would mention an interesting verse in the Noble Qur'an that says,:

* * * * * * *

'And whatever good you put forward for yourselves – you will find it with Allah. It is better and greater in reward. And seek forgiveness of Allah. Indeed, Allah is Forgiving and Merciful.' – The Holy Quran 73:20 and 'Allah does not forbid you from those who do not fight you because of religion and do not expel you from your homes – from being righteous toward them and acting justly toward them. Indeed, Allah loves those who act justly.' – The Holy Quran 60:8.

* * * * * * *

But it was a reminder to him and the Indians than to the British so if and when they were finally expelled from India, they would leave in peace and not to cause untold damage to the Indians, which were a people of many ethnicities and more so, religions, a large fraction of who were Muslims such as those pilgrims from India who he had the good fortune to meet and to get to know better. In fact, it was during the reign of the Mughal rulers and also the Hindu rulers when India saw massive development that could still be seen today even. Moath remembered the Taj Mahal at Agra in India and mentioned it to Mahmud who said it was truly remarkable building and certainly one of its kinds in the world. It was built by Shah Jehan as a royal mausoleum for his wife, Mumtaz

Mahal when she died early and it is also there where Shah Jehan was later buried, beside her.

Moath didn't realize that Mahmud was a smart person; and he later learnt from his friends who said he was an Imam of a Masjid in Melaka and had earlier gone to Cairo to study there.

9

The Old City, Moath and Moshe

Moshe immediately stood up from the wooden chair he had been sitting on in front of his store in the Jewish Section in The Old City in Baitulmukaddis or Jerusalem as he would say it, the moment he caught sight of Moath walking towards it along the passage ways, where many other stores were and many other people who were mostly Arabs and some Jews like him. There were also Arab-Christians amongst them, men and women who were more distinct from the way they wore their clothes. The Church of the Holy Sepulture stood at the end of the alleyway in the Christian Quarter and locked on one side with the Muslim Quarter and the Jewish Quarter. It was past noon when Moath finally got there after arriving from his last stop along the way from Makkah. He surprised Moshe by appearing from out of nowhere, unannounced. And Moshe was very pleased to see him. He never thought he would see his good friend again; they had not seen each other in decades, and other than the pilgrimage to Makkah, his other intention was to come to Baitulmukaddis specifically to meet his old friend, Moshe.

'Shalom,' Moshe greeted Moath and grabbed him in a huge bear hug even before Moath had the chance to reply by saying, 'Salam, my brother, Moshe,' which he did as he was being hugged. 'It's been a while since we last met,' added Moshe. 'A very long while, I must say.'

The break the embrace and still held each other's hand with Moshe smiling widely. 'What has brought you here, my brother, Moath?'

'I have just performed Hajj and am on the way back to my village.'

'Ah, that's very good, very good. And how long are you going to be here? Are you with some people, your wife, too?'

'They are resting in the tent we have set near here, resting. We stopped near Quba near the coast of the Red Sea and put up the night there and moved on just after breakfast this morning to get here.'

'You look healthy...er...Haji Moath.'

'And you too.'

'I have put on a bit of a weight.'

'I wouldn't worry about that if I were you. It's a sign of prosperity. How's business these days?'

'Er...why don't you take a seat here.' Moshe offered his chair and he pulled another one to sit near Moath.

'How's the weather here?'

'It's been fine. And was the weather good from Makkah to here?'

'It was good most of the way except when we got to Quba where there was a sandstorm that forced us to set up camp for the night. It was a wonderful place to stay, which is near the Red Sea.'

Then there was silence; the two men suddenly did not have anything else to say to each other after the initial pleasantries were done. An Arab customer came to Moshe and asked for an item, but he said he had run out of it. 'You can go over to the other store over there; they might have it.'

'Thank you,' said the customer.

Moath then started to notice some Jewish men and women and their children walking in the passage; they looked alien. He knew they were newly arrivals to Palestine. And further up were some Palestinian policemen doing their beat walking along the passageway. They then stopped the Jewish to check what they were having inside their bag. Moshe turned around to also look at the sight. 'It happens a lot here lately,' he said. 'These are Jews from Europe. They don't belong here, but they think it is safer here than in their country there, in Europe.'

'Baitulmukaddis has changed a lot since the last time I was here when I was much younger, at your age now, when your father was looking after this store selling almost the same things you are selling now and you were then such a young man, er...a small boy still in school.'

Moshe smiled. 'Yes, and I still remember you coming and sitting with my late father, Aaron, God bless his soul, who always told me that you were such a good man.'

'I felt very sad when I heard of his death. Did he fall from the stairs in your house?'

Moshe nodded. 'His legs had become weak and he slipped and fell with the things he was carrying to bring here for the cart falling over him. But he was still alive when we found him and carried him on the cart and took him to the hospital where he stayed for a week before he succumbed to his accident.'

'Is your mother, alright?'

'Yes, she is, and getting on in age. She is close to ninety-five.'

'That's ten years older than I am.'

'But Uncle...Haji Moath still looks good and healthy and can walk long distances. I am impressed.'

'Praise Allah the Almighty.'

'Amen.'

Moath sat with Moshe a long while and when Moshe's son, Daghlas came he decided to take Moath to a café nearby to sit for a snack and they continued to talk about ordinary things. Moath marveled at the sight of the Arab Muslims and Christians and Jews living together in peace and harmony like it was since a very long time, but the sight of some new Jews from Europe that had started to appear from nowhere to live in the city and many who were seen walking about and not really mixing with everybody including the local Jews, bothered him. Moshe said they spoke in 'Yiddish'. Yiddish? Yes, it is their type of Hebrew we use here. 'Ibrahini', said Moath. Yes, said Moshe, and I don't know a word or what they say to each other and when they come to my store to enquire about thing and also to ask for direction, etc. Moath look at Daghlas, the young man, like his own grandson, precocious and intelligent but he said he had problems relating to older men from his own group, not that they were too religious, but too insular. This took Moath by surprise because he thought what Daghlas just said was a virtue and not something that was bad. Daghlas also said he did not have much communication with his father and mother, and preferred the company of strangers and older men and sometimes, women, who were Arabs, regardless of their religion, Islam or Christian, like Moath who he said reminded him of his own grandfather, Grandpa Evron who died when he was just a little baby.

Moath was done with Moshe and he did not want to take too much of his time anymore and stood to bid goodbye; and he even offered to pay for the snacks the two of them had taken but Moshe declined his offer and quickly pulled some money and paid for them. They then walked away with Moshe returning to his store to be with his son, Daghlas who was with a customer with Moath walking ahead to Masjid Al-Aqsa to perform the Asar prayers.

He went to the entrance and removed his shoes and walked inside and joined the many other Arabs who were there with some praying and the others just finished it. He went to the back and started to pray, and after he was done with it he left to go to the Temple Mount or Dome of the Rock, to also do the supplementary pray under the stone on which Nabi Muhammad, (s.a.w.) was taken to Heaven on the Buraq. He then chose to leave the small room under the Stone because there were many others who wanted to pray inside it.

Moath decided not to return to his group which was encamped in a park just outside of The Old City in an area called Wadi Al-Joz, and decided to go around inside it to check the stores operated by the Arab Muslim, Christians and also Jews, purely to satisfy his desire to see how they all worked and mostly to see how they related with each other. He saw more foreign Jews walking about and buying things. Somehow, for some reason, they looked foreign to him and they also behaved like they were foreigners who did not speak Arabic like most of the local Jews who could, or Hebrew but in their native Polish language and Yiddish. And they also wore clothes that were different than the local Jews. He then decided to approach them and stopped near a small group of the foreign Jews who were talking with each other and found out that they were indeed speaking in a different language, Yiddish, said his friend,

Moshe, a word of which he did not understand. Moath understood some Hebrew words but those Yiddish ones that entered his ears were totally different than Hebrew.

What was he thinking? Moath did not know what he was thinking anymore as he walked away from the group only to be accosted by another group of foreign Jews, who were also speaking with each other in Yiddish. He just walked on and decided to leave The Old City to return to his tent that they had erected just outside of it. He lay in the tent with his head over his folded arms and continued to think and after a long while started to worry. He was happy to meet with Moshe again after so long and was also happy to see that he was still looking after his late father's store with his son, Daghlas who was barely fourteen years old, but has been trained to look after the store which he would inherit from his father, Moshe, who inherited from his father, Aaron. Aaron did not remember Moath, he said, but Moath remembered him, and he had even carried him in his arms, and felt emotional when he described it to Daghlas in front of his father who did not know of the incident because Daghlas was brought to the store by his father, Aaron, who was Daghlas's grandfather. But Moshe just smiled, and felt like crying. You carried Aaron when he was just a baby boy? he asked Moath who nodded. He then pulled Daghlas and gave him a hug. 'You have grown up now, a big boy, soon to be a man yourself.'

He did not want to buy anything from his store because he knew Moshe would not accept payment for anything he liked and wanted to buy, so Moath decided to go to other stores operated by Arab Muslims or Jews who he did not know so he could look at the things they sold and buy and pay for them. He did not want to get things for free from his friends' store because that would make him feel guilty knowing that they were operating a business and not a charity bazaar. He had a few things in mind of buying to take with the others that he had bought in Madinnah and also Makkah, as souvenirs for his children and relatives and other friends.

He remembered again how Daghlas was still a baby infant when he first met him at the store then operated by his grandfather, Aaron.

And he remembered holding Daghlas in his arms. But he did not look like he was when he was a baby boy; he is now an adult and wearing the clothes that many Orthodox Jews wore like his father with a jacket, black in color and a hat, also black and long hair falling by the sides of his face. Their apparel with the fur hat called 'shtreimel' worn only by such men, also known as Hassidic, because their religious beliefs dictated it, just like many Arab men who would wear the long flowing robes and a headscarves called 'kafiyeh.' It would take a lot of personal conviction for any Jewish men to wear such clothes as it not only required them to be properly attired at all times, but also, or mostly, they had to behave properly, too, in public and to know what to eat, which was only 'kosher' food.

Ghassan and the others who had been away the whole day after they arrived at Baitulmukaddis and set up tents, returned. He entered the tent and greeted Moath when he noticed he was lying on the floor that had been laid with carpet, 'Asalamulaikum.' Somehow Moath had the feeling like they were not able to have him around due to their age difference, and Moath did not take it too personally because he knew he was not the type of people who could get along with many; and only their common goal which was to go to Makkah together to perform their Hajj was what had brought them together and they had succeeded in achieving this goal without facing any problems. His wife, Fatimah was with the wives of the others who had not joined their husbands to go to the city; they preferred to go to the bazaars to do some shopping; but they had not returned. It was not proper for women in his village to be going anywhere without being accompanied by their husbands or close relatives, but here in Baitulmukaddis, their husbands had allowed them to go to the bazaars but not to other places. There were no other places in the city they could go to and the bazaars were all situated close to their carts and tents.

'Mulaikum salam,' replied Moath who turned and looked at Ghassan and the other men who entered the tent together. And even before Moath asked him where they had gone to, Ghassan said, 'We went for a walk around the city – Baitulmukaddis. We'll check The Old City soon. Have you been there?'

'Yes, I have just returned from there.'

The men sat down around the tent on the carpet that had been laid with Hajji Moath laying at the other side and not about to move, since he was not in anyway blocking them. 'Did you see anything? Did you all buy anything?' he asked.

'Yes, a bit, not much,' said Ghassan who was always the first to answer any question Moath would have. He turned to look at the others and asked, 'And you?'

'I have got something, too, just as big,' said Muin who was sitting beside Ghassan and checking the things he had bought. He took one and showed it to Moath. 'I got this one.'

'What is it? A dagger?'

'Yes, in the flea market.'

'Expensive?'

'No, not really. It is an old danger; I got it for such a small amount. I was lucky to get it because I had seen someone in the village having one like this and he said he bought it in Amman and it cost him a lot of pounds.' He then trusted the dagger to Moath who took it and pulled it from the sleeve. 'It still looks good…er…very good like it was just made yesterday and just for you.'

Muin smiled. 'Other than that, I also bought some pieces of cloths for my parents and relatives.'

'I met my old friend, Moshe…' he then said, to change the subject.

'Musa? Moses?'

'No, Moshe. He is Jewish…Hassidic Jew…an old friend of mine who I had not met in a few decades when his son was just a baby boy called Daghlas, who I also managed to see at his store in the Jewish Quarter.'

His friends were not surprised with the revelation; they knew Moath was a good man who mixed with everybody regardless of whether they were Arabs Muslims or Christians and Jews; the only thing he looked in them is their faith in their own religions and not of the persons who they were. And he disdained those, including Arab Muslims who strayed from their religion as much as those of the other faith. And in Moshe and his late father, Aaron, he looked up to them because they are god-fearing Jews – or people, as he would describe them, regardless of their race and backgrounds or religions, as long as they were faithful to their religions and religious beliefs; and in Moshe, now, he trusted that his late father had taught him well his religious beliefs who was also a person of good faith and good character, and who showed a lot of respect to those who were older then he was, a trait that many Arab Muslims and also Christians believed in. And no wonder Moshe spoke well with him when they met earlier at his store in the Jewish Quarter in The Old City.

Moath, who Moshe now called 'Haji Moath' after learning that he had just performed Hajj, was surprised, if not shocked, when he learnt from Moshe that he – Moshe, had allowed his first daughter, Aliyyah to marry an Arab man, who was a Muslim; and the two of them lived in Gaza, but who often returned to Baitulmukaddis or Jerusalem, every year or so, and each time for the first few years after their marriage, which was conducted in the Arabic and Jewish styles, they brought with them another grandson or granddaughter to him. He was ecstatic, as did his wife and other close relatives who welcomed their new relative openly and with open arms. They felt blessed and the Arab man who became his son-in-law was a good man, son of a village Imam who he befriended when he would often drop by at his father's store when he was helping him there, to learn the trade, as it was convenient for him to stop over each time he went to the Masjid Al-Aqsa to pray, before returning to his own father's store in the Muslim Quarter. Aaron must have taught his son, Moshe and also his first grandson, Daghlas well, to follow in his footsteps and remained faithful to their religion; but he was worried if the future generation of Jews like him might not be able to uphold all the rituals and values like his generation. But why did he call himself Daghlas and not other traditional Jewish names? Daghlas sounded too English or western or alien to the Jews and he had not heard of anyone with that name before. Where did he get it? Aaron and Moshe, were good for them, but Moath thought Daghlas and whatever English-sounding names that he had heard of didn't. Moshe did not tell him why he chose his first son's name, Daghlas; and he also did not ask about it and only said, Nice, when he was told of his name at his store earlier. It was his choice. Both, like Aaron, spoke Hebrew well and this was what mattered. Both, like Aaron, spoke Hebrew well and wearing their traditional clothes with the fur hat called the 'shtreimel' was what mattered, for them to observe their 'tzniut', although some days they would be seen wearing simply and with the 'kippah' or skull cap, especially when the weather did not suit them, as it could be extremely hot in the summer here in Baitulmukaddis.

Moath always referred to the city as Baitulmukaddis or 'Al Quds' but Aaron and Moshe and many other Jews called it Jerusalem, the reason being they had different attitudes towards the same city, which was holy to them and also the Christians.

Before Moath left his store, Moshe took a small family album he had in it, and opened to the right page and showed some photos of his daughter's marriage to the Arab-Muslim men, with the Imam and Rabbis attending and posing with the newly married couple with Moshe and his wife. Her daughter, as a Jew did not have to revert to Islam for marrying the Muslim man because they were 'People of the Book' and she and Moshe and all the Jews there knew she could remain in her religion of Judaism and still be married to the man, but their children she would bear for him had to be raised as Muslims. She was clear on this matter and the issue was clarified to her by her future husband's father – her father-in-law and also the Imam and Rabbis, but she insisted on converting to Islam, which was the religion of her husband and it was on her own free will that she decided to convert to Islam, so she could show herself as a faithful wife to him. She was already covering her body in a shroud which was much like the 'purdah' worn by many married women, and she did not have to change her style to conform with the new Islamic faith she had later embraced, just before being married and reciting the 'akad nikah' before her family and that of her husband's.

The Jews in Palestine were especially close with the Arabs who were Christians and Muslims, since ancient times and there had not been any disturbance occurring since the time of Sallhuddin Al Ayubi who recaptured Baitulmukaddis or Jerusalem, that they could think of. And although the Holy City was now controlled by the Muslims, but they shared it equally, for business or religious observations and practices.

Moshe also showed some photos of her grandchildren when they were born and when they were small babies. He said they had his and his wife's features and also her husband's and his grandparent's also with their eyes looking bluish, like his own eyes, that some Arab babies too would have. Their hair was dark like their grandparents on both sides.

'They will be the future of our country, Hajji,' said Moshe.

'In sha Allah,' said Moath. 'In sha Allah.'

'Amen.'

Moath remembered how Aaron, had spoken with him, in Arabic, as did his sons and daughters who were adept to the language and who could also write in it, and Aaron was also an expert in Islamic calligraphy and used to create some for his Muslim friends, he would give for free. He did not want to be paid for creating such works as, he said, it was against his personal principles to charge anyone for them. Besides, he also said, he felt at peace when writing them. Mostly, he gave his calligraphic works to his close friends on their special days, including the birth of their children and grandchildren, so they could keep them and remember him, too. He was better in calligraphy then I was and till today, even in his old age, he was not so capable of creating a calligraphy which was artistic. His works were only his own pleasure, to keep, but not to show around and most of all, to not frame and hang around even in his own house. But he did give away some, but only to his children who did not know any better how to appreciate them for their beauty and style.

It was already late at night and everybody in his tent was fast asleep; but Moath was still awake, very much so; he was relieved to have performed the Hajj, to the best of his ability, and did not know if his Hajj was 'mabrur' or 'wada'; he left it to Allah to decide. But he started to feel at peace with himself when he completed all the rituals and had shaved a bit of his hair at the Valley of Arafat as did all his male friends and the other male pilgrims. And the hair that had been trimmed a bit just above his forehead, had grown back to its usual length, but it is all hidden together with all his hair in a headscarf he usually wore, except when he was sleeping and lying in the tent and amongst men, or in his own house and with his own wife and children, regardless of whether if they were men or women, because they were 'mahram', or females who are classified as the 'unmarriageable kins', that could also sometimes include his nieces, as marriage with them are 'haram' or 'forbidden' in Islam.

And because of his close relations with Aaron, he also knew a bit about his own religion of Islam and that of Aaron's, which was Judaism, a religion he considered to be one that was so very close to Islam in many ways, one of which they value the affinity of the family unit and the type of food preparations they observe with the Muslims demanding that they only ate 'halal' or 'permissible' food with the Jews demanding that their food to be 'kosher' that conformed to the Jewish dietary regulations known as the 'kashrus'. They also knew that Muslims were not allowed to eat with Christians but could put up the night in their homes, but not the Jews, where Muslims were forbidden to sleep in their homes; but Muslims were allowed to eat with the Jews but not with the Christians.

Moath remembered watching Aaron creating one Islamic calligraphy after another and even gave him one, which he had not framed but had kept properly in his home. He had too many of them given to him by others that he had hung in all the blank spaces on the walls of his house in the village, and was not about to hang another. And from Aaron, he got closer to the teaching of Judaism to appreciate it even more when he found that it was so close to that of Islam; and they would go to pray together every chance they could get with Moath going to the Masjid Al-Aqsa and Aaron at the Wailing Wall which was just beside the Masjid. The wall is also known as the Western Wall or 'Kotel' in Hebrew.

Moath could see Aaron standing in front of the wall from the masjid which is at a high elevation and from the windows he could see the wall very clearly and those Jews who were praying nodding their heads as they read from their sacred text. They would meet again after their prayers to go to a nearby café in The Old City to have a snack, and to continue to talk mostly about religion and their families centering mostly

169

on their children including Young Moshe who was as young as his own son, Daghlas, but who was not yet around because Moshe had not got married yet.

Ibrahim, er...er...Abraham? Do you remember him? asked Moshe. Ibrahim? Abraham? Which Ibrahim? Which Abraham?

Moath was not sure which Ibrahim or Abraham, his friend was referring to. He popped up the name suddenly and Moath left wondering who he might be. Is he the one in Gaza? Moshe did not know anyone in Gaza; he was referring to the Abraham, the mutual friend, the Christian guy who used to also operate a store down the road from where Moshe and his father had it, and it was near the Church of the Sepulture, and in the Christian Quarter.

Moath gave out a long sigh as he tried to figure out who Moshe was referring to; he had not heard the name in a very, very long time. He might be their mutual friend, but how come this name had suddenly left his memory? Was he not important in his life? If Moshe could remember him and wanted to mention his name in their first meeting in a few decades, then surely, Abrahim was a very important person in his life and also in Moath's life, too.

I give up, Moshe, sorry to disappoint you; I have completely forgotten his name. Please forgive me, if I have disappointed you.

No, you haven't; he was our mutual friend.

Moath was shocked. He then began to realize that that name somehow sounded familiar and a blurred image of the man's face started to form in his memory after he had tried very hard to dig into it, at a place in his mind that he had hardly visited where many names of people, of places, of incidents had been safely kept because some of them might not be good for his present state of mind. And once he remembered anyone of them, his mind would race back to the time he had spent as a young man in Cairo, er...er...Kaherah and Egypt...er...er...Mesir, to the Haret El Wasser Street all over again.

'He was our mutual friend,' reminded Moshe again, this time with his voice very clear but not sounding annoyed. 'You know him.'

Moath shook his head; the image that had formed in his head that looked blurred suddenly disappeared when Moshe sprang with the revelation. 'I am afraid this name has completely disappeared from my memory, escaped from my mind. I am such an old man, Moshe; you are good with names and can remember those that had disappeared from my own. Who is he...who was he?'

'I am sorry,' said Moshe. 'His real name was Ibrahim.'

'Was Ibrahim?' Moath was shocked. 'Has he died?'

'No. He is still very much alive and well. It's just that he had also reverted to Islam and is now called Ibrahim!'

Moath was relieved; but he still could not remember Abrahim or Ibrahim. 'You have a photo of him?'

'I might have. I'll check.' He then opened other pages in the photo album and found one showing Abrahim, then before his reversion, standing in a group of men, and Moath, too, was in it. 'Here.' He then showed the photo and Moath just stared at it and then zoomed to the photo of Abraham, as he knew him then, who was now Ibrahim. 'Yes, this is he,' said Moshe as he pointed a finger at the image of Ibrahim in the photo. And this is you...remember?'

Moath felt emotional; he had not seen a photo of him at that age, when he was as young as Moshe, and it was taken the last time they met, a few decades ago, when he had not yet got married, but was about to, although he did not know about it then. He inhaled deeply and said, 'Where is he now? Here? Can we...I see him again?' He did not give Moshe any time to answer the earlier questions before he shot some others. Moshe did not nod and Moath started to feel uneasy. Has he died, he asked himself. He did not want to hazard a rough guess. He wanted Moshe to tell him where Ibrahim was and what he was doing.

'He has died.'

Moath stiffen and inhaled a few times and exhaled a few times, inhaling deeply and exhaling deeply, like he was smoking before he stopped, before saying, 'I remember him now after looking at the photo you showed me. And I remember how we got to take that group photo, using a camera your late father, Uncle Aaron bought in Baghdad.'

'No, Amman.'

'Amman in Jordan.'

'My father also shot the photo, snapping the shutter which made a very loud sound.'

No, Abraham did not revert to Islam and had called himself Ibrahim; Moath called him Ibrahim and Moshe called him Abraham; both were his name although his official name was Abraham. His full name was Abraham, formerly from Tel Aviv but grew up in Jerusalem. Moshe did not tell Moath what had happened to him, but Moath later found out from someone else that he had joined some groups in Haifa. He only said 'some groups' which left Moath confused. The man did not want to explain further what he meant by 'some groups'.

Moath had fallen asleep while he was remembering what he had spoken with Moshe at his store, until he lost consciousness and slept off to slumber land. He was dead tired, an old man in his eighties who thought he was a young man in his forties and at the same age as Moshe, but time had taken its toll. His wife, Fatimah wanted her husband left to his own devices and let him go anywhere he pleased since there was no way that he could loiter all by himself in such a city that had all sorts of physical restrictions on the movements of the people there and on visitors. They had camped outside of The Old City and it looked like Moath could only go there to the different Quarter and then return to the camp to rest, pray and rest again before he could get his energy back to go to a coffee shop to sit and read the newspapers they had there for the customers, and also listen to music and songs from the radio that seemed to play mostly old Egyptian songs.

Moath was not given the correct picture on Abraham so his mind became groggy and had to excuse himself from Moshe to walk to the camp that took a while. He wanted to stop at the coffee shop he had been to earlier before entering The Old City, but changed his mind when he heard the call for Adhan; it was Maghrib, so he just found a nice place in the field not far from his tent and prayed there, alone by himself. There were others who prayed in the same park, some by themselves and others in small groups.

It was pitch dark outside and the walls around The Old City was hidden in the light that shone from the moon at the other side casting the whole wall on the west to look black; turning it unto a scene from some unknown entity, unlike in the day when it looked like a castle, where Palestinian police personnel guarded it and at times approached or stopped some Jews to check what they had in their bags and the boxes they carried that might have objectionable objects in them. Some Arab men too were stopped and frisked. And Moath too had been stopped by some of the Palestinian policemen who looked at him from behind and thought he was a young man. He took it as a compliment when they said that to him after he had turned around to look at them. They then let him off not because he was a Palestinian man but mostly because he was such an old man. They had not met with a man like that before who at his advanced age could still walk briskly on his own, like a man half his age.

Next morning, Moath was the first to wake up, before the call of the adhan for Maghrib; he was ready to pray and he had performed the 'tayamum' ablution using fine sand and dust he collected outside his tent, and he wanted to go to Masjid Al-Aqsa to pray there with the crowd, who would be there, with some oversleeping there the night before and after Isyak prayers.

Ghassan was still fast asleep. He patted his body and woke him up. Ghassan then stirred the others in their ten and all woke up almost in unison without asking what time it was; they knew it would be Maghrib soon so they immediately performed their ablution also in the same fashion as Moath and Ghassan, using fine sand and dust from the ground outside their tent. Many other men and women who also slept in their tents nearby had woken and were also preparing to pray, when the cry of the Adhan was called by an unseen man in the minaret of the Masjid Al-Aqsa in the foreground. The Muezzin was the same man who had cried the adhan before from the sound and style he exhibited which boomed throughout The Old City and beyond. The sun started to appear from the horizon hiding behind some tall buildings before it emerged triumphantly, to announce the new day.

Moath, continued to sit in the masjid cross-legged, after the prayers and supplications were over recited by the Imam in the front, who he could not see from the back where he had stood to pray. Many others left the masjid to return to their houses to prepare for their work in the offices and stores. Moath was still thinking of Abraham, or Ibrahim, and Moshe. What fine creatures they were, he said to himself. He thought he was blessed to have them as their friends, and also the others who he had known since he was a small boy and later as an adult and living in Cairo, although he did not want to remind himself of some of them, the Egyptians who had coerced using their style to tempt him from committing some sins that he did not know of how much.

Has his relationship with Moshe been affected by what happened and what he might have said to him yesterday? He felt guilty because when he left him at his store, he felt like Moshe was not feeling good with him coming over to see him, even when it had not been in a few decades that he had last seen him. They had drifted physically with Moshe still holed in The Old City and with him traveling to Cairo and disappearing for so many years that he thought he could be forgiven if he had forgotten about Moshe or his late father, Uncle Aaron, and his son, Daghlas, because of the length of time they had not met and spoken with each other. But he somehow still remembered him and his grandfather, but not his son, because Moshe had not got married when they last me and his son was just a young boy now.

Why must he feel guilty? For not returning to Baitulmukaddis for so long?

Moath and his wife and his friends and their wives in their group stayed another day in Baitulmukaddis before they decided to leave, and return to their village that would take less than a day to reach. This time they were not going to travel beside the Red Sea but inland in the desert. He had tried to visit Moshe at his store, but when he got there, he found out that it was closed; he didn't realize that it was 'shabbat' day, which according to the 'Halakah' their religious law, is a day for the Jews to observe from three minutes before sunset on Friday to the appearance of the three stars on Saturday night, after which they lit candles and recited a blessing. It was something Moshe and his family and the other pious Jews observed with diligence that Moath was not aware of. So he returned to his camp and ordered everybody to leave for their village feeling guiltier for not being able to seek any sort of understanding with Moshe, who also felt the same because when Moath left him two days earlier, he thought Moath was taking with him some anger, if not confusion as to what he might have said or told him. He prayed harder during the 'shabbat' seeking understanding from his friend, who had since been back on the road in his horse-cart, heading for their village. Would they ever meet again? Moath felt disappointed with the outcome of his visit with his friend who he often described as his 'very good friend' without ever mentioning that he was a Jew, just a friend, despite their age difference. Then he realized that the issue arose from this factor, their age difference; with Moshe being the son of his best friend, Aaron who did not have any issues with him until he died, because the two of them were of the same age and who always spoke on the same wavelength, but not with his son, Moshe, who was much younger than Aaron. But Moshe did not have any issue concerning their age differences; he thought the main issues were those that concerned the changed in the whole atmosphere in Jerusalem and the whole of Palestine, in relations to the relationship between the Jews and the Arab majority in the city and the whole country that had affected him a bit, which began to grow even more with the reappearance of Moath. The sudden reappearance of Moath from out of nowhere, after a few decades of absence later turned out to be a rude shock because he had almost forgotten about him, like Moath, too, had totally forgotten about their mutual friend, Abraham or Ibrahim.

Moath liked the way his horse was galloping on the road as they were approaching their village; they had stopped two times earlier for a break and as usual, to pray and to have their meals and snacks and to replenish their food stock. The traffic had become less busy after they made a switch to the village road where there were fewer vehicles, horses, camels, and mules and the desert around them had started to look quiet and deserted with some small towns and villages littered around.

He also like it that the cart seemed to bounce a bit because the roads were not the Macadamized types but just lanes that had widened with use and there were track marks made by wheels of carts. They bounced the cart and with him and his wife in it, and a younger person from his village at the helm.

Fatimah did not say it to him in words, but she made it known to him in some non-verbal way how she appreciated the fact that her husband had become more alert the closer they were getting back to their house, and the problems he had with his eyesight, had become less so; he had not complained or talked about them the last few days. She thought getting to Baitulmukaddis which was the second reason for them to perform their Hajj had brought wonders to his health and she noticed that he was able to walk more briskly than before and the cane he had bought in Madinnah had not been used and put aside like it was not there. And surprisingly, Moath had not mentioned his eyes or health or even the walking stick at all. He lay in the cart on thick carpet and closed his eyes and occasionally opened them slightly to look above at the sky which was clear and there were even some white clouds hanging which seemed to follow his cart as it drove ahead. Fatimah put a thin blanket over her husband's body to pamper him a bit when she felt that the wind was getting to be cool suddenly.

Allah is Great and Allah has blessed us, she said to herself.

Moshe rushed to the camping ground just outside of The Old City, after his 'shabbat' only to find that he was not there; he asked the other campers who were still there and they told him that Moath and his group had left about two hours ago, and was on his way back to his village. Moshe thought he was leaving Baitulmukaddis the next day but he changed his mind and left a day earlier. Now what could he do? He had some issues to settle with Moath but now he was gone and he did not know when they would ever meet again. He felt sorry and then guilty for not being able to come to terms with Moath over some personal matters that he thought might create riffs in their relationship. He then cupped his face with both his palms and almost cried. Forgive me Uncle Moath…Uncle Hajji Moath if I might have caused you to feel bad with me; I had not meant it. He did not know what might have caused Moath to be angry with him, and Moath, too, did not know what might have caused Moshe to be angry with him. The two felt guilty for not having said exactly what they had in mind and chose to be good Muslim and Arab, by now expressing themselves to directly.

But the truth was that there was an issue between them, all that had happened was in their mind. The two had been good to each other with Moath coming to Moshe's store in the Jewish Quarter, a gesture that Moshe thought was very good for him to do considering that he was much older then he was and Moath was also returning after performing his Hajj. The only thing that might have caused the two to feel sorry and guilty with each other was the fact that they did not spend too much time with each other and had just spoken with each other at Moshe's store and a bit more in the sidewalk café after they had performed their prayers at different places. Moshe thought he had not said to Moath enough; and Moath, too, thought he had not said enough with Moshe. Surely, after not seeing each other for some three decades, the two must have a lot more to talk about to share their private feelings. But Moath did not want to ask what Moshe thought at the sight of the so many 'foreign Jews' who had suddenly appeared in not only The Old City or in the Jewish Quarter, but also in other parts of Palestine, especially in the major towns and cities such as Tel Aviv and Haifa, also Hebron and Nablus, where they congregated in droves, arriving from so very far in boats and speaking mostly in Yiddish and not exactly Hebrew; and many did not even speak in any of these two languages, but Polish, German, and Russian!

Moath thought it would not be nice to bring out this issue although he could not fail to notice them and their women and children everywhere when he was in Baitulmukaddis, with some being stopped by the local Palestinian police who checked their bags checking on what they might be carrying in them. He was worried what he might see when he got back to his village if there would be some more of them who had come there to live amongst the local villagers. He had been away just two months or so, and it could happen, he told himself.

Moshe sensed that Moath might have other personal matters to raise with him and not just on the foreign Jews, which he admitted was a major issue and he also did not like the sight of them appearing in The Old City and the Jewish Quarters, with some stopping at his store to check on some things to buy; they all spoke in Yiddish which Moshe admitted to understanding them for just a bit. He preferred to live in the Jewish Quarter and in The Old City and in Jerusalem and Palestine he had known all his life. Maybe his son, Daghlas did not feel the same way as he did and who didn't mind accepting the large group of foreign Jews in their midst, and might even want to see more of them living in their city and Palestine. He was certain his late father, Aaron, too, would not like to see them here as he did. And this was probably what Moath might have wanted to ask of Moshe on the matter, if he also agreed with the sudden influx of the foreign Jews, but who was so afraid to bring the matter directly to him because he did not want to push Moshe to a tight corner and take sides. He did not know Moshe did not like those foreign Jews in their midst.

Moshe returned to his store and met his son, Daghlas attending to a customer; and yes, he is a foreign Jew who wanted to buy something from him. Moshe stopped and looked at the two of them from a distance and noticed that they were talking and smiling a lot, and Daghlas also looked like he was comfortable speaking with the foreign Jew, who had come to their city a few months before so that he now felt comfortable and safe to walk on his own without his wife and children like he did before. And Moshe also had seen him with his family few times walking in the Jewish Quarter, without stopping at his store except for now.

The foreign Jew took away the thing he had bought from Daghlas and Moshe started to walk towards his store and met his son, Daghlas. 'How's business today?' he asked, nonchalantly.

'My first sale.'

'Good. What else did you talk with him about? I saw the two of you were talking a lot. 'Where was he from? Did he say where he came from'

'He said he was from Poland.'

'So he must be speaking Yiddish with you.'

'I understood him a bit. And he has started to learn how to speak in Hebrew.'

'That's good.'

Moshe entered the store to check some items and cut short the conversation he just had with his son which he thought was not going anywhere. Daghlas then turned around and said, 'He said he would like to come back to speak with you.'

'What about?'

'I don't know. Actually, he had come to buy something in order to speak with you, but I told him, you had left.'

'Why couldn't he wait for me to come back.'

'He was here half an hour and had to leave.'

'Did he say what he wanted to talk with me about?'

'No, he didn't. He said he'd rather speak personally with you because the two of you are of the same age.'

Moshe was confused; he did not know what the foreign Jew wanted to discuss or talk with him about. He was anxious to know, when he came by again. 'But did he say when he's coming back?'

'No.'

'Never mind; I am always here, except on Shabbat, and he knows that.'

Daghlas left the store to go to school leaving his father alone to look after it. After he was done checking some stock at the back of the store, he went to the front and sat on the wooden chair to welcome customers. There were many people in the area in front of his store walking about along the passageway, including some who looked different than the locals; they were the tourists from some neighboring countries; they wore modern clothes and not robes like the local Arabs. Moshe wondered what might be the reason for the foreign Jew who had yet not been known to him in person or by his name, so for convenience, he called him privately as 'the foreign Jew', without any malice attributed to it. If he came back, then surely, the foreign Jew would introduce himself and give his name too, so they could communicate and relate better. But somehow Moshe felt he was a very cold and calculated person. This should be normal since

179

he did not know that many persons here; and he would change once we got to know each other. This was what he was thinking.

Meanwhile, Moath and his entourage had arrived at their village; and he started to feel something unusual in himself like he was approaching a strange village. He peeped outside of the cart to look at the place which now looked alien to him. 'Is this our village?' he asked his wife. 'Yes, it is; why?'

'It looks different and strange to me.'

'Wait till we get closer to the village.'

A man from the village, Manaf noticed the caravan and quickly picked up speed riding his horse and headed to the village where some villagers were and immediately announced, 'Uncle Hajji Moath and everybody are back!'

Everybody sprang onto their feet to look at the 'village crier'. One man asked him, 'How did you know?'

'I saw them at the edge of the village just now.'

'If that's so, then we must prepare to welcome them, all of them, new Hajjjis and Hajjjahs back to our village. It's been a long time since they left us, more than two months ago.'

And more villagers sprang out of the olive groves and stopped picking olive seeds while the men who were resting under some date trees, stood up, so now there were about fifty of them, all ready to welcome Hajji Moath and his entourage back to their village in the same way they sent them off more than two months ago. The men brought out their drums and stood at the ready. And they then saw the first cart bearing Hajji Moath now sitting beside the rider, with his wife in the cart whose covering had now been lowered so all the villagers could see her and also everybody else in the other carts behind it whose covers too had been removed. It was a fine day and not yet Maghrib when Hajji Moath returned to his village; they had stopped somewhere along the way to perform their 'Asar' prayers together outside in the desert land, and then had a bit of snacks before riding on their carts on their final lap to arrive at their final destination, at the very place where they were all sent off more than two months ago, in the open space in front of Hajji Moath's house.

And the women immediately cried out the 'Zhagrouta' or 'ululation' the moment they caught sight of Hajji Moath not wearing the Arabic headgear to show that he had performed the Hajj and was now recognized as a Hajji, like the other men and 'Hajah' for the women. Some men rushed to his cart and immediately carried him over their shoulders, with the 'zhagrouta' sounding even more loudly until the sounds rose to a higher pitch and resounding all over the village that stirred many other villagers to peep out of their windows to look at Hajji Moath being carried by the men. And just then, after the group of pilgrims had alighted from their respective carts and were walking towards Hajji Moath, a group of young men appeared to perform the 'dabke' with some musicians hitting the drums and blowing the flute and other instruments, in the same way like they did more than two months ago when they were sending Hajji Moath and the others on their trip to Makkah.

It was now in late January the next year when they finally returned home and in good health which made everybody happy; more so the children and close relatives of the pilgrims who had missed their parents and uncles and aunts, who were now seeing all of them again after so long. All of them had some sort of appearance that signified that they had performed the Hajj.

Haji Moath and his wife, Fatimah and everybody in their group for Hajj were feted with a lot of good food the villagers brought with them from their houses, and because none of them were prepared for the occasion, they had to make do with whatever that they already had with some of the women even trying to cook some simple foods to serve them and to share with everybody who converged around his house. And they talked and talked after the Isyak prayers with the men surrounding Hajji Moath and the women surrounding his wife. It was already winter and it was cold and they sat in front of Hajji Moath's house all wrapped in thick layers of clothes or blanket, to keep themselves warm.

'It was an experience I could never forget in my life,' said Hajji Moath. 'I made the right decision to perform Hajj although I was in my advance age and the task to go there by land riding in the horse-cart proved to be physically tiring, but by the grace of Allah I finally managed it. This second Hajj proved to be more eventful than the last…first time I did it when I was much young, around your age, when I was physically a lot fitter than I am now.'

'Alhamdulillah,' said some of the men as they sat frozen and cross-legged before Hajji Ahmad with cups laid in front of them and a huge 'dallah' of tea that had now been almost finished. His wife who sat with the women near them turned and asked, 'Is there anymore tea, over there?'

Amin, held the 'dallah' and felt it was light. 'It is light.'

'I'll get some more, if you want.'

'That will be okay, Auntie Hajjjah Fatimah. It's already late and we'd best be going soon.'

'It was interesting to hear Uncle Hajji Moath relate his experience performing the Hajj, with more pilgrims from countries that were further away from ours, with some even from The Melayu Land and Jawa and elsewhere that we had not heard of before, especially when he quoted a Hadith or a Saying of the Holy Nabi Muhammad, (s.a.w.): 'All mankind is from Adam and Eve, an Arab has no superiority over a non-Arab nor a non-Arab has any superiority over an Arab; also a white has no superiority over black nor a black has any superiority over white except by piety and good action' and something he created himself, 'Save as much money as you can and make the trip to Makkah when you have sufficient funds, and all of us can send you off on your trip,' added Hajji Moath. 'And make sure you bring along your wives, too, as it makes a lot of sense and you won't be lonely, thinking about them when you are away for a very long time' which often surprised him when he said such things that made a lot of sense because they all knew him as a simple person, not a learned one but one which a lot of common sense and good moral values and general knowledge on the world that he was not stingy to impart to everybody who cared to listen to him speak, especially when he was growing older and not having any daily chores to do, when he would sit alone in the living room of his house on the ground floor or mostly when the weather was fine, when he would go to the rooftop of his three-storey house to sit there and contemplate for hours only to be awoken when the cries of the Adhan was heard.

Someone almost wanted to laugh because he thought Hajji Moath was trying to crack a joke. How could he? He had just returned from Makkah and was looking sober and contemplative; surely he did not have any time to crack any joke on the day he arrived back to his village. And it was getting dimmer outside, in the winter when the lights go down quickly despite it being not so late in the evening. Some thought Hajji Moath had gone mellow a little and none could blame him for behaving like that; but he had just been back less than two hours. They knew anyone who had performed their Hajj would change a lot. And Hajji Moath was no exception. They thought it would be good for everybody in their village to have a man his age and his wisdom to guide the young to be better people and already he had given them some good advice that they all should heed.

He did not mean it; he was serious in giving the advice to the men. So the man immediately refrained from laughing; he merely smiled a bit.

Haji Moath did not see any difference in his village than the last time he was there and when he got to some small towns and other villages along the way he also did not see anything new or different. He did not ask anyone if there were now more outsiders or 'agam', as it was not the time and place for him to raise such an issue. Most probably the men would not know what he was driving at which was to enquire if there were any foreign Jews there who were not in their village before. He was surprised that the problems he had had with his eyes when he got to Quba in Saudi Arabia seemed to have disappeared completely; being back had its own special values and it could be good for his own health. Some of the men and their wives had started to return to their own homes and outside there were still some villagers who were still waiting for their arrival and to help with the luggage and some other things they had bought on their trip to Madinnah and Makkah and also Baitulmukaddis, to see if they needed help to carry them. But some secretly hoped the pilgrims had some presents or souvenirs for them.

They did have some in the form of dates that they had bought in large bags to share with everybody who welcomed them. They may be dates, but not ordinary dates; they were dates from the Holy Land. Some of them were given zam-zam water to drink and a bit more to take back to their houses to share with their relatives, etc. He also realized that he was in Saudi Arabia or 'Al-Mamiakah al-Arabiyyah al-Sau'udiyah' that was formed on 23 September, 1932 when the regions of Hejaz and Najd merged to become an independent state which saw King Abdul Aziz al Saud appointed the first king or 'Al-Malek' of the kingdom.

Moath was also intrigued when he read a bit more on the history of Saudi Arabia where he had gone to perform his Hajj and wondered if his friends in his group and the others who had performed the Hajj earlier knew of it; it didn't hurt to know a bit more of the background of the country where Hajj was performed by Muslims, he said to himself. And when he was there it was barely few years before Saudi Arabia became a kingdom. But what he did not like more was the fact that Saudi Arabia was involved in some disputes with a neighboring country, Yemen, which was also an Arab and Muslim country when that should not have happened, for whatever reasons King Abdul Aziz or whoever might have with each other even if it was alleged that an Asiri prince had gone against King Abdul Aziz a.k.a. Ibn Saud which lasted for seven weeks that resulted in the success of the Saudis after a long campaign which was only terminated by the Treaty of Al-Taif with the Saudis gaining the rights over the territory that both sides had claimed to be theirs. And the other incident Moath had read about that also did not please him, especially in his age and at his awareness was on the diplomatic relations between Saudi Arabia and Egypt that were severed following an incident that happened during Hajj that happened in 1926. How could it lead to the severing of diplomatic relations between two important Arab countries, he asked himself; if those pilgrims who were not Arabs from Malaya and elsewhere in the Far East knew of this, then surely, all Arabs would be blamed, and Islam be looked down upon by the many non-Muslims, especially land was a major issue that often caused the eruption of emotions leading to unnecessary wars; like it was land they had created on their own and from nothing, when it was all God-given?, he asked no one, but of himself, without getting any answer. All these might have caused Moath to suffer some mental as well physical problems that he was not aware of that some of his friends could. But none dared to confront him with the issue lest he might get hurt which could even further exacerbate his problem which might be a temporary issue that many pilgrims experienced.

But some said, Hajji Moath had looked older than he was two months ago, and sure enough in the weeks ahead he started to prefer to be by himself and other than going to the masjid to pray, he almost kept to himself locked in his house, that made his wife worried. He kept asking for Moshe and who Abrahim or Ibrahim was. None knew who they were. And he also started to talk about Aliyah, who was Moshe's daughter who married the Arab-Muslim man, whose name he did not know because he did not ask for it from Moshe, who also did not willingly give it to him when they last met two weeks ago at his store in the Jewish Quarter. He like to look at his watch, but it was not the one he said the Egyptian King Fuad the First had given him; he never showed it to anyone including his wife, so no one knew if it ever existed in real life or just in his fantasy. He only told one person about the watch and showed it to him, but he had died. Yet, the watch he had been wearing was not the type that King Fuad would have worn, but one that anyone could buy in the store. In fact, the watch he had which was also 'Made in England' was the watch his father bought and wore that he took over upon his death. But the tale of his exploits in Haret El Wasser Street in Cairo had some veracity, but it was not the whole truth, but told in some fanciful way to attract those who were his age, who were attracted to his exploits in the city and in Egypt that none of his friends then had been to before, so they took in everything he said.

Haji Moath's memory was lapsing and his eyes, too, were getting blurred and he started to slur when he spoke so he did not offer to lead the prayers at the masjid, and had to grab at the cane he bought on his pilgrimage to Makkah and used it for ambulation lest he tumbled. His wife, Fatimah was worried; she kept praying to God to keep her husband in good health. He was approaching ninety years, and probably the oldest person in his village. The glow or 'nur' he had had on his face many thought and swore they had seen on it many times or each time they met him, had somewhat diminished and he hardly ever smiled anymore. He tried to smile a bit but his face turned into a frown, like they were seeing someone else and not the Hajji Moath they had known all their lives who were lively and full of life.

And some snow fell in the village over the night they returned from Makkah, which covered the land and the trees turning the whole area to cotton white. Even the horses, mules where partially covered by it. When the adhan for Dawn was heard, everybody woke up marvel at the sight to behold; they said it was a sign that Allah had blessed them. So one by one the villages trekked in the snow to go to the Masjid to perform their Dawn prayers with Hajji Moath following suit, but there was something that was not right with his gait and it was made worse by the uneven land that was covered by a layer of snow that he had to walk in that sunk a bit until his ankles were hidden in it. He had to be propped by a villager who was also going to the same masjid as he was, so the two walked together with Hajji Moath not feeling happy about it that he had to be so propped up by a much younger man to go to the Masjid to pray. And on the way back to the house he took out some carpets and put them over the horse that had taken him to Makkah and back and the other two mules he had. He thought that was just a bit of good deed that he could do the horse in return to what it had given him, a pilgrimage that allowed him to perform all the compulsory rituals for the Hajj. In all the horse had pulled the cart he and his wife and their driver for more than three thousand kilometers. He didn't believe that he had traveled this far for his Hajj until someone in his village casually mentioned it to him. He patted the horse and said thanks to it before going into his house.

After breakfast, Hajji Moath rested his body on the wall of the living room which was a common room on the ground floor of his three-story house that he had taken over from his father that was built by his grandfather, so it was already there before he was born in 1850, except that originally it was a one-storey house, which his father had extended to a two-storey house; and when he took it from his father, he decided to further extend it another storey with a flat top; on days that were fine he would go up there to sit and look up at the sky. His family would also go there to have their meals together, and during Ramadan, especially, he would sit there to look at the sky to see how the lights in it started to dim until the sun set, to mark the end of the fasting for that day.

Haji Moath remembered the interesting moments he had had with his family when his children were very young and they would go to the rooftop and from there he could see the land around it, which he owned and beyond it were other houses of the neighbors scattered around his. But more houses were added and between them were now more trees that made the days during the summer and spring beautiful, especially when it was harvesting time for olives. When strong winds blew the nice fragrance from the trees would blow to him and hit his face and entered his nose. He liked it when his young children who went up to the rooftops, to read the Noble Qur'an, together with the other kids their age from the villages who came to him to learn how to read it.

Haji Moath closed his eyes and remembered all those moments that had slipped off his mind for so long when he had other distractions and worries that kept him busy; but now after returning from Makkah he started to feel old. He started to lose interest in what was around him anymore and his eyesight did not allow him to see the wonders of nature and the last time he stood up on the rooftop of his house, he could see more houses around his which was about twenty dunam' wide, or about two hectares, and the olive trees were now very old, some which were as old as his grandfather who would be two hundred years now, and there were also olive trees that were planted when he was a boy by his father, and he could tell the differences in their ages by looking at them, with the taller an sturdier ones, which were planted or were there during the time of his grandfather and the shorter ones, which were planted during the time of his father and the younger ones, which were planted when he was a boy. He too helped his father plan some of the olive and plum trees around their house. And further away were trees that the neighbors had planted over a few generations. He had not seen the oldest olive tree in his village which was beyond the valley and at the foot of a low hill that was said to be more than three hundred years, and it was still bearing fruits. Many people there said they were special as they become better with the age of the tree that bore them.

Haji Moath felt the whole of his house to be especially quiet; and he didn't realize that his hearing faculty was not working well as did his eyesight. He turned to look outside of the window of the room nearest to him and saw the whole land covered with a thick layer of snow. He tried to stand up with some difficulty to go to the window to see outside better and saw all the trees and hills around him to be covered with snow.

There was no one there except for a few horses, donkeys, and mules tied to the trees. But there was one horse that was galloping briskly and then quickly like it was in a state of frenzy; like it was afraid of something that it had seen. Then suddenly a young boy appeared and he walked to the center of the open space and on the snow which was up to his calves. The horse then suddenly turned around and went to him and knelt to allow the boy to climb on its back and sit on the saddle. The boy's face looked familiar to Hajji Moath, like he knew him from somewhere. It was him, as a boy, and then an older man appeared from inside a barn to go to the boy and the horse; he said something to the horse and it galloped away at a nice pace, unhurried with the older man, Hajji Moath remembered to be his own father.

Haji Moath stood frozen behind the window of the living room of his house, staring outside at the sight of him, as a young boy riding a horse and with his father looking at where the horse was taking him, into the distance but not straying beyond the open space so his father could see them all the time. He remembered some verses of the Noble Qur'an and recited them to himself that even his lips did not move, like he liked to do in similar circumstances because it made him feel better with himself and calmed his senses and brought him back down to earth, to help him feel helpless.

* * * * * * *

The Qur'an was revealed by Allah in order for mankind to be guided. Below are fifty-nine instructions that have been directly ordained upon us through the Holy Quran:

'So by mercy from Allah, (O Muhammad), you were lenient with them. And if you had been rude (in speech) and harsh in heart, they would have disbanded from about you. So pardon them and ask forgiveness for them and consult them in the matter. And when you have decided, then rely upon Allah . Indeed, Allah loves those who rely (upon Him).' – *The Holy Quran 3:159*

'Who spend (in the cause of Allah) during ease and hardship and who restrain anger and who pardon the people – and Allah loves the doers of good.' – *The Holy Quran 3:134*

'Worship Allah and associate nothing with Him, and to parents do good, and to relatives, orphans, the needy, the near neighbor, the neighbor farther away, the companion at your side, the traveler, and those whom your right hands possess. Indeed, Allah does not like those who are self-deluding and boastful.' – *The Holy Quran 4:36*

'(Allah) said, "Descend from Paradise, for it is not for you to be arrogant therein. So get out; indeed, you are of the debased.' – *The Holy Quran 7:13*

* * * * * * *

One day, Moshe's son, Daghlas, appeared in front of his father's store, looking like a total stranger; and Moshe could not tell who he was, so he thought the young man was a new customer, or perhaps a 'New Jew' who had just arrived from one of the Crusader Countries in Europe, as he often described them. The man stood there and not certain with the reception he was going to get from his father, who stared at him unblinkingly and all that he could utter was, 'Shalom'. The young man did not respond in like fashion and just stood there like a statue. Is there anything you're looking for, young man? asked Moshe. The young man still did not answer. Ah, maybe he just wanted to come in and find for himself what he wanted, thought Moshe. Do come in and look for yourself, anything you like, he added.

The young man entered the store and came closer to his father and said, and sounding fearful, I am your son, Daghlas!

Moshe stood in front of Daghlas, frozen like a statue. What was he thinking? He tried to think first before reacting to the sight of a young man, now who had just admitted to being his son, Daghlas, and not knowing what to say. And the only thing that came into his mind was 'school.' Don't you have school today? Daghlas kept quiet and ignored the question his father had posed to him; he was more interested to know what his father thought of his new look, now clean-shaven and no 'payot' or side locks that had flown down beside his cheeks since he was a small boy. Moshe did not know what else to say of his son's new look. He just kept quiet. He certainly did not have any nice words or bad words to say of his son's new look.

Yes, I have class, Daghlas finally said. But he did not dare to ask his father about his new look. Moshe only reminded him not to get to his class late and not to also forget to bring the books he had left in the store the day before. Daghlas took the books from the table and put them inside his sling bag and left the store. After he was gone from his sight, Moshe turned around and looked into a mirror by the wall and raised his hands and rubbed the 'payot' he had on his cheeks. Suleyman appeared in front of the store and noticed what Moshe was doing. Asalamulaikum, he greeted Moshe who instinctively replied with the standard, Shalom.

Suleyman entered the store and asked: Who was that stranger who just alighted from your store, Moshe? That was my son, he replied. Your son? I mean, your nephew? My son, Daghlas! Suleyman wanted to freak out but he refrained himself from doing that. His 'payot'... 'payot'?

Moshe kept quiet. He sat on his wooden stool not knowing what else to say or feel at that moment. Suleyman then joined him and sat on another wooden chair in front of the desk. What wrong had I done, Suleyman? he asked, almost sounding sad but not crying. You had taught him well, said Suleyman. But not well enough for him to take my ways; I hope his younger brother, too, would not do this to me. This is what happens when you send your sons to secular schools.

And what did your wife say? I don't know. I have not met her. I am sure she will be distraught, too, like how I feel right now.

There was silence, a very long silence. Suleyman stared at his friend's face. And after a while, Moshe said he needed to close the store to go somewhere for a while. Can I join you, Suleyman asked? I am going to the Wall, said Moshe. I can join you if you want, said Suleyman. That's okay. Or, maybe you can wait here and take a look at my store while I'm away; I won't be away long.

Suleyman nodded. And Moshe stood and walked to the front of the store and disappeared. He walked along the alleyway in front of his store and along few other alleyways until he got to the Wailing Wall and prayed, and prayed. He prayed for God's forgiveness for having made his son turned against him and especially his beliefs. He knew his wife, too, would be distraught with what their son had just done, to not only to himself, but to his parents and people.

Moshe returned to his house later that evening, as the cries of the Adhan for the evening prayers were heard. He entered his house and there was his wife, Sarah standing inside the doorway. And in her hands were the 'payot' that their son had just cut. I'm sorry, Moshe, she said, almost crying. It's all my fault.

Moshe quickly corrected his wife and said: No, it's all my fault; it's not your fault! I hope he will repent.

Daghlas had not returned from school and Moshe and his wife and their second son, Harry who was not well aware of what was happening with his elder brother sat and ate quietly at their dinner table. Harry was done and he left the dining room to return to his bedroom upstairs. And after he was gone, his mother, Sarah, remarked how there were some Jewish men who had fake 'payots' that they would wear at certain times of the day especially on religious days; so she hoped their son, Daghlas would do the same. But, that's not the point, commented Moshe. He has left us; and it's all of my fault. Our fault, added Sarah who then noticed how her husband had not touched any food or drink. You must eat, she advised him. He then took a piece of the shawarma and ate it. The shawarma you cooked tonight is very good, but I have no appetite for it or anything. He then stood up and walked up the stairs and entered his bedroom and opened the door to sit on the verandah facing outside into the cold and dark night with lights flickering from the houses of his neighbors in front of his. Most of them were Arabs who were Muslims and some Christians and also Jews further away with the minarets of two masjid standing at the far distance, at the right and left side of his house. It is already past Isyak prayers and how come, I did not hear the call for the Adhan for these prayers? he asked himself. His wife appeared on the verandah and stood beside him. He asked: Did you hear the Adhan for Isyak prayers, Sarah? I did not. Yes, I did, she replied. It skipped me. I also did not hear the call for the Adhan for the Asar prayers when I was at the store today. Suleyman came and I asked him to look after our store while I went to the Wall to pray. Pray? Yes, for all of us, especially for Daghlas. He said he would be away two days, said Sarah. Moshe got a rude shock. How come he did not tell me? He told me, she said. And where did he say he was going, he asked. Nablus. That's a long way from here. For the weekend?

Sarah nodded and turned around and entered their bedroom with Moshe still standing on the verandah and looking into void. He continued to blame himself for what his son had just done, which to him, came so unexpectedly that he just did not know how to cope with it. He agreed with Suleyman who asked him to speak with Yitzhak. But he, too, had changed a lot from the time he was in Poland to the time he was in Jerusalem, now sporting western-style clothes as did his wife and their children. What good could Yitzhak do? he as Suleyman. Just see him and see what he can offer you in terms of advise, said Suleyman, and see what it can do to make you be at peace with yourself. I was also shocked when I saw your son outside of your store. I'm not sure if I want or if I can find the guts to see Yitzhak, and elderly Jewish man who lived in his neighborhood who he would often visit if he had issues concerning Judaism; and he wished to talk with him on his personal problem which was not really an unusual one.

The next morning, the day was bright and the weather a bit chilly; Moshe walked out of his house and went to the house where Yitzhak lived. He had never been to Yitzhak's house unannounced before, as it was not his type to do that; but since Yitzhak had appeared at his store a few times and also unannounced, he did not feel guilty for going to his house that morning. And Yitzhak who happened to be sitting in his living room on the ground floor looked out and noticed Moshe walking by himself. He did not look like he was going to his store which was at the other direction and there was nothing for him to see at the place he was heading. So he must be heading towards Yitzhak's house. So Yitzhak went to the door and immediately opened it and stood on the doorway to welcome Moshe. 'What brings you here, Moshe?' he asked. Moshe was surprised to hear his voice which was still as strong as it was before, despite his advanced age, being the contemporary of his late father. So the two of them were buddies who attended religious school together and who also got married at about the same time as each other. But Yitzhak outlived Moshe's father who died some five years earlier, which caused Yitzhak to suffer a great deal, more than anybody in his own family. And before he died, Moshe's father asked him to pay Yitzhak a visit as often as he could.

'I hope I am not intruding into your privacy this morning, Yitzhak,' said Moshe.

'Come in.'

Yitzhak led Moshe into the living room and the two of them sat on a different couch.

Moshe told Yitzhak what he had wanted to tell him and he had memorized by heart word by word, on what he had in his mind. Yitzhak sat on his couch and did not show any feelings; he just listened to Moshe reveal his thoughts on his son and afterwards posed a direct question to Yitzhak. 'What should I do in such circumstance?'

'It is not a sin for Daghlas to do that,' said Yitzhak. 'It is his personal decision or was it because of some pressure from his friends or people?'

'I have no idea. I did not speak with him that much when he came to the store in his new look and I was too shaken that I did not want to release whatever I was feeling at that time, on his sudden change. And when I got back here my wife showed the pair of 'payot' he had cut from his head. Why didn't he take them with him, or throw them away? What was he trying to say? My wife and I never mistreated him since he was born.' Yitzhak remained still; he kept quiet and was in full thought, while Moshe waited. 'Did you send him to a secular school?'

Moshe nodded. 'There must be many boys his age who had done this.'

'Yes, and in Poland where I came from…and I am also doing it even when I have reached this stage in my life.'

'But you wanted to come here…'

'It makes no difference. There must be something that's bothering him. Again, there are many Jewish boys and also men who did not have 'payots', but they still wear them, when they felt like it.'

'Yes, they are the fake ones.'

'Even my wife does not cover her hair anymore and is happy to wear a wig.'

Moshe thought about his own wife, who had not come to this and he was proud that she was still covering her hair, especially when she was out, but not when she was inside their house. What can I do with him? he asked.

'Not much; he is an adult and he can do whatever likes. I had noticed it when I was teaching at the university, when the students, male ones, were sent there by their parents and barely one semester or two later, they had changed beyond recognition so when their parents returned to the campus to see them, they almost could not recognize their own children who they had not seen just a few months ago.'

'And my son also did not tell me that he was going away for the weekend.'

'How did you find that out?'

'He told my wife before he left the house in his new look, and after leaving the two 'payots' in the bathroom, when he could have easily taken it with him to throw away. But he didn't do that; he chose to leave them in the house and left it like he had changed completely into a new person.

'You sound scared. Was your wife also scared?'

Moshe nodded. 'She didn't say it in words, but I could guess she was not very happy with Daghlas, who both of us had raised to be an adult.'

'Are you scared if he mixes with girls from other religions?'

Moshe didn't answer. He had never been posed with such a question before until now, so he did not know what to say in his reply.

'Would you be scared if your son, Daghlas…married someone from the Muslim faith? There are many beautiful Arab girls and young women right here in our area, too; and he might have also got to know some of them one who he likes a lot.'

Moshe inhaled a deep breath. He felt like his forehead had some sweat and he wiped it with the ends of the sleeve on his left hand. He then stood up to take his leave. Yitzhak followed suit and followed Moshe to the front door. 'I'm sorry for what is happening to your son,' said Yitzhak. 'And I also sorry for not serving you any food or drink.'

'That's okay. I'm sorry for coming here unannounced like this.'

A young Arab-Muslim woman walked in front of the house with her two teenage daughters, all covered from head to toe, and Yitzhak and Moshe could not help but notice them, too. Yitzhak said, 'Asalamulaikum' and the woman and her two daughters replied by saying, 'Mulaikum salam' without turning to look at him, and walked pass his house with Moshe who was not standing on the ground after stepping on the few steps from the front door with Yitzhak standing at it with his right hand holding the door and looking at Moshe as he continued to walk ahead. 'Take it easy, Moshe; I wouldn't worry too much if I were you.'

Moshe did not hear him and continued to walk ahead until he disappeared behind a house with the cry of the Adhan starting to sound all over the whole area and beyond. Now how would he look at his best Arab-Muslim friend, Suleyman the next time they met? Moshe asked himself this question again and again until he arrived at the front door of his house, and there standing in the doorway was his wife, Sarah who did not know where her husband had gone to earlier. He had been away almost one hour and the day was getting on and she had not yet cooked lunch. She wanted to propose that they ate lunch at the restaurant nearby. But Moshe didn't want to have any of it; he'd rather stay at home and eat whatever they had in the kitchen, if even if was stale food they left some after dinner. Sarah said she would cook some sandwiches instead and he agreed and both entered the house with her going straight into the kitchen and Moshe going to the living room on the ground floor where he threw himself on a padded couch and cupped his face with his palms. Suleyman is a very good friend of mine, he said to himself; how could I take it upon him, for what my son had done, even if he decides to marry a Muslim-Arab woman of his choice, this won't be the first Jewish man to do so? Then he realized why must he go too far ahead to worry about the matter, when Daghlas was only a teenager and he was surely passing through a phase in his life like many young boys his age who often passed such a phase to become better Jews. He was always fond of Yitzhak who gave good advice to him whenever he needed to get some but he tried not to bother with him with senseless problems; but the issue at hand concerning his son, Daghlas not having 'payots' bothered him a great deal and he simply could not bear to see him without them. And he still did not know if what Yitzhak had told him had managed to soothe his mind about the matter; the 'payots' could be grown back or his son could still get a fake one and wear them when necessary. Moshe then decided to put the matter aside and go to his store after eating the sandwiches his wife had just made in the kitchen, and met Suleyman at his store in the Muslim Quarter. But he did not bring the matter to him and instead asked Suleyman about his own sons, if they were doing okay. Sure, they are okay, said Suleyman: They are studying the Nobel Qur'an with an Ustaz who had just come all the way from Kaherah, after he went to Amman in Jordan to teach there for sometime, before coming here, he said. He was surprised with Yitzhak's attitude and he reasoned that he was now so old and was not so strict like he was before when he was Moshe's age, or he would not have said what he had to Moshe earlier concerning Daghlas, who was more like his own grandson that he never had, because he wanted to have one that looked and behaved like him but got somebody else that he did not feel so close to, despite having a few grandsons of his own. And Moshe did not want to tell Yitzhak how he feared his son if he chose to marry an Arab-Muslim woman and revert to Islam, because he already had a daughter who had married to an Arab-Muslim man. But it was pure conjecture on his part and he knew that. Daghlas knew nothing about the fears his father was having because he was having such a wonderful time attending camp with his school buddies in Nablus over the weekend, by setting tents in the open and riding camels and sometimes horses and donkeys with his friend to go up the low hill and down the valley, which was their schoolteachers had planned a while ago, to encourage their male students to get to know each other better. But none of the students except for Daghlas who alone decided to cut off his 'payot' that surprised, if not shocked his teachers and fellow students. They all knew he would let them grow again and it shouldn't take too long before his new 'payot' or side locks appeared again and this time, thicker and darker than they were before. That was what Daghlas had thought would happen if he cut his side locks and let them grow again which was what he wanted to happen. Even his teachers didn't care or mind to ask why he had shorn off his side locks because they knew young male students liked to experiment with themselves especially with their side locks. And he also had not yet had any interest in any girl or had one in mind.

Moshe was surprised that his friend did not ask if he had met Yitzhak, and Moshe also did not want to tell him that he had. And as always, Suleyman had some food with him to share with Moshe and this time it was some falafel that his wife had cook earlier and they were still hot to eat, so they put them aside to sit quietly. A customer appeared in the front of the store and Moshe went to him and sold something he had wanted and taken from the shelf that took Moshe's mind of 'payots'.

Suleyman told Moshe, he knew Yitzhak by his other name. He had another name? asked Moshe, sounding surprised. And how come I did not know that? Who told you? Otto! Are you sure? Moshe asked. Suleyman nodded. Otto Abramowitz! He was my late father's best friend, who went to the masjid and synagogue together and when they were old they met at the coffee shops or sometimes in the Old City in the Muslim or Jewish Quarters to talk. They also grew up together in the village elsewhere, and moved to the place where we now live, with your father..

er…late father, moving in only later, so he did not know the two of them that well to know his real name, the one he was given by his father Navon when they were living in… Poland, too! Suleyman nodded. Yes, Poland but in Lodz not Prague or Warsaw like David did.

This is interesting, said Moshe; I didn't know that. You must be a local historian and a walking dictionary. No, I just remember what was told to me personally by some people; and other than that I am at a loss. I also do not know much outside of the Old City which is less than one square kilometers wide. I have no need to know more than I need to know. But I do care for the future of not only the Old City, but also of Baitulmukaddis or Jerusalem and the whole of Palestine where we have been living all our lives, and it is here where we will all be buried. I am not the sort to flee from the place like some of our friends who had done so, to go to America, to New York City. There are many who have gone there only to suffer from the Great Depression in the 1920s and losing almost everything they had brought with them, all the money, they got from selling their properties, including Aharon and his family of five small kids who took the risks of sailing across the Atlantic Ocean to try and find a new life for all of them, only to suffer and live in squalor and not knowing when they can get to eat again. Aharon last wrote to say he was depressed and regretted his move to go there, but alas, it was all too late and there was no way for him and his family to turn around to come back here with his store over there at the end of the alley having been sold to our good friend. Our good friend? asked Moshe. Who is he? Bassam. Bassam?! How did he get the money to buy the store from Aharon? He got it for cheap because Aharon wanted to be paid in cash and fast. We can go over there and have a chat with Bassam one of these days, if you like. Is he also a Muslim? No; he is Christian. Hmmm…we can make a company then, with him to replace who was it that left us to also go to New York City?

Suleyman and Moshe tried to think of the name of their close friend, the Christian-Arab man, but his name had slipped off their minds. Then the two of them shouted in excitement and in unison; Aswad! Yes, that's his name, said Moshe. The two of them then almost laughed together. I wonder what has happened to him now, asked Suleyman.

Two days later the two of them went to Bassam's store and me him there; and the first question they asked him was, Have you any news on Aswad, my friend? They were surprised to see Bassam suddenly put on a sad face, like there was something not very nice that he had that he did not want to share with his two friends. Is he alright? asked Suleyman. Bassam took a deep breath and then let out the news. He died a few years ago, said Bassam. Both Moshe and Suleyman were shocked. They then recited some verses quietly to themselves and hoped his soul would be at peace.

What happened? asked Moshe. He died on the boat that was sailing from Europe to Ellis Island off of Manhattan Island, and his remains had to be buried at sea. 'Ma Sha Allah', remarked Suleyman. Bassam went on to say that traveling by boat to cross the Atlantic Ocean was very risky and many died on the boat because of a variety of illness. Many of the older people could not stand the long time they were on the boat and especially if it is winter when the temperature was Arctic and extremely cold, said Bassam. You know how cold it can be here in Jerusalem, but in the Atlantic Ocean it could be ten times colder that what we have experienced here.

I can't imagine, said Suleyman. I hope his wife and children are alright and living in New York City. No quite, I heard, said Bassam. Why? Because of the Great Depression, like I said, which saw many who were fabulously wealthy when they were here, became penniless and homeless.

Bassem told Moshe and Suleyman how Aswad had written him a letter he sent just before he boarded the steamship called 'The Gothland', also known as 'The Gothic' somewhere in Europe where he had gone to, to sail across the Atlantic to get to Philadelphia and from there to New York City, he said. But there was no more communication with him and he did not write again after he arrived in Philadelphia where he said he wanted to write to Bassem. And few months later he learnt from a close friend who also went on the same boat with him, who said

Aswad had died and was buried at sea. The casualty rate for travelers on boats crossing the Atlantic was ten percent at times, because of disease and other causes. To make it worse, there were influenza epidemics at times, that forced passengers who had paid to disembark in New York City had to be disembarked in Philadelphia from where they were taken on the train to go to New York City, or anywhere they wished to go to, after being processed in Philadelphia. They had paid quite a bit each to buy a ticket and did not get to their final destination in America. The first class and second class passengers paid a lot more than those who paid thirty American dollars for the deck class which also included food provided to them at the cost of sixty cents per day.

The Gothland was a nice ship, which could carry two thousand passengers, with only one hundred and four in the first class and one hundred and fourteen in the second class while the four berth cabins could take one thousand eight hundred passengers and this was where Aswad sailed because it was cheap at thirty American dollars with food thrown in. Bassem showed the letter written by Bassem which was in very good Arabic calligraphy despite the rush he had to finish the letter, which also told how he had embarked on the ship at a French port of Le Harve, from where he would go to New York City. His wife and children also joined him to sail to America, where they hoped to find their gold and better future. Bassem wondered not so loudly if Bassem had not been able to live a comfortable life in Jerusalem and having a store that was successful? His two friends did not answer the question, but they knew and thought Aswad was indeed a successful businessman who led a comfortable life with a store he operated and having his own house with three rooms for his small family. Yet, there was some yearning in him that forced him to leave all that behind in search for a better future for him and his family. He must have been told by those who had left Jerusalem to go to America that life there was sweet and they were all happier there than they were in Jerusalem. And it was Aswad's wife who later wrote to Bassem to inform him of the death of her husband while at sea. Aswad's wife, also an Arab-Christian with the name of Mary or Maryam, wrote about the time they had while sailing in the Atlantic

Ocean and all of them were very happy and excited to be able to make the trip, and with each day they got closer to their destination, they, especially Aswad who was head of their family became more anxious and nervous at the same time, because they did not know what to expect there. Their friends who were already there said they would wait for them to be processed on Ellis Island off Manhattan Island to take them to their house to stay for a while until Aswad was able to find accommodation for his own family. Everything seemed to be rosy, until the day she found Aswad slumped on the deck and lifeless. He was very much alive and was very talkative the night before, discussing with her their immediate plans when they arrived in New York City.

Suleyman and Moshe returned to their own stores in the different Muslim and Jewish Quarters in the Old City feeling pity and sad at the news on the death of Aswad, as they walked along the alleyways back to Moshe's store, feeling distraught, and whatever plans they might have on their own to also make the trip to America, were suddenly cancelled; they thought it was much better for them to remain here in Jerusalem where they were safe and where they could earn a decent living to support themselves and their families. They felt they were lucky that they had not gone to America to join their friends, with their grand ambitions of making it in a foreign land where many thought the streets were paved with gold only to be met with death and often-times sadness. They were also reminded by a brochure that was distributed which was a report to President William H. Taft, the United States Immigration Commission that was written in 1911 which Moshe still had in his store which he took out from a drawer, he showed to Suleyman, which was in the translated version in Arabic which said: *'The open deck space reserved for steerage passengers is usually very limited, and situated in the worst part of the ship, subject to the most violent motion, to the dirt from the stacks and the odors from the hold and galleys... the only provisions for eating are frequently shelves or benches along the sides or in the passages of sleeping compartments. Dining rooms are rare and, if found, are often shared with berths installed along the walls. Toilets and washrooms are completely inadequate; saltwater only is available.*

The ventilation is almost always inadequate, and the air soon becomes foul. The unattended vomit of the seasick, the odors of not too clean bodies, the reek of food and the awful stench of the nearby toilet rooms make the atmosphere of the steerage such that it is a marvel that human flesh can endure it... Most immigrants lie in their berths for most of the voyage, in a stupor caused by the foul air. The food often repels them... It is almost impossible to keep personally clean. All of these conditions are naturally aggravated by the crowding.'

Suleyman read the passage quietly and then returned the brochure back to his friend and said, That's scary. He then remarked how there had been millions who had made it there, from all over the world and mostly from England and Europe to America, the 'Land of the Free' and there had been many cases from those who were there who had actually made it, except for Aswad, the Late Aswad. May his soul rest in peace, added Moshe who then said, He wouldn't want to take the risks; I am happy and contented living here tending to my small store that had allowed me to live a comfortable life for my family. And I wouldn't ask for more. But I don't know what my son would do if he grows up to be a young man, if he harbors any intention to leave Palestine to go anywhere he desires. Will you stop him? asked Suleyman. Moshe shook his head and said, No! Why should I, if he chooses to go there or anywhere. There are Jews all over the world including in the Far East and South America and in all the Arab countries including Yemen, too, I am told. We are okay living as small minorities in any countries, especially the Arab and Muslim ones, and we have been living here in Jerusalem and Palestine for generations, and feel safe here as in any other countries. Sadly, in Europe, there are many of us who have been criminalized and taunted and even killed for our beliefs, especially in Poland and Germany, and in some others, although they were not what I and you would say, to be Crusader Countries, but Catholic ones at that. We feel safer here in Palestine.

Suleyman returned home late that night. After he closed his store, he walked passed by Moshe's store and found it closed. He had wanted to ask him to go to the Temple Mount with him so Moshe could go to the Wailing Wall, if he wanted to pray there. But Moshe had decided to return home early, to rest. And Suleyman had to walk on to go to the Masjid to perform the Isyak or late night prayers together with the congregation that had gathered there with the Imam delivering a sermon that touched on the future of Masjid Al-Aqsa and Jerusalem. After praying, Suleyman returned to his house and had dinner with his wife; their children had all gone to sleep and the other one Jameel had not returned from school. He told his wife, Zohra, about what had happened to Aswad who she also knew, and his wife as well, and she almost chocked on the food she was chewing. How did it happen, she asked? He fell sick and died and his body was buried at sea, the Atlantic Ocean. His wife said he was okay the night before and was cheerful and was looking forward to arriving at New York City and was looking forward to waving his hand at the Statue of Liberty on Liberty Island and be processed at the center on Ellis Island before being allowed to enter Manhattan and America for the first time. But alas it didn't happen. And what happened to his wife and children? she asked. They managed to enter America and are now living in Manhattan. Where in Manhattan? Somewhere in the Borough of Brooklyn. She said so in the letter she sent to Bassem. That's distressing and I hope she and her children are okay there.

Zohra could not eat anymore and she quickly went to the sink to clean her hands. I'm done, she said. She then grabbed the glass and put some water in it and drank some. She then took a book she had in the drawer in the kitchen and took it to Suleyman. Here, read this, she said. What is it about? asked her husband. It's a book on the experiences of some people, mostly Jews and also Arabs who had gone to America to try their luck there with some meeting with success and some others with failure. Suleyman grabbed the book and promised to read it. His wife the left the kitchen and went upstairs to their bedroom leaving him sitting at the dining table alone with the book in Arabic that she had got from a friend who gave it to her like her friend did not want to encourage her and her husband to even bother to think about leaving Jerusalem to go to America like some other Arab-Muslim men and their families who had also made the trip who even gave her a friendly advise by saying, The pot of gold everyone is looking for may not be across the vast ocean, but right under one's feet, right here in our Baitulmukaddis, our Palestine.

Suleymen was intrigued by the book and he took it to the living room which was beside the kitchen and sat on a couch to start and read it. He liked the photos that were published in it, too, with the men and women and their children looking like the average Arab men and women that one could see in the alleyways of the Old City, and strangely some of them also looked like him and Moshe. He got to the chapter in the book which discussed the three main reasons why there were many who craved to go to America and they were: Economic hardship, political oppression, and religious prosecution. He agreed with some of the points stated in the book but disagreed that one needed to take whatever risks to leave one's country to go so far away and be forced again to speak in a new and alien language, which was English. The young children would be okay to start to learn this language and use it like it was their own mother tongue, but not their parents and grandparents who he thought were already too old to start learning a new and alien language which was nothing near their own, especially Arabic, Hebrew, or even German and Polish. America is not for me, he said to himself; besides he felt he did not feel that he had been persecuted by the authorities here as did his friend, Moshe, who had said that many times to him and to his Jewish friends, too. You only feel persecuted if you feel persecuted, he would say; and I am not about to feel persecuted or even oppressed. It was not easy to leave any place where one had been all of one's life, added Suleyman; and one had to build the feeling of intense hatred in oneself of something or of other persons, in order to get oneself up to another level of existence to force oneself to actually want to just pack up and go away, taking with oneself all that he had created for oneself and adding this to those things that one's parents' and grandparents' and their parents' and grandparents' generations had taken hundreds or even thousands of years to save and perfect. Not for me...not for me, he said again and again to himself as he flicked to the next page to read the next chapter in the book which was fairly thick and his wife had taken pains to read all of it from the marks that she had written on some of the pages, to highlight some facts that were written in them and from what he could feel, she too, did not favor moving away from the place where they were now, unless if there was a massive earthquake or flooding that overflowed that did not recede to make their lives totally unbearable.

Suleyman could not stand the part in the report that said how most of the steerage passengers who had to walk past a narrow space on the deck which was squeezed one both sides by machines and had to walk down the stairways that were steep carrying in both hands their luggage with some of their personal effects other than their main luggage that was waiting for them to collect on the quayside beside the ship later when they arrived at the port in New York City. And they were all directed to go further down to an area that was enclosed in the lower decks until they got in the steerage area where they were to sit at throughout their journey to cross the Atlantic Ocean and being thrown around like pieces of discarded objects on the rough sea which could at times be flown upwards until the ship turn to the left and right endlessly and throwing the passengers on the decks to hit each other with many of them vomiting and feeling sick afterwards. This is now how anyone and especially me and members of my own family wanted to start our new lives in the New World in such a manner and fashion that I think is demeaning to any human being worth his salt, said Suleyman to himself. He almost felt nauseous when he was reading that particular chapter. But most of the time, if those who had made it there to go out of Ellis Island and were on dry land and in Brooklyn and other parts of the City of New York including in Queens and also Lower Manhattan, they would feel relieved and not remember the hardships they had to endure through the two weeks that they were at sea that they considered then to be just a small challenge they had to take in order to free themselves of greater calamity that they were subjected to whilst in their own countries where they were persecuted or felt threatened with anti-Semitic taunts and other physical abuses. Here in New York City they did not have to experience any of that. But for some reason, they, especially the Jews from Europe were told to not go to Harlem or anywhere near it because this place is very dangerous for people who were not Black.

Suleyman did not get it when he got to this part. Why Blacks? We do not have anything against them here in Jerusalem, he thought. And there are many of them who are here and living in peace with the others, some of them were from Somalia, Ethiopia, and other parts of Africa. Aren't the Blacks in Harlem and other parts of America, also people who were originally from different parts of Africa, mostly from the countries in the western parts of the African continent? I wouldn't mind going to Harlem if I am in New York, he said; because I want to see how the Blacks live too. He also did not like it when he read the part on the many contagious diseases that the new immigrants were said to be bringing with them, other than the things they needed to sustain themselves in their new environs, such as contagious diseases such as cholera, plague, smallpox, typhoid fever, yellow fever, scarlet fever, measles, and diphtheria with each of the immigrants being subjected to intense medical inspection at Ellis Island before they were let off to complete the screening process and thus allowed to enter the country, to now better appreciate what the Statue of Liberty was doing when they saw her waving her right hand at them, and holding a torch that was lit in the night to welcome them to their new country. Some remarked how short she was when viewed with their own eyes, compared to her in the many photos that they had seen many times when they were still in their own countries. But at the same time, Suleyman knew why there were so many from Europe who were willing to take the chance to go to America to start their new lives with their families there, and many of them went there for the three reasons as mentioned in the book, and especially for the Jews who felt they were being persecuted by the Nazis who were slowly and surely beginning to control much of Poland and Germany; and they had no choice but to flee from the countries after seeing how their people were persecuted by being who they were, Jews! He could feel for them for wanting to leave those countries in Europe and some of them also decided not to go to America, but to come to Palestine instead where they were welcome by the Arabs, Muslims, and Christians because they needed protection from the Nazis. And he was told that some Arabs in the villages had started to offer the Jews from those countries a place to stay with some others giving them employment. Many of them were wealthy and could immediately live in some comfort in rental houses which they later purchased because they began to feel that they were received warmly by the Palestinian Arabs. Suleyman stopped reading and wondered if he could take the matter up with Moshe or his wife, who was better qualified having gone to school and almost made it to the university had it not been for her parents who married her off to Suleyman, so she did not have a formal university education but some formal education in a religious school and also a secular school, and she might be able to explain to him what was in the book that he had read in some parts but not the rest because he was greatly bothered by what he had read thus far, concerning the many Jews who had started to flock to Jerusalem as they called it, or Baitulmukaddis as the Arabs called it. He did not want to be personal and understand the matter, if there was going to be a problem with them later as their number became larger by the day, from what he could see when the alleyways in the Old City would be crowded by the foreign Jews, as he described it. And he was also told by his friends who were living in the other areas in Palestine especially the cities that had many of them, how their numbers there too had swelled since the last few years when they arrived from countries in Europe, the Crusader Countries in large ships and bearing long banners that said how they were persecuted by the Polish people and Nazis and how they were suffering from attacks of anti-Semitism everywhere that made their lives miserable, and they were forced to come to Palestine and with the others who chose to go to some other Arab countries where they knew they were welcome, because the Arabs, especially the Muslim ones, found them to be amiable and affable especially with the Jews who believed in the family unit and who often stayed close with each other and often did things together, which was no different than the Muslim Arabs who also had similar traits, as did many of the Christians who were also Arabs like him.

Yes, Zohra had finished reading the book, and she knew what it contained and could explain the salient points in it, but she wanted to explain everything to her husband in the gentlest way possible so as not to unnecessarily inflame his emotions and personal beliefs, and more so his personal relationship with the other Arabs who were not Muslims but Christians and also Jews. The last thing she wanted him to do afterwards was to have any ill-feelings towards anyone because what was happening was beyond their personal authority or power; it rested on the shoulders of the political and military masters who had their own schemes and plans that affected the ordinary folks like him.

And once Zohra had described the gist of the contents of the book to her husband, he suddenly felt and beginning to sound morose when his wife asked for his immediate comments on what she had just told or described to him on what was written in the book. Fortunately, it was a factual book and one that was not written by someone with a political or religious agenda, and it sounded sane throughout with the relevant facts and figures. If it was otherwise, she knew her husband would be enraged even after he had read the first chapter in the book.

I can't think of anything to say right now, said Suleyman. I am so afraid that I might say the wrong things, because I do not want to be emotional about it and sound emotional and distraught, too. But the fact remains that we are now living in a new epoch in our lives and not just of ours, but of all our community and country of Palestine.

Zohra was stunned by what her husband had just said. She asked him to follow her to the dining table where she had prepared some local cookies to eat with tea, to calm him down a bit. The trick had worked before and she hoped it would work again this time except that the issue they were having now was not like those they had before that centered around family matters. This time it centered on the future of their family and of the others and the whole of Palestine. She remembered Moshe and pitied him, if her husband had suddenly begun to look at him differently. What did he have to do with what was happening in Palestine or the world? she asked herself, if her husband brought up the matter concerning Moshe. It was not his fault; after all his first child a girl, was married off to a Muslim-Arab man who had given him few grandchildren he was happy to get and said so often, and to anyone who asked about them. His daughter also willingly converted to Islam to be closer to her husband, an Arab-Muslim although she was not legally bound to revert to Islam because as a 'People of the Books' she could marry a Muslim man without converting to Islam; and it's just that her children had to be raised as Muslims which was what she and her husband had been doing.

How do you want me to think? Sulayman asked his wife, Zohra who was now sitting in front of him at the dining table where some cookies were spread on a large plate, with a 'gallah' or kettle of hot tea sitting beside it and a cup filled with it for her husband to drink at his pleasure. He did not touch the cookies or tea. Whatever you say, whatever you do, warned Zohra, remember not to take it out on anybody, must less, to your good friend, Moshe, even if you are provoked.

Suleyman did not go to Moshe's store for one week; he did not feel like going there anymore and Moshe had started to feel anxious and quite nervous too because his friend had never disappeared like that for this long before, unless if he had to go to another place and even then he would inform Moshe on where he was going to and for how long. He then decided to take a walk and go to the Muslim Quarter where Suleyman's store was at, to check if he was okay; he thought his friend might be sick, in which case it would be for him to help him get any medicine he needed or to send him to any hospital he wished. Moshe did not have to walk too long before he got to the front of Suleyman's store. He saw his friend inside working on his ledger book. He stepped forward in the hope that his friend would notice him and greet him. No chance. Suleyman was too deep in his thoughts to check on his accounts that he didn't look up to look at who might be standing in front of his store. Moshe then took a few more steps and made a bit of a sound with his footsteps that finally attracted Suleyman's attention. He looked up and was surprised to see his friend now standing inside is store. Shalom, said Moshe. Suleyman replied by saying, Salaam. I have not seen you in a while, and I wanted to find out if you're alright. I am alright, said Suleyman; and how are you? I'm fine. Moshe then realized that their conversation was not going anywhere and it was cold. The way Suleyman spoke to him sounded cold and unlike him. He then decided to take his leave. I'd better leave now, Suleyman; I am sorry if I had distracted you from your job. He then walked out of the store and left Suleyman sitting on his stool alone with the ledger books lying on the table. He tried to think what he had said to his friend just now, if he had offended him in some way. He realized that his own response to his friend's questions seemed unusually cold and it was unlike him to treat his friend that way. He had never behaved like this before the whole time he knew him since the two of them were small boys; and in fact, they and some other Jewish and Muslim boys had their commission together, after their parents got the okay from their Rabbi and Imam friends in their area who said it was not disallowed but okay to be done together as it was just a formality and not really a ceremony with much or any religious significance. So they had it in the local hospitals and both found themselves lying on the floor of Suleyman's parents' house for a few days while they recovered during which time, Suleyman's mother and Moshe's mother cooked special foods for them to eat, until they were able to wear pants and walkabout like normal boys. So how could two boys, one a Jew and the other a Muslim, who became buddies for so long until both got married and had children of their own and stores to operate, come to this? Moshe hoped it was just a brief misunderstanding that the two could overcome soon, so that they could return to living their normal lives together as friends.

Zohra went to the market one day, not long afterwards and bumped into Moshe's wife, Sarah, and Zohra asked her friend about Moshe and she said, he was okay, except that he did not seem to be cheerful and looking forward to going to his store the last few days. She did not know why or what had caused him to feel like that. Zohra was initially reluctant to explain to her what happened to her husband, but forced herself to do it because she knew the relationship their two husbands used to have was too precious to destroy simply because of what was happening in their city and country and also in the whole region. This took Sarah by complete surprise. Why, the two of them were never political and had never voiced their political views with anyone before, not that they had any to start with, said Sarah. What can I do to help, she asked Zohra who could not provide her with an immediate answer; because she did not have any past experience to relate to that could help her find an answer to the weird problem their to husbands now had, which she thought was frivolous. Just tell Moshe, to be calm and let my husband come to his senses and I am sure he will see your husband again, she said. But at the same time she was not sure how her husband would react, because he too had not been his usual self the last few days and looked gloomy. Most probably he was starting to experience some guilt himself.

The two women then went on to buy few more items for their families, without saying a word, other than to concentrate on their purchases and talking to the storeowner, an Arab-Christian man called Rafiq who knew both the women and their husbands, too, so he was not reluctant to crack a joke about how the two women looked like sisters as did their husbands who also looked like not just brothers, but twins! Yes, we are sisters, indeed, said Zohra, as she hugged Sarah to amuse Rafiq who was oblivious to what the two women were experiencing. We need more people like the two of you and the two of your husbands, said Rafiq. They had known him for years, and could accept a bit of fun, and with Rafiq who was always cheerful especially to women who were older then he was who he treated like his own sisters, too. Zohra and Sarah both liked his personality and style and he didn't seem to have any personal problems and was always cheerful. He had been like that since they first met him after he took over the stall in the market from his father who passed away some fifteen years ago, when he was a young boy, who was never trained to operate any stall, and was forced to do so, and he managed to do it in style and in his own way unlike the other stall owners in the market who look drab and do not smile that much to entertain anyone who came to his store to buy things or even to browse through things and not buy anything. He liked to give some fruits to the children who came to his stall with their parents, too. Zahra knew it was because Rafiq never had a childhood like most of the kids, now that he had grown up and had some children of his own. And before Zohra and Sarah moved away with the vegetables and some fish they had bought, Rafiq asked, is there anything you need, my dear Elder Sisters? That will be all, Young Brother Rafiq, said Zohra, before they walked ahead to join the small crowd of people along the alleyway. The two women didn't realize that going to Rafiq's stall had made their day, and for a while everything seemed to be fine with their personal and common problems all related to their husbands. It turned out that both the women really did not need to buy anything in the market that day; and the only reason why they wanted to go there was to meet Rafiq and make him crack some jokes in order that they could get away from their personal problems for even a while. And it turned out that both had the same reasons to go there to meet with Rafiq like it was therapy that they needed to get by going to the market and all for free. Staying at home while their husbands were away would certainly exacerbate whatever problems they had, before they grew to become larger and even unlikely less chance of going away. The other therapy they had in mind of doing was to cook the favorite food of their husbands, which was – 'maqlouba' the food they first started to like as kids when they would share coins to buy a piece to eat together; it was made with many thin layers of meat and a small portion of rice, with vegetables such as cauliflower, eggplant, potatoes, and also carrots that had been first fried and taken with lots of cream in it and some wonderful syrup so they slurp until their plates and cups were completely dry, and in the background would be some songs by the most popular Egyptian singer or songstress, Fairuz and the other twin male singers from Iraq by the name of Salima Pasha that both of them liked a lot and who would often try and sing some of the songs they had recorded, but only in the privacy of their bedrooms and nowhere else!! Sarah didn't know quite how to cook this delicacy and she had to buy some at the restaurant if her husband had an appetite to have some of it, until one day Zohra offered to show her how to make it and she immediately took a liking to cooking it as often as she could and became good at it with compliments from Zohra who tasted it when Sarah brought some with her to Zohra's house, as it was not against the teachings of Islam for Muslims to eat food prepared by Jews as they are kosher and also halal at the same time. But Muslims are not allowed to sleep in the houses of Jews, but are allowed to sleep in the houses of

Christians, but not eat food they cook and serve because it is not halal, since they eat pork, too unlike the Jews who didn't.

And true enough, when their husbands returned to their respective houses they were greeted with the strong aroma of 'maglouba' that they had not smelled at their houses in a while now. And when they entered the house through the front door they saw their wives at their respective dining tables arranging the plates one that had a huge portion of food. And they sat at the tables and started to help themselves to the food with their wives offering them more until they were full. They then drank the syrup to go with it and slumped to the back of the chair feeling happy. Zohra and Sarah felt happy with the outcome of their experiment that seemed to work. And a few days later they finally saw the end results of their unique experiment when they heard from some 'spies' they had asked to check on their husbands who said they were seen sitting together again and looking like they were happy to be in each other's company again and were seen laughing a bit and hugging a lot like they had not seen each other in a very long while.

Zohra met Sarah at their usual meeting place, the market and shared the good news with each other, by informing each other how their husbands had eaten all the 'maglouba' they had cooked. I know how strange it may seem, said Zohra, But I do hope we would not have to cook 'maglouba' a lot, or often, unless if it is for a better reason. Sarah laughed, but refrained herself from being carried away by laughing loudly because it was not proper for Arab women to do that with the many other women who were walking near the two of the women with their husbands and children.

Sarah felt guilty, after she and Zohra had made the 'maqlouba' for their respective husbands, because she had neglected to tell her how her husband, Moshe had gone to Hebron two days before they decided to cook the food, to go to the Ibrahimi Masjid or Sanctuary of Ibrahim which the Arab-Muslims called or the Cave or Tomb of the Patriarchs where Prophet Abraham was said to have been buried, to attend the 'Chayei Sarah' for the ceremony for the reading of the portion of the Jewish Torah holy book which discussed the life of Sarah who was

Abraham's wife, which was also Moshe's wife's namesake which he undertook the last so many years where he would spend the night in the city to be with the pilgrims who had come from all over Palestine. And he returned to his house a day before his wife cooked the food, to be also a 'welcome home gift' for him for having done the pilgrimage to the Tomb of the Patriarch which he almost forgot to do because he was still reeling over his strained relationship with Suleyman, where he also hoped to pray for it to be mended. He did not tell Suleyman how when he was there for the ceremony, he noticed the many new Jews who had come from Europe, mostly Poland and Germany who were there; they were excited to be able to take part in the ceremony, too, but Moshe felt that they had also come with different reasons some of which had caused Suleyman to feel quite worried. So he and his friend chose to talk about the 'Maqlouba' that their wives had cook the night before, specially for them, but it was not yet then for the two to have them together at one of their houses. We'll do that the next time if our wives choose to cook the 'Maqlouba' again, said Moshe. We'll do it in my house next, suggested Suleyman and we can have the gathering during Eidul Fitri.

10

Moshe and the 'foreign Jew.'

Moshe was busy cleaning and dusting some items in his store when the 'foreign Jew' appeared at the front of it; this time he was wearing not the traditional clothes for Jews like what Moshe was wearing. Moshe was taken by surprised when he saw the foreign Jew standing there; he did not call Moshe by his name because he did not know it yet. Moshe greeted him with 'shalom' in the most casual manner, like how he would call anyone he did not know personally but to strangers, and he was responded in like manner, also in such a cold fashion with an accent Moshe knew that he was not from anywhere in the Old City or in Palestine itself, but elsewhere and most probably, Poland.

'I am David,' he said in Hebrew which did not sound real. So Moshe now knew the foreign Jew's name, David, which was a very common for male Jews so it would be very easy for him to remember. They shook hands but did not hug, and Moshe told him his own name – Moshe, also a very common name for Jews in Palestine, but not in Poland where David had come from. Then there was silence with Moshe wanting to know what David had come there to see him for. He knew David had not come there to buy more things from his store. What did he have in mind of saying? David seemed to be restless; he tried to find the way to say what he had in his mind to tell Moshe, who he guessed could be at least ten years older than he was, but they were of the same height and built and some might think they were even related, not as brothers, but at least, as cousins. But not when David was wearing a jacket that matched with the color of his pants which were dark brown and he had a hat of the same color too, looking very much like a European man of a certain style and stature. There were not many men wearing clothes like that here in The Old City; they may be some in the larger cities but they were mostly foreigners like David. The others were from Poland like him and other countries in Europe especially Germany and even Russia.

'Yes, can I help you, David?'

David found it very difficult to break the ice; he did not know how to look and be friendly and considered Moshe to be a stranger despite them being Jews.

'Yes!' said Moshe.

David turned around and saw quite a lot of people walking in the alleyway with some looking and buying things at the stores. None was looking at him but he felt awkward because it was the first time he was wearing like that, so he felt like he had turned against his religious faith. Moshe began to feel at ease with David who was already starting to feel nervous. It was winter and the weather was cold with everybody all wrapped in bundles, and there was some snow on the pavement that made some people trip when they walked on the snow that had melted a bit or that had frozen like ice.

'Care for some hot tea?' asked Moshe. There was no answer, and Moshe stared at David who was holding his hands and rubbing them together. He then pulled the collar of his jacket to put it up to cover his neck, as the cold wind started to blow. He then nodded. 'Let's get inside where it is warmer.'

The two men entered the store and sat at a wooden table where Moshe and also his son often sat to wait for customers, especially when the day was cold; otherwise, they would sit on a wooden stool just outside of their store. He poured some hot tea into two cups, one he trusted before David and the other for him to drink. He picked his cup and raised it before David who followed suit, without saying any word. And both took some sips of the hot tea. But David was still not in any mood yet to talk despite the eagerness he had exhibited each time he came to the store before and only met with Moshe's son, Daghlas and enquired with him on his father who he said he wanted to talk with. Moshe did not want to say anything; he also did not wish to push David to say anything he wanted to say but was not yet ready to say it. He then took a few more sips of the tea until his cup was empty; and seeing this, Moshe picked up the 'dallah' on the table and offered to pour more tea into David's cup. But he immediately cupped the top of the cup with his right hand to indicate that he did not want more tea. 'Thank you,' he said. Moshe put down the 'dallah' and then picked it up again and poured some tea into his own cup. 'Are you alright?' he asked.

David nodded without saying a word. This made Moshe feel embarrassed and confused. 'Is there anything urgent and important that you want to tell me...or say to me? Is your family alright'

David nodded and then said, 'It's got to do with me, us, who had come from Poland.' He said it very slowly like he was not sure what he wanted to say, if what he wanted to say to Moshe would make sense. He had tried to find the right way to form the first sentence to say or utter to Moshe the last few days so that he could be sure Moshe would not feel offended or angry with him. Moshe was not. He was just confused. He did not expect David, who he had not considered yet to be his friend, just someone from his race, but who had come from so far away, from Poland taking the ship with his entire family, like the many of those Polish and also Romanians and others, from Russia, too that had come to Jerusalem to live in the city and the others throughout Palestine, such as Haifa, Hebron, Nablus and Tel Aviv, but none had come to his store to speak with him on their personal matters, except to get direction or to buy items he sold.

'If you'd prefer to talk with me at another time, when you think, you are in a better position to do so, then I will be glad to see you again, here,' offered Moshe. 'Or, if you want you can see me at the synagogue after the service during Shabbat so we can sit in a café somewhere...'

But just before he could complete his sentence, David pounced on him or chipped or intercut him with, 'No, it's like this. And I think I'd better go, because I might bore you with my personal story and frustrations.'

Some customers appeared in front of the store and one of the men, an Arab man, a good friend of Moshe's called, 'Salam, ya, Musa.' Moshe turned and saw his friend, and stood up to go to him, 'Shalom, ya Hamid.' He then shook hands with him and they hugged each other. 'What have you come here for this time, Brother Hamid?'

'I am looking for the thick shoes you use to sell; do you have a pair for me to wear? This winter has been especially cold for my feet to bear wearing these shoes.' He then showed his shoes he was wearing; they looked jaded and worn but most of all, too thin for walking in the snow.

'These are not winter shoes; they are for summer wear, Hamid.'

'I know that. It's just that this winter, I have a lot of places to go to, or I could wear just these around the house.'

David stood up and walked behind Moshe and tapped his back and said, 'I'd better get going, Brother Moshe. Shalom.'

'Do come back when you are ready to talk. And this is my good friend, Hamid.'

Hamid said, 'Salam' and David said, 'Shalom' and walked away after shaking hands with him. Moshe looked at David as he walked away and turned to Hamid and said, 'Come in; I have a pair just for you.'

They entered the store and Moshe pulled a box from the stack of other shoes of different sizes and took out a pair, made of thick leather, and showed them to Hamid. 'These look perfect. My size?'

'Try them on. Take a seat on the stool here.' Moshe pulled the stool that David had sat on earlier and Hamid sat on it. He removed the worn out shoe on his right leg and tried on the one Moshe handed to him. 'Looks like it fits well,' said Hamid. 'How much for?'

'Just take them! You are my first customer for today; you bring luck each time you pay me a visit even when you did not buy anything from me.'

'But Brother Musa, I cannot do that. You are operating a business. I am not at your own home where you can do that.'

Moshe did not want to say much more; he knew he had offered Hamid to take away those shoes but he declined. Hamid was not happy to receive them because he did not want Moshe that he had come to seek charity, so no wonder, he tried not to go to his store to buy anything because Moshe and even his son, Daghlas wouldn't take any payment for any thing he wanted to buy. But because he could not find the right shoes for him to wear in the winter, from the other stores in the Muslim Quarter or Christian Quarter in The Old City, he was forced to try and get them at Moshe's store here, in the Jewish Quarter, so he could meet up with his good friend again and also visit the Quarter to check out the place where he, too, like Moshe had started to notice the good number of new and foreign Jews mingling with the crowd. Both Hamid and Moshe were the same age, and they knew each other through their fathers who had their stores side by side with each other, except that after Hamid's father died few years ago, the store was sold to another Jewish man. And how did Hamid's late father get to operate his store there in the Jewish Quarter and not in the Muslim Quarter? It had to do with his mother, who was Jewish, whose father had the store as did his grandfather and great-grandfather, but since there was no one in his family who was interested to take over the store because most of them had gone to other larger cities in Palestine and the neighboring countries, where they had studied at the universities there, the store fell in the hands of Hamid's mother and hence, his father, after their marriage.

Hamid looked at the store beside Moshe's but it was not opened yet. He also did not know who operated it or what they sold. His late father sold cloth that some traders brought from the ships at Jeddah Port in Arabia which they said were from the East, and they were of cotton mostly and very good to make robes for the men and long gowns for the women. Hamid's mother, Lila, despite a Jew and married to an Arab-Muslim, but she never converted to Islam and was a staunch Jewess woman all her life and never failed to observe Shabbat and the other Jewish religious holidays and traditions, and her husband and her parents-in-law never brought up the matter concerning the conversion when she was going to be married to Hamid's father, and left it to her to make any decision on the issue. And more than ever, she stuck to the six hundred and thirteen Commandments or 'Mitzvot' mentioned in the Torah, holy book of the Jews.

And she chose to remain a Jew which was fine with them. And Hamid or any of his brothers or sisters, all of whom were Muslims like he was, often took their mother to the synagogue to pray. She would always wear a 'chador' when she started to grow older and after having her second child, and she looked very much like the other Arab-Muslim women so outwardly, she looked like any Muslim women, and she also made sure she cooked 'halal' food for her family and ate such foods when she and her family ate outside of the house, to eat in restaurants. She practiced her religion in her house privately.

'Just take them, Hamid, from me; don't worry about the price; it's nothing. Besides, the shoes have been with me for so long that I might not be able to sell them to anyone.'

Hamid was not sure if he should accept the offer. He put his right hand in his pants pocket and pulled out a few British pound notes and handed to Moshe two pieces of that. 'Here, just take these.' He did not know the price of the shoes, but he thought two pounds would be good. 'Take it.' Hamid paused and waited. 'Take it,' he said again. Hamid then finally gave up and put the two British pound notes in Moshe' shirt pocket. He then went to the side and sat on the same stool again, removed his worn out shoes and put on the new pair. He stood up and walked a few steps to test them, and felt good wearing them. He then picked the old pair and asked Moshe if there was any cobbler in the Quarter that could fix them; they had some torn parts that needed to be sewed. They were still good to wear for another year or so before they gave up and Hamid did not want to get rid of them because he would feel guilty for discarding something that was still good to wear. He could not find anyone there to give the old shoes to, but he also did not want to give those worn out shoes to anyone until they were repaired.

Hamid bid farewell after hugging Moshe again, and left to go elsewhere. He did not tell Moshe where he was going and what he was up to. It was very cold this winter, so he would not go very far from The Old City or Jerusalem. He was happy that his good friend came to visit him and to give him some business today, he thought. Then his mind was brought back to David. What is he up to, he asked himself. He could never guess what David might have wanted to discuss with him about. He looked well dressed and not someone in need of money to borrow and he rented a house in a fashionable district where only those who could afford it, stayed. So the money and borrowing parts were out. When then, he continued to ask himself; it was very difficult to guess or second-guess the mind of someone he did not know; David's mind was hidden in a lot of unusual circumstances and the issues he wanted to discuss with Moshe could very well be related to him and his family coming here. He might have a secret to tell and share. But what could Moshe do to help him in this case?

Some customers came to his store and diverted his attention from Hamid, David, Lila, and the others, which he liked to experience since it was also good for his business that he needed to keep, he thought – for his son, Daghlas, if he chose to take over it from him when the time came for him to decide on what he wanted to do or if he had other things in mind to do, like many young Jewish men, especially, now that they had the advantage of acquiring education that their grandfathers and fathers did not have, then Daghlas could offer the store to his younger brother, i.e., if he chose to take it. But Daghlas's younger brother was unlike Daghlas or their father, and had not shown any inclination in business and he did not like coming to the store even when their grandfather was alive or now when their father was looking after it. Daghlas might go to university somewhere in Haifa or Tel Aviv depending on what his grades would be later and his younger brother, Harry, who was three years younger definitely should not be pressured to make any decision on what he wanted out of his life or would want to do as a career, if he chose to have one. The two of them had been getting good results in their examinations since they first started school.

His last resort was to take over the store. But there were also other Jewish boys whose fathers and grandfathers were operating stores in the Jewish Quarter, but who could not find anyone from their families to take over their businesses from them simply because they had gone to school to receive formal education and as such, thought they had become smarter than their parents and grandparents and who did not want to have anything to do with the stores that their grandparents and parents had looked after from which they were able to benefit by being allowed and able to get some formal training in any place they wished. Some of them had become professionals and worked outside of Palestine, in the neighboring countries, too. And sadly, a few of them, upon getting jobs and mixing with people from other races and religions suddenly felt compelled not to agree with the cultural and religious values that their parents had tried to instill in them. They had started to wear modern clothes, suits, and neckties and even speaking in some European languages such as English, French, and whatever else.

Moshe feared that Daghlas and Harry, both his sons he had mistakenly given English or English-sounding names, when they were born, because he had thought that it would be easier for those who they might mix with, could remember them better compared to the ancient Jewish names that were difficult to pronounce and even spell. But Moshe was okay. The Arabs called him Musa for Moses. And he did not mind being called by those names by some close non-Jewish friends. But so far both his sons had not shown any inclination to 'leave the flock' as he described it and he had not decided on what actions he would take to solve the problem if it appeared that they were starting to lose faith in their religion. Moshe had also not discussed the matter with his wife or anyone in his family, yet, but he would like to seek advice from the Rabbis (Rabbe) on the matter, if he had the time.

Ah, maybe this is the problem that David had wanted to discuss with him too, but who was reluctant to say so, yet; because, he like, Moshe, too, would not like it, if they had to bear their souls with anyone even with brothers and sisters, and what more with strangers. And David did not have anyone from his own family to whom he could bring the matter or problem to for advice and he had not yet got a local Rabbi who he could approach. There were a few Rabbis from Poland who had also fled the country to come to Palestine, but he did not want to take his personal problems to them. He felt more comfortable talking to someone who was not from Poland, like Moshe, who somehow attracted his attention because he felt Moshe was old enough to understand him, as an older person, and as a Jewish man, who had lived all his life in Palestine and whos ancestors had been in this land for ages. He did not when David would come back to his store to speak with him again? He might even ask David to speak with a friend of his named Rabbi Cohen, who might be able to help him if his problems concerned religion that Moshe would not be able to comprehend, if they were posed to him by David. Rabbi Cohen was still a young man, at the age where David was at, so they could talk with each other like brothers. But Moshe thought he ought to give David a chance first to see what the problems he had were, and see if he could offer some advice or he would just get Rabbi Cohen to help him out. It was the first time when he was faced with such a dilemma and he wanted to take it in great strides. He was also surprised that a perfect stranger saw in him some qualities that he thought he had as a religious counselor that he was not and never could be. The best thing that he could do was to give him some general advice like someone who came to him complaining he had a bad headache for which he would prescribe some aspirin to take and have a good rest. The advice had worked a few times for some of his friends and relatives and also strangers like David who popped in at his store with their personal problems. And for those medical problems that were too immense for him to undertake, he told them to go to the nearby clinic operated by Doctor Aziz, an Arab man, who studied medicine at the University of Al-Azhar in Cairo, Egypt, a young man with a promising career in medicine, not yet married but engaged to an Arab woman who was studying at the same university as his, but who still had another year to study before graduating after which they would be married at her village in Gaza.

Moshe bumped into Rabbi Cohen at the synagogue, outside of The Old City, one day, where Moshe happened to be because he had some business to do near there. He walked out of the synagogue long after the prayer service and bumped into Rabbi Cohen who was walking alone, slowly like he was not in any hurry, to go home. 'Shalom. And what brings you here, dear Moshe?' he asked Moshe in Hebrew. 'Shalom, Rabbi Cohen. I have some chore to do in this area and decided to go to the synagogue...' he answered also in Hebrew. 'I have not seen you in a very long time, Rabbi Cohen.'

'Me, too. And how have you been? How's your business? I must go there sometime.'

'Not bad. In winter everything is slow with less tourists.'

'And this winter is especially bad, isn't it, with the snow falling almost every night. Be careful when you walk; the roads are slippery especially in The Old City where they are made of concrete. Someone almost slipped down but he someone else managed to grab him by his hand, the other day.'

'Were you there?'

'No, someone in the congregation told me about it.'

The two of them walked along the sidewalks for a distance before Moshe said he had to go to the other direction with the Rabbi going to the right. 'I hope to see you again, Rabbi,' said Moshe.

The Rabbi shook Moshe's hand and they started to walk at different directions. Moshe thought of David, but there was nothing yet for him to bring the matter concerning him to the Rabbi. He thought, maybe, after he had met with David again, he would know what to do with him or his problem if the Rabbi could help him out with it.

Moshe took a ride in the bus to go back to his store, after he was done meeting some traders near the synagogue to order some new stock for his store to sell, and to take over from his son, Daghlas who replaced him while he was gone. He tried not go be away from the store too long because he was told by Daghlas that he had a special class at school and needed to be there on time.

Daghlas spent his time reading his school books in the store when he was done seeing some customers who had come to look for things; some bought things from him and he was delighted to be able to sell them while his father was away. Moshe appeared at the front of the store carrying in his hands some small boxes and also bags full of things he had bought from the Arab trader earlier. He looked at Daghlas and indicated that he could leave the store to go to school, without saying anything that would be redundant. Daghlas quickly packed his books and notes and put them in a sling bag and started to leave the store. 'What time will your class be over?' asked his father. 'Around four. Why?'

'You don't have to come here from school; you can return to the house and help your mother there.'

Daghlas nodded and said, 'Shalom' and left without hearing his father returned the greeting which he did almost by heart with no sound coming out of his mouth, with only his lips moving a little. Daghlas then returned to the store with his father wondering if he might want some money. No, he had just left his jacket and took it from the side of the store to wear it and walked out of the store again. Moshe removed his jacket and hung it at the place where Daghlas had hung his jacket earlier.

Moshe remembered something, but he forgot to ask his son if David had returned to ask for him. Maybe he hadn't or his son would have said so. But he didn't. Daghlas could not have easily forgotten to tell his father if David had come to see him when he was out with the traders. Moshe told him not to worry about David; he ought to worry more about his business and the store and his business.

Snow started to fall outside of the store and in no time the whole pavement outside the store was covered in a thin layer of snow; and those who were walking on it, quickly brought out their umbrellas or hats, and started to walk properly lest they would slip off it and fall to the ground.

But he looked like a university professor, thought Moshe when his mind was taken back to him; he did not look like an ordinary person, and certainly not a laborer or a simple-minded person; he looked like a scholar from the way he behaved himself and even from the way he walked. But how could he tell if David was a university professor? He had not met any university professors in Palestine. He had only met some schoolteachers when he sent his sons to school. He had not been to any university in the country before to know how the professors behaved and spoke. David was a mystery to him. He had to tell him what he wanted to discuss with him about and he also had to tell Moshe who he was, because Moshe was not the type of person who liked to ask anyone their personal details, because it was his principle in life not to ask those questions and for the same reason, he did not expect anyone to ask his personal details. He'd rather talk with strangers on issues of the day or anything on earth, except their personal matters. So, he had so many 'good friends' but whose names and personal backgrounds he did not know. And they, too, did not know his name or what he did until they found him at his store, and only then they realized that he operated the stall, but for how long and why he was operating it, they did not care to find out directly from him. They only learnt about those matters from other persons, or his two sons, when they came to the store and Moshe introduced the boys to them.

Let our lives be a mystery to others and their lives be a mystery to me, he often liked to say and explain when some friends asked if he knew so and so, or the person who was tall and liked to wear a hat. Who? Moshe could not tell who the person was from the description his friend described him. It could some nameless persons. And what did they do for a living? He could not say. He was not interested to know more than the person he met and not what he was and what he had done before he met him at his store or even the synagogue or the Wailing Wall and sidewalk café, etc.

His own father had taught him not to be a nosey person; he himself did not care to know the names of the persons he met, what they did, and especially how many children they had. He'd rather let time tell him all those details and from other persons who might know the persons he was referring to. And this trait was imbued into Moshe by his father since he was very small. So Daghlas, did not know David other than the name, which he learnt from his father who found out about it from another person. Or was it from the person, David himself, who might have told Moshe his name – David. And he and his father, too, did not know who David was or what he did for a living.

And it turned out that David indeed was a university professor in Poland for many years until he decided to call it quits to flee from the country with his wife and their children to come to Palestine where he expected to be welcomed by the locals, be they Muslim or Christian-Arabs and other Jews like him. He and his family were immigrants who were seeking a better life and to live in safety. He and his family did not speak Hebrew or Arabic like the locals but he would try and learn the languages. He and his family spoke Polish and Yiddish, which was still handy when he wanted to communicate with the local Jews who understood him when he spoke Yiddish, although not much because the two languages were totally different and had few words that were understandable to those who spoke Hebrew. He could even memorize some verses from the Noble Qur'an and even recite them as well as any Arab man, such as...

* * * * * * *

'O you who have believed, do not consume one another's wealth unjustly but only [in lawful] business by mutual consent. And do not kill yourselves [or one another]. Indeed, Allah is to you ever Merciful'. – *The Holy Quran 4:29*

'And if two factions among the believers should fight, then make settlement between the two. But if one of them oppresses the other, then fight against the one that oppresses until it returns to the ordinance of Allah. And if it returns, then make settlement between them in justice and act justly. Indeed, Allah loves those who act justly.' – *The Holy Quran 49:9*

'O you who have believed, avoid much [negative] assumption. Indeed, some assumption is sin.' – *The Holy Quran 49:12*

'And do not spy or backbite each other. Would one of you like to eat the flesh of his brother when dead? You would detest it. And fear Allah; indeed, Allah is Accepting of repentance and Merciful.' - *The Holy Quran 49:12*

'Believe in Allah and His Messenger and spend out of that in which He has made you successors. For those who have believed among you and spent, there will be a great reward.' – *The Holy Quran 57:7*

* * * * * * *

They made him feel free of his own fears and worries, and he liked to say that to his Arab friends and also some of the Jewish ones including some Rabbis who thought he was doing the right thing.

Moshe did not ask for these details from David personally, as it was not his nature to do that; he learnt about him from a brochure David had given which he did not dare to read in his presence when he appeared at his store one day, when the snowing the night before was very bad that there were piles of snow on the roads and some in the alleyways in The Old City and the Quarters, where Moshe had his store. He did not expect David to come to his store in such weather conditions walking in the streets that had been piled with snow, and some more continuing to fall. But he did and managed to appear in front of his store, frozen in the cold so that even some hot tea was not able to heat up his body. He had to wipe it with his bare hands to make himself feel warm, and still wearing the overcoat and woolen hat.

Moshe kept the brochure on David and only read it when he got back to his house later that evening. He also showed it to his wife, Sarah and son, Daghlas and the three of them sat before the fireplace in the living room of their two-storey house outside of The Old City, frozen, when they realized who David was. And by then Moshe too had known what he had wanted Moshe to do for him, a favor that he found to be difficult to do. He'd try, he promised David; he'd try, although he did not know exactly how he could do that. After all David was a university professor and Moshe just a small-time businessman who operated one small store in the Jewish Quarter in The Old City and in the City of Jerusalem. And sadly, he had not been out of Jerusalem and had holed himself up in The Old City since he was a young boy when he first helped his grandparents at the store and when he was older when he helped his father there, and who took over it from his father after he died. The furthest he had gone out of Jerusalem was to go to Jericho, to visit his relatives during a festival, but that was a very long time ago. He did not think he had missed anything by not going anywhere outside of Jerusalem, and was happy to be holed in The Old City which to him was his world; where there was everything he needed to do and observe his religious duties. He did not need to travel anywhere because he feared he might be tempted to do things that were against his religion. And after his marriage, his wife, too, did the same and only went anywhere with her husband and not by herself or with other women.

But he allowed his first son, Daghlas, to go on field trips with his classmates, so that he could be prepared to face the world, which his father, Moshe, thought had changed since the time he was Daghlas's age, and that it would go on changing until the world he once knew disappeared. Like Moshe, Daghlas too spoke and wrote in Arabic well, other than Hebrew, but Yiddish was something he had heard fairly recently when some Jews from Poland appeared from out of the blue and mixed with them, who spoke in the language, they found too foreign to understand. Daghlas also spoke and wrote in English that was taught in his school. And he didn't mind when his son went to the Muslim Quarter to meet with his friends who were Arabs but who also spoke in Hebrew but not writing the language, which they learnt from mixing with Daghlas, although their level of understanding of the language was not very high; they used it sparingly and only when Daghlas came around. They made an unofficial agreement and agreed to speak in Hebrew with Daghlas who would speak to them in Arabic so that they could test the proficiency of each other's language amongst themselves.

There were also some Jewish families living in the Muslim Quarter where the Arab-Muslims and Christians would mix with their Jewish friends over tea in the café and oftentimes ate together, to talk and sometimes discuss business, before they went on their separate ways to go to their Masjid, synagogues and churches to pray, when the time came. Moshe liked to watch them when they were at their best joking and talking about everyday things, but he did not dare to join them because they were mostly older men than him. They were also his father's friends who felt very sad when his father died like they felt the wall had collapsed on them. He hoped Daghlas would be like the Jewish men who sat with his Arab friends when they were the age of his grandparents and the men who Moshe could only watch from a distance and when he had occasion to go to the Muslim Quarter for an errand or to deliver something an

Arab had purchased from his store that he could not carry because it was heavy for him to carry.

But lately some of the Jews living in the Muslim Quarter left the area when they felt it was not as safe as it was before and that his son who used to go there stopped doing so and he met with his Arab-Muslim and Arab-Christians at school and at times, in the cafés or restaurants where it was safer. But their relationship which was friendly and close before suddenly became cold and soon all of them did not meet anymore with each having their own after-school activities with their own groups or races. Moshe noticed how in the beginning his son behaved in an unusual way and hardly spoke with him or anyone including the customers who came to his store; he would treat them less friendly and Moshe feared if he continued to behave like that many of their customers would not come back to buy at his store. So he reminded Daghlas to forget about his friends when he was in their store and treat all the customers cordially and nicely, even if they did not buy anything. Daghlas tried to do as what his father had told him to do, and he managed to behave well with the customers, except for the few who were their regulars and family friends, but later he slipped into his own world and spoke sparingly and started to read, which was good since he managed to improve on his examinations results because of that.

Moshe's close friend, an Arab man by the name of Suleyman said, Ah, your good son, Daghlas, has grown up; don't be too worried because he is not a young boy anymore but a young man! Suleyman said he should know about young boys and young men, because he had five of them, who were now not like they were before when they were young boys; they all have acquired their own tastes and had views of their own on anything. What Suleyman said made him think hard; and over time he believed in what his good friend had said. They spoke in Arabic with each other mostly, but Suleyman sometimes broke into Hebrew, the little bit of the language that he knew, to stress a point which he said he could not very well say it in Arabic, like the many other Arabs who could speak in the language in various degrees of perfection, with some who were as good as the Jews themselves. Suleyman always like to congratulate

Moshe for speaking in Arabic like any Arab man, if not better than most of them, because he did not know how to speak in the language in any other way, but in the formal way.

A week after Moshe met David at his store when the later found it difficult to tell Moshe what he had in mind of saying, he came back to Moshe's store and this time he came with the specific intention which was to discuss something important. Last week he had tried to be brave to confront Moshe and he had succeeded and had met Moshe at his store. It was still winter and the snow was not any less bad; on the contrary, it had become worse with the sleet which made walking on the cobbled alleyway slippery and dangerous. He had snow shoes on, so it was not so bad.

Beit Ur al-Fauqa which means 'Upper House of Straw' is a small city to the east of Jerusalem and twenty-one minutes driving from Jerusalem; and this was where Moshe lived or about twenty-three kilometers, from each other, a distance which was not long, and easy to drive since the road linking the two areas was quite good and not so congested. But it could be tiresome at times especially in winter when there was snow and ice, or when there was a festive holiday for the Arab-Muslims and during Ramadan before that, when there were many travelers and all sorts of vehicles, the more modern types and the traditional ones with horses, mules, donkeys, and also camels clogging the road. Moshe did not like to be stuck in traffic and tried to avoid such days when the road was clogged. But the view was stunning, especially in the evening when he drove back to his house and could see the sun setting and the lilting sounds of the Adhan for the Maghrib prayers that came from all the Masjid in the areas he was passing through during which time he would slow down so that the sound of his car did not cover the sounds of the Adhan.

Sometimes he would drive to go to work or for most of the time he would commute. He had a small car he bought from a neighbor who sold it to him for a good, fair price, he said, because his neighbor, an Arab man wanted to move out of the area to another city; he said his children were now older and were married so he decided to move to Hebron where he did not have any need for a car to get around. But what the Arab man did not say was that there were now more Jews living in his area which was considered to be exclusive for the more affluent, and he did not want to ask Moshe who he had known since they were small kids. And Moshe too did not want to ask the reason why his friend, wanted to go to Hebron, where everybody knew had a large Arab-Muslim population and that his area in Beit Ur al-Fauqa now had more and more Jews coming to live in it especially those who had come from the Crusader countries, as he described them. He almost wanted to give away the car, an English model called an Austin, but Moshe said he wouldn't accept it if he did not pay for it. In the end they decided to do some barter trading with the Arab man giving his car for some things Moshe sold in his store. And they shook hands to seal the deal.

And to his surprise, Moshe learnt that the guy from Poland who had wanted to meet him, too, lived in the same area, but in a posher residential area, further up from his own, and their houses were not so far away with hardly ten to fifteen minutes of driving. But David had not contacted him again at the store and he did not want to go to his house, unannounced, as it was not proper; besides the two were not yet good friends unlike the Arab man who sold the car to him, who he could see whenever he wished, and vice versa, and that had happened on numerous occasions. Even their wives and children knew them well, and would talk with each other on a host of things, except recently when they started to feel coldness in their relations. Their children, too, had not met each other. Their wives, too, did not go to the market together. The foreign Jews from the Crusader countries presence had brought about such a situation when they flaunted their wealth that they and their ancestors had acquired in the hundreds or possibly thousands of years since they fled Palestine even before the time of Jesus Christ, while it could not be denied that many of them were indeed Ashkenazis, and those who converted to Judaism and called themselves Jews. One of them was David himself. Everybody in the area and Jerusalem where they had gathered knew this especially the local Jews who could not feel much empathy for them, even when they practiced their common religion and perform all the rituals in the synagogue and celebrate their festivals when they came.

Moshe became more alarmed when he found out that David and his family were living not so far away from him in the area, not so much because he lived in a house which was at least two or three times larger than his and was renting from a local Jew, because he could afford to pay for the hefty rental fee, and also the fact that he was interested to buy it from the owner of the house, for a higher price because he had grown to like it as did his children and wife.

Some of Moshe's Arab neighbors had left, including Jamil and some of the local Jews, too, had left or were contemplating moving elsewhere, to areas where there were more people of the same type as them. Moshe could not do much because the house he and his family were living in was his that was handed down to him by his father who was bequeathed it from his father, and it had seen many renovations over the last one or two hundred years when their ancestor built it using his own bare hands on a piece of land surrounded by desert when not many people had ventured to build their house there, in a village where friendly Arabs had lived for generations, and since biblical times.

He wanted David to take his own sweet time to come and meet him. But the longer he remained missing, the more he became anxious and suspicious like he had come to bring bad tidings although he had found out that David was a former professor at a university in Poland, so there was nothing sinister that he wanted to bring to him. Maybe he thinks you are distantly related to him, said one of his friends in the Jewish Quarter who he had shared his story concerning David. Who knows? said Moshe; except that he is not tall and I am quite so. He made sure he did not use the expression of 'short'. He had also seen David's wife near their place and someone told his wife that her name was Lila. Moshe's wife was Sarah, but they never spoke with each other when they bumped into each other at the market, a couple of times, because Sarah thought Lila who did not understand Hebrew felt worried if the locals especially Jews knew she was from Poland, like the many others. She looked like someone from Poland and could not look like any local Jew like Sarah and her friends.

One day, David popped out to Moshe's house. He had found out that Moshe lived there from some people who he had met, fellow Polish like him who had lived in the area much longer than David, and who knew Moshe, although not personally. He decided not to go to Moshe's store in the city, but meet him at his house, although it was not a proper thing to do, to just appear in front of his house unannounced and uninvited. He did not care; at least, here, he thought he did not have to travel twenty-three kilometers taking public transport, since he did not have a car yet, and since he also did not have a driving license either; and he waited outside of the door. He froze there not from the cold but by some fear he had created in himself. After a while, he moved forward to knock on the door. It was around nine in the morning and not too long later, he was told David would be leaving his house to go to his store.

David waited and not long later, Moshe appeared in the door and he was shocked to see David standing there. 'How did you know I live here?' Moshe asked. 'Someone told me you lived here and since I live not too far away, I decided to come to your house. I know it's not a proper or civilized thing to do, please forgive me.'

'That's alright. Want to come inside? It's cold.'

'That's alright.'

'Just come in.'

David walked the few steps and entered the house with Moshe holding the door and quickly closed it because he did not want cold wind from outside to enter it. He was wearing sleepers and not yet ready to go to his store.

'Have a seat. Do you take tea?'

'That's alright.'

David sat on a sofa made of thick leather and felt warm. He did not remove his overcoat because he did not want to give the impression to Moshe that he wanted to stay long.

'Let me take your overcoat,' offered Moshe.

'That's alright; I won't be long.'

'Is there anything I can do to help you? Sorry for asking; but I got the impression that you have something inside your mind of telling me or saying to me.'

David nodded and waited a while before he finally exposed why he wanted badly to meet with Moshe and more so to speak with him. 'It's a long story, and sorry for making a nuisance of myself and for keeping you in some unnecessary suspense. As you know I have just come from Prague, that's in Poland. And I am with my children and wife and we are Jews like you, and also unlike you.'

Moshe did not sit; he chose to stand up at the other side of the room which was gloomy because the shades had been pulled down. 'That's okay. And I learnt from the brochure you left with my son, Daghlas for me, that you are a university professor in Prague.'

'No. Warsaw.'

'Sorry.'

'I taught at a university in Prague but moved to Warsaw later. But I have left the university and am not a professor anymore.'

'I have not met a professor before. Sorry if I did not show my respect to you the first time you came to the store and then the second time, and just now here...'

David ignored Moshe and continued to think what next to say. Moshe waited. 'How many of us are here in this city and in Jerusalem?'

Moshe was taken by surprise by the question and he did not know why he asked it, and why from him, of all persons!?'

And before Moshe could find the answer or guess one, David pounced with, 'I heard that there are so many now in Jerusalem and other major cities.'

Moshe nodded and was relieved that he did not have to answer David's question which he did it himself; he just nodded in agreement. Still, he did not know exactly why he asked the question and what he planned to get from the answer which he already knew.

Then suddenly the Adhan sounded and Moshe immediately asked David to stop. Why? asked David. Let the Adhan be heard undisturbed, he explained. It was something new to David who did not know of the respect the Jews had of Islam and the rituals their good friends performed on a daily basis and the adhan was one of those rituals that all Jews respected and stopped doing anything they were doing and stopped talking whatever they were talking to let it pass. He mostly found the lilting sounds of the Adhan that came to his ears five times a day to be a sign of the Oneness and Greatness of God, the Almighty, and they helped him and his other friends of his own faith, to calm down and stop thinking and worrying about worldly things. He explained that to David when the Adhan was done, and stillness returned to the area where they were at.

'Thank you for explaining me about it, the Adhan and the call for the Muslims to pray and what magic it does to them and you,' said David, 'And I am sure I will appreciate it better now that I know what it means to the Muslims and to you, too. I have not heard the Adhan sounding like this before I came here; in Poland I did not hear it. It booms like the sound comes from all directions. There are not many Musalman… er…Muslims in the cities where I lived.'

'They do, because they are four Masjid in this whole area and the Adhan is being cried from each of them, so you hear the sounds from four directions.'

'So you must know the Priest…'

'Imam. And Muezzin. Yes, all of them, since we were small growing up together here.'

'Muezzin?'

'The person who cries out the Adhan, and without fail every day… five times a day!'

'You know all of them, the Imam and Muezzin, too?'

Moshe nodded. He then suddenly remembered a saying of Nabi Muhamad, (s.a.w.), and recited it, not for David, but more for himself, 'Every one of you is a shepherd and is responsible for his flock. The leader of people is a guardian and is responsible for his subjects. A man is the guardian of his family and he is responsible for them. A woman is the guardian of her husband's home and his children and she is responsible for them. The servant of a man is a guardian of the property of his master and he is responsible for it. No doubt, every one of you is a shepherd and is responsible for his flock.'

'Beautiful words, there, Brother,' remarked David. 'You wrote it yourself?'

'How could I? They are sayings of Nabi Muhammad, Peace be upon Him…as related to the Prophet's companion, Sahih al-Bukhari.'

The other sayings of Nabi Muhammad, (s.a.w.) Moshe liked to read them to himself and to some of his friends from amongst the Arab-Muslims, Christians, and also Jews, so some of his Muslim and non-Muslims jokingly called him Ustaz Musa. And true enough he would often dispense free advice that made him sound like he was an Islamic Ustaz, which is an honorific title usually given to experts or scholars of Islam, because he exhibited a vast knowledge of Islam.

* * * * * *

"The most excellent Jihad is that for the
conquest of self." (Bukhari.)
"Allah will not give mercy to anyone, except
those who give mercy to other creatures."
(Abdullah b. Amr: Abu
Dawud and Tirmidhi.)

* * * * * *

This made some of the Arabs, Muslims, Christians, and Jews secretly think Moshe was going on the trek or personal journey to Islam, although he would scoff at them saying that having some or a lot of knowledge about Islam did not make him any less a Jew who upheld the true teachings of the Torah that he, too, was an expert in, or at least knowledgeable which formed one of the most important aspects of the Jewish holy book, from the Book of Exodus that the Muslims called 'Taurah' that he had memorized by ear when he was a small boy and read all the Ten Commandments each time. He had the need to do so mostly to remind himself if he had gone astray from his religious beliefs, even slightly, doing so in the original text, Hebrew and not in English that he did not know by heart except by reading the text, which he preferred not to do, and he knew he had no reason to do so.

* * * * * * *

1. I am the Lord your God.
"I am the Lord your God, who brought you out of the land
of Egypt, from the house of slavery." (Exodus 20:2)
2. You shall have no other gods before Me. You shall not make
for yourself an idol.
"You shall not recognize other gods before Me. You shall
not make for yourself a carved image, or any likeness
of what is in heaven above or on the earth beneath or
in the water under the earth." (Exodus 20:3–4)
3. You shall not take the name of God in vain.
"You shall not take the name of the Lord your God
in vain, for the Lord will not leave him unpunished
who takes His name in vain." (Exodus 20:7)
4. Remember and observe the Sabbath and keep it holy.
"Remember the Sabbath day, to keep it holy. Six days you shall
labor and do all your work, but the seventh day is a Sabbath
to the Lord your God; you shall not do any work, you or your
son or your daughter, your male or your female servant, your
animal or your stranger within your gates." (Exodus 20:8–10)
5. Honor your father and mother.
"Honor your father and your mother, so that your
days may be prolonged in the land which the Lord
your God gives you." (Exodus 20:12)
6. You shall not murder.
"You shall not murder." (Exodus 20:13)
7. You shall not commit adultery.
"You shall not commit adultery." (Exodus 20:13)
8. You shall not steal.
"You shall not steal." (Exodus 20:13)

9.   You shall not bear false witness.
"You shall not bear false witness against
your neighbor." (Exodus 20:13)
10.   You shall not covet your neighbor's wife or house.
"You shall not covet your neighbor's house; you shall not covet your
neighbor's wife or his male servant or his female servant or his ox or
his donkey or anything that belongs to your neighbor." (Exodus 20:14)

* * * * * * *

Moshe was happy and relieved that David had come to his house
where he got a good idea of what he was driving at although even then
it was sketchy. He seemed to feel lonely and being a former professor
of a university in Poland for many years, he needed to speak to some
people who he thought he could relate to, some people who he thought
were on the same wavelength and intellectual level as he was. But Moshe
didn't think he fit the type of persons David was mixing with at his
university; he was not much of an intellectual and had never been to any
university to study. He studied Judaism, and almost became a Rabbi. He
thought the responsibility to be a Rabbi would fall onto his son, but when
Daghlas grew up he drifted away from being interested in becoming one,
much to his chagrin and consternation. He blamed himself for not being
able to guide Daghlas to the right path that he himself had not able to go
on, because he did not possess the right quality to become a Rabbi like
some of his friends who later became Rabbis and who were very happy
and contented to lead such a life.

David excused himself after spending a bit of time with Moshe at
his house and started to become restless and guilty for intruding into his
life and taking too much of his time too. Before he left Moshe's house,
he asked if he could see Moshe again, but at his own house where he
thought he had some important and interesting materials to show him.
Moshe was not reluctant to accept the offer although he hardly ever
visited the houses of other people including those of his close friends,
often choosing to meet with them in cafés or restaurants or other places.
He agreed to come to David's house a few days later. He hoped he would

239

not be intruding into David's house and family space when he was there, to listen and discuss with David whatever he wanted to discuss with him and to see what important and interesting materials he said he had that he wanted Moshe to see.

Before David left the house, Moshe told him his sons were in school and his wife was inside the room.

Moshe went to his store and opened it. His friends who operated the stores beside him wondered why he had come to his store a bit late; it was close to noon, they said. They knew he had never been late to open his store, usually at around ten in the morning. So that day he was late by two hours. And it could not be due to the weather because it was such a fine day, even though it was winter and very cold but the snow the night before had stopped and the sun that had disappeared for a while had suddenly reappeared to brighten the whole of The Old City and much of Jerusalem, that Moshe, too, had seen when he was approaching the city when he was driving to his store. He had also not driven in his car in a very long time, but because he was held up for a while at his house by David, he forced himself to drive in order for him to get to his store faster, or else if he took the bus, he would be there an hour later.

Fortunately, business was brisk that day and despite not being able to open his store at the usual time, but some two hours later, he had good business and many customers; many of whom he had not met before came to buy things from him; and he thanked David for making his day at the store. There were some Jews from Poland too, but he did not ask any of them if they knew David, a former university professor in their country, who might be well-known amongst some of them. And he had promised David to get a small group of local Jews to meet with him so he could meet them and exchange ideas with them. Moshe said he could try to arrange for the meeting in David's house. And only after the last customer had left his store, did he decide to think about the promise he had made with David when he visited Moshe's house earlier in the morning, so Moshe now had a good idea on why he had chosen Moshe and not other traders in The Old City to approach; because David said he had made an investigation and observation and found that Moshe seemed to be an amiable person with the right personality and attitude who might be of help to his cause, which even at that point Moshe had not actually known for certain what it was, other than that David, a former university professor in Poland now a refugee in Palestine living in the same residential area, but in a more posh part of the area and was renting a large house for his small family because he could afford it. Not because he wanted to show off his wealth but because he was offered a good rental rate for the property, which was also in a mixed race area, with a lot of Arabs who were Muslims, Christians, and Jews, some of whom were refugees from not only Poland but Bulgaria and Russia and elsewhere who had come over a period of years, long before David did.

But for the meeting, David asked to meet with only local Jews like Moshe, and not those refugees. He said he had a reason why he wanted to meet and discuss and exchange ideas with the local Jews and not the refugees. Moshe said he could get around fifty persons, so that David and his wife, Golda could prepare refreshments for them. David said his wife, Golda was a true Jewess but her ancestors had left Palestine a century or two earlier and she had lost ties with them if they were still living here, in some remote village whose name she had long forgotten and over the years. Her family members had acquired Polish identity and who could now not speak Hebrew but Yiddish like David himself. But in the last few years, David had started to learn Hebrew on his own so he hoped to be able to speak and communicate with the local Jews in the language they knew – Hebrew. He was afraid the thick Polish and Yiddish accents he had might cause the local Jews to not able to fully understand what he was saying.

When the time finally came Moshe managed to invite about fifty persons, all males and mostly Jews like him, with some who were less faithful to their Jewish faith. There were some Christian and Muslim Arabs, too, who Moshe had announced to David and got his approval to invite for the talk held in the living room of his house, on the ground floor where all the furniture had been removed so that all the men sat around the spacious room, sitting cross-legged as it would not be possible for him to provide each with a chair to sit on. Everybody had their coats removed and put in the side room, so they were comfortable sitting in the room which was heated by old-style heaters with firewood.

David sat on one side with Moshe sitting beside him. David's wife, Leah was in the kitchen and Moshe brought his wife, Sarah to help with the cooking. But they were never seen in the living room or introduced to the guests.

Moshe gave a small speech to introduce David to the crowd who comprised mostly of those men who lived in their neighborhood with a few from the neighboring areas. Many of them had seen David there before but they did not know who he was and were anxious to know what he wanted to say. Being a former professor, he naturally managed to attract their attention to the gathering he had wanted to organize to allow him to speak with them and in this way, they could also get to know him better. There was no one who was from Poland like David or Bulgaria or Russia there. And after Moshe was done with his brief introduction, David spoke. He first introduced himself as a former professor at a university in Poland and who had conducted research on the Jewish communities in his country and the other neighboring ones. He also mentioned the First Zionist Congress that was held at the Stadtcasino, in Basel in Switzerland in 1897. And he followed with a talk on the Masada, the League of Nations, and so on. By then some of those who were present had started to figure out what David was driving at and a few of them were beginning to feel restless. Moshe tried to put on a stoic face and allowed himself to continue listening to see where David wanted to go with his presentation. Then one of the men, turned to look at the other beside him like he was not happy with what David had said so far; he was a staunch Zionist supporter, but no one knew that because he never said anything about his politics and continued to work for his own small company in Jerusalem.

The meeting did not end well as David had expected. A few left before it was over. Moshe stayed with the last group of only thirty people. He did not like it when one by one of the men stood up and without saying a word, grabbed their overcoat and walked out of the house into the night, with some continuing to talk with each other and could be heard by those inside the house where David and Moshe were. Someone was heard quite clearly saying that David, who he suspected was a pro-Muslim activist had come from Poland to divide the Jews in Jerusalem, until his voice became faint and what he was saying became intelligible. But the tone of his voice said everything that he needed to say.

David tried to continue with his speech, but gave up after a while when he felt tired and the others in the living room did not look like they were keen to know more about what he had said. They had sat there more than an hour and had eaten the food that was served, and were tired. It was also now late at night. The last Adhan of the day for Isyak had happened an hour earlier.

After everybody had left, there were only Moshe and David were the only ones who were still sitting cross-legged in the living room. Moshe felt bad for not being able to get the right crowd for David to talk to, and the questions that were posed to him during the question-and-answer session were too personal. What was he up to? most of them asked themselves, and among each other after they had left the house and far away so that what they were saying was not heard by David and Moshe.

Moshe walked with his wife, Sarah, back to their house and it was close to midnight with snow piled on the sides of the road which was clear of vehicles. They decided to walk to David's house because it was not far away from their own. Both of them kept quiet and said nothing because they knew what they said could be heard by David and his wife, too.

David sat on the floor of his house and felt disappointed that his good intentions had been misconstrued by many of the men and he did not blame Moshe for bringing those who were not appreciative of what he was saying. His wife came into the living room and sat beside him. 'I thought you did a very good job, David,' she said, and touched his hand. David did not say a word and tried not to think about the gathering and his speech. It was a very long speech that touched a lot of sensitive subjects close to the Jews and he knew it. But what the others did not know was that he was looking far ahead, at the future of the Jews, not only, of those who lived in Jerusalem and Palestine, but elsewhere in the whole world and what might become of Palestine not too long in the future. As an academic and professor he had conducted thorough research on the subject and wanted to remind the men on certain things. But they didn't seem to care.

Moshe and his wife, Sarah continued to walk and when they realized that they had left David's house far behind, his wife, started to talk; she asked, 'How did you think the gathering and talk went?' Moshe shook his head slightly and tried not to give his wife a verbal answer. But she knew what it was. 'I felt sorry for David. I felt sorry for his wife, Sarah.'

'What did you talk about with Sarah?'

'Nothing. About the food she was offering the men. They ate everything, so she did not have to do much cleaning.' She laughed a little while Moshe smiled a bit, and both continued to walk a bit more until they got to the front door of their house. They then entered their house and once inside, Sarah turned to her husband and asked, 'What will you say to David if he asked you about the gathering?'

'I have to think about it first. But before he asked me, I will ask him what he thought of the outcome of the meeting, the gathering.'

'And...'

'I will also ask what he intends to do next with his mission.'

'Mission?'

'Yes, it seems like he has a mission, a grand mission to do something for his community of Jews not only in Jerusalem and Palestine, but all over the world, to remind them...'

'To remind them? I don't quite understand.'

'I don't know...'

David did not sleep in his room; his wife returned to their bedroom and went to sleep, while her husband chose to remain seated in their living room. He then lay down on the floor and covered himself with an overcoat to keep his body warm now that the fireplace was not lit anymore. He did not want to think of the men and their behavior and attitude, or of the long speech he had tried to give them.

The night was pitched dark and at three in the morning he was still not able to sleep; he kept still and not moving all this while except that his mind was racing replaying the speech he gave earlier, from the beginning to the end that took one and a half hours. But why was I able to speak to them for this long and with no one bothering to stop me or to ask me any questions? he asked himself. They all seemed to be transfixed in what I was saying and when food was served they all ate it until the plates were cleaned and the tea in the three large 'dallah's were dry. Maybe they were transfixed by what I had said and knew what I was saying after all and did not dare to stop me to ask any question. But what could they ask me? Nothing. There were some general questions in the question-and-answer session that lasted for thirty minutes and I gave all the right answers. There was no real argument and I did not hear anyone disagreeing with me. But when there were two persons who were sitting beside each other started to move and leave the house, the others followed suit until thirty left, and then twenty left. In the end there were only ten of us left including Moshe and me. Surprisingly, the Arab Christians and Muslims stayed till the end of the meeting. But they did not ask any questions. I thought they were the ones who would not like what I was saying and would take their leave, but in a very polite manner. Ah, maybe it was too long, my speech; I should have shortened it to half the length just before the guests Moshe brought with him began to become uneasy. Or, maybe they had other things to do and it was getting late.

With this thought, and self-explanation, David began to feel a lot better with himself. He knew he had not hurt anyone's feelings; Moshe said my speech was okay; it did not touch anything sensitive or the Arabs – Christians and Muslims were the first to feel so, and would have said so, but in a polite manner; and I can accept it if they had felt that way, because they must want to look at the whole issue from their own perspective, being Arabs and regardless of whether they were Muslims or Christians. On the contrary they were the ones who had stayed till the end of the meeting and who had greeted me good night, and shook my hand before walking out of the house to return to theirs. That was close to midnight three hours ago.

David then heard someone walking down the staircase inside his house. He turned and looked at the door and his wife, Leah appeared.

'You better get to the bed,' she said. 'Don't worry about what happened; you tried your best. And wait a while before you know what happened. It might be for the better for all; and those who had come must have surely thought your speech was dragging too long and they simply had to leave. Can't blame them; for Sarah and I were also tired waiting in the kitchen and listening to your very long speech from there.'

'What did she say about it?'

'She liked most of it. It makes sense, she said. But those who came were not the type of people who had the discipline to listen to a very long lecture of the type they give in the universities to their students. This is not a university and they are not students.'

'Maybe I should change my style and approach from being a professor to being a normal person, and speak in the style they understand.'

Leah nodded. David then stood up and both of them left the living room to climb up the staircase and entered their bedroom. They opened the two bedrooms where their children were fast asleep and closed the doors. They are the future of the Jews and of Palestine, said David to himself. He then remembered the King David Hotel in Jerusalem that he had passed a few times before but never entered it or went anywhere closer to it; he looked, stared at it from a distance. It was opened in 1931. Interesting hotel, he said. He knew something about it even before he came to Palestine and wondered how it looked like. Now he knew. He wanted to go there someday to enter it. It shouldn't be very expensive to go inside and sit in the bar and order a glass of wine or champagne and look at the crowds who frequented there; it must be totally different than the crowds he had seen in the bazaars in the Old City or anywhere in Jerusalem or Palestine. It was on Julian's Way in the city center in Jerusalem, and it overlooked the Old City and Mount Zion. Interesting, he said to himself as he remembered the hotel which was seven stories tall. He had counted. He had also heard of the Sharkey Brothers who built a series of hotels in the major cities in Southeast Asia, but not this one.

So, two days later, David went to the hotel that bore his name. He entered it through the main entrance and went straight to the bar and sat on a wooden stool; a waiter immediately came to him to ask for his order. A glass of wine, he said. He looked at the bar and saw a sizeable crowd of people who were mostly Jews and British people speaking in soft tones, so he did not know which language they were using, most probably English, he guessed. There was laughter. The waiter returned to him from the other side of the bar and put a glass of wine in front of him and asked, if he needed anything else. No, that won't be necessary for now, he said as he grabbed the glass and took a small sip of the wine. He forgot to ask the waiter by the name of Lateef, if it was a locally-made wine or if it was from England. He then stood up when he saw some brochures about the hotel stacked on some shelves and went to them and took one and returned to his seat to read what they were writing about the hotel where he was now. Hmmm…it was opened in 1931, and it was built using limestone that was gotten from Palestine itself. The hotel was founded by a wealthy Jewish banker from Egypt by the name of Ezra Mosseri who was then the director of the National Bank of Egypt, along with other wealthy Jews in Cairo providing another forty-six percent of the investment on the hotel, about five percent more with the purchase of some shares by the National Bank itself to build the hotel. The design of the building and its interiors were inherently European but it had influences that would visually have a 'Biblical' style and also reminiscent of the ancient Semitic style with the look and feel of the glorious period of King David for which the hotel was going to take its name after. An interior decorator by the name of G. G. Hufschmid was assigned to design the interiors of the hotel and rooms and he chose motifs which he found in the early Assyrian, Hittite, Phoenician, and Muslim buildings. David himself could not comprehend what he was seeing when he was outside of the hotel and later when he was inside it, because the motifs of the building, walls, and everything had some familiar traits in them, which he only much later and after researching in books, saw photos and illustrations which he guessed where the designs that might have come from that the brochure of the hotel did not mention.

Interesting, he said to himself, that the design of the hotel and the motifs the designers had used blended with the overall surroundings of the road known as Julian's Way and the whole City of Jerusalem, and in fact, the whole of Palestine, too, which to him indicated how the owners of the hotel had wanted to show and promote the unity of the people, Arabs and Jews, who he thought and hoped would remain that way, for ever and ever, in peace and harmony. He wondered, who might be the Julian whose name that was given to the road in front of the hotel! That's very English, he said. There was never a Prophet Julian, that he knew or had read of!

After reading the brochure, he looked at the other waiter and asked, if he could keep it as a souvenir and the waiter just nodded and said, Sure, take it. David put it in his brown leather briefcase. This was the briefcase he used when he was teaching at the University of Warsaw that made him look smart, like an intellectual; and he knew he looked like one, especially when he was wearing suits and an overcoat when it was cold and a hat to match. He remembered how his friends, Moshe and Suleyman had told him they had never been inside of this hotel in all their lives, despite being born here and growing up here, in fact, they had seen the building rising when it was being built in 1929 until it was completed two years later, from land that was vacant, they said. It would surely be something that he thought he could mention to the two of them, if they met up again. But so far he had not said when he would come by or for what reason. There was no need for him to make an appointment to meet anyone of them because here in Jerusalem as in the whole of Palestine, no one did that as it was not a British thing to do. One can just drop by at their friends' house or office anytime they wished. Initially David did not like that setup, but he had accepted that to be the norm here, which was perfect for him because he could not be charged for taking advantage of their friends' hospitality and kindness. They were operating their stores, so anyone can just drop by at anytime of the day until they closed, and if need be, he could buy something in the stores, as an excuse to go there to meet any of them, whenever he liked. So David did not feel guilty each time he wanted to see Moshe and Suleyman or the other Arabs and Jews at their stores in the Muslim, Christian, or Jewish Quarters, if he wanted to. And he had done that fairly often without even buying anything from them, which sometimes made him feel a bit guilty.

Suddenly there was a commotion. He turned to look at the main entrance he had entered from earlier and noticed a group of British soldiers all armed with their officers and a large car come a complete stop on the porch outside of the entrance. He tried to see who was being chauffer-driven to the hotel. He noticed the Union Jack at the front, left side of the vehicle and guessed that the person must be someone of high standing. The man alighted from the vehicle but David was not able to see who he was because his view was blocked by many people who surrounded him. He then caught a glance of the man but it was not who David guessed: Not Ramsey McDonald the then Prime Minister of Britain who just won the general elections in 1931. The man might be a senior officer or even the British ambassador to Palestine, he guessed. He did not want to ask anyone at the bar or in the lobby which was now crowded with guests of the hotel who were also excited to see such a commotion happening. His tenure as a professor of a university, and hence, his status of a scholar did not allow him to be excited about anything.

David sat at the bar a while more and drank all the wine that was in his glass and paid for it and left the hotel feeling happy and relieved that he had been to such a hotel that was then a premiere hotel in the whole of the City of Jerusalem and also Palestine where only the senior British officers and wealthy folks in the city and country could come for their personal pleasure. It was a meeting place for such folks, and definitely not for people like David, who told himself that that was the first and last time he would ever go to this hotel because he felt so out of place the whole time he was there with no one looking at him or wanting to have any conversation with him.

He walked out of the hotel and was not greeted by a vehicle like the other guests who came in large limousines and were chauffer-driven; while he had to walk a distance until he lost sight of the hotel. He then decided to enter a small restaurant and sit inside to have his lunch there which was cheaper. He got his order but did not immediately eat; he took out the brochure of the hotel and read that it had hosted some prominent international political personalities such as the Dowager Empress of Persia, Queen Mother Nazli of Egypt, and also King Abdullah the First of Jordan. It was also a refuge for exiled heads of state such as King Alfonso XIII or Spain abdicated from his throne in 1931, in the same year the hotel was opened for the first time and King George of Greece, among others. They all must have felt very safe there getting full protection from the British who were occupying Palestine.

That would be something interesting that he could bring to the dinner table in his house to discuss with his wife, and how a minor staff at the hotel had told him in secret that it was also where the civilian government and military command of the British Mandate in Palestine were headquartered, because they thought it was a very safe place for them to be. And he definitely could not take her there, because, she, like him, could not stand the way everybody there behaved, like they were watching some Hollywood film. He remembered seeing 'Garden of Allah' and 'The Sheik' and 'The Son of Sheik' and knew the main characters in these films well and not be able to relate to any of them. They were White characters, mostly British whose government had colonized many Arab countries and affected tremendous changes in them, but which had hardly shaken their belief in themselves and in their own cultures and religions, especially Islam, and had discovered many ancient artifacts from the times of the Pharoahs or 'Firaun' as the Arabs themselves would call them, and looting some to be shipped back to England for public display and further investigation; and Americans, too, who jumped onto the bandwagon, being mostly those with English heritage and the adventure spirit that their ancestors had inculcated in them, in their fantasies however weird it may seem to be, and who had chosen to go to the Arab countries, and others in Africa and Asia, and not being able to see how they could fit in any of them, like what he was feeling right then.

David sat at the dining table in his house with his wife putting on it a large bowl of 'hummus', she said. David hardly knew what it was, and had to be told of it. That was the first time his wife had cooked the food, which was very Palestinian but the Jews, there, too, had liked it enough to claim it was also their own. They shared the same cultures, values and food tastes, thought David, but he was not sure if the hummus his wife had just cooked for dinner for his family would taste as good as some hummus he had taken in the sidewalk cafés and restaurants before. But it looked like hummus, he thought, so it must taste like it. 'I learnt how to make hummus from a recipe an Arab woman at the restaurant gave me,' said Lila. David caught a strong whiff of the hummus the moment Lila opened the lid of the bowl and it smelled like hummus, like the type he had taken earlier. And it looked like hummus too, he said. Lila poured some hummus for him and their two children and sat in front of David across the table. 'It tastes better with plain water and not wine or syrup,' she said.

'Is is difficult to make it?' asked David.

'Not really. It consists of just a few things – chickpeas, sesame tahini, olive oil, lemon juice and garlic; just these five ingredients, with some salt and pepper to make it. Or it can take other spices such as sumac, cumin, or smoked paprika.'

'What spices did you put?'

'Salt and pepper, this time. I will try with other spices the next time I cook it.'

David had a spoonful and ate it and said, 'Hmmm…' His wife knew what that meant, while their two sons, took small scoops of it at a time each until their small bowl was clean. Lila noticed even before they started to ask for another helping, and she dutifully put some hummus in their plates. 'Yes, it is good…very good', he remarked as he swallowed more hummus. 'We never had hummus in Poland; it was not a common food with our people there.'

Lila remembered something, but could not tell what it was. 'Did you forget something,' asked David.

'Yes,' but I can't remember what it was.'

'Salad?' David guessed. Lila nodded and stood up and rushed to the kitchen and brought another bowl of salad for her family to take with the hummus. 'Hummus certainly goes better with salad; how could I have forgotten about salad!? The best thing with hummus is that it can be taken at anytime of the day and also night like now...'

So in the end David did not mention to his wife that he had gone to the King David Hotel earlier in the day but he told himself he would tell her of how he had met some important British dignitaries who arrived at the hotel later when they were back in their bedroom to sleep. He was definitely not going to sleep on the carpet in the living room of their house again tonight. The only thing that might cause him not to sleep well was how he did not dare to ask Lateef, the waiter at the hotel, or anyone there, if he could go up to the rooftop of the building so he could look at the scenery around it, to see the whole City of Jerusalem from that vantage point. He knew they would not be able to entertain him, with such a request, knowing that he had just ordered and taken a glass of wine. It would have been different if he had gone to the restaurant and taken a full meal, for which he might not be able to pay with all the money he had had with him in his pockets then. So he made sure he took with him, a glass of wine to his bedroom to take in case getting to sleep was difficult.

In the end what kept him awake that night was not things that he thought would keep his mind racing. He took the glass of wine and went down to the living room and lay on the carpet and drank a bit of it. He remembered what the waiter at the hotel, Lateef, said was the reason why he wanted to work there as a waiter was because he could go to work everyday and get paid. He did not drink liquor though. He had seen a lot of happenings there, one of which that happened to an English man who got drunk and had to be propped up by two British soldiers who took him to the car waiting at the porch of the hotel, and drove him to the Jerusalem Airport, because he did not want to be sent back to London. They revived him when he was in the car by slapping his cheeks with wet towel. He did not want to be sent back to England because he liked it here so much and had a girlfriend, an Arab Christian woman, who his superiors thought might be a spy. Spy?!

David did not get it. An Arab Christian woman, a spy? For who? And this was the part that made him not want to go to sleep, because he feared that there might be some British officers at the hotel and elsewhere where he had frequented, who might have seen his less casual ways, who might think that he, too, might be a spy! David did not enquire with Lateef about the Arab Christian woman or the English guy who had to separate because his senior officers thought he was getting close to a local spy, and started to feel uncomfortable being in the hotel and that was why he thought he'd better leave it, before any untoward happened there. And he could not help but notice the few times when the local police officers stopped and frisked the luggage and bags carried by some Jewish men, especially when he was in the Old City. Fortunately, none of them saw me or they might stop me and frisk me too. I also learned from the local Jewish men I bumped into in the stores or restaurants, that most of those Jewish men were 'new arrivals', meaning they had just arrived from Europe, some also from where I came from, Poland. Most did not have a valid reason to be here other than to escape persecution there and in other cities in the countries the Arab-Muslims called the 'Crusader Countries'. I could not blame them for saying so, as it was a fact that most of them were Crusader Countries who had at an earlier time came to Jerusalem, Palestine, and other Arab countries to control them for years and even generations, including Egypt, Jordan, Iraq, etc. David said he could accept these as facts as a scholar and might not agree with the assessment if he were just a layperson.

The wine glass he had was dry and he tried to drink even the last few drops that were still stuck in it; and he was too lazy to wake up to walk to the kitchen of his house which was barely a few steps away from where he was lying on the floor of his living room. He thought if he did that, he would not be able to sleep a bit more until the sun rose for the break of dawn, when he knew the first cry of the Adhan would be heard soon. He had gotten used to it by now and had accepted it as a sign that it was a new day for him to face more uncertainties with his mission that he did not yet feel he had accomplished. He had not told Moshe or Suleyman and some others what he had in mind to tell them. And most likely, he would never be able to tell any of them what he had in his mind that forced him to come to Jerusalem and Palestine at this time. He

253

then decided to write his thoughts in case he did not get to do what he wanted to do so that his sons and perhaps their sons could take the issue with them to share with whoever they felt like sharing them with. They could also later on decide by themselves if the notes were of any historical value and might seriously consider getting a publisher to publish them in the form of a book, a memoir of his life in Poland and Palestine, if they thought highly of what he wrote in his notes. He had bought two thick books with blank pages but he had not written a word in the first one other than to write his name and the city he was in, Jerusalem. That was two weeks ago, when he first met Moshe, Suleyman, and the fifty or so persons who came to his house and sat right here in the living room for two hours. He felt sorry for keeping them there for so long. But at least he hoped they enjoyed the food his wife, Lila and Moshe's wife, Sarah had prepared for them, which was mostly food they ate in Poland that they had not tasted before. No one complained about it so he and his wife and Moshe's wife, assumed they all liked it.

11

Moshe and Suleyman.

Moshe was busy in his store, unpacking new consignments of things that had arrived in small boxes. He opened the covers and pulled some things out and arranged them on shelves that were not full. His business was good lately. It was not yet lunch time and he could finish arranging the new things he thought. He had totally forgotten about the talk or speech David gave a few days ago, and he also had not seen him around or knew if he would drop by. At the same time, he was anxious to know from David what he thought of the crowd and of the speech he had given that touched some interesting and important subjects all concerning the Jews. Some of the things he had said, were controversial in nature that had never been uttered by anyone before, at least by those who he met regularly at the store or synagogue and other places, like the sidewalk cafés and restaurants, etc.

Today was another day just like any other for Moshe and he did not know what business awaited him, but yesterday was a good one with many customers, most of whom he had not seen before; all were Arabs, but some were not Muslims, but Christians, from the way they behaved, dressed, and spoke, and he could also tell that they were not locals, meaning, from Jerusalem, because they looked like tourists, and could very well be from Syria from the accents they had when they spoke with each other and mostly when they spoke with him. He did not ask where they were from. It was not his nature to intrude into their personal lives and private spaces unless they willingly told him where they were from, because in this way, they thought Moshe might be able to offer them a better price for the things they were interested in, which was a fact, because Moshe had a soft spot for those who had come so far and chose his store to purchase things, which often times were brought in from their own countries but they didn't know that, until they got to Jerusalem and to his store, when they learnt of it. The things were not made in 'Damsyik' or Damascus, or they would know that. But were made in small factories away from their capital cities by artisans who had been making them for ages using the same tools and techniques to make them that were handed down to them from their great-great-grandparents' time. And the customers he had yesterday were all foreign tourists, from Syria and some from Iraq, who had wanted to come here to visit the religious sites including the Temple Mount, Masjid Al-Aqsa, and the Church of Holy Sepulchre and the others, including the Church of Nativity and the place where Jesus Christ was born.

Suleyman appeared in front of the store, as always with a frozen face that belied any emotion, and kept it inside his heart, like he often said; and he looked at Moshe where he knew Moshe would be at that time, near the shelves to arrange and rearrange things, hoping that Moshe would feel his presence and turned around to greet him. But Moshe was too busy to hear the faint footsteps he made with his leather sandals as he approached the store, because the sounds were mixed with those of the sounds made simultaneously by the footsteps of many others who were walking on the alleyway outside of his store. Suleyman then called, 'Busy again, as always, huh, Moshe, my dear friend?' Moshe did not turn around; he knew whose voice it was and replied, 'Want to give a hand, my Brother Suleyman?'

'Really?'

'I'm joking. Have a sit. I am about done. Yes, is there anything I can do for you today, Suleyman? Were you at the gathering at David's house two, er...three days ago? I did not see you there. You said you were coming.'

Suleyman entered the store and helped carry a few things and put them on the shelves. 'Yes, I was there, sitting at the back.'

'Oh, how come I did not see you there?'

'I came in late and entered the room from the back and sat hidden by some people.' And before Moshe could ask him what he thought of the gathering and especially the speech given by David, Suleyman gave a statement or comment that surprised, if not shocked him. 'I thought the gathering ended up to be very good.'

'And the speech he gave?' Moshe was done with his job or rearranging the things on the shelves and he sat on his wooden stool and panting a bit. He used the ends of the sleeve of his right hand and wiped his face with it.

'I thought it was good; indeed, it was good, even when he spoke in the little Hebrew that he knew, but he managed to deliver what he wanted to say quite well.'

'Really?!' Moshe poured a bit of tea from a 'dallah' to two cups and offered one of them to Suleyman. 'Come over and have a seat, Suleyman.'

Suleyman approached him and pulled out a stool and sat near Moshe and they began to sip the tea which was still hot. 'And what were you saying just now, Suleyman? I didn't quite get it.'

'I thought the speech David had given was very interesting; and I fully understood what he meant to say, and I also fully support it.'

'And what exactly did he mean?'

Suleyman was taken aback by the question. How could Moshe not know it too, he thought. 'Well, David feared for the future of Palestine and the future of the Arabs and Jews who have lived in this country for centuries. Jerusalem, too, is more than five thousand years old. And it had withstood a lot of issues but this time, it may not be able to remain as it is…'

Even before Suleyman was able to finish his statement, Moshe interrupted him by asking, 'What do you mean by that? I don't get it!'

'David must explain further what he had in mind; but from what I could deduce from his speech, he feared that outside forces are out to destabilize not only Jerusalem, but the whole of Palestine; and not just the whole of Palestine, but the whole of the Arab World of the Middle East as a region, too.'

Moshe took a bit of time to digress what he had heard from Suleyman and was still not sure of what he had said or meant. 'Please explain again the part on the whole of Palestine and the whole of the Arab World and the Middle East. I am a bit confused by that, even when he was speaking. Did you think the others also understood what he said, in the same way you said you understood him well?'

Suleyman nodded; he then took another sip of tea while Moshe waited. 'I'm not so sure about the others, but I can think that what David had said had sunk into their heads, and some may have felt groggy afterwards because they were forced to think ahead, very far ahead, beyond our time; and things could be worse than what we can imagine now, what can and will happen in the future when all of us, you and me, are no more around. It's people like your children, my children, and David's children or our grandchildren who have to suffer for the failures of people like us…'

'Did he say what would happen in the future to our Jerusalem, er… Baitulmukaddis, Palestine, the entire Arab World, and the whole of the Middle East, as we know it?' 'He did not say it exactly in words, but he merely expressed his own fears, based on his research findings and what he had managed to get, when he was still in Poland and working as a university professor at a university there. He is a learned person who can think very far ahead of all of us here. He happens to be the first university professor I ever knew in my whole life. No university professor had come our way here in The Old City or in the Jewish and Muslim Quarter; he was the first and maybe the last of such persons to come and try and relate to people like us.'

Two Arab customers entered the store and one of them, a woman asked, 'Do you have any leather purses?' Moshe stood up and went to a shelve and said, 'Here are some.' The customer went to the shelve and looked for a few and liked one of them. 'Where is this made and how much?'

'That one is made in Ramallah, and it's for three pounds only.'

'I'll take it.'

Moshe wanted to wrap the purse but the women said, 'That's okay; I will use it straightaway.' She then paid for the purse and she and her husband walked out of the store. Moshe then returned to his stool and sat on it, to resume the discussion he and Suleyman were having earlier. 'Where was I? Where were we?'

'I thought the description of what life was like in Poland was interesting, also because he had lived in the country most of his life until he came here, what, barely a few months ago?!'

Moshe nodded. 'He said less than four.'

The two of the men went on to talk about the topics David discussed with the group in his house, starting with life in Poland for Jews like him, and then he talked about the Masada and the First Zionist Congress held at the Stadtcasino in Basel, Switzerland from 29 August to 31 August, 1897 and attended by two hundred and eight delegates and twenty-six press correspondents, convened and chaired by Theodor Herzl, the founder of the modern Zionism movement. The last item he discussed was the League of Nations. All these could not have been discussed by him separately but only if they are connected together. We could see where he was driving us to go to with him, to the future of Jerusalem and Palestine, the Arab World, and the Middle East, our own future too, if we live long enough to see what he feared would happen, God forbid!

Moshe remained stoic and pretended not to be greatly affected by the explanation given by Suleyman, which had become crystal clear. At the meeting, he only heard words flowing out the mouth of David, without being able to make much or any sense of what he said, much less, what he meant. Now he knew for the first time, and he began to feel scared and worried. 'I know what happened at the Masada,' said Moshe. 'But roughly, like all Jewish boys and girls who were told of it when we were young; and what he explained was a lot clearer and deeper. It was described as the First Jewish-Roman War which occurred from 73 to 74 C.E, and around a large hilltop where the Jews where stranded and blocked by the Romans who camped at the base of the hill in Judea, until the Jews could stand no more and one by one, they decided and agreed to commit suicide by flinging themselves over the side of the hill. It was tragic how the Jews decided to end the siege of Masada in this way. But they had to because they did not want to be captured by the Romans. They were led by Eleazar ben Ya'ir for the Jews and Lucius Flavius Silva for the Romans. And he said, according the Jewish chronicler, Flavius Josephus, he mentioned, the Jews their nation would be beyond the Euphrates River, would one day be joined together with all Jews in an insurrection. But unfortunately, in the end, there were only nine hundred and sixty Jewish Zealots who stayed to confront the Roman army there, at Masada. Josephus also said that when they, the Zealots, were trapped on the top of Masada and with nowhere to run or flee, the Zealots believed that it was the will of their God, that they should all die together.'

Moshe was very emotional when he heard Suleyman relate the incident on the Masada and what it meant to him when he first heard about it as a boy. 'The fact that they manage to stay there for a long while and during that time, they managed to stave off the Romans, was stunning, stunning indeed, don't you think, Suleyman?'

Suleyman nodded and added, 'For many years, they managed to live on the hilltop by creating and making everything they needed to survive, was a phenomenal feat. Have you seen the hill?'

Moshe shook his head. 'Have you?'

'Yes, from afar. There were nine hundred and sixty-seven of them, Zealots.'

'Not nine hundred and sixty?'

Suleyman shook his head to indicate a negative answer. 'And the Romans had more than ten thousand soldiers, or auxiliaries and slaves, too. Nine hundred and sixty died when they jumped off the cliff, and seven were captured. Two were women, who were unknown, and five children.'

'It was tragic because of how they had chosen to die, in a mass suicide of the Sicarii rebels and resident Jewish families of the Masada fortress,' added Moshe. 'Will that happen again in the future, like what David wanted to suggest?'

'How? Where?'

'Muslims don't do such a thing.'

'You mean, the Jews? Or Christians? There at Masada, again?'

'It was what I could surmise what David, wanted to suggest…'

'David? How ironic when we looked at how it was another David, the King of an earlier time who had rested at the hill, after fleeing from his father-in-law, King Saul.'

'And the two women, who survived because they did not join the others to commit suicide, had hid themselves inside a cistern along with five children. They were later captured.' added Suleyman.

Moshe had wanted to discuss the next topic raised by David, which was on the Messiah, but had to stop when the Adhan appeared and he had to allow Suleyman to perform his prayers, which he did at the side of his store, as did some other Muslims who happened to be walking along the alleyway in front of it. And when Suleyman was done he returned to the store and sat on the stool and continued their earlier discussion.

'I learnt a lot from David, from his short speech that day, you know, Moshe, so I was happy that I had attended it.'

'Me too, especially when he discussed the Messiah. He is a scholar so he gave views and facts that not many of us laypersons would know…'

'With him mentioning the Messiah, I got the impression that there would still be more Jewish individuals who hold authority and immense power who would use it, not for the good of the religion, but also of the world, and…'

'And??'

'And who would drive other Jews to the New Masada!!'

Moshe was stunned. He didn't expect that his friend would see that from the way David spoke on the two subjects, the Masada and Messiah. But that was how he felt or started to feel as he had not ever thought of it before.

'Wasn't he brilliant?'

'Indeed. Indeed. But why didn't he just say so directly?'

'He wanted all of us to think for ourselves.'

'The most interesting thing on the Messiah he said was how he, or everybody, meaning all Jews, including your good self, Moshe, did not know when or how the Messiah or 'Mashiach' as you, Jews would say it, will ever come, or in what way, and during which incident; nor whether he will be in the form of a charismatic human figure or if he is a mere symbol of the redemption of humankind from the evils of the world. He also said, your religion of Judaism teaches the Jews that every individual human being must live as if he or she individually, has the responsibility to bring about the messianic age.'

Moshe suddenly paused and he tried to remember all the things that he and his friend had discussed about the speech David gave few days ago. Did all Jews know them, he asked himself, while Suleyman waited? 'What are you thinking now, Moshe?'

'Many things. But...but, why didn't anybody here in our city say that?'

'There may have been some who had said that, but not to people like us; but to students at the universities where they teach. We are not university students; we are ordinary folks, small traders in this market. And what good could he do if he were to speak before students and professors like him anyway?'

'You have a point there.'

They then went on to talk about what life was like in David's native Poland from where he had just come from, barely half a year ago, yet, he had exhibited a strong grasp of not only Hebrew he said he had learned while in Poland, but also Arabic he learned from mixing with the Arabs here in Jerusalem. 'There are approximately ten million Jews living in Europe, which comprised two percent of the total population of Europe,' said Moshe, from the figures David gave. 'This number should represent not more than sixty percent of the Jewish population in the world today which David estimates to be less than sixteen million. The majority of them in prewar Europe are located in Eastern Europe with the largest group of Jews living in Poland, where he came from, with about three million. The second largest group of Jews is found in the Soviet Union, with slightly more than two and a half million, followed by Romania, with about eight hundred million. The Jewish population in the three

Baltic states totaled a quarter of a million and in Latvia about two hundred thousand.'

'But what he did not say was David's family or ancestors might have come from here, in Palestine, too, or if they were converts to Judaism, so no wonder he spoke in Yiddish there and studied Hebrew a few years ago and is able to speak it with limited vocabulary. I see that he does not have features of Jews that I know...'

Moshe did not want to smile; and he also did not like to discuss and dwell on anyone's personal features; but he admitted that he had given that some thought too, but he did not or would not say it in the same way as his friend just did. Yes, he also thought David was not a pure Jewish man, but his heart, maybe so.

'And I suppose even according to Islam, the Jews were scattered all over the world so they may benefit the others; and that is why there are so few Jews in Jerusalem and the whole of Palestine and who are happy to live in the midst of the Arabs and whoever, they like in other parts of the world. There are even small communities of Jews in the Far East, including in Malaya,' explained Suleyman. Moshe had heard about that too, but hearing it again and this time coming directly from the mouth of his good friend, he suddenly felt there was something amiss in his life, living amongst the Arabs in The Old City and in Jerusalem and Palestine where his own ancestors had lived all their lives, many never got to go out of the country to see them with their own eyes, other than to read about them in the newspapers and other literature. Some had not even been to Haifa or Tel Aviv, much less to Damascus.

Moshe and Suleyman, behaved like they had since they were small boys who grew in the same village, who would speak in Hebrew, sometimes Arabic, and sometimes, in both languages using words from the two languages in the same sentence and only they knew what they wanted to say. And when they were older they wanted to try and speak English that was used by the British officers but with a few of the words in this language they knew then. They did not care if they sounded funny, but only they knew what they meant, although it didn't mean anything in proper English. Both of them decided not to learn the language of the colonialists, because they did not want their soul to be sold to the 'devils', as they would describe the British then. Good morning, Moshe would ask, and Suleyman would answer, 'Good morning, to you too, Moshe. How are you today? said Moshe, and Suleyman would answer by saying, I am fine! And they would laugh at each other's joke. It was not a joke; what they said made sense except that they said the same things again and again and this was what made their exchange funny, but only to them, and not to the others who sometimes heard what they were saying, but who did not know what they were saying about because they did not understand a word of English.

But when they met, they often greeted each other with, Salaam or Shalom, depending who said it first; if Moshe said it first, it would be, shalom; and if Suleyman said it first, it would be, Salaam. Sometimes, they would hug each other. When they were older the need to do so and not only when they were young, they would just jump onto each other and fall on the sand, or in the snow when it was winter, and rolling in it until they were done and had snow all over their bodies, and sometimes hidden in the pile of snow if the snowfall earlier in the night was heavy. Fortunately, all the light bruises the two of them had when they were boys disappeared over time, because they were light.

But when they grew older they decided not to make fun of the English because the English as a race were not responsible for the actions of their political and military leaders and rulers. The two of them did not have any dispute on this fact and did not dwell on it. But they decided not to learn how to speak and write in English because they feared if they did that, they would lose their soul, and become less Arab or Jew which mattered to them more than anything in the world. They didn't care about others who learned the language and started to speak with each other, not only in private but also in public. Who were they trying to impress, they thought.

Suleyman then realized that there was no one at the forum, yes, they were now describing the meeting, discussion, or speech given by David as such and not just a gathering, but a forum and wanted to ask him why he was forced to leave or flee from Poland taking with him his family. He would certainly have some good and valid reasons for fleeing the country of his birth and a place his ancestors had lived for many generations. But Moshe, was of the view that it was not proper for him or anyone to ask David such a question because it was not polite, unless Suleyman asked him the same question in private, instead of in front of everybody. Moshe would not dare to ask David the question even in private because he did not like to pry on anybody's private affairs. The brochure David had given him had some information on his background in teaching at the university in Poland but it did not describe his political and religious attitudes or thinking, and certainly nothing on the reasons why he fled Poland, leaving a lucrative job as a professor there and most likely, some properties, too.

They were now walking along the sidewalks in their residential area and were approaching Moshe's house and further away where Suleyman had his. It was also near the place which used to be an open field where they liked to play as young boys in the thick of winter where snow would cover the field, and where they would fall in it, sometimes hitting some hard objects that caused the two to suffer bruises. You remember this place, Suleyman? asked Moshe when they were there near the open field, which was no more because some people had purchased the land to build their houses and other buildings. Suleyman nodded. But the field is no more here, he said. It would be good if it is still here. Why, asked Moshe, so you can throw me in the snow in winter? That would be a very good idea, said Suleyman. Instead of getting bruises this time, I could get my bones broken. He also said he did not like to live in Rehavia, which was a predominantly Jewish community so he decided to move to our area, which he said was mixed and there were Masjid, synagogues, and churches. He thought it was a good place for his children to grow up so they may mix with boys their age. They also began to wonder if his name was indeed David because from the way he said it, it didn't sound right. Or, maybe it was the way how the Polish like him say it, Moshe added. Moshe said he had been to that area before and also found it difficult for him to relate to the people living there. They were mostly wealthy people, and not so far away was the King David Hotel where the more affluent and foreigners, who were British officers and their wives and children stayed, and where those who worked in the city would come to have their breakfast, lunch, or dinner. The British soldiers mostly wore khakis light brown in color and a bit faded, too, which stood out from the locals who were mostly wearing flowing robes, with their women in gowns and who were often wearing dark glasses when they were outdoors with their arms exposed, as opposed to the Arab and Jewish women who hid them in long sleeves. It was a very expensive place to stay or dine, I am sure, said Suleyman; I have never set foot in that exclusive area, not even once. It's seven stories…and looked grand like a palace, all washed in white. Maybe we should go there someday, Suleyman, added Moshe. Why? Just to go inside it and see how it looks like inside and how it feels to be there. Who knows if we might bump into some powerful British military and political officers there! Would they allow us in? asked Suleyman. Hmmm…That, I'm not sure, said Moshe. And both of them almost laughed at their joke, their fantasy.

They laughed and continued to walk along the sidewalk in late evening just before the cries of the Adhan from the four Masjid could be heard. And Suleyman had wanted to get to his house to perform the Maghrib prayers with his family. Suleyman then remembered their other childhood friend, Aswad, and he asked, do you remember our good friend, Aswad? Moshe did not. Who, he asked. Aswad, our good childhood friend, who also used to play with us in the snow; his parents' house was just over the low hill over there. He pointed at the low hill but it was not there anymore. In its place were some buildings that were build at least thirty years ago, when they were all very young. Ah, I think I remember him now, said Moshe. He was the guy… Christian guy, remarked Suleyman, before Moshe could even finish his sentence. I did not want to say, Christian, but a slim and tall guy. And I also did not want to say he was a slim and tall guy, but a smart guy; smarter than the two of us. Where did he go? Moshe could not remember, but Suleyman could and he said, I heard his parents decided to go to America and take him along and with his two brothers, too. America? asked Moshe. No, I did not know that.

Aswad was a Christian Arab who Suleyman and Moshe knew when they were young boys and not yet in school. After a few years they went to school but with Aswad going to another school for the wealthy, so in time their relationship became distant due to the pressures of school and Aswad's father was increasingly wealthy and became so much so by the time they were around ten, Aswad and his family had left Palestine to go to America, to New York City to live in Brooklyn, where there were many Jews living. Aswad never returned to Jerusalem or Palestine and even if he was to suddenly appear before them, they would not be able to recognize him. They also did not have any photo of him, but he might have some of them, because his father had a box camera he used to take photos of Aswad and his friends.

But Moshe and Suleyman did not think their friend would ever want to come back to Palestine anymore; and he might have gone to visit the Wailing Wall and his relatives who the two did not know. And even if Aswad had visited Jerusalem and come back he would go to the Christian Quarter where he had relatives and friends working at their stores. He would not recognize the two of us, said Suleyman. We have not changed that much, said Moshe. He could recognize us if he sees us again. You think so, asked Suleyman. I don't know.

They parted ways and Moshe entered his house; but before that he hugged Suleyman, which he had not done in many years. The reflections or the trip back in time they had earlier concerning the time when they were small boys, and then involving Aswad brought a lot of emotions pouring into his head and he felt he could hug his friend again like they used to do before. Suleyman kept quiet and after they broke their embrace, Suleyman continued to walk for about half a kilometer to get to his house. Just then the Adhan for Maghrib was called from four angles.

Moshe took out a book he had which he bought at a flea market in the Jewish Quarter, which was on Poland and the history of the Jews there, that he had not had the time or occasion to read. Now the occasion had come and he decided to take it out to read it. He had dinner and was not able to sleep. It was around ten at night. He opened the book at random and found a chapter in it and read it silently. It was written in

Hebrew and was a thick, fat book that had seen better days, having been owned by someone who was a university student or professor, because no one else would want to keep such a book. There was a name of the owner written in the inside page but that was torn, so he did not know who had owned it, before he did.

Even if it was in Arabic he would still have bought it, but not if it was written in English. The chapter was on the life of the Jews in the major cities in Poland where their population was large and overall, they formed the largest minority in the country. And over time they managed to lead in many or all aspects of intellectual, cultural, and political life there. They even created institutions and networks to spread their influences in those fields, and indirectly caused the creation of a race that was rich in intellectual tradition and creating leaders in all fields with some of the more prominent Jews starting to dabble in Zionism and Socialism, which Moshe disdained, being a Palestinian. They spoke and wrote mainly in Yiddish.

Moshe then flick the pages and found a chapter on Czar Alexander the Second of Russia; it intrigued him. What has the Czar got to do with Poland and the Jews he asked himself. He found out from reading the chapter, the Czar was assassinated in 1855. And the Jews in Russia and Poland were exposed to some attacks or organized massacred called Pogroms which was an organized action that happened after the assassination of the Czar. And as a result of that, some two million Jews decided to leave Poland and the countries in Europe and Russia, to save themselves from the Pogroms. Moshe then started to think that this might have caused David to leave Poland to come to Palestine where he was now. It was what he was guessing but the truth could never be known unless David said so himself. They were mostly the more modern Jews and not the Orthodox ones, and who took the initiative to distance themselves from the more modern Jews, in order that they would be away from harm's way and be able to protect their religion of Judaism.

Moshe's eyes suddenly widened when he got to the passage that said, the Zionists were trying to promote the idea of mass immigration out of Poland and they encourage the Jews to migrate to Palestine instead, where they thought they had a claim over it! While at the same time the other faction called Bundists were trying to unite the Jews especially those in Eastern Europe to fight for economic reform, while other Jewish leaders tried to encourage all Jews to assimilate with the local population, the natives of the countries they were living in.

He flicked the pages and found one which described how after the First World War, Poland became an independent state where there were large numbers of Ukrainians, Jews, Belorussians, Lithuanians, and ethnic Germans. Unfortunately, over time it made Poland a place that was not safe for many Jews especially when a series of Pogroms and laws that were deemed to be discriminatory to them were introduced that, in the end, caused the growth of anti-Semitism, which made it impossible for the Jews to leave the country. The three million Jews who lived in Poland were the largest minority group there.

Moshe who did not know much about the happenings in Poland suddenly realized if what he had just read was true of David who had sought and got the opportunity to leave or flee from Poland with his family while they could.

So, this could be the reason why David left Poland, said Moshe to himself and how come he did not know about Poland before he read the book he had bought at the flea market months ago? he asked himself. But could he also be an Ashkenazi Jew, too? Moshe became confused. He had heard of such people and learned a bit about them. He needed to learn about them a bit more before he could come to a better conclusion as to who they were. There was a passage in the book he was reading that caught his attention. It told him something new and interesting when it said that little was known of the Ashkenazi Jews before they were expelled from the Mediterranean. Mediterranean? He thought they were expelled from elsewhere, like Russia. Now he knew it was the Mediterranean Jews and not Russians who were forced to settle in Poland and it was long ago during the Twelfth Century. And the more interesting part was how they were said to be genetically and closely related to each other as distant cousins, either as fourth or fifth cousins, according to a professor.

But Moshe really did not care about them, as long as they professed the religion of Judaism and practiced all that the religion subscribed, as much as he also did not care if his friends were Arabs and Christians or Muslims, as long as they respected each other. Maybe David had good intentions for having the gathering or meeting or forum, because he had brought to his attention some issues concerning who they were and why there were so many Jews in Poland and other countries.

The clock on the wall of his living room sounded: It was four o'clock. Didn't have to go to his store tomorrow? No. It was Sabbath and he closed his store on this day. He would stay at home and pray. He then decided to put down the book beside him and laid down on the floor and sleep, for as long as he could. And soon, his wife would wake at six o'clock, which was barely two hours more and she would definitely want to check on her husband to see if he had woken up. He should wake up before six o'clock, like he did everyday because the Adhan for Maghrib prayers were heard, which never failed to wake him up. Sometimes he woke up on his own even before the cries for the the morning prayers for Muslims were heard.

Adhan was cried shrilly as always from the Muezzins in the four Masjid around Moshe's house and he welcomed it. He was still very sleepy having just slept for less than two hours but he decided to respect the call and wake up and sat on the floor by leaning on the wall until it was done. Then he heard sounds of footsteps, made by his wife walking down the staircase and it got louder and seemed to be approaching where he was sitting. She appeared at the doorway and looked at her husband and asked, 'Did you get a good night's sleep?' Less than two hours, he replied and told her he had been reading the book. She turned to look at the book sitting on the floor beside him and said she would prepare breakfast, and turned around to go to the kitchen.

What did I read just now, Moshe asked himself? He had forgotten what he had read. He tried to remember and all that he could remember was 'Poland', 'Ashkenazi' and 'the Mediterranean' and nothing more. What connection did they have with each other? David? And what had David got to do with them?

It was still dark outside and just a bit of the light started to appear, with the rising of the sun over the horizon, which he could not see because it was blocked by the roofs of his neighbors' houses where a field was and where the horizon was visible with the sun rising every morning when he was a small boy. He remembered Aswad. Where could he be now, he asked himself. His wife did not know Aswad, because she was not from the same area but further away, and had never met him or his family who were long gone from the area where they were, because they left it for good to go to America, to New York City to begin their new life in the Borough of Brooklyn where there was a large community of Jews of the Orthodox persuasion, who liked to live amongst themselves and many, if not most were immigrants from Europe, particularly, Poland and other countries including Russia, many of them who were Ashkenazis and Khazars, too, who were said to be converts to Judaism, an issue Moshe hope he could get David to explain further, on his own accord and without any prodding from him, because he did not like to ask personal questions such as on this matter, which was unlike him to do. And he also did not want his friend, Suleyman to ask David on his behalf; he left it to Suleyman to ask the question, if he so chose to do. But why was there any need for his friend to want to know about Jews if they were Ashkenazis or Khazars? Suleyman had brought out the issue with Moshe once and didn't like to know the answer, to it, because to him a Jew is a Jew! So what was there to ask? And for now Moshe did not know when, if ever, he would meet or bump into David again; he had met with Suleyman at his store and other places few times, but David had gone missing. Was he angry with Moshe for bringing in people to his house who did not appreciate what he had said in his speech or lecture? He did not have any answer to that; he thought he had tried his best to get as many people to listen to him, but he did not know what they were expecting to hear from David. He was not the only Jewish man from Poland who was living in their community; there were some others; the only difference between all the others and him, was that he was a former professor of a renowned university in his country. And this might be the only reason why they wanted to meet him and to listen to him to see if he had brought some news from Poland, which was also their country to share, if the situation there had changed since they came to Jerusalem and Palestine, and if they could return to their country, to live there again on their properties they had left behind. Many were disappointed when they did not hear David say anything to that effect and what he said were on issues that they did not find to be interesting, unlike Moshe and Suleyman and a few others who thought they were interesting issues, because they were not related to them directly as they did not come from there, but those who had lived all their lives in Palestine or that their ancestors had come from elsewhere for many generations ago, so they did not have any direct connection with Poland; some also did not know how many Jews were living in the country, up to three million of them.

12

Moshe and Suleyman on Jabal Suba.

It was a fine day, sunny and bright and not so cold despite the winter which was ebbing and in a few more weeks it would be early spring. Snow had cleared a bit on the pavements and ground except for the hilltops where there was a bit. Moshe and Suleyman decided to climb on their horses, to go to Jabal Suba, the conical hill that stood at seven hundred and sixty-nine meters from where they could see much of Jerusalem – or Baitulmukaddis, to look at the view of it and around them, from the height, on the clear day. They had done that many times when they were young and sometimes with Aswad, before he left the trio. Jabal Suba or 'Suba Hills' had an Arab village of not more than five hundred inhabitants living in one hundred and ten houses. It is ten kilometers west of Jerusalem. Even though the village had its history that was mentioned in some ancient text, there was no Jew living there. But the two men still had to wear thick jackets because they feared if the temperature were to suddenly go down, as it could, they would be prepared; besides it was always cold on the hilltops even in summer and when there were winds blowing too. For now, the weather seemed to be very fine and they did not have to wear the jackets that they had with them.

It was not Moshe's idea to go there, but Suleyman's who suddenly felt that they had not been there in a long time; and besides, he wanted to take his horse for a ride, for him to get some exercise. Moshe liked the idea and jumped on it and felt it was also good for his own horse he had not ridden on long distances. But sadly, Aswad was not with them.

The last time they rode their own horses to the top of Jabal Suba was more than thirty years ago, said Moshe. Thirty-five, said Suleyman. Did it matter how long ago? asked Moshe. It didn't, said Suleyman. Their horses then were not the ones they were riding on now; they were new horses. Their old horses had long died and were given decent burials.

It took them a while to get to the top of the hill from their village in Beit Ur al-Fauqa, riding for ten kilometers, and stopping at three places to rest and to have snacks. They pitied their horses for having to bear them on their backs, but they seem to enjoy the ride too because it was good for them, from being literally locked in the barns or ridden around the village most of the time. No wonder when they knew they were going on a long ride, they got excited and ran around Moshe and Suleyman, before they hopped over them.

And once they had arrived on the top of it, they stopped, perched on it to marvel and wonder at the sight in front of them, of Jerusalem that now looked totally different than what they had seen when they were young boys; it had more buildings around it and now almost covered the Temple Mount and The Old City, which looked tiny even when they were looking at them through a pair of binoculars Moshe had brought with him which he shared with Suleyman. Moshe asked Suleyman to look slight to the left and he could see The Old City but not inside of it. Amazing, said Suleyman who had not used binoculars before. It was the pair Moshe had bought from a tourist who did not want to use them anymore and sold to him for a small price he did not want to accept; but in the end they decided to trade it with another item he was selling in his store, to the delight of the tourist, who looked like he was from Nottingham in England. He said he was a researcher at a university there.

But Moshe had not gone to the top of Jabal Saba just to view the areas around it; he wanted to go there to reflect on his past and to see what the future held for him and his family and the people of Jerusalem and of Palestine. And he also wanted to trace the trips the two had made when they were young boys together with Aswad who was not living in Jerusalem anymore, but at least, the two could try and remember the times they had together. So they stood on their horses for a while. Suleyman then lowered the binoculars and handed them back to Moshe. He then climbed down from his horse to let the load off it with Moshe following suit. They let the two horses run about to relieve themselves of the burden of having to carry their owners. Moshe and Suleyman did not like to say they were the 'owners' of the two horses; they liked to say, they were their friends. They then found a boulder and sat on it, still staring at Jerusalem in front of them which looked faint, but clear to their view. Jerusalem, Baitulmukaddis, said Moshe almost to himself. This was the boulder the two and Aswad had also sat on many times before.

Suleyman then remembered something. He then pushed some of the bushes beside the boulder at his side and showed the scratch marks he had made more than three decades ago with his name and those of Moshe and Aswad's. See these? he asked Moshe who had almost forgotten about the scratch marks they had made. He turned around and looked at the marks and remembered them with the year, 1909.

It was clear how Moshe and Suleyman were looking at the scenery around them that focused on a city which was close to five thousand years old, from different views; Moshe called it Jerusalem while Suleyman called it Baitulmukaddis; and both were correct; the city was for the Peoples of the Book, Jews, Christians, and Muslims. Both stared at the sight around them and thinking of how lucky they were to be able to live in such a city that not many in the world could get to do, even if they were given the chance to come and live there. Many might want to come over but not many could afford to stay there; they had to be born there to know what it was and what it meant. Ironically, those who had been given the opportunity to be born there had chosen to leave it. Aswad came to mind. But he was a mere young boy who was taken out of the city to go to America to live in the Borough of Brooklyn in the City of New York, and it was a decision that was not made by himself but by his parents. Moshe hoped Aswad would one day return to the city, even as a visitor, so they could meet again. He must be successful there in New York City and probably dealing in the business of trading in gold which the Jews there were good at, and hopefully, a staunch Orthodox

Jew like Moshe hoped he still was. He thought he was still a staunch Jew like he had been, but he might have gone astray a bit over the years of growing up in uncertain times and in many uncertainties that life had shown him, from being a young boy, to a young man, and now a happily married man with three children all grown up to become their own individuals and who would soon go on their separate ways. Hopefully none would take the long journey by boat to cross the Atlantic Ocean to go to America, where he knew some of the young men had gone in the last few years, all without saying goodbye, not telling anyone why they had made the decision to go live in a new country they had not been to before and learn how to speak a new language that many were not familiar with, except for some who had been in close contact with some of the British who were occupying Palestine, from a long time ago to the establishment of the British Mandate of Palestine in 1922.

What was Suleyman thinking? He had been quiet and was staring at Baitulmukaddis, not saying what he was thinking of then, whether he was not happy with the sight of the many Jews who had come not only from Poland but from other countries, too. And he had not said anything about David, one of the Jews who had come from Poland, and he had also not said why he decided to leave Poland to come to Palestine, which was exactly the opposite of what the other Jews who had chosen to leave Palestine to go to America, like Aswad and his family had done.

Moshe had told Suleyman that Jews mostly liked to move; they hated to stay in one place; so no wonder they could be found in various populations in almost all the major cities in Europe, which Suleyman called, Crusader Territory or Region, so they could mix with the locals. Moshe had to explain that it was stated in their Holy Torah that it was this that had been ordered by their God for them to do. But why were some of the Jews who had been there for ages, wanting to return to Palestine or to go to America and elsewhere?

All these questions that had crept into Moshe's and Suleyman's private thoughts they had not thought of before, but they knew these were the same type of questions that many other Jews and also Arabs were asking themselves. Maybe David could give them the correct and right answers to them, that they themselves could not because the whole matter was beyond them and their limited intellect.

The day was fine, then suddenly cries of the Adhan for Zohor were heard coming from all directions especially from the Masjid on the ground in the villages where there were two of them and others further away in the other villages. Because they were perched on the top of Jabal Suba, they could hear the cries booming and reverberating. It caused Suleyman to stop wondering; he immediately picked some fine desert sand and did the ablution with Moshe watching. He then went to the side where there was a space that was even and started to perform his prayers. The two horses that were running around stopped like they were ordered to do so. They could tell if the cries were of the Adhan or noises of people talking loudly with other and knew how to stop doing what they were doing until the cries stopped.

Suleyman did a long supplication after the prayers and once he was done, he went back to the boulder to sit. 'Isn't it time for lunch, Moshe?' he asked. There was food in the side bag on his horse. 'I have some with me. Want to have some?'

Moshe nodded and the two sat to eat lunch. Suleyman gave something for the two horses to eat and drink and they showed their full appreciation by neighing loudly a few times to their 'friends'. He patted them a few times on their back and said to them, 'Good job, my friends.' He held a string of prayer beads on his right hand called 'tasbih' and continued to touch each of the beads so the string turned in a circle as a counter to the supplication he was reading or saying to himself by heart.

Then it was time for them to talk again after being quiet for a long while. Suleyman remarked that they had 'let the angels stay for so long', now that they were gone it was time for them to talk; but he chose not to bring up the matters that they had been discussing for a while now after the gathering at David's house a few nights ago. He proposed that they talk about food, Palestinian Arab food and Jewish food; both had similar flavors and taste. And both of them liked their food. The first type of food that came to Moshe's mind were 'hummus' and 'falafel'; Suleyman said he liked both. What about 'maqlouba', asked Suleyman, and Moshe said, That too, and why not? They are all good, tasty, and above all very nutritious. They are made from a few layers of meat and rice. And Suleyman added, 'And fried vegetables…. cauliflower, eggplant, potatoes, and also not forgetting carrots, too. (Maqlouba' means 'upside down' in Arabic, which Moshe knew, and said it was then topped with fried nuts or fresh herbs to make it even more tasteful, and very easy and cheap to prepare. But most of the food available in Palestine for the Arabs and Jews to eat were also available in most if not all the other Arab countries, too.

There was no denying that the two seemed to share the same passion for food and who would eat together and the same things that they could get at the sidewalk cafés and restaurants, but till now they had never ever talked about food in such a way before like they were cooking in the kitchen. The only reason why they strayed from their normal everyday discourses that mostly centered on what they were doing and how their business was doing, today, in the warm winter day when it was bright and sunny, and now well-fed with food they had brought with them to the top of Jabal Suba, they decided unanimously to talk about this subject. They did not say it in words, but they thought they had had with the forum and tried to analyze it as much as they could and also as deep as they could but in the end, they realized that all that they could do was to guess or second guess what David had in his mind of saying; and this could only be determined by he himself, not by Moshe and Suleyman. But they enjoyed the discourses they had created post-forum to see later if what they had guessed matched with what David had in mind of saying in his speech.

Food was never that important to the two of them other than it was for their subsistence and not as a topic to discuss and deliberate upon in such details, they thought; but that day, they were forced by circumstances and liked it when they, for the first time, spoke with each other about such things that they had taken for granted for too long with Suleyman surprising Moshe and vice versa when they admitted to each other how they would often cook at home for their families. Both cooked shawarma a lot and often took some to their stores to eat for snacks or for lunch because it was easy to prepare and keep in their lunch bags to carry around. And only sometimes did they find food at the sidewalk cafés and restaurants to eat for lunch if they had to rush to their stores and did not have the time to cook. Or when their wives were away at their parents' house with their children. Shawarma with lots of gravy, said Moshe, seconded by Suleyman. They don't cause any man to become fat, eating them, said Moshe, because they are nutritious and do not have a lot of fats. Look at me, he added, I have never been fat in my life; and you too, Suleyman, or Leyman as he would often call his friend, when he felt closer to him, or especially when he wanted to indicate to him that he was not being serious and might be joking, except he did not want to be described as a funny person. He liked to remain serious and stoic in any circumstances, because he was trained to be that way by his father and grandfather, a trait that he had inculcate in his sons, too.

The sun had dimmed a bit and the temperature was starting to become cold again. Moshe went to his horse and grabbed his jacket and put it on. He then went to Suleyman's horse and grabbed his jacket and took it to Suleyman who put his on. Both felt better now and not chilly like they were earlier. There was silence. Both looked at the sun that was going down into the horizons they could see from the hilltop. By now much of Jerusalem and The Old City had been covered by thick fog. It was time for them to turn around and ride their horses to return to their homes in the valley below.

Both of them felt better after taking the ride to the top of Jabal Suha where they had spent close to two hours, arriving there just before Zohor, and throughout the whole time they felt like they were at another place altogether, like it was not in Jerusalem and not in Palestine, from where they could not see anyone in the valley below them, except for buildings that were more now than they were before the last time they were there perched on the top of the hill. It would soon be Asar, and Suleyman planned to do the prayers in Masjid Al-Aqsa and later to give his horse a bath and a good rest for the night.

And as the two were approaching the cities and villages along the way from the hill top back to their village, they started to catch whiffs of the sweet aromas of foods cooked by the women in the houses whose kitchens had smoke rising from them; the women were busy preparing food or were heating food to serve their families for dinner.

There were so many types of delicious and palatable Palestinian food such as 'Ka'ak Al-Quds', 'Sfihaat', 'Shorbet 'Adas', 'Chicken and freekeh salad'. And Jewish food, such as, 'Hummus' and 'Tahini', delicious 'Israeli Falafel', divine Israeli 'Shakshuka' and a popular Middle Eastern salad 'Tabbouleh' and wholesome Israeli salad. The Israeli foods list ends with appetizing bread from Israel and the world's popular Middle Eastern 'Shawarma' and 'Kebab an also 'lafa (or, Taboon bread). And for the Jews they had the 'challah' bread which is an Israeli bread traditionally baked for holidays and 'Shabbath' and taken with drinks such as 'sahlab' and 'arak', that are served at different times of the day or night or during holidays or everyday that they had accepted to be theirs regardless whether they were Arabs or Jews that their ancestors had cooked and perfected using influences they received from the countries around them as far as Egypt where the 'kebab' was said to have originated from.

They thought it was good to talk about food, and thinking about it, when they were on the top of the hill where the aromas of those foods were not present and what was left was their imagination. And now when they were back in the valley with the hill hovering above them at their back, a good ten kilometers away and with the light of the day having dimmed considerably, feeling tired, exhausted, and also hungry and thirsty, the memories of those foods made them even more excited to be back at their own homes, where they could sample some of them.

The cries of the Adhan for Maghrib were sounded and coming simultaneously from all directions. Suleyman and Moshe prayed quietly for their personal safety at being able to return to their village where their wives and children were waiting.

Before they rode on in different directions when they got to a junction, Moshe asked his friend about the trip. Suleyman said he enjoyed it; and he'd like it if they could go up the Jabal Suha again, and if they had the time, he wouldn't mind if they camped on the top of the hill for a night or two so they could marvel at the sight of the valley below them in semi-darkness and in total darkness to experience the wonders of nature and what God had offered Mankind to savior, and to be with Nature. Moshe said it was a good idea; and it was not too late for them to do it at least once before they became too old and too weak to ride their horses for long distances. Suleyman patted the neck of his horse and thanked him for the good and enjoyable ride to the hill and back. It neighed. We make good friends, he told the horse. He turned to Moshe's horse and thank it too in like manner but was not able to give it a pat on its neck because it was a distance away from him. Moshe did the patting for him. They then greeted with 'Shalom' and 'Salaam' and rode off in different directions and soon both disappeared in total darkness with the sounds of the feet of their horses making the noise 'clip-cloping' as they trotted slowly back to their 'friends' houses along narrow village lanes that had some snow at the side that was melting, with Suleyman and Moshe feeling triumphant at their success in climbing the hill and getting reconnected with their past, although they, especially Moshe was tinged with sadness because Aswad was not around to make a trip for the trio to conquer together. It was not a place for many to go to under any circumstances, unlike the two who had some good and valid reasons to go there.

Suleyman could not sleep that night despite being tired; he just could not close his eyes as he lay on the couch in his living room on the ground floor. He remembered Salehuddin Al Ayubi, the Arab hero, who recaptured Baitulmukaddis from the Crusaders and won their hearts because he did not exhibit any aggression against any of them even when he was triumphant. However, he did not like it when the Crusaders called him Saladin. What name is that? he asked himself. Even Moshe despised the name. The Crusaders had gained control over what they called Jerusalem for over eighty-eight years, a very long time by any stretch of the imagination, and by the time Salehuddin Al Ayubi died in 1193 CE he had managed to create an Emirate which stretched from Tunisia to Iran destroying all the countries along the way, and all the while exhibiting positive traits, humanity, and humility to those he had vanquished without torturing and further reducing their stature as humans.

Meanwhile Moshe was thinking of Aswad again. Why was he thinking of him? Moshe didn't know; he didn't care to try and reason out why Aswad had been occupying his mind for a while now and all that he could think of was how they had spent a lot of time together as young boys together with Suleyman. Then suddenly, he was missing from his life; he and his parents did not inform anyone in their village that they would be leaving to go very far away from everybody. So no one knew exactly when they left their house, because it happened one day when everybody else was busy with their own chores to worry about them. Besides Aswad's father was not exactly what one could call a friendly person. He liked to keep things to himself, which was okay for everybody who lived around him, as long as he did not do anything harmful to anyone else. But he knew deep in his heart, Aswad would return to Jerusalem to check out the place, and he supposed that Aswad was now a successful businessman living in Brooklyn in New York City. He, however, never thought that he would like to go there to live. He was happy to live here in Jerusalem, all his life. But he was not certain if his son, Daghlas, might be keen to go there when he grew older than he was now. That's his life, he said to himself; and if he so chooses to go out of Jerusalem to lead a new life in New York City or anywhere in the world, the decision would be for him to make, as long as he was happy and was capable of managing his own life.

13

Moshe, Suleyman, and David

Moshe worked in his store by himself like on any other days before for what seemed to be a long while. And suddenly a surge of customers converged on his store looking for a lot of things. He had not seen such customers before, looking like they were from very far, from some countries in Central Asia and most likely Muslims too from the way they were dressed, with the men in large turbans and the women in long flowing robes and speaking in a language he could not understand that sounded like Farsi. They seemed to like everything they saw and wanted to buy everything they held. Moshe remained quiet and allowed them to browse the items on display on the shelves and on the floor. They did not bargain which Moshe found to be strange; and they paid for everything at the price Moshe said and in the end each of the Japanese men and women, amounting to a dozen of them left with a large bag full of things they had bought from him. Moshe thought it was his lucky to have such a large group of customers early in the day who hardly said anything. They were traders themselves in their country, who bought things to resell in their stores, so they knew how not to bargain because they knew the prices Moshe had given them were very reasonable indeed and they could still make a tidy profit from what they had bought, items that would surely attract the attention of the buyers back in their countries.

But Moshe was not able to call it a day despite having made some good sales that day; he had to replenish the stock on the shelves which was almost bare with new things to sell. It was tiring because to bring them out from boxes that he had put in the storeroom behind the store. It tired him a bit and he stopped to have a drink and then another drink to replenish his body with fluid, and later on with some food for lunch that his wife had prepared this time, shawarma sandwiches, his favorite food for lunch with a few other pieces to take later and also to share with Suleyman if he came by, who also sometimes brought more shawarma or falafel to eat together. He had had some falafel yesterday and a change to shawarma would be a nice change to take with some water he had got from a well near his house that gave mineral water that came from underground and fresh. Some of the villages alleged it to contain unusual purities that were good to cleanse the body with. It was free as the well was not owned by anyone but the public and was dug long ago by someone who had lived in the village who had long died of old age. He felt good that day with his business and with himself; he attributed it to the ride he and Suleyman had made to the top of Jabal Suha. If his friend came by again, he wanted to make sure he asked him to go back to the top of the hill again. Surprisingly, his body did not feel any sprain or muscle pull riding for ten kilometers from his village to the hill and another ten kilometers riding back to the village. But he did give himself a self-massage of his calves that had inflamed a bit. Other than that he was okay.

David had not been to the Old City in more than a week, but it seemed longer because he had spent too much time worrying about the speech he gave to the local Jews and Arabs; and he was worried to meet with Moshe to ask for his comments on it, lest if he might say, it was a horrible one. The others who attended the forum in David's house had disappeared. They did not know what was expected of them at the forum and afterwards, because Moshe did not tell them what the purpose was for attending it other than to listen to 'someone from Poland' speak. Initially they were all not too excited with the invitation, until Moshe said the person from Poland was a professor at the University of Warsaw; this made them wonder a bit more on how they ought to behave and to wear, although there wasn't any real need for all of them to worry about what to wear, simply because they usually wear the same clothes almost everyday, their traditional wear and Suleyman who agreed to attend the gathering because he could not decline any invitation from his good friend, Moshe, who mostly wore the Arabian robes and hardly any western clothes.

So David decided to go to the Old City where he said he wanted to meet with Moshe, and if possible Suleyman, too, to seek their views and feedback on his speech at the forum which they did not have the time to do immediately after the forum as it was already too late for David to hold them back any longer.

So David appeared in front of Moshe's store and saw him writing something in his ledger book on the sales he had made earlier. He stood there for a while before greeted Moshe with, 'Shalom.' It did not sound like Suleyman or anyone he was familiar with. Moshe replied the greeting in like manner and looked in front of his store and was surprised to see David standing there by himself. 'Do come in, Mr. David.' David walked in and Moshe offered him a wooden stool to sit on. 'Here, have a seat.' David sat and remained quiet which caused Moshe to start to worry. 'Is there anything wrong?'

'I just had to come and talk with you, Moshe. I hope I won't take too much of your time. Are you busy? I saw you with some customers from Central Asia, I presume at your store and did not want to disturb you until you were done with them. Where's your friend, Suleyman?'

'Oh, he has his store in the Muslim Quarter. Want to see him?'

The three of them sat in a sidewalk café in the Muslim Quarter, after Moshe's son, Daghlas came to take over the store from him. He and David then walked to the Muslim Quarter and met Suleyman at his store and he joined them to sit in the café. David thought he was better there because there were not many Jews, some who might have been at the forum he gave. Moshe and Suleyman did not know what else David wanted to say to them this time. Suleyman's store was not so far away and his wife was looking after it with his eldest son.

David started to ask the two what he thought of his speech that night, and Suleyman said it was interesting. Moshe, said, it was very interesting. But how come many did not feel that way, he asked. Most had not expected what he wanted to say and were not prepared, said Moshe; besides, many had to leave because they lived further away in the village, at its edge, and had come on horses, mules, and some in carts, and as it was in winter and snow was falling quite heavily in the areas where they were living.

Moshe especially liked the information on the University of Warsaw David had studied at and went on to teach there for many years until he became a professor. It was the largest and most prestigious university in Poland, established in 1816 and had more than forty thousand students and offered more than thirty different fields of study at the fifteen faculties. He apologized to David for not respecting him the first time and the second time he came to his store, because he did not know who he was then, and was shocked to learn that he was a university professor at the university. Suleyman said he was impressed with Moshe's memory and could explain in every detail on the university just from listening to David talked about it without even jotting the information down and by remembering it by heart, a bit of it Suleyman said he could remember.

David was happy to hear Moshe talked about his university and he went on to further explain that during the First World War, Warsaw was seized by the Germans in 1915. He was a young university lecturer then, after graduating from the university a few years earlier so he knew what life was about not only in Warsaw, the capital of Poland, but of Poland itself and found himself together with the other teaching staff out of work. However, in order to pacify the Polish people, the German, Austrian, and Hungarian leaders allowed for some liberation of life in their country, which was in accordance with 'Mitteleuropa' which was a concept they used whereby they permitted several Polish social, cultural, and educational groups or societies to be reintroduced in order that they did not suffer any backlash from their action to control Poland by military force. The Polish language was reintroduced and the professors were allowed to return to work. However, the number of lecturers who were allowed to return to work was deliberately reduced to around fifty persons only. The reason being to not let them to feel patriotic and start to create a national movement to free their land, our Poland, said David.

They had ordered a 'dallah' of tea and had taken sips of it in their own cups that were laid on the table in front of them. Suleyman was at a loss as to why David was talking about his university and the fall of Poland to the Germans. He tried to guess what the main trust of his point was but still couldn't. He assumed his friend, Moshe had started to get a grasp of what David was going to say. The two of them did not blame the others for leaving the talk at the gathering because David was speaking in his own style, that of a professor and the others were mostly laypersons that did not have the capacity to look at the issue beyond their personal everyday experiences. The two hoped they would soon know what David was driving at, and when that moment happened, they would appreciate him better.

David then repeated what he had said about how after the First World War, Poland became a democratic independent state with minority populations, that included Ukrainians, Jews, Belorussians, Lithuanians, and other ethnic Germans. However, the country became a hostile state for many Jews when Polish nationalism crept into the minds of the population that finally created anti-Semitic sentiments amongst them following a series of pogroms and other laws that were discriminatory to the Jews were legislated. This forced many of the three million Jews to leave Poland for other countries that were safer for them to live in.

David said this with a stone face, but Moshe and Suleyman began to get closer to his heart, the main reason for the forum he gave at his house that was not clear then, but it was now. So now they could guess why David and his family had to flee from Poland, to save their lives. They couldn't believe that the Jews who had been living in Poland for ages, or at least since the Middle Ages when the Crusaders moved through Europe in the Thirteenth Century with Jews seeking safety in Poland where with the laws passed by King Kazimierz Wielki or King John Casimir the Great in the early Fourteenth Century, they were able to thrive and become good citizens so that by the Sixteenth Century, eighty percent of the Jews in the world could be found in Poland, where they became prominent members and leaders of society in various endeavors and social and cultural activities, so much so that they were even able to introduce new religious movements known as the 'Hasidim', which was a sect in Judaism that emphasized the mystic, praying, and another reformation movement called the 'Haskalah' that did not exist before. However, unbeknownst to many outside Poland, the Jews who were successful and wealthy were small in number and were merchants and bankers, with the vast majority comprised of the poor and whose fortunes became worse when Poland came under the control of Russia and they were forced to eke a decent living working as traders, and as semi-skilled craftsmen in the traditional and new industries such as the textile industry and so on. Many were forced to become shopkeepers getting low wages and a few took up farming, while the rest were destitute. And over time, those cities that had a sizeable Jewish community became the cultural, religious, intellectual, and artistic centers of Jews in the world who then developed an extensive and varied network of institutions for cultural and literary institutions and charitable bodies to help other Jews who were not as lucky as others who were. The side affects of all these developments saw the emerging of religious trends introduced by religious elders who competed with each other and introduced new political theories and ideologies that distracted many Jews in Poland, including Zionism and Socialism which were all discussed in greater details in many books, journals, and even stage plays, but which were all written in Yiddish and not in Hebrew.

That was the history of the Jews in Poland, said David which was brief as it was, but dramatic no less. Both Moshe and Suleyman although not students of history, were still attracted to the fears that the Jews where forced to experience living in a foreign land called Poland, where despite their large number, were still being slowly persecuted until they were forced to leave the country to go where they hoped to get a better life for themselves and their families.

Maybe they were lucky to be living in Jerusalem and Palestine, thought Moshe. The last political upheaval they had in Jerusalem was during the time of the Crusaders that ended with the sudden appearance of Salehuddin Al Ayubi or Saladin so now they were able to live in peace and harmony with each group divided according to their religion or

Judaism, Christianity, and Islam, yet, were able to live with each other. And this was what had drawn David to come with his family.

A waiter came to their table and asked if they needed anymore drinks or food. David looked at Moshe and Suleyman to ask them if they needed anything else, but both shook their heads slightly to indicate that they did not need anything else. They had had a lot to eat and drink over the last two hours they had sat there. Moshe and Suleyman did not want to think that the waiter had come to shoo them away because the crowd at the café was not big and there were many vacant chairs and tables. They would have gone earlier if this was not the case.

David felt very exhausted; the explanation he had given the two seemed simple, but it took a toll on him. He sweated a bit despite the cold weather outside. He also had removed his overcoat and hat to make himself more comfortable. Moshe took the bill that was left on the table by the waiter earlier but David immediately grabbed it from him. 'I'll take that,' he said. He remembered he did not mention the fact that Poland was under colonial rule for one hundred and eighty years until 1918, because it would sound dramatic, but just could not find the place in the discussion with the two, to bring up this matter.

The three walked along the side of the road to return to Moshe's store in the Jewish Quarter passing many Arabs who were Christians and Muslims who were strangers, but still greeted each other with 'Salaam' or 'Shalom' and were responded to in like fashion. Two of the men who greeted him along the alleyway were those who had attended the forum at his house. They stopped David to tell him how sorry they were because they could not understand fully what he was saying; they did not want to hurt his feelings by saying his speech in his style of Hebrew was confusing and to make it worse was his foreign Polish-sounding accent, so they only knew a fraction of what he had said. David was quick to apologize to the two for making them sit for close to two hours to listen him speak on topics which might have been too difficult for them to fully understand, and also the fact that his Hebrew was not so good. The men then walked away and allowed David to move along with Moshe and Suleymen in the other direction. Although they did not say it, but the Spanish Flu that broke out in 1918 that caused fifty million people around the world to die with many in Palestine and Poland, that also caused some of their relatives and friends to die, seemed to be far away from their mind as they tried to look ahead to their future, to the future of Palestine and the whole world... David was old enough to remember the outbreak of the epidemic, and he was already an adult but not Moshe and Suleyman who were still young and had no idea of what it was when it happened. They were bundled out of their villages to live in the rural areas where their parents thought they would be safer.

Moshe and Suleyman did not know if David would continue with his lecture; but they were willing to listen to him because they felt sorry for him, for being forced to leave Poland and come to their city and country, where it was peaceful. They did not want to ask him about that. But they would leave it to him to decide if he had more to talk about and they were willing to sit with him and listen.

What was inside David's head? Plenty! He had a few more things to bring to the two before they knew what they were getting into and he did not want to be so direct in discussing the pressing issues that concerned the two of them and everybody in Jerusalem and Palestine and the good relations they had had since the arrival of Salehuddin Al Ayubi.

Moshe and Suleyman returned to their stores while David decided to take a walk to the Wailing Wall to pray even though he hardly ever went there because he did not feel it was good for him to pray before the Wall which he considered to be a part of the Masjid Al-Aqsa that the others didn't know. He knew because he had conducted a study on the history of the Wall and the Masjid. Besides, it was a fine day and it didn't make him tired to walk the distance to go to the Wall and spend some time there after which he said he would take a horse-cart back to his house. It would be about sunset by the time he got to his house where he hoped to read more on the First Zionist Congress held at the Stadtcasino in Basel, Switzerland in from 29 to 31 August, 1897 that he had mentioned a bit at the forum he gave in his house which he had to cut short because it didn't seem to get a lot of attention from his guests who did not know much about since it happened so long ago when all of them were not born yet. In Jerusalem and Palestine there was no literature or book on it that anyone here could read. He hoped Moshe and Suleyman would be more interested in the matter from the way they had shown a lot of interest on the topics he talked about with them earlier at the café.

David was much older than Moshe and Suleyman, at fifty-six years old and he was born in 1880 in Warsaw, so when the First Zionist Congress was held in Basel, Switzerland he was a young man, a student at high school at seventeen years old. He never heard of the Congress when it was held, but maybe...just maybe, his grandfather and father had gone to Basel to attend it, not as participants but observers, meaning they were at the venue but not in the hall where the Congress was held. So they knew more about what happened in the Congress from what was shared to the public and from some of the participants who attended it, who they had met during the lunch and dinner break and also in the street cafés on the weekend that the Congress was held.

At seventeen years old, David was alert to what was going in Warsaw and Poland and what the colonizers were doing to their country, and mostly to the Jews, including him. He was a bright student too, and was destined to gain a place to study at the University of Warsaw a year or two after the Congress. He might even had bumped into Theodor Herzl, who came to visit some of the Jewish leaders before and after the Congress. But he could not remember well, if it was him or his brother who looked like him. Theodor was born in 1860 so he was twenty years older than David when the Congress was organized and he died seven years after it at the young age of forty-four years in Reichenau an der Rax, Austria-Hungary and was buried in Döblinger Friedhof, Vienna in Austria where he majored in Law at the University of Vienna, and was described as 'Father of Political Zionism.' Many alleged him to be so, but the early beginnings of Zionism could be attributed to other Jewish religious leaders who had the same idea, many of them religious such as Rabbis Yehuda Bibas, Zvi Hirsch Kalischer, and Judah Alkalai, promoted a range of ideas that were described as proto-Zionist ideas before him.

He remembered the time when he first enrolled at the university with the other students, lining up to register for the first time as a student, a university student, he kept reminding himself and walking like he was floating now that he was one of the many hundreds of students who had just joined the ranks of students of the same university. He did not care and did not want to know how the others felt having registered as a student and becoming one, if they, too, like him, were walking on air the whole day until reality came crashing down on him, when challenges had to be faced when they came along. He dreaded it when he realized that the 'fatality rate' of students who did not make it in the first year was not so high but was still there; he hoped he did not become one who did not get through the first year. But at least he had given that a thought even if he knew he would not become a victim of his tardiness and would pursue his education there and graduate from the university. He had no plans post-university; he might pursue a graduate degree or find employment as a teaching staff there.

It felt good to be a student of the University of Warsaw, he thought.

Theodor had already graduated in Law at the University of Vienna, he said to himself, and he had gone underground, joining some groups which were left-leaning, whatever that meant then, so no wonder he later became what he had become afterward for organizing the First Zionist Congress in Basel in December, 1897 when David was twenty years old and had just joined the university in Warsaw. It would also be good if he could further his studies at the same university for his masters except that his German was not good; he spoke Polish and Yiddish. He had never been to Vienna or Austria before, but his parents had been there a few times, driving there a distance of six hundred and seventy kilometers and taking more than a day to get there passing through lush forest and some plains, enjoying the beautiful countryside; but they often drove through Krakow, in Poland, where they had some friends where they would spend a bit of time, before driving on in their old Russian-made vehicle that took a long time to get there because it could not run very fast. At least it was better than riding horse-driven carts, they thought.

David did not sleep the whole night because his mind was feeling active with the flashbacks occurring which brought him back to the time when he was a student at the University of Warsaw and his reminiscences of Theodor, who he never met; but his parents did, and told him what they thought about him. Did he ever want to be like him? he asked himself. No, he never did want to do that because he was not impressed by the description that his parents had of him; nor was he ever impressed by what he had done at the Congress. David had carried the thoughts and memories of Theodor the whole of his life until now when he was in Jerusalem and meeting with Moshe and Suleyman. Theodor had long died in July, 1904 and buried in Vienna, dying at a young age of forty-four years, followed by his wife, Julie Naschauer, who died soon after. He took out a copy of an old German newspaper, the Der Judenstaat, when Theodor wrote: 'The Jewish question persists wherever Jews live in appreciable numbers. Wherever it does not exist, it is brought in together with Jewish immigrants. We are naturally drawn into those places where we are not persecuted, and our appearance there gives rise to persecution. This is the case, and will inevitably be so, everywhere, even in highly civilized countries – see, for instance, France – so long as the Jewish question is not solved on the political level.' He then made his first trip to Jerusalem in October, 1989, a year after the Congress, where he sought to be recognized as the founder of Zionism, and on 29 October, he met Wilhelm II for the first time in Mekveh, but the meeting was brief, but still historic. They met up again the second time on 2 November, 1898 on the Streets of the Prophets in Jerusalem, where David said he would go soon, now that he had remembered the name of the street in the city where he was in now, to see it and mostly, to feel how it was like back in 1898 when Theodor, was there. There might be some people there who would remember the meeting, and if they were in their twenties, they would now be in their sixties or early seventies, and not too old to forget the incident. He had seen many old men in the streets and alleyways in the Old City especially and other parts of Jerusalem who might be witness to the meeting between Theodor and King Wilhelm the Second.

He had been to Mekveh once; it was a small city near the Mediterranean Sea and about seventy kilometers from Jerusalem. He went there with his wife because they also wanted to visit Tel Aviv and see the Mediterranean Sea, and sit on the beach looking at it.

For some unknown and strange reason, David preferred to call Theodor Herzl by his first name and not his surname.

The next day, David strolled along the street and saw some old men, Arabs and Jews. He tried to study them to see who might have any news or information on the meeting of the two men; and surely from looking at some of them, they would have been alive when the meeting took place. But how could he approach any of them to ask about it? He went to a sidewalk café and sat at a table, and beside him were two elderly Arab men speaking with each other in Arabic, which he did not understand. Then the men switched to speaking in Hebrew that he could understand a little bit. They stopped to drink and chew some local food. One of them turned out to be an Arab Christian and the other, an Arab Muslim. It was quite clear that they were talking about the weather that now had become fine with the winter spent and early spring just starting. They did not wear thick jackets over their robes as did David who was wearing western-style clothes and looking like a foreigner or tourist, with his hat. He removed it and put it on his lap because he did not like to put it on the table because he feared there might be germs in his hat for sure.

He tried to start a connection with the two Arab men by turning to look at them to indicate that he was keen to communicate with them. The Arab men did not realize they were being stared at and continued to talk with each other. The waiter came to ask for orders from David; he spoke in Hebrew for tea, hot tea, he said. No food? No. And a while later the same waiter reappeared from the back of the café and put a cup of tea on David's table with a small 'dallah' made of bronze. He poured some tea in the cup and left with the Arab men still talking to each other. Then suddenly one of the men stood up and said something in Arabic and hugged his friend and left. David thought this might be a good chance for him to break the ice by introducing himself, by saying something to the Arab man who was now sitting alone. He took a sip of tea from his cup and stared in front of them at the men and women walking along the alleyway. He then turned around and smiled at David and asked, 'You from England?' speaking in English that was heavily in his Arabic accent. David was relieved; he said, 'No.'

'And where are you from?'

'Poland. Warsaw, Poland.'

'That is very far away from here.'

David nodded.

'I have been wondering where you might have come from, with my friend, and he said he could not tell either.'

David was shocked that the two Arab men were talking about him earlier and not about something else more mundane. He then decided to talk straight and asked the man, 'Do you live around here?'

'Yes, all my life, I was born here, and I do not know how much longer I will be alive,' he said almost trying to make fun of his long life. 'I am eighty years old, you know? But I am still able to move around on my own, unaided.'

David then realized that the man might know something about the meeting between Theodor and King Wilhelm the Second that took place when he was not a young boy, but a young man. 'Were you here in 1898?'

'Oh, yes, I was in the early thirties then. Why? Is there anything special happening?'

'Theodor and King Wilhelm the Second...'

'Ah, I remember that...the meeting of the two that happened in a building along this street over there; there were many people... But I did not know what they were doing and talking about until I read about it in the newspaper the next day...'

'You have such good memory...'

'Such events had never happened here before, so I can still remember it.'

David learnt from the man that Theodor had discussed with King Wilhelm II about the First Zionist Congress held in Basel in August, 1897 and a few months later he came to Jerusalem to meet the King. Theodor told him what they did in the Congress which, among other things, was for the Zionists to undertake the formation of the Zionist platform; the foundation of the Zionist Organization; the adoption of the 'Hatikvah' as its anthem and the adoption of the most of the previous 'Hovevei Zion' societies, with the suggestion of the establishment of the people's bank. The last resolution was to elect Theodor as the President of the Zionist Organization and Max Nordau as one of the three Vice-Presidents.

David had read about it in the newspapers in Warsaw, and he liked to remind himself of those resolutions, to refresh his memory. He was glad to have met the Arab man who had all the time in the world to speak with him on the meeting of Theodor and King Wilhelm II, although he did not care so much about what the two had said other than what was reported in the local newspapers in Hebrew and Arabic. He didn't ask for the Arab man's name and the Arab man also did not ask for his. They shook hands when the Arab man, who was a Christian man, said he had to go and left David to sit on his chair all by himself to finish the tea in the 'dallah' and to wonder where he would like to do next, which was to wander around the place and to visit the building where the meeting took place, as it was a nice and fine day, in the early spring there. He was surprised to see that both Arab men looking the same with the same facial features and wearing the same clothes, robes and speaking in Arabic but they were Muslim and Christian, unlike the Jewish men who had their different clothes to wear and also language they were speaking in who could be determined to be Jews even when they were young, because of that. However, he was told by some Arab Muslims that the Arab Christians had started to wear different clothing, especially the women but also men, who now were wearing more western-style clothes that the earlier generations of Arab Christians did not, just like the Jews in Poland and also he, himself – who realized that he too did not look like his father and grandfather when it came to wearing everyday clothes. Will it be much worse for the Jewish men in America, David asked himself. There were a lot of Jews in New York City who mostly lived in the Borough of Brooklyn, many were of the Orthodox persuasion.

The day was fine in the Streets of the Prophets where David was sitting in another sidewalk café and having another small 'dallah' of tea.

This time he had a piece of shawarma sandwich and falafel to eat for lunch he got from the café. He saw some British soldiers walking about in the streets, some of who could speak in Arabic and were seen talking to the local shopkeepers and the members of the public who knew them, from the way how they interacted with each other, in a very casual and friendly manner. The British had been in Palestine for so long they felt comfortable with their presence.

'How are you, mister?' one young boy asked the British soldiers. 'I am fine, thank you. Have you eaten?'

Did he know what he was asking the British soldiers? David asked himself; Maybe not. The soldiers did not respond in English; they responded in perfect Arabic, to say they were fine and had just taken lunch in the café further down. One of the soldiers then patted the Arab boy's head before he walked away, the boy feeling excited to have made communication with the British.

There are not that many women in the public space, David wondered to himself; and even if there were women, they were mostly with their husbands and hardly any of them could be seen walking alone, even with their children. He also noticed that in the Jewish Quarter the scene was the same with few Jewish women present.

David felt happy to have met with Moshe and Suleyman and had spoken with them a bit in the café, but he hoped they could meet up again. He had returned to his house in Beit Ur al-Fauqa and it was night. He opened a window in his living room to let in some cool breeze as he had felt warm after walking a lot the day earlier. In his hands were some books and old newspapers on Theodor and others, including some pages he had jotted down notes on in Yiddish that he had wanted to do since he left Warsaw a few months earlier. He did not know if it was for him to later turn into a book of his personal adventures living in Jerusalem. He stood up and pulled some books from his shelves; they were very thick and one of them was the Noble Qur'an and the other, The Bible. He opened the Noble Qur'an which was written in Yiddish that he brought from Poland where there was a small Muslim community and started to read a chapter in it that he had picked at random, and quietly.

The Adhan was heard and he stood up to look at the minaret in the distance but there was no one there who cried it, and stood there until it was over.

David, again did not sleep in his bedroom leaving his wife there, who had not yet realized that her husband was up other than that as a former professor for many years he was constantly yearning to acquire new knowledge and must engage anyone who had knowledge to share even from amongst who thought they did not have any to share, but David had a way of getting even a little bit of knowledge from them, especially from strangers he bumped into for the first time.

With the Adhan for the last prayer for the Muslims done for the day, the night became silent and still. There was something stirring in David's mind. He wanted to talk to Moshe and Suleyman about who Theodor was, but the subject had different dimensions to different people. He did not want to bring up the matter Theodor had brought to the Congress because there would be some who might not be able to appreciate it.

David learned that Theodor had written in his diary how he had founded the Jewish State in his speech to the Congress in Basel, an idea which he said was too early to know if it was ever going to happen. It could not happen over night, but given time, it could happen, i.e. by introducing the right institutions. He was greeted with loud roars of laughter from the participants who were expecting to hear something light from him, like how the Jews or the World Jewry should learn how to live wherever they were at, where even as a tiny minority they could serve their local communities and countries and succeed in assuming the leadership in many fields of endeavor, including in charitable bodies. Theodor mentioned the need to form institutions such as a people's bank known as the Jewish Colonial Trust, which was going to be the instrument for the promotion of Zionism all over the world, an idea which was again taken up for a discourse in the Second Zionist Congress held in Cologne, Germany in May of 1898, which finally came into existence in the Fifth Congress when the Jewish National Fund was established with the purchase of a piece of land in the 'Land of Israel'. And later the Zionist Commission was established to promote the economic well-being of the Jews specifically those living in what he then described as the 'Land of Israel'. The Commission was headed by Chaim Weizmann.

David had read the passages on the early beginnings of Zionism and their leaders' goal in achieving it which was to establish the 'Land of Israel'. At that time, he did not think it was tenable or useful, but he kept an open mind to it and hoped if it did happen it did not cause untold hardship to everybody, especially the Palestinians whose land it was that the Zionists wanted to take away. When he remembered this part, he immediately felt a strong shiver running down his spine. He almost collapsed. He immediately lay down in case if that happened, so he was ready to fall, and did not hurt himself.

David did not expect to experience any of this when he told himself to go to Jerusalem for a while, rent a house for him and his family, and meet as many local folks as possible and learn a thing or two from them, concerning the 'Land of Israel' that Theodor had said that had not yet come to fruition despite the many years that had passed since the First Zionist Congress in Basel in 1897. Then he realized why he was there. He could come to Jerusalem on a trek to find something on his own without the company of his wife and children but he chose to bring them along. He was not going to emigrate to Palestine and live in Jerusalem or at any other city in the country; he had other things in mind about what he wanted to do and achieve. He felt like he needed to do something. And that something was in the ways and styles that he thought were how Theodor had used to fashion his personal goal and to attract attention to it, despite meeting with dead ends. He was not an important person or dignitary but he somehow managed to trust himself and finally managed to attract the attention and support he needed until he succeeded in achieving his initial goal which was to organize the First Zionist Congress that attracted a lot of attention from the right persons and the media; that was good enough for his ideas to be further developed until it came to the stage that some others could handle them, especially when he died seven years after the Basel Congress with his ideas dying with him. His goals were lofty, but he still managed to turn his personal goals into the common goals of the entire Jewish fraternity, not only in Europe, but elsewhere too, involved the World Jewry.

David especially liked the part when Theodor went to Istanbul in Turkey which was the center of the Ottoman Empire or 'Uthmaniyah' as the Turks called it. He thought it was his good luck when he came to know Count Philip Michael von Nevlinski, who he thought could arrange for him to have a meeting with the then Sultan, Abdulhamid. That was on 15 June, 1896, or more than thirteen months before the Basel Congress. He had wanted to meet with the Sultan in order to discuss his personal ideas on how to go about achieving the establishment of the Jewish State. He, however, failed to get an audience with the Sultan but he still managed to meet with some senior officials of the Palace including the Grand Vizier of the Court to who Theodor presented his proposal, by representing the news organization he said he was working for, which was 'Neue Frieie Presse' or New Free Press where he worked as a journalist. He was also a writer, a playwright, and mostly a political activist. He said the Jews would be willing to pay the foreign debts incurred by the Turkish government and not only that, they could also help the country to regain its financial footing, but on the condition that Palestine would be turned over to the Jews to become their own homeland. He knew it was a preposterous idea, and one which he himself knew was not tenable and might even be taken as a joke, but he persisted and put on a thick skin and went along with his dubious plan that in the end did not work.

David smiled widely when he got to the part in the book where there was a chapter on Theodor that dealt with this matter; and he, as a professor, too, would not have done such a thing. Or, maybe, if he was not a professor and a lawyer like Theodor, he might have also done similar things. And no wonder David decide to resign as professor to come to Jerusalem and try and copy what Theodor had done, in the hope that he could convince some people and then many more on his plans on how to deal with the Palestine matter vis-à-vis Jewish matter too! And he now felt like laughing at the achievements that he had managed to get, from being able to give a talk in a forum in his own rental house, where about fifty persons from different religious backgrounds came to listen to him, to the second forum or gathering at the sidewalk café in the Muslim Quarter with only Moshe, a local Jew, and Suleyman, an Arab-Muslim, both small traders in the respective Quarters, to listen to him. But the two listened to him very attentively. He knew the two men had started to get what he was driving at.

Moshe and Suleyman only studied in their religious schools and taught by their Rabbis and Ustaz and never received any secular education but they were aware of things and were not interested in worldly possessions and subsisted with whatever they got from their stores, never trying to make too much profit from any of the items they sold, as it was sinful to them to take more than necessary from anything they sold. Moshe only wrote in Hebrew and Arabic while Suleyman wrote and spoke and wrote in Arabic, so it was not easy to spell his name in Yiddish or English – as there were a few ways that he could do that, 'Suleyman', 'Suleiman', 'Sulaiman' and so on; or 'Solomon' in Hebrew. But David had never had occasion to call any of them by their names. The opportunity never arose, and his relations with them were still formal and not yet cordial or that friendly. But he could tell the two of them were smart individuals, and acquired knowledge from the unique education they had had since small, and now only read the sacred text of their respective religions which they claimed to contain any information and knowledge they wanted, so they were constantly on the right path that, hopefully, would lead to their 'Jannah' or 'Heaven' when life on earth ended for them, as living is a transient state of existence and not the only place for them to exist. Being a Jew himself, David knew the feeling, but at times when he was not guarding his senses, he felt the two were too extreme in their views and acceptance of their religion which he was too, earlier in his life until he got to the university where he was exposed to secular education that believes in the obvious and not in the mind and beliefs. And now, he felt like it was his duty to try and do something before what Theodor wanted became a reality because if it happened, life will be very unbearable for not only the Arabs but also the Jews, who will be locked in a situation that would be very tough for them to extricate themselves from.

What am I saying? David asked himself when his thoughts had taken him to the part when he started to question his own personal beliefs. He then decided to put the books back on the shelves from where he had taken them from, and lay on the floor that had been laid with thick carpet, to try and get some sleep. It was already four o'clock the next morning and soon the Adhan for the dawn or Maghrib prayers for the Muslims would be heard.

Soon the Adhan was heard coming from a few directions but David was too tired and sleepy to wake up. His wife came to the living room after being woken by the cries of the Adhan, saw him lying on the floor in the living room, but she was not willing to stir him because she knew he had returned to the house very late last night.

I am anti-Theodor…I am anti-Theodor…I am anti-Theodor!! David kept hearing this in his head as he lay asleep, as the sun started to appear from the horizon that was now being hidden behind the roofs of houses around his, but the light had started to brighten the living room where he was sleeping. His children had already gone to school, being taken there by their mother, so David was alone in the house until his wife, Leah, came back from the school.

David woke up; he opened his eyes to look at the living room now lit in bright light. He felt groggy and steadied himself as he tried to wake up to sit on the carpet and lean his body to the wall so now he appeared in a dark silhouette with the bright daylight coming through the window. He remembered again the words that entered his mind, his dream; or was it his subconsciousness state that made him hear the voice appear in his mind. I am anti-Theodor! What does it mean? he asked himself. I am anti-Theodor?! But David also remembered how Theodor, initially was pro-assimilation and wanted to see all Jews in Europe live together with the natives; but his attitude took a sudden change when he became political, after dabbling in theater and writing when he produced some plays that had no Jewish ideology in them. And as for David, he did have strong feelings towards the idea that all Jews in Poland and also in Europe should stick with each other so they could collectively create leaders in all fields from amongst them. That was when he was still a student at the University of Warsaw. When he became a faculty member of the same university upon graduation from it, his attitudes changed dramatically, without him realizing it at first, but after he got married, when he became restless knowing how he had, at an earlier time, as a bachelor, had such thoughts on how the Jews ought to have the 'land for themselves' regardless of where it was, either in Poland or somewhere in Europe. He never thought of Palestine then.

His wife opened the door from outside and immediately turned to look at her husband who was now sitting frozen on the carpet that he was sleeping on earlier, except now he looked disheveled. 'You need to wash yourself, have a bath or shower before having breakfast. I'll warm it, in the meantime,' she said as she entered the house and walked straight to the kitchen, with David doing as told and soon he stepped on the staircase to go upstairs. Leah heard him open the door – and from the sound it could be the one for the bathroom. And not long later, she heard the water shower spraying water. She knew her husband was having a shower, while the bread she had on the stove had become quite hot. She took it to the dining table and put the pieces of bread on it and waited for her husband to come down and have his breakfast.

David was quick to have his shower that morning; he made a re-appearance on the ground floor by walking and almost stamping his bare feet on the staircase that shook a little. He then went to the dining room and sat across the table from his wife who had by now poured some tea into a cup for him to drink with the bread and jam. She decided to give him and their children a western breakfast that morning because it was easy to prepare. She looked at her husband who was now tidy except that his hair was still damp. 'Are you going to keep your hair long again, David?' she asked. David chewed the bread and could not give her a vocal answer, so he just nodded. And when he had swallowed the bread with the jam on it, he said to his wife, and without looking at her, 'But it won't be too long like my university days. It won't be good to have a long hair here in Jerusalem,' he added.

She then stood up and was getting ready to go upstairs to clean the room and bring soiled clothes to wash leaving her husband at the dining table to fantasize about how he was going to be the person who would confront Theodor and his plans for a better life for the Jews, not only those who were in Poland and the whole of Europe, but for the World Jewry without realizing that his fantasy was taking him on the verge of madness! He thought Theodor was lucky to die young at the age of forty-four, and if he had lived longer, chances were he would be confronted with his cynics and skeptics and also a person such as him, who did not favor Jews to be placed in a special land for themselves, regardless of whether it was a state, or an area in the ghetto, where many of their ancestors had lived when they first arrived from everywhere to go to Poland and other countries in Europe and America and the whole world including in many Arab and Muslim countries. David preferred the Jews remained where they were, and tried to live in peace and harmony with the local population.

The three pieces of bread that Leah had put on the plate for David to eat for breakfast that morning were gone. And David was full. He took a few more sips of the tea until the cup it was in became dry. He froze on his chair. He did not want to think about Theodor anymore; he had had enough of him. He wanted to think of something else; he wanted to stay at the house and later in the afternoon take a walk, or take the horse he had just got for himself for a ride to nowhere special, just so that he could run away from his usual or normal environment and think about nothing special or spectacular.

He told himself that he liked it here. He also liked to be back in Poland. And he liked it everywhere he had been to in Palestine! He remembered how Theodor, too, was at the stage in his intellectual and artistic development when he would reject the values he held earlier and became an entirely a different person, who craved for attention and who forced himself to excel in writing and in the theater, that became elusive, that he develop the idea for the creation of the 'Jewish State' when he got to this stage when he wanted to say and write something spectacular and dramatic as well as preposterous. Even the newspaper he was writing for then refused to entertain him and refused to publish anything he wrote that touched on politics. He was then forced to write and distribute pamphlets about 'A Jewish State' that targeted some people who he thought believed in his ideas, especially from amongst the left-wing students at the university where he studied Law and graduated, during the time when the charge of being 'anti-Semitic' had been hurled by many Jewish leaders and elders on those who look down on the Jews, for no reason other than for them to be Jews.

And was this what David was now doing? trying to talk to some people, any people on his views?

Yes, later in the afternoon after the call for Zohor prayers, when David was feeling better and well-rested he decided to take his horse for a ride. He did not know where to take the horse; he wanted the horse to take him anywhere it liked. And it seemed to know exactly where to go to, to a local synagogue, where a Rabbi was sitting outside and trying to tidy the place by cleaning the land of some litter. David saw him and told the horse to stop. He said to the Rabbi, 'Shalom, Rabbi' and was replied in like manner. 'What brings you here?'

'I am going where my horse takes me,' said David. 'And he has brought me here to your synagogue. A nice place. Must be old.'

'Not really; just three hundred years old.'

David did not laugh because he did not think the Rabbi was cracking a joke. 'But it looks new.'

'We had it fully renovated a while back.'

'That's good.'

'Why don't you come in and take a look at it.'

David said he had to go off. 'I'll come back later, Rabbi. Shalom.'

'It's such a fine day, and must be good for riding around. Shalom.'

'Sure is,' said David. He then ordered his horse to move on and both went ahead until the Rabbi could not see them anymore except for the dust that the horse' legs had forced to fly from the dry ground. The Rabbi known as Rabbi Gilad spoke Arabic, Hebrew, a bit of Yiddish, and also Aramic, the language used during the time of Jesus Christ; and he was not very old, half that of David.

So in many ways the two were the same. But here in Jerusalem and Palestine, David had never encountered anyone who said bad things of the

Jews; on the contrary, non-Jews, meaning Arab Muslims and Christians, hardly ever had any bad feelings towards any Jew. Everybody here seemed to be happy to be with each other. They could see that especially during the harvesting of olives when the Muslim and Christian Arabs would be with the Jews picking the seeds from the trees to be made into olive oil and other products, a tradition they practiced hundreds of years ago many of them would mix and help each other in joint religious and cultural activities; they could be seen in the way they carried themselves every day buying things in each other's stores in the Old City, where despite being divided into the Jewish, Christian, and Muslim Quarters, there were many people from the other religious faiths or religions who lived in the quarter that were not attributed to them. Even in sidewalk cafés, coffee shops, and restaurants they mixed freely eating food sold, which all ate, with the Muslims who favored halal food being able to eat food served by the Jews which were kosher, and hence acceptable by the Muslims, too, except those served and sold by the Arab Christians which was not halal, because they consume pork that the Muslims did not. And it was not strange how the Jews and Muslims have the same word to describe 'pig', which is 'kazir' and 'khinzir' respectively, as well as many other words which are similar in Hebrew and Arabic such as although their pronunciations are different.

David found it a little too much to watch the first time he came to the Old City especially, and also at the other parts of Jerusalem, because the scene of the people from the major different races and religions, who were mostly Peoples of the Book, of the three Abrahamic faiths could live in such a manner. He sat on a chair in an outdoor sidewalk café staring at them as they went about doing their daily chores and stopping to greet each other in Arabic and exchange pleasantries and sitting to have snacks together. It was just too much for him to see and bear. But it was an interesting sight and observation he experienced when he got to Jerusalem few months ago. He could not see such a phenomenon in Warsaw or Poland where the Jews stuck amongst themselves in ghettos and other communes while the small number of Muslims, mostly Arabs lived amongst themselves and who went to their own religious schools.

And of course there were also some characters who he found to be at the wrong place, who spoiled the sight. They were the British soldiers, army officers, administrators and their families with children, that made the scene look odd for him. He did not like that. He even suggested how the presence of the British who were controlling Palestine under their so-called British Mandate of Palestine they imposed in 1922 to be untenable and downright rude and illegal. They behaved in different styles compared to the local Arabs and Jews and spoke in a language that was totally alien to the land. But the locals ignored them and many did not have anything to do with them in their everyday lives and who did not have any direct communication with any of them except for their political leaders who did have some interaction with each other. Yes, the British were the people who brought some modernity to Palestine such as the train service that currently had a line connecting Jaffa, which was close to the Mediterranean, to Jerusalem with construction beginning on 31 March, 1890 and completed in 1892 that was sixty-five kilometers long with a ride of fifty-one minutes, so it was mainly for the transport of goods, with so few of the locals who could afford to take it because they did not have any need to travel on the train, and who preferred to travel on horse, mule-driven carts, on horses, donkeys, and mules.

It would be interesting if I were to take the ride from here in Jerusalem to Jaffa, said David to himself; he did not want to any anyone who was near him if they had already taken such a ride. Most probably not!

Moshe and Suleyman never mentioned to David about the Basel Congress or the First Zionist Congress organized by Theodor Herzl from 29 to 31 August, 1897 in Basel, Switzerland; so he assumed that the two had not heard of it, a good ten years before the Russian Revolution, led by Vladmir Lenin and a group of revolutionaries, the Bolsheviks, that took place in 1917. It was when the group of unlikely people comprised of mere peasants and the working class people of Russia. Their aim was to overthrow their ruler, Tsar Nicholas the Second to form a new government with Communism as their main political ideology and calling themselves the Soviet Union. He was old enough to be aware of what happened in Russia then, but he was not aware of the character calling himself Vladimir Lenin, who sprang from nowhere, as far as he was concerned, who managed to garner a lot of support from the ordinary masses, to follow him and cause the collapse of the feudal system in their country, which had done them a lot of good as far as David was concerned. The outbreak of the First World War in 1914 three years earlier gave the impetus for the masses to go up against the ruling class and the autocrats who had been treating the peasants like slaves.

David also wanted, and was anxious to know, if they had heard about it and wanted to know what they thought of it. But they didn't have any idea what it was. David did ask about the Congress but they registered blank faces and he did not prod them on the matter, except with the old Arab Christian man who he bumped into at the sidewalk café or coffee shop near where Theodor had met with King Wilhelm the Second in 1896 who knew about this meeting. He also did not know anything about the Basel Congress because it was a private meeting and mostly likely not announced to the general public. But did Moshe say he was born in the year the Congress took place? He was in his early forties; he could very well have just been born, as was his good friend, Suleyman. So how could the two of them know about it? David realized that and remembered how he was just a sixteen-year-old boy at that time; or seventeen, and even then he was not fully aware of what the Congress dealt with and did not know what Theodor said in his speech, and only came to know about the details later when he got to the University of Warsaw a few years after it happened, i.e. from literature that was written about it that he could lay his hands on at the university and in old newspaper cuttings, etc. He also did not discuss it with any other students, either Jewish like him or Poles, at the university. His parents who had gone to Basel to watch the Congress from outside, also did not take up the matter with him; they brought some literature on the Congress that David got the opportunity to see; he only got them after they died and by that time he was already a professor at the university where he had graduated from. He met his wife, Leah at the university when he was teaching there and she was a staff member at the library. She was ten years younger than he was and they got married a few months after meeting with each other, and she still continued to work at the library until they had their first child, a boy who they wanted to call Theodor, but he changed his mind at the last minute and chose Leah's father's name instead which was Douglas, a name of someone in America who Leah found in a book she had read in the library, and thought it would be interesting; and her husband, David agreed, so their son could have an English or American name to hide his identity from strangers, when he grew up in another country and most likely in America. David and Leah did not know if they had made the right or wrong decision on the name of their first-born which might have been out of fear or foresight. David was a Jewish name, and they knew it, which had become so Anglicized but Douglas was not. There was no Jewish man who had such a name, which to them was too English or American. They also wanted their son to learn how to speak and write in English. Something other than Yiddish and Polish the language that they did not understand, or Hebrew, if that would not be too much for them to force their son, then so small and being carried in their arms sometimes by grandparents and who had not spoken a single word or sounds other than to say something unintelligible when he felt thirsty and wanted milk; and other than 'Ma'…'Ma'…and…'Pa'…'Pa'…to call them' that did not indicate that the boy was precocious, but much like the other babies his age who could do the same thing like he did.

And he did know a Muslim man when he was in Poland who he and everybody else called Hajji in Budapest, but there were more living in Wilno, Nowogródek, and Białystok Voivodeships. And they were Lipka Tartars who ancestors had come to Poland in the Fourteenth Century. And in the early Twentieth Century, some of the younger men and women joined the Christians who sought refuge in America where they settled in the Borough of Brooklyn where they establish a Masjid to serve their community. He knew an elderly Muslim man who everybody called Hajji because he had performed his Hajj once and he found him to be an affable person who spoke very good Polish, Arabic, and also some Yiddish with whom he communicated. He was probably the only Muslim man David had met in Poland. David did not know if Hajji was still alive or not; he had not seen him in ages, and he was already in his mid-sixties so he might be in his nineties now and looking like the many Arab men this old that he could see in Jerusalem and other parts of Palestine where he had been and who did not care for the world anymore and who seemed to be longing to make their final trip to meet their Creator, Allah! Would I also come to the point in my life when I feel like how they all feel? David asked himself this question. This was not the first time he ever asked himself such a question; he started to do so since he had come to Jerusalem. He had never thought of it the whole time he was in Poland where the situation was different than it was here in Jerusalem, or in Palestine where everything was different. He liked it that he had come very close to the beginnings of civilization; only that those in Europe who some Arabs called the Crusader countries, could never come to accept the fact that they were indeed not living in reality but in fantasy. David knew he was in such a collective fantasy when he was there; but his attitude changed dramatically when he saw old Arab men and could not tell if they were Muslims or Christians all by themselves sometimes walking with a pronounced hunch and not looking up and moveing along the passageways by themselves sometimes with the aid of a stick for balance. David remembered his late grandfather too, had walked like that when he was in his eighties, and he was still a small boy then. He wanted to sympathize with the Arab men walking with a hunch but after thinking about it, he decided not to feel sorry for them; they had come to that point in their lives when everything was useless; they could be taken to their graves. And for Muslims, he knew their graves were simple with almost nothing of value and opulence that could be displace regardless of who they were when they were alive, unlike the others whose relatives could build expensive graves for them that cost more than what it took to build the house of the average person. That's not good, he remarked, and added how he too did not want his grave to look extravagant, but simple.

14

Omar arrives in Baitullaham

Omar finally arrived in Baitullaham or 'Bethlehem'. He looked thinner than he was when he left his village about two weeks ago and the clothes he wore had faded a lot. He thought he looked older the last time he saw his face in the mirror. He prayed to God for allowing him to arrive in the city in good health and above all, the horse that had taken him there was also in good spirits and good health, and this mattered to him, lest he should feel guilty beyond belief if it was not. He had changed a lot but he didn't seem to realize it, until his close relatives said so. They should know because they had not seen Omar a while to notice the difference not just in his appearance, but mostly in attitude. He had lost a bit of weight.

Omar was indeed glad that he had finally arrived in his ancestors' village in Baitullaham. It was such a long journey, he said to himself, one which was not only physical in nature, but more so, in spirit; he found out and learned a lot on his journey that took ten days, which was a few days more than he had expected due to the delays he encountered and the nights he had to spend in the empty desert where there was no one except for the birds that flew around him and his horse, Qawiun, meaning Strong. If it was not strong, it would not have survived the journey. And now he said he would leave the horse to its own device to let it rest a bit while he did as his father had told him to do which was to get rid of the carpets and the things he had given Omar to take to Baitullaham. He had not yet realized what the real duty was he had to perform here other than to come here. There must be much more to it.

He felt a sense of triumph, and the first night he spent in his relatives' house he felt he was like an ancient Arab adventurer, Ibn Battuta or the Italian adventurer, Marco Polo whose adventures he had read of when he was a young boy in books that his father had given him to read; he would be open to adventure like he was when he went or was sent to Cairo in Egypt by his father, Omar's grandfather, before he was born. He brought the books with him so he could spend time reading them again, he thought. He had read a bit of them while on the journey he had just undertaken when he spent nights in the desert. He thought it was amazing how Ibn Battuta was only twenty years old when he undertook the journey in 1325 to 1354! Omar was a few years older than he was; and his father went to Cairo. Ibn Battuta only wanted to travel to Makkah to perform his Hajj which was the fifth Pillar of Islam, but in the end, his travels took twenty-nine years before he finally returned home and as such, he had traveled seventy-five thousand miles and visited forty-four countries, most of which were Arab or Muslim ones in what was described then as 'Dar al-Islam' or 'The World of Islam.' Omar became nervous each time he came to the parts when Ibn Battuta was experiencing danger, and he would sweat when reading the passages. He paused a long time before he was brave enough to continue to read. He looked around the place he had stopped for the night and looked at his horse, Qawiun, who was fast asleep, and at the land around him, which was bare and dark with faint light from the moon shining. He did not want to look at the trees and hills because they might appear to look like apparitions. Ibn Battuta was attacked by bandits a few times and even almost drowned in a ship that was sinking, was caught by the soldiers of the ruler and brought to him to be beheaded! But he managed to escape all the dangers to continue on with his journey where he got married and had few children with different women. The climax of his adventure and life was when the Sultan of Morocco or Maghribi, when Ibn Battuta issued a royal decree to get him to talk about his personal adventures to a court scribe so that it could be handed down through the generations of Arabs to learn how he had done what he did in close to three decades of his life that finally appeared in a travelogue with the title of, 'Tuhfat al-anzar fi gharaaib al-amsarwaajaaib al-asfar', which translated to 'A Gift to Those Who Contemplate the Wonders of Cities and the Marvels of Traveling.' It was described as 'Ibn Battuta's 'Rihla', or Ibn Battuta's Journey'; Marco Polo traveled from 1271 to 1295 with the book on it travels called 'Il Millione' (The Million) which was not written by him but as told to Rusticello da Pisa!

Do I want to write a book of my own personal's adventure too, Omar asked himself? I can write it myself from the notes I have written while traveling from my village to Baitullaham? because there would not be any ruler who would want to get his court scribe to talk with me on it, so I have to do it myself, he added. But then, who would want to read about it since I was not kidnapped and never nearly drowned while on the journey! He smiled when he thought of it. He knew he was not serious. I am nothing compared to Ibn Battuta or Marco Polo, he said to himself and almost laughed at the thought. But he liked it when the thought came to him because he thought it was interesting and a harmless thing to do showing the circumstances he was in at that time. He imagined what his horse, Qawiun might have thought if it could think and express himself; he was sure his horse also enjoyed riding with him to go places that the two of them had not been to before, despite the hardship he had given to it and also to himself. Am I going mad, going bonkers? Maybe! Ma Sha Allah! He still did not know what his father had in mind when he asked him to go to Baitullaham, and such haste that he did not have any time to think and discuss it with him. He had to go, and to go fast! Why the rush? The only time he had to rush was when he was late to go to school and he had to be stirred by his mother, take a quick shower, and run to his father who was already waiting outside on his horse, the same one who later bore Qawiun. He had been dreaming and the dream did not end early and it passed the time when the Adhan for the dawn prayers would start. That much he knew about why he was late; that he had had a dream that lasted too long and it would not end if his mother had not woken him up. He never knew what the dream was till today!

He only said, there was a good reason for it to happen; like there was a good reason for him to be where he was then, sitting along in the middle of nowhere in the vast desert with his horse. The desert which was as wide as he could see and the broken only by the horizon and the sun he saw in the day and the moon he saw a bit of in the night because it was not a full moon when he started to ride from his village and it would late disappear as the days progressed. And of course, he also had his companion, Qawiun who had been especially kind to him throughout the journey. The food he had been given and packed by his mother had been eaten and he had started to eat from any sources; from the village food stalls or make some on his own using the items he had purchased from the stalls and from villagers he had met along the way who spared food for him to eat. There was water from the stream to drink as much as he and his horse liked and to also wash themselves with; he would dip himself in the water for a long time until he felt fresh and was ready to go on. Or, maybe his father had asked him to go on the arduous trip as a penance for him to pay, for something he might have done, or to ask him to take a test, a physical and also a psychological one, to see if he deserved to be his first-born son benefitting of carrying on with his family name, and to also later be given his properties when his father became older and had no need to worry about such things anymore.

Omar became more confused and decided not to think about anything anymore; he wanted to rest and to lie on the carpet in the house for a while. He might get a good idea of why he was here in Baitullaham from his uncle, who should know what his father had in mind for him to do there. So far he had not said a word since he arrived here; he wanted Omar to have a good rest before he informed him of the tasks he had been assigned to do by his father. His father's face was blank the last time he met when he bid farewell to him; now his own uncle's face too was as blank as his father's then.

Omar's uncle, who was his father's younger brother called Yunus did not look like his father, Munir. He had not seen him in a while and almost did not recognize him when he met him again when he knocked on the door of his house to announce his arrival there. It was not much

of an arrival, with no one knowing when he was arriving; they only knew
he was coming, and did not expect him to be there outside of his uncle's
house. 'Are you looking for someone?' asked Yunus.

'I am here to meet my uncle, Yunus,' he said. 'Is this his house?'

Yunus thought Omar was a stranger and had not met him before.
'Yes, I am Yunus. Your uncle? Who are you?'

'Omar. Omar bin Munir.'

Yunus was taken aback. 'Omar? My Omar? Are you sure you're our...
my Omar?'

Omar pulled Yunus' hand and kissed it and the two then hugged
each other. Yunus' wife, Manal appeared from the kitchen and looked
at the two men hugging. 'Ya, Allah, Omar; is that you?' she almost
shrieked. The two men released the hugging and Omar rushed to his
aunt and kissed her hand. 'How could you remember him, Manal?'
asked Yunus.

'I held him as a baby and I saw him grow up to be a boy,' she
explained. 'How could I forget who he is? Do you still have the mole on
your right arm, Omar? Here, let me check.' She then held Omar's right
hand and push up the loose sleeve of the sleeve of his robe and there it
was the mole. 'Here! How can I forget it? It has grown larger.'

'Of course, it had to grow larger now because he is not a baby or a
small boy anymore,' said Yunus.

'You were too busy with the farm and your horse, to worry about
him.'

'You must be very hungry now, huh, Omar?' said Yunus. 'He then
turned to his wife and asked, 'Can we eat something now?'

They then sat in the living room and ate together.

'Did you know why your father had asked you to come here, to
Baitullaham, Omar, my son?' asked Yunus.

Omar nodded; he could not give a vocal answer because he was
chewing some food in his mouth. He was relieved to know why. But
Yunus too did not know anything more than to look after him. 'That's
all that he asked me to do.'

'He also wanted you to be with your wife and two children at her parents' home. I will take you there today. In the meantime, eat some more and take a rest.'

'Where is their house? It used to be very near here.'

'They have moved to a larger house and sitting on a larger piece of land. Your wife, Hanady and your two children, Ilham and Thaer are fine. They got here a month ago.'

'Ilham looks exactly like you, Omar,' chipped in his aunt, Manal. 'And I am pleased to have met them again, here in Baitullaham. They dropped by a few times since coming here last month, you know!'

Omar felt very sorry for himself for having totally forgotten about them, his wife and two children, for most of his journey. He blamed the many distractions he experienced traveling along with his horse for that. He looked outside of the window and saw Qawiun running about chasing his own shadows. He then said, 'Qawiun needs something to eat and drink. I'd better give him some.'

'Who? You have a friend with you? Why didn't you bring him in earlier to eat together,' said Manal.

'He's my horse, Auntie Manal.'

Yunus and his wife they realized they had not asked Omar about his father. 'And how's your father and your mother?' asked Manal.

'They're fine, Auntie. And they have sent their 'salaam.'

'Mulaikum salam,' said Manal and Yunus.

Yunus helped Omar get rid of the carpet and a few other things Omar had brought all the way from his village of Kafr Ad-Dik. Long before he arrived and he had been paid in advance for them, so Omar had no need to worry about the consignment. His duty was to look after his family and his uncle would take him there once he had rested. No, he did not need any massage; but he could do with sitting in the 'hammam' or steam room to cleanse his body, and Yunus said there was one nearby where the two of them could go to and sit there, together. This they did and both sat in the hammam until they felt light with a lot of fat burnt from their body. But it still did not make Omar feel any easier because he still did not know why he was sent there. What was the mystery about?

he asked himself again and again the whole time he arrived here and even when he was sitting in the hammam. Most likely, some of the sweating he experienced sitting in the hammam was due more to his anxieties than the heat inside the steam room.

Omar felt it was like an anti-climax to his journey he had spent a while on and to get to the final destination without any surprises. He met his wife and two children at their grandparents' house which was about ten kilometers from Yunus' house later that day, and he felt like he was not welcome there either, except that he would now have to help his parents-in-law toil on the farm until he received further instructions from his father, via his uncle, who did not know anything else to tell Omar, other than to remain here in Baitullaham until further notice. How could the journey be more interesting than the destination, he asked himself as he was riding on his horse to view the land around his parents-in-law's properties which was wide and there was also a stream running through it, and he told Qawiun he would take him there for a bath, other than to take his wife and children on a ride in his carriage to go further away from the house to look at the area and to go to the city and mostly, to the oldest olive tree he had been told about by some people he bumped into along the way. He had heard about the tree that was more than four thousand years old and wanted to go there one of these days. His wife and children had not seen it either, so they could bring along food to have a picnic there. That would be fun indeed, he said. And he had discussed the plan with his wife, Hanady, who thought it was a good idea so they could spend some time together as a family. What was it, the olive tree? Al-Walaja, said his wife. How far is it from here? Ten kilometers. That's not too far, said Omar. We can get there in an hour, riding at a nice pace and stopping at some interesting places along the way. No rush; we'll take our time and leave from the house in the morning, and make sure we get back here late in the afternoon, before Asar. We stop where we are to pray and have a snack and to rest. And for Qawiun to rest too. He has rested a bit since arriving here. And he seems to be restless because he has been used to running everyday since we left our village two weeks ago. She later admitted to him by saying their two children had grown restless because they had been holed up in the house for a long time and it was good for them to be able to take a ride to go somewhere. Omar agreed. Gosh! he said; What he would have done if not for the very old olive tree he wanted to see and now the trip to go to Al-Walaja had become a trip for their family to be together, for bonding, which they often did when they were in his village. They would go places just for the trip and to look at what they had there in those villages some of which were very ancient that had many archaeological remnants for them to appreciate and understand and to seek knowledge. And where did he get the idea from, to travel even for short distances? His father, Munir had taken him and his brothers and sometimes, nephews, on rides in his horse-drawn carriages to go to the neighboring villages and towns to visit his friends and mostly strangers, to show his children the vastness of nature and to encourage them to appreciate it and not take it for granted. It is beyond the scope of their schools to teach this sort of education that was not available in their syllabus. They normally did not go too far away from their house and his father made sure he drove them for at the most one hour on his carriage before stopping often for praying, wherever there was one, or sometimes in open space. His father never said a word on the reasons why he liked to take his sons and nephews along, whenever he could and had the time; but he told his younger brother, Yunus whose sons, too, had come along on such trips whenever they came to visit him and stay with him for a few days or even weeks at one time.

Omar then realized that the reason or reasons why his father had sent him to Baitulloaham was for something that he had not yet told his Uncle Yunus. There must be something that he had not found the words to share even with his own younger brother. He even asked Omar not to take the main road, but the side road, passing deserted land with almost no village or small towns. It was an order he found funny if not weird to follow. Everybody wanted to travel fast to get to his destination, but Omar's father wanted him to take his own sweet time to go to Baitullaham. The roads would safer for Omar to take to get there, and along the way he could become closer with his horse, and with himself and his God, although he did not say so in words. Omar knew his father's style of disciplining him and his brothers. He also did not show much affection to his own children, like most Arab men who frown upon the exhibition of intense feelings. Even with the deaths of their close relatives and friends, they were not allowed to show any emotion, lest, they were said to cause the deceased to suffer in the Hereafter or 'Jannah', that the Ustaz or Religious Teachers often taught the students since they were very small as prescribed by the Noble Qur'an. Omar's father and those of the others he knew, too, subscribe to such a belief without question and that had served them well when they grew up to be adults and have children of their own to look after and be carbon copies of themselves in many ways. But lately, under the British Mandate of Palestine, some Arab men and also their wives had shirked on their duties and became more open-minded and allowed a lot of leeway for their children to transgress some of the edicts passed by the Council of Religious Elders or 'Ulamak.' But in the Munir household that Omar was a member of, they still practiced what their Ustaz had taught them since small and were not about to change what was taught to them. Only a small number of Arabs had become a bit 'modernized' and started to wear western-style clothes by the men who often go to the major cities; while some were those who had the opportunity to go to other major cities in the Arab World, especially Cairo where the mixing of the genders was not frowned upon. Some were even speaking English amongst themselves, not only in public but also in private much to the delight of the British officers and administrators. Munir did not want any of his children to become like those men and boys he had met in the city who had studied in the schools operated by the English where the medium of instruction was English, and who were quick to adopt their ways. Had there been any Arab Muslim men or boys who had left their religion to take the religion of the colonizers? Munir did not think so, as that would take more than speaking in English and the wearing of their clothes for anyone to want to do that. But Omar's father didn't mind speaking in the little English he knew by greeting the English he knew by saying, 'Good evening and, how are you, sir?' and not much else. The funny part was that he was responded to by the English men and women who spoke in Arabic that they had learned from Arab teachers their senior officers had engaged so they could communicate and relate with the local Arabs better. And surprisingly, Munir found out, there were some English men who were Christians from the Church of England who had reverted to Islam, married Arab women and used their new Arab names with some even starting to wear the Arab robes and looking much like any Arab men themselves, especially when they had grown up and having children of their own.

That night, Omar could not sleep; he sat outside and looked at his horse which was fast asleep because he got tired running around the compound after Omar unleashed it. He ran round and around like a mad horse, excited to be let loose and stopped only to drink. Later in the evening Omar took it to the stream and gave it a nice bath by dipping it in the water and scrubbing its body to clean it of the dust that had collected on it the last few days using soap he used for himself. The light from the moon was not strong as it was toward the end of the month when the shape of the moon had turned to a narrow crescent. There was stillness.

Sleep came to him easily when he was on the road, because he often exhausted himself from the traveling in areas he had not been to before and who was often by himself and with his horse, Qawiun. By the time they decided to put up the night at any isolated place the two of them were too dead tired to have any time to stare and marvel at the 'wonders of nature' and appreciate the beauty of it, with Qawiun feeling lost because he did not seem to know where it was going, ahead and never turning back to return to the barn at Omar's parents' house they had left earlier. Munir had spoken to him before he left their village to look after his son, Omar well, like the horse understood what he was saying as it grabbed some food from Munir's outstretched arm and ate more than he needed to sustain himself through the day. It knew Munir was a kind man who often overfed him, but when he did not stop feeding him and patting him, it knew what he had in mind; it was for the horse to go on a very long journey. Munir also made sure to get a cobbler to replace the shoes on Qawiun with a better and stronger set that made a loud noise when the shoes hit hard surfaces, which to him would be good not only for the horse but mostly for his son, Omar, with the continuous noises they made that sounded like music that changed in tones and volume when they hit different types of surfaces along the route they were going to take. The sound the horse made galloping added to the sounds of the winds and the leaves rustling in them added with the sounds of sand being blown away by the winds that created a symphony of music to the ears, so thought Munir. The sound or music could be good for the soul, too, if his son could take that to this level. There was not even the cry of the Adhan to indicate to him the time, so most of the time he lost the sense of time, and had to depend on the neighing of his horse who told him when it was time to pray, and after looking at the sun, he made the decision on which prayer to perform and cried the Adhan himself, before praying by himself prostrating on the barren desert ground or sometimes under the shades of trees or shrubs. He did not want to bring a watch. He left it in his house in the village and wanted to totally surrender himself to nature to guide him along when time was of no substance as there was no schedule to do anything for him to make for himself, other than to go on with his journey and to do a few daily chores along the way, bathing only when there was a stream that he could find.

'I am from the village of 'El Mutallah,' Omar would tell those who he met along the way from his village to Ramallah, saying it proudly because he knew that many of them had heard of this small village and who could not guess where it was. Maybe his features that were finer than most Arab men his age and in how he wore his robe or 'jubah' and in the way he spoke the Arabic language which had a particular accent and intonation and diction, all peculiar only to those who were born, grew up, and lived there for most of their lives. 'It is small village, built of stone, containing about one hundred Christian of the Druze persuasion,' he would add, and sounding like he was reading from travel or tourist brochures distributed by their tourism agency. And it is situated on slope of hill, near a large stream, surrounded by land which is very good for farming.' El Mutallah which literally means 'The Lookout.'

With that explanation and description of his village from where he had come from, he was certain the strangers would have a very good idea of the village and who he was and why he had come from so far away from the northernmost point in Palestine to be there now amongst them in their village, but which did not have the advantages like those they had in Omar's own village. 'The Jews called it 'Metula,' he explained. 'And it is a bastardized version of Arabic, from the sounds or mispronouncing of our original Arabic word or name. It is near the sites of some Biblical cities of Dan, Abel Bet Ma'akha and Eyon that border the state of Lubnan or 'Lebanon' as the English would say it.'

Omar didn't feel guilty if he sounded too condescending with his tone. He had been asked the same question many times and he thought it would have been a lot better if he had written a catalogue and made many copies that he could distribute to them who asked from where he had come from. He was joking, of course. But at times he felt awkward when no stranger asked him that question, like they didn't care from where he had come and why he was there in their village or what he was doing traveling in such an isolated place that had not seen foreigners like him passing by. It was all his father's idea, he explained when asked who or what had brought him there. He wanted me to travel to Baitullaham taking side roads so the trip could become a journey of self-discovery, to proof my worth as a man. Some of the strangers had not been to Baitullaham and were stuck in their isolate and remote villages all their lives and there were many elder men who had even died without ever leaving their village where they were born and who also did not know that Palestine was now under the British Mandate that was created in July, 1922 under the Balfour Agreement. And he did not want to bore his newly-found friends, strangers for the first one or two minutes, and after their first thirty minutes, had become close friends or buddies and later on, brothers and sisters in Islam, by mentioning how some mosaic pavements were somewhere hidden in his area that dated from the time of the ancient Roman and Byzantine periods in the history of their country, or how some foreign travelers by the names of Buckingham and Victor Guerin who had lost their way and found themselves there, described how they had met some Christian Druzes; but they did not call the village like the Arabs there did, but 'Metully' or 'Methelleh' or 'Metelleh'. Some people had told him tales of the exploits of the two men from the Crusader states in Europe and how they had strayed from their path while riding their camels and ended up in his village in the early Nineteenth Century. But they did not say or put on record if they had enjoyed the time they spent with the locals there. They were definitely not really of the Ibn Batutta or Marco Polo type of adventurers but mere travelers who broke away from their groups to find themselves in strange areas. He definitely did not want to inform his 'friends in Islam' about how someone in his village had told some people a story of an alien space ship that had landed there a few hundred years ago and who lived with the locals without them realizing it, for a while and even got married with some of the local women, who were then not yet Muslims as the story happened before the advent of Islam or even Christianity or Judaism. Why? Because he did not want them to laugh at him, because as Muslims, they were not allowed to say such things about the adventures of space aliens flying in their futuristic spaceships called by some Englishmen as the UFOs for 'Unidentified Flying Objects' even though they were mentioned and it was true that they existed, but no one should dwell too much on the subject who were described as 'Sky-Gods.'

Omar had never had the opportunity to inform anyone before about the village where he had come from, and he took the chore of doing it now, for 'his own brothers and sisters in Islam' to understand and appreciate it; at the same time, it was refreshing to his own self to know of it too.

Days later, Omar and his wife and two children went to Al-Walaja and they sat under the oldest olive tree, not only in the area but the whole of Palestine. They enjoyed sitting there and thinking of nothing. His horse that had pulled the carriage from their house in Baitullaham, was now running about, oblivious to what Omar was thinking. The tree was more than four thousand years old and it was definitely much older than the religions of the Peoples of the Book – Judaism, Christianity, and Islam. He was proud that he was now sitting right under the tree, taking shade in the hot sun in early spring. There were other people there too, some sitting under the same tree with them, and the others sitting everywhere; with some of them who did not seem to care too much about the significance of the tree, except that it was shady. It didn't look that old they thought; they had seen many olive trees like that. There were also some other visitors to the area who were sitting in groups on mats they had laid down and eating snacks. At the other side some men and also women were praying in the open. And why did he suddenly remember this particular verse from the Noble Qur'an? that says: 'And the servants of the Most Merciful are those who walk upon the earth easily, and when the ignorant address them [harshly], they say [words of] peace" – The Holy Quran 25:63.

Omar got home just before sunset and just in time for the Maghrib or evening prayers. That day he decided to do it outside of the house, to be close to nature; after seeing the olive tree and sitting under it for a while he felt bliss at being able to do so. It was a tree that had lasted for so long; but a human's life cannot be that long; it is fleeting and during that short period of time one needs to be careful and not go astray. And with that he did his ablution on the ground by scooping fine desert sand and cleaning the parts of his body that needed to be cleaned, although there was a stream not so far away and water in the well at the back of the house, but he still chose to do the ablution, naturally, to satisfy the desire that had swelled inside of him while he was driving back on his cart and being pulled by Qawiun.

He was happy to be allowed to take a seed from the olive tree which he put in his pocket and when he got home he immediately found a good spot where he dug a small hole and put the seed inside the hole where he hoped the seed would grow into a plant and then a tree. It was not for harvesting but to be used to provide shade, and if there were seeds, he hoped he and his relatives would pluck them and turn them into olive oil for personal use. He thought it would be magical if that happened, if a tree which came from the oldest tree in the whole of Palestine could grow in another tree in the compound of his house in Baitullaham, it would be great, and a present from God Himself, he thought.

He sat on the prayer mat on the ground after performing the Maghrib prayers and read a very long supplication or 'doa' to thank Allah the Almighty and his parents, and their parents and all his relatives for having brought him to be what he was now. And to end it, he asked for their forgiveness if he had done anything untoward and had not heeded their call to become a pious Muslim man and obedient son. Amin.

He wiped his face with both palms, rolled the prayer mat, and went to Qawiun and patted his body and said something to it, and said sorry for not including it in his supplication he read to himself earlier which he now said to it in his heart as the dim light from the sky started to become dimmer and dimmer until he was hidden in the partial darkness surrounding the house and the whole area. The horse gave a loud neigh like he heard what Omar had said in his heart and agreed with it.

Before he left, Omar put the prayer mat on Qawiun's body and took it inside the barn to spend the night. He had no plans for tomorrow; it would be determined on what his Uncle Yunus would do or his father-in-law said, if he needed an extra hand to help him in the farm. It was not yet the olive harvesting season. His father-in-law, Hajji Ayoub, knew not to disturb the peace his son-in-law wanted and to be with himself and his family. He liked it when he said he wanted to take them to see the old olive tree earlier in the day which he did. And no one in his house asked him what he thought of the tree and how he felt sitting under its shade. They wanted Omar to tell them what he felt about it, but chances were, such an incident would not happen because they knew he was not the type of a person who would introduce new topics for discussions and who also hardly ever answer questions posed to them in any great length. His answers he had given in the past were all short and brief, not that they didn't know that, since his father, too was of such predisposition as was Yunus; and his own children had been taught never to give long and winded answers and be brief with them and to also never ask questions to strangers and even relatives.

Omar discussed with his wife if they should take their next trip as a family to Ramallah, the Jews called 'Ramle', so see the place and perhaps to meet with some of her friends who lived there. That would not be such a bad idea, she said; and she suggested that they should stay there a night or two to look around the city and its environs instead of returning to their village the same night. Omar gave a thought while his wife waited and then agreed. Not a bad idea, he said; And how come I never thought of that? he asked. That's because you have some of your close friends living there and I do not, he added.

Hanady liked it when what she said or suggested to her husband was accepted; and she deliberately put out the suggestion to him to see or to test if he would listen to her views. Arab women generally did not like to do that, because they liked to play the subservient women, who were faithful to their husbands while they play different roles as mother to their children and hardly or ever got to do anything for her family, including asking her husband to agree to her views. Most were happy to play the roles as mothers to their children as prescribed by the Noble Qur'an and Sayings or Sunnah of Nabi Muhammad, (s.a.w.) without question. But Hanady would never tell her parents that it was her idea to bring her husband to Ramallah with their two children, to spend a night or two there; and it was all her husband's idea, so they did not get the wrong idea on what sort of a women they had brought to the world and teach her the values in Islam for any woman to behave. And so when they finally left their house in the morning her parents knew it was Omar's idea and good enough they welcomed it and thought it would do wonders for his family, to be able to spend sometime together to do their own thing and especially in Ramallah where they would meet with some of Hanady's close friends who had also married and had two children each so they could relate better with each other, now as parents to their own children and with husbands who were also responsible people.

The distance between Baitullaham and Ramallah is thirty kilometers and taking the cart pulled by Qawiun would take two to three hours, depending on the speed Omar wanted his horse to run. If he ordered it to gallop at a nice space, it could take four hours. Knowing Omar, his father-in-law knew he would want to take a leisurley drive to go there and might even take six to seven hours with two, three, or even four stops along the way to stretch and to have snacks and most of all to allow him and his wife to find a Masjid to pray.

So it was Omar again who brought out the idea for him and his family to go to Ramallah over the weekend, when they were having dinner in the living room cum common room. Omar thought after a while his wife's family would have dinner and other meals together with him in the kitchen to show that he had returned and not in their common room where they normally entertained visitors or strangers and not a member of their close family or distant relatives who dropped by. Omar tried to tell his wife for them to have meals in the kitchen but he did not have the guts to say so, because he thought her father and mother would be slighted because by making him have meals in the common room. It was their way of showing their respect to their son-in-law. And it would be even worse for Omar if he were to suggest that he bought a house for himself for his family somewhere in the same village or in another because this could be taken differently by his in-laws who might think that they did not respect him as their son-in-law who had already bore them two grandchildren. It's all very confusing if he were to explain to foreigners, the few he had met before, who would expect him to live on his own now that he had a family, but not amongst the Arabs who liked to live with their family in Majdal Bani Fadel village and in some there were two or three generations of them living under the same roof even when they were said to be wealthy with some other relatives living in Qabalan and Beit Dajan villages, situated east of the City of Nablus. And further away, was the village of Deir Yassin that had even less people living there who were mostly Arab-Muslims. And even if he was married to Hanady, he would still not enter the house of his in-laws, if she was not around. If his mother-in-law and his sisters-in-law were there, it was forbidden by his religion of Islam, which was stipulated succinctly in the Noble Qur'an that he had read again and again that he should never be in the same enclosed confines with women other than his own wife and mother, grandmother, sisters, and close relatives. And personally he was happy with the setup and had never transgressed the edict, because he took women to be special creatures to walk upon the earth and as such they should all be given the special treatment accorded in his religion.: 'O you who have believed, do not enter houses other than your own houses until you ascertain welcome and greet their inhabitants. That is best for you; perhaps you will be reminded.' – The Holy Quran 24:27.

This advice was taught to Omar and his brothers, all of his cousins, and others by their respective parents and Ustaz religious when they were still small, to heed the advice more so when they were older, so they teach their own children the virtues of such an edict. In this way, many untoward events that could cause unnecessary personal issues concerning thefts and personal misdeads had been avoided.

So on one fine day, Omar and his family left the house in Baitullaham to ride on their horse-driven carriage with Qawiun pulling it to take them to Ramallah, a distance that normally took two hours but he decided to take the unchartered roads and see what they could find along the way; it was to show his wife and mostly their two children how life was like and to be closer to nature, because to him the destination was not the only thing to look forward to, but the journey itself that could bring a lot of surprises like what he had experienced along the way from his remote village on the northernmost part of Palestine to Baitullaham that took him an unusually long time to get to, but he was not undeterred and did not aim to speed up his horse so they could arrive at their destination faster. Meeting strangers who first appeared as strangers, then friends were what excited him the most on the journey. And he looked forward to meeting more of them on this particular trip which was not the same as the last one because he had with him his wife and two children so his relationship with the strangers could not be the same as before; he had to safeguard his stature as a husband and father before the strangers and could not express himself too much, lest his family could be looked down upon by his personal indiscretion. He knew his limits.

And sure enough along the way he met with many strangers for the first time and they got on along very well and even decided to accept their offer to put up with them in their modest houses for the night with Omar's wife helping with the household chores and cooking with the stranger's wife, who was a little older than she was. They had four children of their own all grown up with the eldest son married with his wife now pregnant with their first child. They hoped it would be a boy, like all Arab men who wanted their first-born to be a boy so he may carry on his family name, like Omar who was Munir's first-born and a boy, too.

Ramallah turned out to be a large city with many Arab who were Muslims with a sizeable number of Christians who live together peacefully with no known discord that the elders could remember, since the biblical times. It was far away from Baitulmukaddis so political and military activities were not known there since ancient times.

They then finally made it to Ramallah and after stopping at a restaurant to replenish themselves, and buy some food to give to Hanady's friend, as a present for having them as their guests for two days, they went to their house and were greeted warmly. They did not know Hanady and her husband and their two children were coming but they welcomed them anyway, and happily.

Omar liked the break and would be with his wife's friend's husband who was called Zakariyah, to go to the city to visit places of interest and met some of his friends who were Muslims and Arabs and they would sit in the cafés to talk. Zakariyah was a native born and had never left Ramallah except once when he went to Baitulmukaddis so he could pray at Masjid Al-Aqsa, he said. He and some of his friends rode on their horses to go there and back to Ramallah. Zakariyah told Omar that living in Baitulmukaddis was not for him; he said he could not stand the life people there led with everybody rushing everywhere, compared to here in Ramallah when life was at a much slower pace. He also said he didn't care if he and his family did not have much as long as they had enough to live and be pious Muslims. He wanted to send his sons to the religious schools so they may become Ustaz themselves. Omar said it was a good decision and if he had the inspiration from God, he, too, would want to send his own sons to such schools; but it would have to depend on what they wanted to do with their own lives when they grew up a bit more to know what it was that they wanted to do or be in life - their lives, he stressed.

Zakariyah pointed out that the city had a population of more than seven thousand Muslims, five thousand Jews, and more than one thousand Christians all living peacefully with each other; their mayor was Sheikh Mustapha Khairi. And in 1927 it suffered an earthquake and he took Omar at the site where it happened. Both stood still near the area to recite their prayers for those who died in it. 'We're lucky we didn't have such natural calamity like that,' said Omar. 'Ours is a very small and isolated village close to the border of Lubnan. That's our world and all we care for.'

'And you have come from so far away, my brother,' said Zakariyah. 'How long did it take you to get here?'

'Actually I went to Baitullaham from there and then from there came here. It took a long while because I chose to take the sideroads and did not rush to get here and took my own sweet time.'

'Why?'

'So I can see the beauty of what Allah had given us. And the same with my trip or journey from Baitullaham to Ramallah, when we, my wife and I decided to take the side and uncharted roads to get here and we spent a night along the way when we could get here in one day. I feel sorry for those who died in the earthquake. I did not know of it because it seemed to be very far at my village to know what happened here in Ramallah and even Baitumukaddis. We are closer to Lubnan than to Palestine.'

'If it could flood at the Pyramids in Giza in 1927 and also at the Holy Kaabah, earthquakes can also happen here or anywhere,' added Zakariyah. 'I was lucky that it was far away from our village. But I could hear the noise and feel the shaking in the ground that rattled the bottles in my house and topple some things, too. But fortunately, no one was hurt. I thought I was dreaming or something shook the bed I had outside the house to take an afternoon nap, to wake me up. But there was no one there. Even my donkey was not around, or it might have caused my bed to shake to wake me up.'

'Has it done that before?'

Zakariyah nodded. 'He liked to do that to remind me the time to pray when the Adhan is heard.'

'Good donkey. My horse, Qawiun, too, does that when it sees me sleeping for a long time in the day.'

'I would like to take a ride with you on Qawiun and me on my donkey, tomorrow to look at the villages nearby.'

'That would be swell indeed. I'd like that. And Qawiun, too, would like that. And from what I have seen of Ramallah, I think you're lucky to be born here and to grow up in such a place where there are people of different races living side by side and in peace. In my village there are so few of us and most of us are Muslims, a few Jews, and almost no Christians. But we get along with each other well. There have also been some inter-religious marriages.'

Meanwhile, Omar's wife, Hanady took her sons to go to the market with Zakariyah's wife, Zeynab, where she was entranced with the designs of the embroidery they were making and selling there. She wanted to buy a piece or two, and Zeynab managed to bargain for a better price. 'This piece looks good on you, Hanady,' said Zeynab. 'You can put it over your body or use it to cover a table in your house. This is where I always get my embroideries. They are cheaper here than elsewhere in the whole of Ramallah. And my mother and grandmother, too, came here to get theirs.'

They then walked to other parts of the market or bazaar to look at what the stores were selling. 'My mother knew the mother of the person who made the embroidery you just bought and also his parents who used to make them in their store too. So they have been doing it for generations. It's only people like us, my people, who were not good with them so we have to buy some from people like them. But I am not embarrassed because each of us have a talent that we are good at; they are good at what they do and we are good at what we do, which is to buy these from them, or they would not have customers to buy what they make.'

Hanady almost laughed but she refrained from doing that because she was aware she was in a crowded place and it was not proper for Arab and Muslim women to express such feelings in public and also in the privacy of their own homes. She then pulled one of the embroidery she had bought from the bag she was carrying and Zeynab helped to put it over her body. 'I can't buy anymore because I already have a few at home, some I had bought months or years ago but never had the occasion to wear. I kept wearing the ones I liked and until they are torn and I will not pick another to wear, like the one I am wearing now. I have been using it for the last ten years or more. It was given to me as a present for my wedding that I had put away until I remembered it and started to wear it. I also gave away to a few or my relatives for them to wear since I had too many to keep. You really do not need to have in your possession that many scarves or clothes; I have a few coverings I wear like this one I wear when I go out and nobody cares what I wear underneath it.'

'True. There is no need to show off to everybody, every stranger what we have in our possession; all we need are just a few clothes to wear. I bought the embroidery to give away to my mother and sisters who are back at home. Any embroidery that is made here in Ramallah must be pretty. Besides, Ramadan is around the corner and soon it will be Eid Mubarak, so they can wear them or use them to decorate the house with.'

The two women had not seen each other in a long time; the last time they met was at the wedding of Rahimah and Zeynab and her husband attended it, and now Hanady had two boys who are not so young. The first one is around ten, she was not sure; he did not want to ask Hanady about it. She calculated the wedding was more than ten or eleven years ago, and she had her first child a year later and if her calculations were correct, the boy, Ilham might be ten years. He looked like a ten-year-old boy and was in school. But he looked intelligent too, and mature that made the guessing of his age to be a bit difficult. It would be easy for her to ask Hanady Ilham's age but she did not want to do that because tradition forbid her from asking direct questions of such personal nature. And Rahimah, too, has not asked her any personal question of herself and her family, despite being good friends, who knew each other when they were small. She and Zeynab preferred to talk about other things; there were a lot of things that they could talk about other than on themselves and their families, much less on their respective husbands who were now riding their horse and donkey to visit the neighboring villages. They promised to return to the house before sunset so they could pray together in the open.

Omar and Zakariyah stopped for Zohor prayers in a small town and they prayed in an open land facing towards Makkah in Saudi Arabia, as always. After that they decided to go to a restaurant to have something to eat and to rest. They had given their horse and donkey a place to rest under a shade of a tree whose leaves were lush. Both had had enough to eat and drink and they were lying on the ground to wait for their 'friends' to tell them to move.

Zakaiyah told Omar that it was like this in Ramallah as in the whole of Palestine even since the British Mandate of Palestine in May, 1922, with the Palestinians living away from Baitulmukaddis a.k.a. Jerusalem. The other small cities had not experienced much change, except that both Omar and Zakariyah had noticed the influx of many Jews from outside of their country, especially from the former Crusader countries, as they described them. They were the countries in Europe. And a few of them had started to buy properties in Ramallah and elsewhere and from newspaper reports and also from the radio they sometimes heard when they were in the restaurants in the cities, there were now Jewish enclaves where they lived amongst themselves and hardly ever mix with anyone mostly Arabs who were Muslims and also Christians. Zakariyah, especially did not know why there were there and what they were doing there. He was not aware of the anti-Semitic sentiments in some of the former Crusader countries of Europe that had forced them to flee to come to Palestine where they were given special attention and support by the local Arabs, who sympathized with their plight and tried to do whatever they could to help them find a way of life here. Because they thought their presence here was only of a temporary nature. They made sure no one heard what they said. He knew there were spies working for the British. So far he had not seen any British soldiers there, but he still feared if there were spies from amongst the Arabs and Jews who might be working for them by providing information on those Arabs, especially from the Muslim community who might have some negative attitudes towards the British. So he made sure he kept his voice low so only Omar could hear him speak; low tones that were drowned by the sounds of horse or donkey-driven carts on the streets in front of the restaurant where they were.

Omar received a rude shock with the revelation given by Zakariyah who was being frank with him. He knew his friend wanted to remind him of the dangers that he might find himself in if he was not careful. 'Everybody has been speaking in such low tones, since the British Mandate of our country' said Zakariyah. 'And all of us have a good reason to do that because we do not know who might be turning against us, our friends and strangers alike. And I am not accusing you who have come from so far away, to want to spy on me. And I am not saying that you are a spy for the British. I am just trying to warn you to be extra careful in who you meet and who you speak with.'

Omar was even more shocked when Zakariyah insinuated how strangers to his village and to Ramallah who had never been there before, who had come there for the first time were often suspected to be 'spies' although he, Zakariyah knew Omar was not such a person. Why? Because he had come with his wife, a good and dear friend of his own wife; and if not because of that, he everyone else in the village and in Ramallah, too, would suspect him of being a spy that he was not. 'Ma Sha Allah!' Omar almost shrieked as they were riding back to Zakariyah's house, where there was no one to look at them and who could hear what they were saying. And suddenly, Omar thought he could look at the faces of some people in the restaurant and on the streets who were staring at him, although this was just his imagination. So now he knew why his friend wanted to take him for a ride away from the village so he could talk with him about the matter that he had never thought of before. And what would he say to his wife when they were back in her parents' house in Baitullaham tomorrow? He definitely did not want to stay in Ramallah a day more; and from the two days he planned to stay there. He now said he would leave Ramallah after spending just one night. It was going to be a long day and night henceforth, and he could not wait until tomorrow morning after breakfast, to leave on his carriage to return to his in-law's home which was, at the moment, his home too, i.e. until he got a house for himself.

And along the way back, Zakariyah mentioned to Omar how there were spies in the early years before the British Mandate of their country. Two of whom were involved in espionage who were assisted by the British and it was purely to fight the Uthmaniyah rulers or Ottoman Empire in Palestine, where they were now. The organization was known in its Hebrew phrase 'Netzah Yisrael Lo Yeshaker', which translates into English, as 'the Eternal One of Israel will not lie' or in short, 'Nili' which sounded almost like the River Nile. It was the British code name for 'An Organization.'

Zakariyah took a deep breath as he galloped his donkey along, as the sun was dimming in the horizons and with Omar riding his horse at a slow pace beside him. He turned to look at him and saw him frozen on the saddle. They had been riding back to Zakariyah's house for an hour. Omar could not wait to get back to the house, he said, so he could have a shower or a bath in the stream near the house. He brought out the matter on the bath, because he had had enough of the talk about spies and how some in Ramallah might even think he had come there to spy on them. His wife, Hanady would be shocked if she was told of this; but he had not intention of telling her what Zakariyah had told him just now in the restaurant and while they were riding.

'I did not mean to scare you, Omar,' Zakariyah added. He felt uncomfortable and uneasy too looking at his friend now looking nervous.

'How was your ride?' Zeynab, who was Zakariyah's wife asked Omar the moment she saw him climbing down his horse outside of her house and beside her was her husband who was already standing on the ground beside his donkey. Omar did not answer the question. And her husband quickly answered it, 'It was interesting, wasn't it, Omar?' he turned to look at Omar who just nodded. He felt his face froze. He felt his limbs numb. But he tried to remain calm. And he was thus saved when the cries of the Adhan for dawn prayers started to be heard. 'Ah, it is Maghrib; shall we go to the Masjid over there to pray? And you can meet some locals who are there too.'

Omar did not answer. But the silence said to Zakariyah that he would do as he had proposed. Omar did not even mention the gazelles (ghazal) he had spotted on the trip to Ramallah and a few more on the way back; they were far in the distance. And he also caught sight of some sunbirds or 'iidafat' flying over him. They were Palestine's national animal and bird respectively; but Zakariyah was not fond of them because they could not be kept as pets and he like many Arab men preferred and liked to keep eagles or 'nasir' which they put on stands they made themselves and seldom keep them in cages. The well-trained ones were allowed to fly on their own because they knew when to come back. But those 'nasir' that they allowed to fly on their own were mostly those that were born to older eagles they had kept so the young 'nasir' knew where they were born and who reared them since small and also who trained them, so they always knew where to return, usually late evening before nightfall. Zakariyah liked to take his 'nasir' birds for long walks in the desert and riding on his horses or donkeys with the eagles when the weather was fine. But he reared the 'nasir' for fun and not to used them as commodities to sell in the market to make money from them. He disdained anyone from doing that; the most he used those birds to entertain him and his sons who he hoped could be compelled to also like rearing them in the same way that his father had, giving him his love for such birds for which he was grateful, because they had given him a lot of thrills to look after their welfare and well-being and treating them not as birds but as 'friends' or 'sadiq.' To him the eagles or 'nasir' sometimes could be better friends than those who walked on two feet.

But not Omar; who never showed any affection or interests for such creatures, because from where he had come from eagles were rare and could only be found very far away in the hills from his village, so he never knew them and how to treat them; even when he saw some at Zakariyah's house, he almost ignored them. He did not notice any eagle at the house when he arrived there; he only saw them the evening before he left the house to return to his own. Oh, they left to go anywhere, they wanted, said Zakariyah; and sometimes they would be gone for days. Once one of them did not return for a week and I thought some people had caught it and stole it. But here in Palestine as much in all the Arab countries no one steals 'nasir', because they are all God-fearing people. And what happened to the eagle, Zakariyah? asked Omar. Nothing, he replied; it just flew wherever it wanted but there were strong gales that took it further away and it did not know how to come back to this place; and it took a week to get here. And at one of its feet was a note. A note? Yes, a note! Who wrote it? A good fellow wrote a note and tied it to its foot. And what did it, the note say? It said my 'nasir' had gone to Damsyik! Damsyik?! Damascus! But that's in Syria! Precisely. I was shocked. How could my 'nasir', my eagle fly so far away? It must have been blown by the strong gales. I have never been to Damsyik in 'Suriyah' and my 'nasir' had been there before me! Imagine that! I can't. I have still not gone to Damsyik. Neither I, said Omar. Damsyik from here, said Omar, must be more than eight hundred kilometers, if I'm correct. I have not the slightest idea, said Zakariyah. I was just glad and happy that my 'nasir' managed to return, to find its way back here; and I prayed to Allah for its safe return.

And how did the good man in Damsyik know your eagle had come from Ramallah? if I may ask, asked Omar. He did not guess, said Zakariyah; he must have read the note I had written on a piece of brass which I tied to the foot of the bird to say that it is from Ramallah, here in Palestine. I see... and did it have a name? No. I did not favor giving my eagles any name. My horse is called 'Qawiun' and I also let it go on its own, so he would run everywhere. Has it ever gone astray and disappear for long periods? No, not that I know of. Besides, in my village, there is really no place where it could go. Why? Because it is almost bordered by hills. I have also taught him not go to astray even especially when he is let loose. It is difficult to be a bird, said Zakariyah, because it does not know the weather condition and if it rains, it might not be able to find any place to hide itself; or if there is a sudden gush of wind or gale then the bird can be thrown off-course and be taken to a place it is not familiar with. And sometimes, they could get hurt from falling onto the ground with their feathers torn. Once my eagle brought a gold ring and I became anxious because there was no way for me to return it to its owner. What did you do with it? asked Omar. I consulted the Ustaz at the Masjid and he told me to surrender it to the authorities to let them deal with it, and if they see it fit, they could pawn it and use the money to give to charitable bodies to spend. Was it expensive? Not really about fifty pounds. That's quite a bit, I must say. I pity the person, a woman, I believe, who had lost the ring. But there was no way for my bird to steal it from the woman's finger. She must have dropped it… Or, it might have been taken from a corpse! added Omar, even before Zakariyah could finish his last sentence when he wanted to say, if the ring might have been dropped in a field and my bird did the right thing by picking it and taking it to him to decide on what to do with it.

I have no use for such things, said Zakariah; I wouldn't even want to give it to my wife; and she would definitely not want to take it if I had given it to her to wear because she would ask me where I had got it, and if I had found it. In fact, I do not encourage my wife or all my daughters to wear gold. And, as you know, it is also 'haram' (forbidden) for Muslim men to have gold on them. My wedding ring is made of bronze. Mine too, said Omar.

After the Maghrib prayers, Omar did as he had told Zakariyah, which was to have a bath at the stream; and he went there with his horse. He first poured water over its body to freshen it. Qawiun was thrilled to be thrown cold, fresh water Omar had scooped in a pail from the well near the stream. And he also poured some water over himself. He was glad he could take his mind off what Zakariyah had said to him earlier in the day. He meant well, he thought; it was just for general knowledge; of course, what he said was history and it happened before the British Mandate of Palestine and also during the First World War, thought Omar as he continued to wipe his body with a thick towel. Zakariyah meant well when he said those things, he thought.

338

Omar had the Isyak prayers in Zakariyah's house and afterwards, he and and the others had dinner together. This time they had it in the kitchen with he and his wife. Hanady liked this as it indicated that they had been welcomed not as guests, but as members of their family.

Omar could not sleep well that night after returning from the riding to the neighboring villages outside of Ramallah; he was surprised that his friend, Zakariyah found it necessary for him to remind him of such dangers that he might face when he least expected it. He thanked Zakariyah for that advice. And he decided not to travel on uncharted roads on his way back to Baitullaham, but to take the main roads linking the two cities, so that he could feel safe; besides it was already getting dark. The new moon was full and it shown bright light over the whole area as he traveled on his cart and pulled by Qawiun, who was now moving at a fast speed with the shaking of the cart that made his head move all around and the prayers he was reading in his head going with it. His wife and two children were lying on the cart at the back. Omar wanted to arrive at his house before ten o'clock. He, however, did not tell his wife what her best friend's husband had told her earlier in the day; and the reason why she was tired and he asked her to lay in the cart on thick carpet with their two sons, was because Zeynab had taken her to many places while Omar and Zakariyah were not around and their sons had been playing with each other running around outside of the house, and became exhausted. And Zakariyah did not see them off in the afternoon after Zohor because he had to go somewhere to help his friends.

'I hope you can come back soon,' said Zeynab to Hanady and Omar, before they left on their horse-cart.

'In Sha Allah,' said Hanady.

In Sha Allah, said Omar to himself; Maybe not, he added; maybe not. He knew he was trembling when he said that, but fortunately, no one could see it because he was wearing his robe and an overcoat to shield him from the cool wind that would hit him as he rode along, as the sun dimmed and the winds getting cooler and cooler. He was sure glad that Zakariyah was not around at the house to see him off because he would feel nervous if he was. And for the first time, Omar did not want to think of the moon, to think about how bright and full it was in the new month in the year, and how lovely the whole area he was passing by, like he used to do before, especially when he was riding alone with Qawiun from his remote village to Baitullaham a trip that took them about two weeks to achieve. But he wanted to start thinking about what his uncle, Yunus and his father, Munir had in mind to make him do, with his father sending him to Baitullaham to stay with his own family and be with his Uncle Yunus, who had not yet told him why he was there at his house in the first place. Did the two of them have any conspiracy to force him to do something that he did not want to do? But what possible agenda would they have for him to be a part of? It was difficult to read their minds; they were men who had few words and who hardly shared their thoughts and even his mother could not guess what his father was thinking; the same with Yunus' wife who had grown to understand her husband's peculiar traits and who never would want to bother with him anymore and to let him be with his own world.

Riding back to his house seemed to be very slow and long even though Qawiun was speeding fast with the sounds of the shoe it was fixed with hitting the road with such ferocity hitting the road and creating different sounds that should be music to Omar's ears, but this time, they did not mean anything to him. He pitied his horse for providing him with good company and creating some interesting music with its feet as it hit the ground but he was not in any mood to appreciate it.

Omar's wife suddenly woke up; she found it surprising and wondered quietly why Qawiun was speeding so fast. She peeped through a hole in front of the cart where her husband was and asked, 'Where are we now?' Her husband did not hear her because the sounds of the horse hitting the ground and the other sounds created by other carts and horses and occasionally motorcars driven by some British men and their women, was too loud; Omar did not hear what his wife had said, so she asked him the same question again, 'Where are we?' and this time she made sure she said it louder than the first time. Omar heard her this time and said quite casually, 'We'll be back in about thirty minutes. Why? Do you want to stop? How are Ilham and Thaer doing back there?'

'It's up to you, if you feel like you want to stop, so we can stretch out a bit and have some food and drinks. I can wake up the children. Qawiun could do with some rest too, and to have something to eat and drink...'

'We can stop at the next place where there is a restaurant, but we cannot stay long there. We eat, and go. The light will start to dim soon and I don't want to be back at the house after dark. We just missed a restaurant a few minutes back.'

Omar found a restaurant by the side of the road along the way and immediately stopped. They found an empty table outside of the restaurant which was full and there was a lot of noise of people talking in Arabic, which at times sounded boisterous and wanted to avoid it as much as possible. And there was also a lot of smoke coming out of some hookahs the men were smoking. So that was why Omar chose a vacant table outside of the restaurant and not any of the few that were vacant he could see inside. His wife made the orders of some food and tea and they ate quietly. The radio was playing some familiar Egyptian songs he was familiar with and tried to listen to the lyrics and enjoy the music, too. Then the song stopped; it was interrupted by an announcement made by a male reporter. Omar ignored it but not for very long when the announcement related to the arrest of two men in Ramallah who were suspected to be spies; they were Arab men who had lived in the city for many years, but they turned out to be Jews who spoke good Arabic. But Omar was not able to listen properly what the radio announcer was saying because his report was broken by the sounds of sibilance and also cracking due to the poor reception. He stood up and went to the back of the restaurant to wash his hand and training his ears on what was being said by the reporter in the radio. It was clear now that two Arab-looking men had been arrested by the Palestinian police who suspected them for being spies. This gave Omar the shivers.

'What was that all about?' asked Hanady the moment when Omar was approaching their table. 'Did I hear right, that two Arab men were arrested?'

'Nothing,' said Omar as he sat on his chair, and as the radio started to play the song again, that was interrupted just now. He took a sip of tea from his cup to cool himself down. The other customers, who were mostly men, were all oblivious to what was happening. And they did not hear the news to worry about what had happened in Ramallah; they were in their own world.

Omar had heard it wrong; the two men were not Arabs who lived all their lives in Ramallah; they were British men who knew how to read and write in Arabic and who had lived in the city a few years; and they were from the British spy agencies who managed to infiltrate into the society pretending to be religious teachers who had come from another Arab country and the report did not say which. They could be from Egypt or Libya. They were young and mixed with the locals and who also often ate in the sidewalk cafés and restaurants eating with their bare hands and drinking 'chai' and 'qahwa' as much as the locals; and sometimes they also did the dabke dance with them in feasts held in the villages during weddings and other festive holidays. One of them even played the role of Imam and gave sermons in the Masjid during the Friday prayers. So naturally, their arrests shocked many of the locals who did not know who they were and why they were there amidst them. There arose some suspicions when some local Arabs found their interpretation of the verses from the Noble Qur'an and the 'Sayings' or 'Hadith' and 'Sunnah' to be wrong. But the laypersons could not tell it, except for some men from Ramallah who had just returned from the universities in Egypt and Jordan found out and they were the ones who lodged reports against them with the authorities. They had learnt about the existence of spies working for the British when they were in Egypt and the other countries who were later detained and sent back to England, and who knew their modus operandi, which was what the two spies in Ramallah were doing that fooled the locals for a long time, before they were exposed and arrested and subsequently sent back to England by the British authorities in Palestine, from where they had come from; and perhaps be given some recognition for having done a good job whilst during the whole time they were in Ramallah and elsewhere in Palestine where they must have got some important information that was useful to the British.

Omar read about the scandal and the two men from the reports in the local newspaper he managed to get from a store he had stopped to buy some snacks for his children the next day after he returned from Ramallah. But he did not show them to his wife who had said how her best friend, Zeynab had listened to the speeches and also sermons or 'khutbah' they had given in public in their village and others and found them to be erudite and knowledgeable indeed. They did not know better and he also did not want to disappoint his wife if he told her about who the two men where. He wanted the issue to die down a little before he brought the matter to her attention and in the safe confines of their house in total privacy so she may not feel disappointed with the revelation and accept the fact and not be emotionally affected by it. He also hoped with the arrests of the two men, other spies could be exposed and detained and stiff action taken against them as there must be so many of them throughout the country of Palestine as did the other Arab countries around it.

He was surely glad to be back here in his own home, and away from the incident; but he was not sure if anyone here would be arrested for the same reasons; he swore he had seen some men, Arab men who always wore new robes and whose faces where covered with thin hair and mustache which was unlike the other men including he whose facial hair was thicker and darker, while the men had lighter hair on their faces and most probably on their heads, too, except that no one could see it because it was always hidden under their headscarves. They were stylish for the locals and often did not sit long in the restaurants or sidewalk cafés, and often appeared like they were in a rush. Or maybe, just maybe, they did not want to be exposed by mixing with the locals in an intimate fashion that would expose their true identity.

Omar did not want to think of them because he lacked the true facts and he definitely did not want to guess who they were. They could be nice people from the big cities such as Jerusalem, Haifa and Tel Aviv and so on who were here for a specific reason, and only they knew what that was. Omar then felt guilty for assuming that they were 'spies' when they might not necessarily be so. They could be nice people who wanted privacy and wanted to be left alone. But they looked wealthy from the type of robes they wore which were definitely not those that were sold in the open markets and bazaars, but from abroad. Omar had a robe looking like that made of fine cotton that his father had bought when he went to Amman in Jordan that he had not worn before; he wanted to wear it on special occasions such as the Eidul Fitri or Eidul Adha or at the very least to attend weddings of his close relatives or friends. He then sought God to forgive him for thinking so negatively of the few strangers who he thought he had seen a few times, but who he personally did not know and could never know who they were and what was their identity and what they were doing there. And none of them had ever greeted him with 'Asalamulaikum' when they bumped into each other along narrow alleyways or in the small restaurants, because they did not look anywhere else but within themselves and they also spoke sparingly, and only with each other or to the waiters to place orders and to pay whatever they had eaten or drank. They looked very fair, which often meant that they were people of high academic standing and who might be knowledgeable in Islam who did not have much time to communicate with the hoi-polloi to ask what they were doing and if they were okay, and so forth; they had a lot of things in their heads to worry about.

And sure enough not so many days later, Omar learnt one of the men he had seen before had been approached by the security officer when he was sitting alone inside a restaurant which was not full and was asked to follow them to go out through the back door and get inside a car. That was what his friends who happened to be inside the restaurant had told him. But still his friend could not confirm the reason why he followed the security officers who were in uniform. This is what I saw, his friend told him; but I did not know for what reason why the man who looked different was taken away in the car. Omar became more confused when he did not hear any report in the radio or the newspapers the next day and through the whole week after the incident happened.

From that day on, Omar made sure he did not wear nice clothes, and used the old robes he had worn many times; they looked exactly the same, because it was the habit of most of the Arab men to not flaunt their wealth in the form of the robes they wore, but chose to look like each other; the only difference between them was their piety and not in the way they flaunt their wealth which he suspected had started to creep into the psyche and mentality of some of their fellow Arab men who would also allow their women to wear more gold than necessary, with them also doing the same, but not so much as it was still forbidden for them to wear gold on themselves, only silver and bronze, on their fingers and only one ring and not two or more. So far no one had breached this rule or edict in Islam, which was good to him. But from what he had heard from some of his friends who often went to the large cities in Palestine such as Baitulmukaddis, which some of them had already started to call Jerusalem, Haifa, Tel Aviv, and more so in Cairo in Egypt and Amman in Jordan and Baghdad in Iraq, some of the men were already showing and flaunting their newly-gotten wealth not so much by the way they wear their robes, but in the form of the motorized vehicles that they had bought from some British officers who had left their country upon the termination of their services in the respective countries, although some of them had also started to wear robes that were made of fine cotton and specifically made for them, and not those that anyone could easily buy in the common markets and bazaars anymore and they would go there driven in their motorized vehicles when earlier on their parents and grandparents had gone there riding camels, horses, donkeys, and mules and sometimes, driven in carts.

Omar still remembered and always asked himself not to forget to remember the incident that happened when he was just a small boy and was still being carried by his grandfather, who took him to a funeral of a very wealthy Arab man in the village near theirs. The deceased had many camels, goats and other animals and many acres of land where he grew olive trees. He got some of his workers to pick the seeds to turn into expensive olive oil to sell in the big cities only, because the villagers could not afford to buy any of it. However, when he died, he was still buried in an almost nameless and featureless grave just like the others who had died earlier and was laid near some of them, who had worked for him and also his father and grandfather. Omar was still a small baby then but the incident remained in his mind and got stuck there, and it was one of the most indelible moments in his entire life that he considered to be of a high significance, so much so that when he grew up he somehow refused to entertain the thought that in order for him to be successful or very successful, he ought to improve on his personal skills so the could use them to enrich himself and in the process force him to challenge himself to do better than the others of the same age as he was then, and in the process to, cheat his way to get or achieve what he wanted to do or was forced to do by hidden forces, which he usually meant to be 'Satans' or the 'Devils' that were lurking in his mind so that he may become their representative on this earth. He had seen over the years, some of his friends and the others who he did not know personally who had fallen prey to the dictates of the unknown and unseen Satans and Devils who forced them to do the bidding for them, in ways that they could not comprehend or realize before it was too late before a few of them, started to repent and turned their lives around upon seeking advice from some Ustaz, who gave them advice that allowed them to become part of the overall society again, while the others who did not do this, continued on their road to self-angradizement and personal achievement and forgetting in the end, what awaited them was no more than a small piece of land the size of their bodies or corpses or remains to allow them to lie till eternity when their souls were raised to confront their Makers, which in Omar's and the Muslims' case, was Allah Ta Allah, or Allah the Almighty!

Omar sat alone outside the barn where his horse, Qawiun was lying sleeping inside. Occasionally he could hear it neigh softly. He almost cried when he thought of what he had experience and seen with his own eyes, as a baby and when he grew up to see many Arab men going in the ways of the Satans and Devils. He continued to sit there frozen and hidden in the dark. Then he realized that his trip to Ramallah had a real purpose that he had not envisioned before until he got there and now when he reflected on what his good friend, Zakariyah had said and did with him, and especially with the arrests of the few people, the spies of the British who were detained that he had heard of from the radio and in the words written in the newspapers he got the day after that. And he also knew or wanted to think why his father, Munir had sent him out of his village in the far north of Palestine close to Lubnan or Lebanon, to come to Baitullaham, but not in the exact words that his father could describe it himself.

His father was a simple man of some means; although he could be described as rich or wealthy, but certainly not fabulously wealthy as some other men in his village and in the nearby ones, who had more properties than his father did. Maybe his father had never wanted to become wealthy more than he could be and had gotten now. Wealth in the Arab mentality or psychology was seen in the form of having many children and grandchildren and not in the form of gold, money, or other worldly properties, because the world was not their final abode but Heaven or 'Jannah' was and this was where all Arab-Muslims and other Muslims spent most of their time to try and get there by whatever means, which mostly meant for them to be as pious and close to Allah Ta Allah as possible. He was grateful for the teachings he had received from his Ustaz or religious teachers and not those who viewed the world from a totally different angle, those who taught in the more modern or secular schools who forced the students to perform well so they may become successful in life and gain many economic benefits from their secular education.

Yes, I was Ibn Batutta in some way, he said to himself. And I am also Marco Polo in some other ways. They went on their journeys through many lands they had never been to before or knew they existed; and they were compelled by their desire to see the vastness of God's Earth, yet, with their immense achievements that had been recorded and recognized by many till long after they had died, and they did not benefit anything for themselves, other than the satisfactions that they might have got from having travelled through all the lands and meeting so many people who were unlike them…

Omar did not finish his sentence that had formed in is head; he did not want to think that he was like the two well-known and world famous adventurers and travelers, an Arab man and an Italian man, who had traveled far and achieved a lot; he had only traveled in his own country and had seen changes happening to it, especially in the people, the strangers, and had now started to worry for them. There were more and more foreigners now living in his country with many more who were expected to come in droves in ships from the Crusader Countries of Europe, and who in time can cause his country and people to change, hopefully for the better. But he was not certain if his country and people could handle the influx of those foreigners and their families and their tall stories that they had started to tell and even write in books to seek pity from the Arabs....

Then suddenly his thoughts were disrupted by the sudden neighing from his horse, which he knew was a signal that the morning sun was about to rise and the cries of the Adhan would also soon happen, for the time for the Maghrib prayers. Qawiun never failed to neigh every morning wherever he might happen to be at, in his village or elsewhere. Omar looked at the distant horizons and saw what he thought was faint light coming from under the horizon. He then stood up to welcome the first rays of the sun and the sound of the Adhan. He scooped some fine sand from the ground and perform his ablution by the 'tayamum' fashion in place of water that was abundant in the stream or well near him. But he chose to do the ablution using sand instead. And after the cries of the Adhan were over, he performed his Maghrib prayers and as always facing 'Qibla' towards Makkah in the distance, and crying a bit as he did that towards the point all Muslims turned to pray from where they were all over the world and whose bodies were laid so they face towards it when they die. He didn't realize that going to Baitullaham where he was now and then to Ramallah where he had just been earlier, would be such a suspenseful and traumatic experience for him personally; he just could not describe it in words how he felt and share it with anyone, lest he would be deemed to be a spoiler of fun or heretic he said he was not.

His father, Munir, must have told Qawiun why he wanted it to take me to Baitullaham, because his father liked to talk to him more than he did with Omar, who he hardly ever spoke with on anything; and everything that he needed to pass on to Omar had to go through his mother, who relayed the messages to him including the trip or journey he would take to Baitullaham. If only his horse could speak, he thought… and not that he had not asked it if his father had told him something, or anything on the trip, he would have said so, only if he could speak other than to neigh or bray and sometimes smile widely to bare his white teeth, which Omar often took it to mean that it wanted to have his teeth cleaned, which Omar often obeyed and did as 'told' by brushing it with a large brush he had bought at the market specifically for this job which happened every two to three weeks or when the situation demanded it. It was not the other brush he had to clean its coat which he also had for Qawiun's personal use and sometimes for his other horses, donkeys, and mules.

Omar, too, spoke with Qawiun, but not as much as his father who liked to 'talk' to it a lot; but now when it was with Omar in Baitullaham, his father must feel lonely with no horse to talk to. So the two of them, Omar and Qawiun were stuck there until further instructions he got from his father, through his younger brother, Yunus, who he had not seen since he returned to his in-laws' house. And he wanted to take that as both good and bad news at the same time, if his presence there could be described as 'a blessing in disguise' much like his trip to Ramallah. He then went out to check on the seed from the very ancient olive tree he had got from it that he put in the ground, to see if it had grown even a little over the last few days he had not seen it. It didn't look like the seed had grown into a seedling, or anything that showed that it was growing. It needed time and more water, so he got some from the stream which he thought was fresher than the water in the well and poured over the spot where the seed was inside the ground. He then took the pail with some more water in it and offered it to his horse to drink. Thank you for the rides, Qawiun, he said to the horse, and all the rides you had given me even before we left our village to come to here, Baitullaham. I'm sure we will be taking more rides in the near future, together. I am so sorry if I have to bother you, my 'friend', my trusted 'friend.' You are 'strong', so that was why I decided to call you, 'Qawiun.' Omar then gave the horse a strong hug at its neck.

He then remembered the small village of Deir Yassin and thought, maybe, he could go there for a day's trip to see the small village with so few Arabs who were all Muslims, like him, as a diversion from his dreary life full of uncertainty and not knowing what else his father had in mind for him to do other than to come to Baitullaham, and stay here with his own family. Hmmm…Deir Yassin; sounds like an interesting place to visit, he said softly in 'Qawiun's' ear. Did you hear me, Qawiun? We can go there one of these days, just to see it; and this time only the two of us will go there and you won't need to pull the cart.

Qawiun brayed to indicate that he had heard Omar and agreed with the idea, which sounded good. He then gave a loud neigh that startled Omar and the other camels and donkeys nearby, including some which were sitting or standing on the land of their owners that were littered around Omar's in-laws' house where he was currently staying. Thank you, Qawiun, said Omar to the horse; 'Shukran'. You have been such a very good horse; and you are my best friend, too; remember that!

Omar did some work on the exact location of Deir Yassin later that night after having dinner with his family. He sat alone on the rooftop of the house, which was where he always went if he wanted to have some privacy. His wife and in-laws knew that so they did not disturb him, except for his wife who would show up carrying a tray with snacks and a small kettle or 'dallah' full of coffee or 'chai', for her husband to take. Their bedroom was on the third floor, which was a flight down from the rooftop. The moon was full and Omar decided not to light an oil lamp; he liked to be bathed in the soft light from the moon, to look and feel like he did not exist. His wife went to him and put the tray down and left as quietly as she appeared without uttering any word. She knew her husband wanted to be left alone with his own thoughts. But just before she disappeared at the door, Omar called out and said, 'Deir Yassin.' It was not a question; it was not a remark, or a comment. Omar's wife, knew it was directed to her and it sounded like he wanted to know if she knew of the place and where it was at, being a person who lived all her life in the village where they were now.

'Why?' she asked, after stopping and turning to look at her husband from the bottom of the stairs. 'You want to go there?'

'Is is a nice place to go to?' he asked without replying her questions.

'Yes, it is; it is a village, not a large one. It only has about two hundred people. Why?'

'I am thinking of going there, but with my friend, Qawiun, but just for a day trip.'

'When? Tomorrow? I can prepare some food and drinks for you to take.'

'I'll let you know when...'

His wife nodded and turned to walk into the third floor of the house, leaving her husband alone in the semi-darkness. He poured some coffee and sipped it. Omar had done some research on his own on Deir Yassin and found that it was five kilometers from Baitulmukaddis and there were many side roads, which were narrow that passed through many old villages with fewer inhabitants, which attracted him; so he thought of taking these roads with Qawiun galloping and not riding in a rush. Then he realized that the only reason he wanted to go to such a place traveling through the areas from where he was to Deir Yassin was because the villages along the way were all very small with so few inhabitants. They were all like the village in the northernmost part of Palestine he was born and grew up in, and he might have remembered those interesting times spent there all his life now that he was away in Baitullaham, and wanted to be in such surroundings where camels, horses, donkeys, and mules roam not leashed by their owners, who he wanted to describe as their 'friends', like Qawiun, so Qawiun, too could find some friends with them. And he and his horse could leave in the morning and go to Deir Yassin to arrive there before Asar or afternoon prayers after stopping at some places along the way to meet with some locals.

Omar knew what 'Deir' meant – a monastery and 'Yassin' was named in honor of a local legend, Sheikh Yassim. And all the houses there were built of stone and mostly enclosed in a small area called 'Hara' which meant 'The District'. And there were remains of some ancient building that the locals called 'Deir' too. And there was also an area that sat in a valley from where the place was and where the Jews lived called Givat Shaul. The Field Marshall Edmund Allenby of the Royal British Army, had brought his men to storm a fortification built by the locals on 8 December, 1917 and the next day Baitulmukaddis fell to the British. Omar got this information when he found a thin book on the early history of Palestine that was written before the British Mandate of Palestine in a small store he had stopped at on his way back from Ramallah and knew about the village and its colorful and dramatic history, which was also why he was eager to go there to see it for himself.

A small village in the middle of nowhere with so much history!?, Omar said to himself, that had withstood the test of time since the Era of Uthmaniyah (Ottoman) till now. And to get there we have to pass through Jaffa, another interesting city that I had heard of before but had never been there, until now. I am glad I am here in Baitullaham. My father, being the man that he was and has been, must surely want me to experience life to see more of our country, Palestine and meet and mix with many more people to get to know them better, to allow me to grow up into an older man who is wiser and full of life.

Now Omar thought he knew why his father had sent him off out of his small villages so he could be on his own and not pampered like he had been all his life even after he had got married and had two children of his own. Was he ashamed of me? asked Omar, of his father, who might have such a thought that Omar felt in his mind. I don't know…he may be right…I don't know…was all the answer that he could think of.

15

Epilogue: With Douglas in Ramallah Park and on Broadway.

I went around the City of Amman in Jordan in September, 1999, after the function at the Khalil Sakakini Cultural Center (KSCC) in Ramallah where they showed the first film I produced and directed and also wrote called, 'Seman: A Lost Hero' and a few other television features I wrote that were shown on Malaysian television. But because I finally arrived in Ramallah after the event I did not get to speak in the forum on my works with the audience who probably had seen some film and television drama productions from Malaysia, and I won't be surprised if they could see much Malaysia in them. Actually, all my works had a bit, if not a lot, of Malaysia in them because I made sure of that. I took some photos and also did some sketches of the city compared to the many films made by Malaysians, which are mostly those that they copied from popular Hollywood and Hong Kong films, with some almost exact copies, so they called them a 'tribute' to those films.

And this is compared to the works by other Malaysian film directors and producers who gave scant regard for such matters so most of their works that have been shown in the cinemas and on television do not reflect Malaysia, but mostly their fantasies about living or life in the west, which they had seen in many American productions with some even producing their fake Hollywood stuff to share with the audiences in Malaysia who are excited to see them, because of their lacking in the understanding of films and what they should be encouraged to see in them.

I returned to the hotel where I had stayed before I went to Ramallah with two Malaysian embassy officials who drove me there, and who also got my visa to go there, albeit after the function at KSCC, which was just across the street from Ramallah Park where the Roman Amphitheater is, where there are many stalls selling souvenirs. I decided to check out the ancient Roman theater to see what it was like and found nothing of interest except for the fact that it is old, very old and oddly enough there were also some parts of statues of Roman gladiators that were placed near walls some with their heads missing. Most of the tourists I noticed were local ones from the way they spoke in Arabic and some foreign ones who were eager to take photos. And on the back of the stage, was a large photo of the newly-installed King Abdullah, who ascended to the throne upon the death of his father, King Hussein.

The whole area around the small hotel was busy with life and there were also many restaurants where I could buy food to eat. and once I was done with touring here, I decided to take a cab to go up a low hill to see the remains of more ancient Roman buildings which had collapsed leaving only their sites where tall structures or pillars could be seen. From this strategic spot I could see most of the City of Amman, which had mostly low buildings and few tall ones. On one site, was where some locals told me was where the refugees from Palestine were located.

I then got another cab to return to the hotel and along the way I noticed an area where they had stalls and it looked like a flea market. So I decided to stop there and entered the area and saw a lot of things they were selling, some old and others very old, but I was not sure if the objects that looked very, very old were actual authentic objects that had historical significance. I guessed they were copies fashioned from some original artifacts. I did not buy any because I feared I might be stopped at the airport and would have to spend time trying to tell the officers there that the objects were copies of some of their country's historical artifacts. I bought some not so very old books which contained some information on the history of the country of Jordan and the others around it, especially of Palestine so I could read some of it when I was back in my hotel room which was nearby. In one of the books I noticed a chapter mention of the refugee settlement I had just seen from the hilltop with some photos of the houses that looked like shacks where the refugees lived, but I did not have any plans to go there; I was happy to know that such a refugee camp or settlement existed exclusively for the Palestinians. And I also had another book, where there was a chapter on the First Arab Revolt of 1936 that happened for three years before it was quelled by the British forces. It was officially known or referred to as the 'Great Revolt', a nationalist uprising by the Palestinians who grew angry with the state of their country after being forced to live under British rule for so long starting from the British Mandate of Palestine in 1922. So this year in 1999 was seventy-seven years ago. Of course, I was not born yet in that year; and my father, Puteh bin Sulong was only twelve years old, being born in 1910, or before the First World War. The Arabs demanded independence from Britain which was a fair 'request' that was left unanswered and unaddressed. Finally, the Arabs were forced to seek justice by taking up arms. What they mostly did not like was the British policy of allowing more and more Jews from Europe to immigrate to Palestine, before that a sizeable number of Jews who had assimilated with the local indigenous Arabs for centuries were happily seconded in the country to call their own, with no grand designs to ever want more political roles in the governing of the country for the establishment of the 'Jewish National Home'.

I looked at my watch and found that it was still early for me to go out again to have dinner at a restaurant nearby so I thought I could lay on the bed to continuing to read a bit on the chapter, on the First Arab Revolt which I found to be intriguing, and learnt how the dissent by some Arabs was the direct result of the influence the Arabs in Palestine got from the rebellion of the Qassamites as a result of the killing of their leader, Sheikh Izz ad-Din al-Qassam that happened a year earlier in 1935 which followed the declaration of the 'Palestine Day' by Hajji Amin al-Husseini on 16 May, 1936, who also called for a General Strike to be done against the British in Palestine. It was however, met with a lot of resistance from

the Jews, who were mostly the new Jews who had arrived from Europe
to Palestine who had by then managed to establish the stranglehold of
some parts of Palestine in areas where they were the majority with some
individuals rising to take the mantle of leadership for their community,
such as Ben Gurion who described and compared the uprising to fascism
and Nazism. The growing economic power and opposition to the mass
immigration of Jews from Europe and the fears of the Arabs with greater
presence and the influence of the English, their language, and lifestyles
had begun to attract a considerable number of Arabs to start to lead the
lives of their colonizers. Mostly, the English's identification with Zionism
all of which had started to show itself in many forms so that those Arabs
who were living in the major cities in Palestine and in Jerusalem or Tel
Aviv and Haifa could not see until it was too late for them to finally
realize it. It was okay in the Old City where the Arabs professing the
Muslim and Christian faiths who managed to live along well with their
Jewish neighbors as did their ancestors in the earlier many generations,
but not those Arabs especially Muslim-Arabs who lived in the remote
villages who did not have many Jews living amongst them.

I kept telling myself how all these things that I have just read
happened more than thirty-six years ago with the rebellion; and I was
first hearing about it now that I was in Amman. I had never heard about
it the whole time I was in Malaysia growing up in Melaka Town, the
British called Malacca Town, like it never happened before or ever. Why
didn't I know of it when I was still there when I was growing up studying
in primary and secondary school?

I would read all of the chapter and maybe find a whole book on
the First Arab Revolt because the chapter I just read did not contain
all the information I needed; but it helped me to get to know what it
was all about. Couldn't this episode in the history of the Palestinians be
turned into a feature film that could be released throughout the Entire
Muslim World or EMW, at least? I don't think Hollywood would be
keen to produce it, because they cannot grapple with the concept of
heroes and crooks or protagonists and antagonists in film, unlike those
they had become familiar with and knew how to create from stories in

history or from thin air using nothing more than the wild imagination of their scriptwriters. They had also done so by turning a pig into a major Hollywood star, whilst the more interesting and important political leaders who they did not favor could never be given such recognition by them in the form of films or documentaries and limited television drama serials to show to the worldwide audiences. But when can we expect to the get Arab and other Muslim leaders to do likewise by creating their own system so that they could highlight the heroism and virtues of some of their old political, military, intellectual, religious, and artistic leaders to profile in major feature films and other works including stage plays and songs, to be appreciated by those who now live in the EMW, in place of those heroes that Hollywood could create. I went to study film in graduate school at Columbia University in New York City, and I know this can be done, but the Arab and other Muslim leaders only knew how to write memorandums or memoranda and write lengthy useless speeches to give in the United Nations General Assembly (UNGA). The leaders of the major countries in the west, some of who have United Nations Veto power, never attended or bothered to listen to or care about. This had gone on for decades since the expulsion of the Palestinians from their ancestral land in 1948. I have gone to the UN once to listen to the then deputy prime minister of Malaysia Dr. Mahathir Mohammad speaking in 1978, sitting in the visitors' gallery at the back of the hall on the first floor. I found the hall to be virtually empty as was the gallery where I was sitting at with five others at the most. Did his speech ever get to the pages of the local New York City newspapers and on television the next day? Definitely not. Maybe his speechwriters were not good enough for him to say anything which was of any significance for the average American to care about. The only time any Malaysian ever got anything covered on the front-page of the New York Post was when the newly appointed Malaysian ambassador to the United Nations, one, Zain Azraai, came to the city and he deliberately parked his official car with the UN plates on the front and back of the limousine in Times Square which was then a seedy area, not like what it was now, for a few days until the newspaper reporters and cameramen got a whiff of it and wrote a story on the car being there for days, with a photo of the car on the front-page of their newspaper. Ambassador Zain got what he had expected to get in the American media, but he never got any reception for his speech he had given in the UN or anywhere through his tenure as Malaysian ambassador to the UN, as did Mahathir, even two years later, after he became prime minister of Malaysia and had many other occasions when he had to deliver speeches which, unfortunately, sounded like his old ones with nothing new. This happened at the same time more and more Palestinians and later on other Arabs in other Arab countries had started to be equally persecuted. What good does the UN and all the speeches leaders such as Mahathir and his ilk could give there or anywhere in America and the rest of the world, do to promote a better future for the Palestinians and other suppressed people of the world? Nothing! I could have easily written speeches for any of the Arab and other Muslim leaders to read in the UN or anywhere, especially in the Organization of Islamic Conference (OIC) biannual conference that is held by rotation in the fifty-seven member countries, while their wives or the 'first ladies' of the fifty-seven countries take some time to do some shopping to take things back to their own countries flying in official jets.

I don't think in order to solve any major political problem especially one that had been happening for so long and involving millions of lives, some of who had been mercilessly killed or bombed to smithereens, cannot be done using speeches in the UN or OIC conferences or by sending repetitive and boring memos to the American Embassies in the respective countries, or by throwing stones at armored vehicles of the Israel Defense Force (IDF) only to be met by them sending more missiles to destroy vast areas in Gaza Strip and the West Bank. There are other more effective ways that the Arabs can use to solve their problems, one of which is to stop creating more problems amongst themselves, so that if given the opportunity, they wouldn't be killing each other and sadly, by using arms supplied by their common enemies, too.

My thoughts were broken when someone from the other building shone a piercing light into my room through the window I had left open, so I decided to close it and then went out to go to the Ramallah Park to sit there. From there I could see the Roman Amphitheater where I had gone to earlier to see it at a close range and to take photos and do some sketches. I left the hotel and crossed the Ramallah-Faisal Street to go to the park, passing by some souvenir stalls where one was selling a 'gambus' guitar of the Arabs and other souvenirs. I found a vacant seat and sat there. It was not yet time for dinner so I had to sit there a while before having it. This time dinner would be falafel and some water, that should be filling and I would be happy to have another taste of it before I fly out of Jordan to return to Malaysia where falafels and other Arab and Palestinian food are sold in special restaurants operated by some refugees from Palestine and other countries including from Iran too. Having falafel and other Arab food may not be difficult in Malaysia as in most major cities in the world, including New York City where there are now more Arabian restaurants offering them.

One falafel, to go, I said speaking in English to the Jordanian man at the restaurant who was about my age but he had some hair on his face and a mustache while I was clean shaven. I used to have a mustache but it was not as thick as his. I was the only customer at the counter so not long later he got the order and handed it to me. I paid and walked back to the park and sat on the bench where I had sat earlier to enjoy my dinner, albeit a simple one, while the sky was dimming and soon the call of the Adhan from the nearby Masjid would sound, and there were already some men who had converged on the Masjid to prepare for the evening or Maghrib prayers. The Masjid did not look new and I suspect it might be at least one or two hundred years old. It sat right in the city itself so it was very convenient for the locals to walk there to pray and then return to their places to resume work. There were also many apartments on two-story shop lots where the owners and whoever lived in them could step out and pray in the same Masjid so it did not feel like they had to take the trouble of going to a Masjid, if it was somewhere else, built in the middle of an open ground like many of them that one could find in Malaysia. The Islamic authorities liked to have their Masjid built in the middle of nowhere, sometimes on river-banks and away from the community.

The falafel was fine and the water I had in a small plastic bottle was finished. I was full. The Adhan sounded and more men from the surrounding areas surged to join those who were already inside it to pray. The sky did not seem to dim very fast here in Amman; it took a while before night would fall in this month of September, when it should be late Fall. I did not have to wear thick clothes or jacket the whole time I had been to this country, because the temperature never went down that low. In fact, it was like spring time in America where I was used to living through the four seasons, and it felt like it was May there.

The night came thirty minutes later when the street lights were lit and I was starting to disappear in the darkness because I was hidden under the shade of a tree with a lot of leaves, that was good to sit at in the day, but certainly not in the night.

Daghlas came and introduced himself again, like I had not met him before or knew who he was. I had met him and knew him rather well when I was living in New York City, when I would move from one place or borough to the other starting with Manhattan and then to two different parts of Queens – in Sunnyside and later to Astoria, where the neighbors were mostly the working class while I was in the 'studying class', as I would describe what I was then. I became the 'traveling class' when work forced me to fly to different cities around the world to attend film festivals, seminars, and conferences where I would be invited to either show my works or show the gift of the gab that I thought I had, talking about films mostly.

Daghlas and I got to work immediately and skipped exchanging pleasantries since we already knew each other in New York City. Do you remember, Ephraim? he asked me. Who? Ephraim? Who is he? Where is he? Is he with you? Your son?

Daghlas was never the funny guy, I should know as he did not laugh at my feeble attempt at cracking a joke, which again fell flat. Do you remember David? he asked. David? Who is he? Where is he? Is he with you? Your son?

Now Daghlas knew I was trying to crack a joke but again it was not a very funny one. He knew I didn't mean to bully him with repetitive words, a trick used by comedians in early Hollywood films. Of course, I knew David, but not in person; I knew him because Daghlas had told me about him, and he was his late father, Moshe's, very good friend, the guy from Warsaw who came to Jerusalem in the 1920s. To be exact, he was a former professor at the University of Warsaw. He looked lost the first time he came to live in Jerusalem, and he did not have anybody who he could call friends, and he got attracted to Moshe for some reason, probably because Moshe who is Daghlas' father, had a store in the Jewish Quarter in the Old City. And because of that David did not feel like he was intruding into Moshe's private space because his store was an open space for anyone to walk into to buy things or to just browse. Moshe was such a fine man who didn't care if anyone came to his store just to look at any of the things he sold.

Ephraim, was indeed his original name, said Daghlas. I was intrigued by that, with the name I had just now heard from Daghlas' mouth. I only knew David but never Ephraim, but again, I only knew this colorful character by name only because Daghlas had mentioned him to me many times when we were in New York City, where he was still living and had come to Amman, because he wanted to travel by land to Tel Aviv, now in Israel, as anyone knows. Ephraim Lieberman, he added. Now David looked more Jewish in my mind with this name that Daghlas had told me and that confused me a lot because I now had to see him and his face from this name and not as David. I could picture him in my mind when we were talking about him. There were some photos of him that Daghlas had shown me when we were still in New York City when we would meet at Earl Hall, which was near Dodge Hall, where the Film Division in the School of the Arts was, and where I was studying at that time, when I was in the 'studying class' while Daghlas was in his 'working class', as he would describe it. He still considered himself to be someone in this 'working class' so he never left Brooklyn, since he first arrived there in the 1940s, just before the breakout of the Second World War.

Maybe I should write about Daghlas in a different way. Why? I have the feeling like those who have not got the idea and thought he was the same age as me; they are wrong; he was the same age as my late father,

Puteh bin Sulong who was born in 1910 and about the same time as Daghlas was born. I did not know where my father was born at, but I knew where Daghlas was born at – in Jerusalem. My father died on 15 September, 1998 at the age of eighty-eight years. Daghlas may have been eighty-eight years old the last time I met him here in Amman, but he seemed to be very active and youngish-looking and when I first met him by accident in New York City, he was in his late sixties. So in many ways he had been a father figure to me, which I might need because I was halfway around the world in New York City, from Malaysia, and divided by a distance of twenty thousand kilometers. At that time, communication by phone was expensive and I only made just one phone call to Malaysia per year and wrote letters that took a while to arrive at the addresses in Malaysia, so writing was necessary and I did it quite often writing to my father and some friends. I however, never sent him any photos of me the whole time I was studying at Columbia for two years living in the city and in Boston following the knee surgeries I had at two hospitals in the city – once at St. Luke's Hospital for a biopsy, where Dr George Unis diagnosed me has suffering from a 'Giant Cell Tumor of the upper left tibia' which was near the campus and two times at the Memorial Sloan-Kettering Cancer Center, where Dr Ralph C Marcove operated on me to remove the benign tumor in the upper left tibia and filling it some plastic cement that had been scrapped off the tumor. I had to walk on crutches after the first surgery or biopsy, through the third surgery when my left knee was reconstructed and a Cuepar knee prosthesis was inserted into it that forced me to continue to use crutches for so many years.

Daghlas was an old man. I knew that because he was the same age as my father. I did not feel offended when he turned and left me sitting on the bench in a diner near the Columbia campus on 110th Street, between Broadway and Amsterdam Avenue, where I was living in a university dormitory called Harmony Hall. He asked if I had sprained my leg, because he had seen me coming to the diner. Many people had guessed I had slipped on slippery ice on the sidewalks or had sprained my ankle while skiing at Aspen in Colorado. They thought I must be from a wealthy family who could afford to go to an expensive ski resort to ski. And although the doctors at the two hospitals had said that the tumor was benign, but there was still a chance for it to metastasize to my lungs and other parts of my body so Dr. Marcove prescribed that I took x-rays of my left knee and lungs every year for fifteen years. Fortunately, nothing of happened until 1994 or five years before I came to Amman when I was declared to be medically safe from such an eventuality from happening. I was also able to walk on my own with no crutches but with the prosthesis still in my left knee that was left there permanently.

So it was the diner, tumor, and age difference that brought the two of us together. I began to notice the accent he had when speaking in English, although I too had a bit of it, especially when I was not in the company of Americans and I normally try to speak in American accented English, and got a thrill when I called Americans on the phone and they thought I was a local like them. I had to tell them I am not an American, but a student from Malaysia. Malaysia? they would ask. And where is that? But strangely, Americans who I bumped into in the streets or behind counters in department stores and in the university thought I was Japanese, and had come from Japan to study at Columbia. Even Daghlas too thought or suspected I was from Japan. And when I said I was from Malaysia, suddenly his face lit. Chinese? he asked. No, I'm Melayu. Muslim? Yes, 'alhamdulillah' (Allah be praised!). He then started to speak in Arabic which I was not good at. But it startled me to hear an old American white man speaking very good Arabic. He then said in English how he had actually come from Jerusalem in Palestine which is now in Israel. Did I detect some regret in his voice when he said that? I'm Jewish and my name is Daghlas, he said and sounding like he was going to make a very long confession to me. I then began to feel guilty and uneasy because I really did not have the time to sit there in the diner to listen to a perfect stranger pour out his heart and soul to me, all for noting and for being someone who was studying at Columbia and who came from so far away, from Malaysia that startled him earlier. I was then just about done eating lunch and wanted badly to go back to the campus where I was having a class. Because of that he could not hold me any longer and had to allow me to go. But before I was able to pay my bill, he called out to the staff at the counter to say he could put it in his bill. He then asked for my phone number which I gave him, but I didn't expect him to give me a call.

I walled on along on the sidewalk along Broadway with a backpack on that had some books and note books and other personal items, got to the campus and entered it through the south entrance where I went ahead and got to Dodge Hall and took the elevator to the fifth floor. I bumped into my instructor for The History of Motion Pictures, Andrew Sarris who also wrote a column on film review in The Village Voice, and got to my class. There were already some students there and more came to wait for the instructor to arrive. I was not prepared for the class and hoped he did not turn up which was a rare case as such an incident had never happened before.

I returned to my room at 602 Harmony Hall as the number indicated was on the sixth floor, and the Hall was along the same 110th Street, between Broadway and Amsterdam Avenue on the Upper East Side, bordering Harlem and divided by the Morningside Park, feeling exhausted. I thought I might have been under the weather because I had been out a lot that day. Now I could do with some rest in my small room. I would cook my own dinner using a hot pan, and go to sleep, after watching a bit of television.

The phone rang and it was Daghlas. I could not say I was sleeping and could not speak with him. I knew he had something that he wanted to tell me, a secret, about his life in Jerusalem. And like they say in the Screenwriting 1 course I took from Frank Daniels, an instructor and co-chairman of the Film Division, who himself came from Czechoslovakia, the plot thickens. And true enough from the moment I heard Daghlas' voice I knew he needed to see someone who he could share his deepest secrets with. I knew someone who had come from Jerusalem before the Second World War would have some things he wanted to share. And as a former reporter with Utusan Melayu in Malaysia, I had been approached by many strangers who came with interesting family secrets and personal stories to share that they wanted published in my newspaper. I did not have to search for them; those stories came to me. All I had to do was just listen to them and write what they had told me, and if the stories were interesting, I might even get a byline for the report the next day.

Daghlas said he wanted to meet me again somewhere. He was now known as 'Douglas'; the sound of it was still the same as in his original name, but there was just a slight difference in the spelling. He said he had to do that so the Americans could write it better. And he got it changed legally in the courts.

So that was how I got to know Douglas better and began to appreciate what he had to say. He became more expressive and less secretive after he found out that I was majoring in film at Columbia. He also told me that he had a good friend called Gary working and living in Malaysia. Gary Braut was a Jew, an Orthodox Jew. Where in Malaysia, I asked and he said Kuala Lumpur. He had a factory where he reconditioned spare parts of automobiles he got for cheap in America and shipped them to his factory in containers. His workers who were mostly from Bangladesh reconditioned them and they would later be shipped back to America. Years later I would actually meet him in 2007 in Kuala Lumpur; in the city, if not at the Perdana Peace Foundation conference at the Putra World Trade Center (PWTC) whose chairman, former Malaysian prime minister Dr. Mahathir Mohammad organized it and invited many speakers from all over the world. Gary was there at a counter he had opened to give gifts to selected guests and visitors to the conference. He wore the traditional Jewish costume with a black hat and was assisted by some of his staff from his factory. He told me was in Selayang in the state of Selangor. He offered me a small gift and invited me to go with him to see his factory during the break at the conference, but I declined because I wanted to be at the conference to record video and take photos. We communicated later and I agreed to meet him at his factory in Selayang and was surprised to see just how large it was. The many workers he had there were mostly from Bangladesh. There were also shrines of the major religions he had built on the ground floor of the factory. A few years later after I got to know him better and having met him mostly at his factory, he invited me to come along on his factory jaunt for his staff to go on a day-trip to Pulau Pinang or Penang. There we visited the Jewish graves and the only synagogue that had been closed and was now a camera store. We also went to the E&O Hotel to meet with a very old Jewish man who once worked there. Gary had heart problems and received treatments in hospitals in Kuala Lumpur including one in Beijing, where he had gone a few times, until January, 2012 when he died. He had asked me to produce a documentary on him with a title he specifically chose which was, 'A Big Fat Jew Who Loved Malaysia,' and I managed to do some video recording of him in his factory, including a personal interview where he spoke about many matters. I later met his younger brother, Bradley, when I returned to New York City, who had contacted me by email upon Gary's death to seek some information on him because he did not leave a will and I gave Bradley the interview I did with Gary to see if there was anything in it that would be valuable to him. Unfortunately, fifteen years after Gary died, the factory closed. There was no one who could manage it and his Malaysian-born son, whose mother was a Malaysian-Chinese was too young to be able to handle the business that his father had built and managed for so long. I was quite stunned when Gary told me how he had married off his first son with his first American-Jewish wife, a Jew like him, but not an Orthodox one, to a Melayu and Muslim woman from the state of Sabah in Malaysia, and they lived in San Francisco. A few years after their marriage that was conducted in the Islamic manner, they gave him his first grandson.

So my association with Douglas extended for many years and different phases in my life, from a student to a small-time filmmaker in Malaysia. We continued to communicate with each other much better when the internet and email services were available. That was how we planned to meet here in Amman because he too had planned to come here to travel by land back to Jerusalem as a pilgrimage to the place where he was born in and grew up. We did not plan to meet in his hotel, but here in Ramallah Park which was across from the small hotel I was staying at. I was also about to fly back to Malaysia in a day's time. In Manhattan, we would sit on benches in the park and sometimes on the dividers on

Broadway where they had some wooden benches, when he had some things to do around the area. Many times I would also meet him in restaurants, which he made sure provided 'halal' food, in Brooklyn, near the Long Island Railroad station which was very convenient for me to go to with the subway system being so dependable. With the drop of a token I was on the train heading there.

But I had never asked Douglas why he decided to leave Jerusalem and come to America and live in Brooklyn, especially since he now said it would have been better if he had not left Jerusalem or Palestine, as he still described the country instead of Israel. I then decided to seize the opportunity to ask this particular question before it was too late as he was getting on in life and it might be easier to give me a better and more truthful answer than if I had asked the same question, say, twenty years ago. His answer to my question was succinct; he was told by some of his friends, his age or older, that life in New York City, especially in Brooklyn, was a lot better for Jews like him than in Jerusalem where they had a very large and close-knit community and could support each other. That was why he decided to make the arduous trip to America and ensconce himself in Brooklyn where he felt safer. Did he feel in any way threatened when he was in Jerusalem? I asked. His father, Moshe had a store and was doing okay; in fact, the store is still there and is attended to by his younger brother and his own children in the same place in the Jewish Quarter in the Old City. And I supposed when he returned to Jerusalem in a few days' time, the first place he would or should visit is his family store. And the next place would or should be the store once operated by his father's best friend, Suleyman, who had also died a few years after Moshe did. His store is operated by his first grandson from his first son. Douglas said. Yes, that should be the first two places he should visit when he got to Jerusalem and after that the Wailing Wall to pray before it. His own children had visited their family store the few times they were in Jerusalem, but somehow Douglas did not. At his age when the intense guilt he had with him for deserting Jerusalem or Baitulmukaddis as he would sometimes describe the Holy City, had long subsided the more he felt like he was an American man than a

Palestinian man, and also before it was too late. And after the Wailing Wall, he would go to visit the graves of his parents, Moshe and Sarah who he never seen since he left for America on the boat he took from Le Harve in France. It was right after the Paris Colonial Exhibition that opened on 6 May, 1931 at Bois de Vincennes. He also managed to visit that because of the delay in his trip, so he had two days to visit Paris and the Exhibition which was held for six months and attracted about seven million visitors. It was purely a public relations initiative by the French colonial government to feebly attempt painting their government in favorable light after they had colonized many countries, especially those in Africa. And they brought some representatives from each of the countries France had colonized to be put on display, too, to showcase their culture and arts.

Douglas, or Daghlas then, was not immensely impressed by what he had seen at the Exhibition. He thought it was a feeble attempt orchestrated by the French Crusaders, as he described it, to whitewash all the ugly deeds that they had committed against the people of color who were not of the same stripe as them, to pillage their wealth and to develop their own economy. He felt nauseous after visiting the few booths and had to leave to return to the harbor to wait for the ship he had booked a ticket for himself on to take him to America, where some of his friends were eagerly waiting for him to leave Ellis Island, and go to Brooklyn, where he would start his brand new life there as an American Jew.

Douglas had never been inside the Columbia campus and I offered to take him for a short visit there. So the next day, the two of us strolled inside the campus while I described to him the buildings that we saw and when we got outside of Dodge Hall I told him that this was the place I was studying at where the Film Division was. He did not know that Columbia University was named after Christopher Columbus, and it was renamed from its original name which was King's College; and in fact, if the forefathers of the country had their way, the name United States of America or U.S.A. would be U.S.C. for United States of Columbia, the name that they did not choose over America, with Columbia being the alternative name that they had shortlisted. Really? he asked. Not many Americans knew this I said. And this Columbia campus was built when some gangster groups donated a vast sum of money in the 1920s, to move it to its current location from King's College which started with eighteen students in a church in Lower Manhattan, to grow and develop to become one of the première universities in America, and an Ivy League one at that. You must be a very smart scholar, he said, and you certainly look like one, especially with your hair long and in the style of Albert Einstein. Douglas was not a funny character and never told jokes, so I did not take what he had said to be one; and Gary who was an incessant joker who liked to exaggerate things to thrill himself, especially with numbers, had never said that to me, even though he was told that I had gone to study at this university which he said he knew what sort of a university it was.

Douglas and I then found a nice place to sit, to rest as he was getting a bit tired, due to his age, which was not yet seventy, outside of Dodge where there were some students from the different departments or divisions in the School of the Arts of which the Film Division. Milos Forman was the other co-chairman of the Film Division, I said; and Douglas surprised me when he said he had seen Milos' film, 'One Flew Over The Cuckoo's Nest' when it was shown in 1977 and liked it; and he won an Oscar for Best Director. And he had also watched the film, 'The Message' and 'Lion of the Desert' when they were shown in a cinema in Brooklyn where he lived. I saw the first one in the Odeon Cinema in London in August, 1978 and the second one when I was living in Sunnyside, Queens in 1981, I said. Did you like them? I asked. He nodded; they were good for all, not just for Muslims and felt sad that Anthony Quinn should have won an Oscar for Best Actor but he didn't because he was playing the role of an Arab Imam. So I thought the two of us had at least some things in common, and the more we talked, the more things would be added to the 'List of things both of us like'.

Nobody would know you are a Muslim man, he said. Because you look much like a Japanese man – a smart Japanese man, if not a brilliant Japanese man, he added. Yes, but when my hair was very long, most Americans thought I was a Native American man. Oh, you do, he remarked. I first thought I was sitting beside a Japanese tourist the first time I met you in the diner over there on 110th Street. But you spoke in English so well, I heard when you gave your order to the waiter, so I thought you could not very well be a foreign Japanese tourist or visitor, but a Native American, except that there was no Native American who lived there that I know of. And I was certainly shocked when you said you were a Malaysian and that was the first time I had ever heard that there was even a country going by that name. I later checked the location of your country, Malaysia on the map I have at home. I was shocked to see how far it is from here to there, around twenty-two kilometers. How long did you take to fly from there to here? I said, twenty-four hours with one stop; but I made three stops, one transit stop in Dubai in the United Arab Emirate or U.A.E, and then eight hours in Brussels and the third stop was London, where I stayed for two weeks to stay with some Malaysian friends who were there to study. That was during Ramadan; and did you fast? he asked. No. Because you were a traveler, I suppose! Douglas may be a Jew, but he also knew a lot about Islam, and spoke Arabic better than most Muslims in Malaysia, who hardly spoke the language. If he were to wear the Arabic robe, he could also pass as one. Yes, he had known some Arabs who lived in New York City who had also come from their countries in their own search for the peace and security that their countries could not offer them and their children. We mostly met after their Friday prayers at the Masjid in Brooklyn, he added and we would go to the nearby halal restaurant to have lunch together. Not, in Astoria in Queens, where I used to live I said, so we had to cook our own food and rarely ate out except for breakfast and snacks when we would have cookies or cakes and fruits with coffee or tea or soda.

How did Gary Braut get to come to Malaysia? Douglas suddenly asked. He probably knew I had wanted to ask him more personal questions. I said, he was in the Navy when he was young and then he opened a factory in Hong Kong but closed it after five years or so to reopen another one in Malaysia where he found the place and country and its multiracial mix to be more conducive to his business and where he could go anywhere wearing his Jewish garb and telling how he was a 'Jew' or 'Yahudi' as the Melayu people say it. He had never once been subjected to any sort of racist taunts being a staunch Jew and looking pretty much like one. I told him a few times the Muslims in Malaysia didn't care who he was; besides, he looked like a foreigner, a tourist, if he walked around in his Jewish garb and the Muslims could not tell if it was so, or if it might be a fashion. However, even after fifteen years of living in Malaysia, Gary still could not speak in the Melayu language other than a few words, such as, 'Alamak!' which could translate to be, 'Goodness gracious me!' or 'My goodness!' as it was just a slang word which literally translates as 'Oh, God…Oh, Mum!'

The next time I met Douglas was in Brooklyn, in his neighborhood and true to his tradition, he never invited me to visit him at his own home; we decided to meet at the subway station where he picked me up. The first stop he made was the Jewish Seminary, where he said Gary had studied, from the group photo of Gary and his school friends in it, and true enough the building in the photo looked exactly like the one I was seeing. The photo must have been taken in the 1960s, said Douglas. I had already lived there and passed in front of the Seminary many times, and I had even thought of sending my own two sons to study here, but after discussing their future with my wife; she is an American-Jewish woman who was born here in Brooklyn, I met barely a year after I arrived here. But we got married two years later when I was said by her parents to be old enough and responsible enough to be their son-in-law, and I accepted their decision with open arms to also allow me to mature faster knowing how I might become somebody's husband and son-in-law soon, and found for myself a better-paying job. They were also not Orthodox Jews like me then, so we got along well even before I got married and more so soon after, when I moved into their family house until I had two sons when my wife and I decided to purchase a house for our own family. It was not very far from her family house, and walking distance from the Seminary, where Gary had studied before he joined the Navy. But I liked it here living in Brooklyn where there is a large Jewish community, where there are many kosher restaurants and even as a secular Jew, we still needed the bonding we can get with the whole community here, many of whom had their grandparents and parents coming to live here as refugees from their respective countries in Europe and elsewhere. And yes, you can say that this is the largest Jewish community not only in the City of New York but in the whole of America. And yes, I have met some Jews who had also come from Jerusalem and other cities in Palestine such as Haifa and Nablus, and when we met up or bumped into each other, we would speak in Arabic. So that's how I can speak in a language other than Hebrew and English. I started to learn more formally when I got here and applied it when I mix with the others here and all over the city, who do not speak much Hebrew or Arabic. It's a nice city to live in, he added, and you must have made the right decision to come to the city to study film when you could have gone to Los Angeles to study at a university there, as it is closer to Hollywood. Oh, but there is no Ivy League university in Los Angeles! Did that matter to you if you had studied at a university that is not an Ivy League one? I told Douglas that I didn't know about Ivy League universities; because in Malaysia, any university is good as long as one can get a place to study in it, because there were so few universities in Malaysia when I was studying there, and I only knew about the eight Ivy League universities you have in America after I got to Columbia. The only reason why I wanted to study at Columbia was because it was in the City of New York and where there were not that many Malaysian or especially Melayu students from Malaysia. Why? he asked. Because the truth is, if there were many of them in any university in America or anywhere in the world, it means that that university they were studying at must be a bad one, or a non-competitive one, like they liked to describe such a university here. And at Columbia there were only a handful of Melayu students with most doing their doctorates and were sent there by their universities in Malaysia where they were lecturing before and where they would return to resume their jobs as lecturers, except now they would be given higher pay and better posts at the faculties they were attached to. I did not want to tell him that my application for a Malaysian government scholarship was rejected because they did not want Melayu students to study in such universities so no wonder most of the Malaysian students in America were studying at some of the most non-competitive universities because the Malaysian government and their officials thought by studying at such universities they would not fail. I also had to work as a reporter for a Melayu language newspaper for a year before my appeal for a scholarship or loan was accepted which finally allowed me to enroll at Columbia, thus creating Malaysian academic history for being the first and only Malaysian to have studied film at such a university. But I did tell him, albeit reluctantly, how I had written a script for Frank Daniels' Screenwriting 1 course during my first semester in the Fall of 1978, which I finally handed in May, 1981, because I had taken a one-year medical leave, approved by the two chairmen, called 'Papier-mâché' and received a grade for the course. When I got back to Malaysia in the early 1990s I sent the script to a major studio in Hollywood, but received no response. But some years later I found that the same studio had released a feature film that closely resembled the story in the script I had written for Frank, for a short film. The studio went on to produce three more segments of the film and collectively made two billion dollars, including the sale of merchandise related to the films they produced. Douglas was startled and quite shock when I told him of this. I thought he would receive it with a pinch of salt, but he felt truly sorry for me. I said I could blame the Film Division for not teaching a course in copyrighting so the students leave school knew how to protect their works. I feel so sorry for you, Mansor, he said. But is there a way for you to take the matter up with them? he asked. I have the original script, I said, but it's not enough. I may have the original letter I then wrote on my manual typewriter, but it was not good, because I did not adequately use legal ways to protect my intellectual property. But I still do not know where I have put the original letter.

I later went on to explain to him about the two VHS tapes of my scripts that were produced by the first private television station of Malaysia called TV3 called 'Basikal ku' (My Bicycle) and 'Kadir dan Kim' (Kadir and Kim) which I wanted to submit as my master's theses project, which I sent to a former classmate, Ron Nyaswaner, but he and the then chairman of the Film Division said they had not received them.

I had sent them in a package with twenty American dollars in stamps at the post office in the Dayabumi Building in the center of Kuala Lumpur City, but the package was not delivered; and I suspected that the postal clerk did not send the package off and took the money which was quite a large sum at that time in 1986. If the package had been delivered I was certain I could have been allowed to graduate from the university with my Masters of Fine Art (MFA) in Film Directing. But that didn't happen. And I told him I was not worried by that because I could still proceed with I wanted to do except that looking for funding to produce big films was virtually impossible. I had established myself as the most prominent film critic of Malaysia and a film essayist who wrote both in English and the Melayu language for most of the newspapers and magazines published in the country, and was invited to even review films on Malaysian national television. The Malaysian national film agency called Finas was established in 1981, they were dominated by unqualified officers who used the agency as their private travel agency, where they would attend film festivals and markets abroad at government expense and who did not develop the industry. Even the Finas Act of 1981 that was passed by the Malaysian parliament was bad; it could not be used as the basis to develop the Malaysian film industry.

I knew what I had told Douglas was a boring topic, but he seemed to be attracted to it. He said he watch so few films since he arrived here from Palestine and he chose those that were special to him, so he told me again about 'The Message' and 'Lion of the desert' he had seen, which I had also seen, and said he liked them a lot.

Douglas later explained that there were one million Jews in the city and half of them were in Brooklyn alone which represented a quarter of the total population of this Borough. But what I really wanted to know was what he had managed to discuss with David a.k.a. Ephraim Lieberman since Douglas had mentioned his name, even without me bringing up the matter concerning him, and from the little that I knew of him through my conversations with some people in Ramallah and Jerusalem, he was some kind of a guy who came from Warsaw in Poland and a former university professor who found a lot of inspiration from

Theodor Herzl although not a great big fan of his when he was young and before he organized the First Zionist Congress in Basel, Switzerland from 29 to 31 August, 1897.

Yes, I knew Uncle David who later told me his real name as Ephraim Lieberman, said Douglas, and Ephraim, said it was okay for me to leave Jerusalem to go to Brooklyn, where I am right now. Why, I asked. Because if that was what my heart told me to do, then I should just do it without question. Did your heart tell you do to this?, I asked. Yes, many times, but I was too young to be able to make the move; which I could only do when I was older and more capable and most of all, when I was legally able to obtain my passport on my own without my parents' consent, and I got it expeditiously; and when I first held my Palestinian passport, yes, it was a Palestinian passport and not an Israeli one because it happened before the establishment of the Israeli state in 1948, I felt like a free man, like I still do now.

And what did Ephraim want to achieve by asking your late father, Moshe to get as many people as possible to come to his house outside of Jerusalem, to listen to him giving them a lecture, which I was told was not so successful because most who came were the laypersons and not the scholarly type that Ephraim had wanted to meet, but who was afraid to go directly to the universities in Jerusalem or other major cities in Palestine then to attract the attention of some prominent Jewish scholars and students, to listen to him, if indeed he had something unusual and important to say to them. It seemed that only your father and best friend, Suleyman, the Arab-Muslim man had the time and guts to listen to him, and even then Ephraim did not say much other than to say the obvious and nothing spectacular. Now I am asking you, if you had indeed discussed anything with him and if he had said anything of substance and importance that you can share with me now that the matter or his concerns have become moot, because Theodor, as he would call him, is long dead and the state of Israel had been long established? We are in September, 1999, so that the state is now how many years? Fifty-one long years!

I was thirty-eight years when the state of Israel was formed and had been in Brooklyn for many years and already had two grown-up sons in grade school, secular school, said Douglas; and there was merriment and celebrations that went on till late at night on the day the United Nations officially declared Israel to be a member state of the United Nations, U.N. Most of the Jews in my neighborhood could not sleep; all stayed awake to await more news till the next dawn, and during that time we danced like we had never danced before and drank until some actually got drunk and fell to the ground. They were that silly.

I can fully appreciate and understand why they did that, I said. But what really was Ephraim trying to tell or say to the people in Jerusalem that he found very hard to say to anyone in words; he only tried to express himself using vague innuendoes and other imageries that no one understood and even Moshe and Suleyman found to be vague.

I did not get from Douglas then when we were in New York City, what Ephraim had told him. But now in his advanced age, and with us sitting on the concrete bench in Ramallah Park in Amman, Jordan, he finally decided it was okay to tell me what Ephraim had told him then when they were in Jerusalem or Baitulmukaddis. He said Ephraim had tried to visit his father's store but he was not there at that time, and met me instead, so he thought as a young man then, I was in a better position to better appreciate and understand what he had in his mind to say, that my father and Uncle Suleyman could comprehend because they were in a different age group and would not be too keen to know what the future lay for their city and country like I could. So he entered the store and sat with me at the desk and spoke in great length on the real issues he had wanted to convey to the men he had met and the others he had tried to speak with, which was how.

Douglas said Ephraim was in awe of what Theodor had done for himself and his race, and despite the odds, he still managed to achieve what he had set out to do, which he did not see happen because he died seven years after the First Zionist Congress in 1897 and was buried in Vienna, and Israel was finally formed on 14 May, 1948 or forty-one years after he died, by the Zionist leader, Ben Gurion following the expiry of the British Mandate of Palestine the next day. And the United Nations finally accepted Israel as its new member on 11 May, 1949, with some provisions, especially for the country to determine its borders, which it never did and to also allow Arabs who had been expelled from their villages and lands in the 'Nakhba' or Dispossession of the Arabs, to be allowed to return. The 'Aaliyah', which was a counter movement of Jewish Diaspora living all over the world returned in droves to replace the Arabs who had vacated their lands, caused the leaders of Israel then to not able to commit to the two most important provisions stated by the United Nations.

Theodor Herzl's body was later exhumed and taken to Israel to be reburied there as a hero and Founder of the State of Israel. It was precisely what Ephraim had tried very hard to not see happen, and he also died after the establishment of the state of Israel, which caused him to feel more alarmed and scared to the fate of the state itself and the people who were disposed in the act called the Nakhba, which saw seven hundred thousand Palestinians being evicted from their ancestral homes that they had lived in for many generations with most of them crossing into Jordan to live in refugee camps till today and some others scattered all over Europe and some even made it to America.

What happened?, I asked Douglas. What actually happened with Ephraim and what did Theodor aim to achieve and do when he was alive? Douglas took a very long pause; and he tried to think hard to remember exactly what Ephraim had said to him what he thought he could do which was the direct opposite of what Theodor wanted to do. He was a low-achiever, said Douglas. Who? Ephraim? No, Theodor, said Douglas. This is what Ephraim said to me of his assessment of the man, who studied Law at the University of Vienna but never practiced as a lawyer; instead he became a journalist and not a prominent or influential one. He then dabbled in the theater as a playwright and still failed to attract any attention to the theater-goers. And in an act of desperation to call attention to himself, he decided to cry out to demand a separate state for the World's Jews. This finally managed to trust himself to the limelight when some Jews who had not dared to say so in public but who held similar views in private, because they feared being chastised or booed by their own kind, then realized that their fantasies could become a reality and they began to support for such a call and also the caller, Theodor Herzl.

This was how it happened?, I asked, for the call for the creation of the state of Israel? Douglas nodded. Did he support it, too? I was referring to Douglas and not Ephraim. Yes, and No!, he replied. And I said this then and I am saying it now. Because I had lived through the times and tribulations and also lived amongst the Palestinians and I should know a bit more than anyone from my own race, who were in Europe who were persecuted by the people in Poland and more so in Germany from the Nazis and in the Holocaust, which had nothing to do with the Palestinians.

And he wanted to oppose that?, I asked. Douglas nodded, and felt unsure if he did not support his stand when Ephraim told him about his. It sounded sane; it sounded the best option. Creating a new state anywhere in the world, Ephraim thought was a huge gamble and campaigning and counter campaigning he thought and foresaw then could lead to terrible consequences, no one then could envision or imagine. And we had seen what had happened since 1948 till now and we were in 1979 then and now in September, 1999 there is still no certainty as to what the real impact would be on the grandiose plans of Theodor, who did not live to see the amount of carnage that had happened in the Gaza Strip and West Bank during the Six-Day War or Yom Kippor War of October, 1967. And even as far back as in 1919 when some prominent Jews in Europe and also in America, were not in favor of the creation of a special state for Jews to live in because they would still be surrounded by Arabs and other Muslims in the region of the Middle East. They released a statement condemning such a move, by saying: *We raise our voices in warning and protest against the demand of the Zionists for the reorganization of the Jews as a national unit, to whom, now or in the future, territorial sovereignty in Palestine shall be committed. This demand not only misrepresents the trend of the history of the Jews, who ceased to be a nation 2,000 years ago, but*

*involves the limitation and possible annulment of the larger claims of Jews
for full citizenship and human rights in all lands in which those rights are
not yet secure. For the very reason that the new era upon which the world
is entering aims to establish government everywhere on principles of true
democracy, we reject the Zionistic project of a 'national home for the Jewish
people in Palestine'.*

And whose side were you with?, Douglas asked me. I was confused
a bit by such question that had never been posed to me before, so I
tried to find an answer by saying, I am not Arab. Yes, he said, but you
are Muslim, too. Does that matter?, I asked. He kept quiet. He knew
he would be returning to Jerusalem again, and for the first time since
he left the city and Palestine in the 1930s, so he managed to escape the
Great Depression that many other Jews and Arab-Christians were stuck
in for years, until they finally manage to heave a sigh of relief when it
was finally over, so they were now able to live a less depraved existence
in their new country that did not offer them much future, except maybe
to their children who were born there and who were not aware of why
they were there, until they grew up to become adults and when they
were told about the era of uncertainty that their parents had to endure
to allow them to live more peacefully in Brooklyn, where unfortunately,
according to Douglas, where there were some Jews and their families who
had pulled up the roots that they had planted there, to make 'Aaliyah'
to return to the Homeland of the Jews and take up Israeli citizenship,
like some of his immediate neighbors whose parents or grandparents
had taken so much trouble to leave Jerusalem, Haifa or Nablus in the
then Palestine, to travel in ships to cross the Atlantic Ocean and come to
America, only to have their grandchildren and children make the reverse
trip back to what was now known as Israel!

But Douglas going to Jerusalem was not part of his 'Aaliyah' but as
a mere tourist, because, he said, he was originally from there, Jerusalem
and he considered himself to be a Palestinian and a Jew. He knew the
place outside of Jerusalem where his father owned a house there where
he grew up in, was now gone to make way for new housing projects and
his younger brother had to move to another house to live with his family

with three children, all of whom had now become more religious and pious, which was not a bad idea, except that he might not know how to deal and relate with them anymore, when they meet again after so many years.

I flew back to Malaysia taking the same Pakistan International Airlines (PIA) from the Queen Raina International Airport (QRIA) outside of Amman where I could still see the few Iraqi Airways planes sitting on the tarmac after the airport in Baghdad was bombed in the First Gulf War that also destroyed much of Baghdad and other parts of Iraq as well while Douglas was heading by land to return to Jerusalem by taking the bus and trains to get there, in pretty much the same way he had traveled earlier to get to Le Harve from Jerusalem in the 1930s. I felt a sense of relief when my PIA plane landed safely back at the Kuala Lumpur International Airport (KLIA), while Douglas wrote an email to say his heart pounded until he thought it might just pop out of his chest the moment his bus arrived at a spot at the edge of Jerusalem when he caught sight of the Dome of the Rock, near where was the Wailing Wall or Western Wall and the Old City were. So much had changed, he commented. Everything had changed, he added. I am not returning to the Jerusalem I once knew, but to a New Jerusalem I had never been to before. There are now more buildings around the city, no doubt, and also more local Arabs and Jews wearing western-style clothes than before, but many of them are tourists from outside of Israel or Palestine. I do not know which is which anymore. So it was good that he had chosen not to fly direct to Tel Aviv from Kennedy Airport in Queens, New York, and then to Amman in Jordan by flying there from Tel Aviv after a short stint in Jerusalem. But instead he chose to fly from Kennedy Airport straight to Amman and then travel to Jerusalem by land and then to Tel Aviv, also by land, to see what he could see along the way, and fly off back to New York by flight from Tel Aviv on El Al, the national airline of Israel.

And now instead of seeing Palestinian police constables riding on the Raleigh bicycles and occasionally stopping Jews who had just arrived there as refugees, there were now many soldiers from the Israeli Defense Force or IDF, who were stationed everywhere. He feared if he might be mistaken for an Arab. He knew and was told by some friends in New York City that he did not look like a Jew if he was in Israel again.

Douglas took some photos with his cell phone and sent them to me from where he was inside the Old City, and I could see the alleyways I had been to earlier and the Masjid Al-Aqsa in the background. He then took some more photos of the store where his father operated with him helping him, which still looked exactly the way it was, he said. I might have been to the place before when I was there, but I was not sure which was the store he was talking about. And in one of the photos, there was his younger brother, Harry, standing in front of the store, looking old and taking the image of his father, Moshe, who had said it before that he still preferred to stay on in Jerusalem and not go anywhere, regardless of whether it was in Palestine or Israel. Are you happy living in America?, his brother asked Douglas. He was not sure of what to say. At least, when I die, I can be buried right here in our ancestral land, said Harry. But we also have large plots of land to bury our dead, in New York City with one large Jewish cemetery in Brooklyn, too. We're closer to God, said Harry. Douglas started to feel guilty for deserting his younger brother and he did not want to get into any disagreement with him, as they were all going on with age, with Harry's first son, who is Douglas' first nephew who was already married to a local Jewish woman who had borne him four children, two boys and two girls, who are now adults and were leading their own lives elsewhere in Israel leaving Harry to live with his wife, Pamela, an American-Jewish tourist and pilgrim, who came to his store and not long later got married, and who started to call her husband Harry, a typical American name, to change it from his real Jewish name of Haim, meaning 'Life' that his father had given him when he was born that Douglas had known all his life, until he found out about his younger brother's new American-styled name of Harry. Harry's or Haim's wife, Pamela was not at the store because she hardly come by to give her husband a hand there. She preferred to stay at home to tend to their house and to prepare food for her husband and herself and sometimes their children and grandchildren who came over to stay for a few days, especially during their grandchildren's school breaks.

But at least they are doing okay, said Douglas in his last email to me, which I received when I was already back in Malaysia and trying to work on a small video project I hoped would be selected for some international film festivals like the film I had produced that was shown in the Fajr International Film Festival in Tehran in February, 1994, five years before I went to Ramallah in September, 1999. And the next day I received another email from Douglas who said he was already approaching the Ben Gurion Airport in Tel Aviv and was going to fly back to New York on the national airline called El Al with the non-stop flight taking around ten hours. I replied by saying I will plan to come to New York City again in a few months' time, so we can meet up again somewhere near or inside the Columbia campus, and again sit outside of Dodge Hall.

That would be good, he said. And that was the last email I had received from him, because he died two days after arriving in New York City of heart failure, and his eldest son, sent a message to me to inform me of his father's demise. I felt very sad and could not think well the next few days worrying about him and seeing his image that I had saved in my camera and also mind, when we last met in Amman in Jordan.

Douglas said he gave up visiting Deir Yassin after he was told that the name of the village had been changed to Givat Shaul or something, a name he had not heard of before which he did not have any real connection with; and all he knew was Deir Yassim where he used to have some school friends who were Arab Muslims and also Christians who he used to play football on the sand with and sometimes did the 'dabke' dance when there were festivals there.

My thoughts were brought back to the time both of us were sitting on the wooden bench in the road divider at 114th Street between Broadway and Amsterdam which was just beside the Columbia University campus and sat there alone, where we had spent a bit of time talking about all the characters he knew in his 'past life' as he would describe it, and the places in Jerusalem and Palestine he grew up in as a boy, who did not have any dreams of leaving the city and country that he had grown up to like for which he thought there would never any country that would come close like them; and he definitely did not have any weird fantasies like some of his friends and their parents who did not think twice about leaving Palestine, to go to Europe or America to seek a new beginning for the lives, in a new country. He mentioned many names, of friends and relatives and their friends and relatives who appeared so real in my mind when I imagined and tried to see them as though they existed, although they were only characters that he knew and wanted to remember, because all of them had in more ways than one, helped to give him the life he had led in Palestine, to his 'new life' in Brooklyn, in the City of New York that had changed his whole attitude towards the world and the city and country he had grown up at.

Vehicles light and heavy passed by in both directions and people, some who were students walked along the sidewalks on both sides of the street. There were food stalls at the junctions that were now also offering 'halal' food, but I did not feel hungry; not did I feel any desire to leave the bench I must have sat on the last few hours, at least, because I could tell the first time I got there it was bright and the sidewalks were quite empty; then everything changed and the whole area was enveloped by darkness that had come early because of the weather which was close to the end of autumn. I then realized that I had not worn a thick jacket but a light one for outings in the day when there was sunlight. Now the temperature had slumped down and the wind had turned cold. And people did not walk slowly and casually like they did earlier but more briskly to rush to the subway station or the bus stop and stand in the enclosed area there.

I stood up and turned at the direction of the Columbia Bookstore but it was already closed; I thought I could go there and grabbed a university sweater to wear, or anything that was thick to wrap around me. It was closed, because it was already late. I turned at the other side and saw some stores which were still opened and I went there to see what I can find that I can wear, to keep me warm, like a sweater or even an overcoat and also a woolen cap to cover my head. I had never ever worn any overcoat, the whole time I was in this country, and I preferred to wear light jackets even in the thick of winter, but somehow this time I felt I needed one; I felt very cold and frozen. So I had no choice but to try and find one and pay for it at whatever costs. The stores did not have overcoats, but there were some parkas. I immediately grabbed one that fitted my size.

I was relieved that I had managed to get them and immediately wrapped myself in the new overcoat I had just bought and the woolen cap now covering my head that kept me warm and comfortable. But I was still reeling from what Douglas had also told me in his last email which was the main reason why he decided to return to his village or his parents' old house near Jerusalem, which was to go to a spot near the woods to dig something there where he was told by Ephraim, he could find some books, notes and small personal items that were dear to him, and some photos, because of the sentimental value and not because of the price. He was shocked to find that the whole area had been leveled and new buildings built on the site, and the developers probably had piled a lot of dirt or earth to prop up the ground before constructing the buildings that now houses more Jews who had come from all over the world and probably some from Brooklyn, too. He said, he stood near the spot for a long while before turning around to return to Jerusalem to stay in a small hotel not far away from the King David Hotel on King David Street, which he could see from the window of his room and to stare at the sight around it. Why didn't he book a room in that hotel even for just one night, he asked himself. But it was already too late for him to stay there because he was leaving by bus to Tel Aviv tomorrow morning to catch his El Al light back to New York City. But he promised to himself that should he make another trip back to Jerusalem, he would definitely want to stay at the King David Hotel even for one night; after all it didn't cost too much, just around one thousand American dollars! That's not too expensive. And if he had got the room for just one day, he would make sure he stayed there the whole day and not go out, except to eat in the café or restaurant down the road where good Arab food were cheap and very tasty. And he would lie in his padded bed the whole night watching local television until he fell asleep. He knew because Ephraim had told him how he had also gone there once, but he did not stay there for the night; he went there to see how it looked like in the inside and to get the feeling of being there. He went straight to the bar and bought for himself a glass of wine, when all of a sudden there was a commotion at the entrance when some limousine stopped in the porch and many British officers swarmed the vehicles which were carrying some British dignitaries who he could not recognize. They then walked into the hotel and disappeared behind the walls leading to their rooms or suites. Ephraim then admitted he left the hotel and walked along the street then known as Julian's Way where he found a small restaurant or sidewalk café and had his lunch there because it was a lot cheaper to eat there than to have his lunch at the hotel he might not be able to afford. He had earlier told Ephraim Lieberman had died during the Second World War when he was in his late sixties and was buried in Jerusalem.

Douglas' father, Moshe said he had heard a loud blast coming from where the King David Hotel was, on 22 July, 1946 when he wrote to him a letter to describe the horror and fear everyone had when the hotel was attacked at the southwestern corner which caused chaos and confusion even at where he was at that time at his store in the Jewish Quarter. Douglas received the letter from his father at his home in Brooklyn, a few weeks later when he reported that ninety-one people died and forty-five others were badly injured in the attack which was later attributed to the Zionist paramilitary terrorist group calling themselves the Irgun Tzvail headed by Menachem Begin, after the earlier attempt by another paramilitary terrorist group called Irgun was foiled by Haganah who informed the British military authorities about it. Moshe also told his son how the Irgun paramilitary men had impersonated Arab waiters at the hotel carrying three hundred and fifty kilograms of explosives they hid in milk canisters and placed them in the hotel's coffee shop and fled the same way they entered the hotel, before anyone could take notice of them. Explosives were timed to explode at precisely at twelve-thirty-seven on that afternoon. The damage was extensive. And Ephraim, had told Moshe, he had been to the hotel more than a decade earlier and sat at the bar which was also on the spot where the bombs exploded.

And it was also near the spot at the hotel where Douglas went to and stared at the southwestern side of the hotel what had been reconstructed earlier. He said, he could only wonder what might have happened on that fateful day of 22 July, 1946, if he or his father or Ephraim were there trying to have some class and sipped some wine, they too would become victims of the aggression. Fortunately, that did not happen and he was happy that he was now able to stare at that part of the hotel that was completely destroyed by the blast that also killed ninety-nine people who happened to be inside it comprising of Arab Muslims and Christians and also Jews and some foreigners and also British. And in the 1980s, Menachem would later become a prime minister of Israel.

Douglas told me about his visit to the hotel and staring at it from a distance and fantasizing about how he should stay there if he came back to Jerusalem the next time, even if it cost him a bit to pay for the one thousand American dollars they charged, for a night's stay there. And he was also aware that in 1922 the population of the Jews in Palestine was just seventeen percent that of the Arabs and other non-Jews, but in 1948 when the state of Israel was established it had rose to thirty-three percent and had taken the matter up with me during one of our meetings on the wooden benches near the Columbia University campus, but we did not dwell on it. I mentioned how in 1948 the Apartheid state of South Africa was also established.

He said he thoroughly enjoy traveling by land from Amman in Jordan back to Jerusalem which took him three days because he decided to stop at two places along the way and he marveled at the sigh of the major cities in the Arab countries that had been developed. But he did not make it to Baghdad which had been attacked in the First Gulf War with many parts of the city destroyed completely, but the president of Iraq, Saddam Hussein were quickly rebuilding the city. I had specifically asked him to make the trip to Baghdad so he could tell me personally what he thought of it, because I remembered a painter friend of mine from Malaysia who said some painters from Malaysia were invited for an exhibition that happened just before the First Gulf War, and they left their paintings there because they were not able to have the time to take all of their works with them. So, I was told Baghdad had developed into one of the most modern cities in the Arab World, but that was not good for its enemies. And I told Douglas, who agreed with me, how most of the Arab countries were developing nicely and in no time the whole region of the Middle East would be fully developed and the Arab World, would overtake Europe in its development to become the new center of culture of the world. But this was not good for the enemies of the Arabs who had to find ways to ensure that that did not happen, so they aimed to destroy Baghdad and the other major Arab cities to turn the whole country and their people back to the stone age. And where would that leave Israel, if Baghdad and the whole of the Arab region became super modern? They would not be as what they are today. Douglas was stunned by what I had told him but he reluctantly agreed with my personal assessment. You're smart, he said; How come I or anyone had never thought of that? Because they did not study at Columbia!, he added, but without laughing because he said he said that as a matter of fact! No one had said that to me the whole time I was back in Malaysia, I told him, but as a joke! Who could say that to you in Malaysia? Why? Because everybody wanted to think they were smart, when they are not! And most of them were the elected officials some of who never even completed High School! Malaysian politics had gone to the dumps, I told him; it is a cesspool for those who had nothing to offer, but everything to gain!, I added. They have destroyed the development of the New Malaysian Cinema I had been trying to help develop for the country so that it could be a strong competitor to Hollywood that had got stuck in the old ways and no one in Hollywood had the gumption to try and be able to take it to the Post-Hollywood Era. You see, what the Entire Muslim World needed is to establish and develop their own cinema I called, the New Islamic Cinema that focused on different themes and issues and stories, those that Hollywood could never ever come up with. We have the audience in the fifty-seven Muslim countries that were in the OIC which statistics say total close to two billion inherent who have different levels of economic development and colorful history and culture that can cause many new types of stories to emerge in the form of films, documentaries and television programs. But their filmmakers were only good with the 'Monkey See, Monkey Do' mentality and to produce 'Fake Hollywood' films, I added. Didn't you know some old films produce in the Silent Era of Hollywood had Arab men in the lead, such as 'The Sheik' and 'The Son of Sheik', with Rudolf Valentino playing the lead in both the two films; and when he died most American women cried. You should do a remake of 'The Sheik', he suggested, and not as a normal film, but as a 'silent film' and in black-and-white.

Douglas was stunned by what I had just told him and I remember him freezing for a while before I heard him inhaled deeply, before saying, That makes sense.

Then he started to change the topic and asked if I had been to Makkah and performed the Hajj. I said I have been to Makkah but only performed the Minor Hajj. I was flying back from New York City to Melaysia in January, 1981 and stopped at some eleven countries one of which was Saudi Arabia and performed the Minor Hajj. How about your parents? he asked. My mother performed the Hajj with my grandfather, her father and my youngest sister, Saadiah, but my father didn't go with them. It was in 1971, I continued, and I was in Form Six studying at a private college in Petaling Jaya in Malaysia, and went to the port to send them off. And when I returned to Melaka during the school break, my father was alone in the house and he would cook. I didn't know he could cook. And he prepared some lunch and laid the dishes and rice on the table. But I did not eat anything and I did not know if I was protesting; there was this voice in my head that told me not to take it and I walked to the road side and sat in a stall and had something which was my lunch. I then returned home and my father didn't ask me where I had gone to or what I had done there, and he looked at the table and saw that the food he had cooked and laid on the table was not disturbed. He then put them dishes inside a cupboard to put them back for dinner that night. I told Douglas I always remembered this incident and I feel very sad and thought I should not have done that to my father, and I did not know how he might have felt when he saw the food he had cooked and laid on the table untouched. He might have forgotten about the incident, but it stayed with me, and each time I remembered it made me very, very sad. And where did you have dinner that night?, he asked. I think I had it at home eating the food he had cooked earlier for lunch, I replied. But that still did not absolve the sin I had committed on my father for treating him so badly by refusing to eat food he cooked and lay on the table.

And I couldn't help laughing when I wrote the email in reply to the one he had sent me earlier that said this like I could see him slumped on the bed in the hotel and all covered by a thick blanket like me who was wrapped up in the overcoat and woolen cap as I stumble to walk to the subway station further up at 116th Street which was the Columbia University subway stop. It was not easy for me having to walk on two crutches.

And I sat in the train, the Number One Local, heading south to Times Square where I had to switch to another train that would take me to Sunnyside in Queens, where Douglas would take the other train to take him back to his home in Brooklyn. And I also remembered the others that he had also mentioned to me such as Omar, his father, Munir and his Uncle Yunus and Hajji Moath who he said had died in 1920 at the ripe old age of ninety years. Of course, these were not their real names, but those I invented because Douglas or Daghlas or the strangers in Palestine I bumped into who told me tales and stories of some friends and other people they knew without ever mentioning their true names or where they were born in and grew up at, and I had to find the right places for them to live at. The notes I had written were also jumbled that some of the names were not legible even to my eyes. But I did not have any real intention to write a screenplay based on the stories I was told because they were all jumbled up with no decent or plausible plot for me to create a story with.

I remembered the Hadith, Douglas often recited to me, when I first met him in the late 1970s in New York City until I left the city to return to Malaysia in January, 1981. He didn't say it but I guessed it was his most favorite of all the Hadiths of the Prophet. I met him again in April of 1990 when my first feature film called, 'Seman: A Lost Hero' was shown in the Rivertown International Film Festival in the Twin Cities of St. Paul/Minneapolis, which I attended and I would later take the Greyhound bus from there that took one and a half days to arrive at New York City, where we planned to meet on the Columbia campus where we sat inside of Earl Hall because it was chilly outside. Why I chose to take the bus instead of fly?, he asked. Because I like to take my own sweet time to travel by land across America like I had done earlier on the Los Angeles to St. Paul/Minnesota that took two days, and during which time I could meet so many people who were mostly in the working class and sometimes, students who could not afford to fly, or once in a while some Amish folks. Didn't you also say, your film, 'Seman: A Lost Hero' was nominated for Best Film in a festival in Portugal? Yes, it was also supposed to be my Masters' thesis film, but I declined to submit it to the School because I was reluctant to graduate, by submitting it; I wanted to create a better film that would be my thesis, instead of coming out with a fifteen-minute film as my thesis, which was no thrill for me to do, I said. Many others managed to graduate by producing a ten to fifteen-minute film, but I did not find that to me exciting for me to even consider doing. I just did not want to graduate and thus severe my ties to the School and Columbia, I added. Did you attend the festival in Portugal? he asked. Yes, I did.

I was surprised that Douglas also knew about the Malaysian man who lived in Hollywood, in a house that looked like a mansion. He operated few Malaysian restaurants there and other cities selling Halal Melayu and Chinese food. He did not graduate from university where he was majoring in business studies but he did well. He returned to Malaysia and married a Chinese woman whose husband had died, who he knew before he went to America to study. She had three children; two girls and a boy who he adopted and brought all of them ot America after marrying the woman and with all of them reverting to Islam, to uplift their lives and now living glamorously. The couple then adopted two young children the man found huddled by a street in a deserted area who were Hispanics, and another two children, one a white girl and the other, a Black boy who they later found in the same fashioned. All of their adopted Chinese and white and Black children were registered as Melayu who he gave pure Melayu names instead of stylized and Anglicized ones that was favored by most of the Melayu these days. So they were Salma, Fatima, Hamza and Saleha, Salleh, Hamidah and Hamid.

Later on the man's wife gave birth to quintuplets, with three boys and two girls, and were celebrated because there had never been anyone who gave birth to five children in Hollywood before. They were truly blessed. I did not ask Douglas where he learnt about the Melayu man. I just said to myself I would go to anyone of their restaurants to have something there and see if I could bump into them. He was also from Melaka like I was. Yes, I did check the internet later and found some stories on him and his family with some photos of their children, taken after the birth of their quintuplets, so they now had a dozen children; five boys and five girls whose names started with the alphabets 'A, B, C, D and E' for Ali Samad, Badrul Hisham, Chairel Shah, Dia Rashida and Esma Yati, respectively. Nice and original names, I thought for Melayu born in America, or in Hollywood, I thought.

Yes, I told Douglas and myself that I thought it was nice for me to travel in this way, while I had the energy to do it, and I did it again in April, 1999, when my short film, 'Coming Home/Kuala Lumpur' was shown in side screening in another film festival in Taos, New Mexico and I traveled to the city also on the Greyhound from Los Angeles that took more than two days. And from there, after the festival, I went to New York City and met Douglas another time, also at Columbia which was very convenient for the two of us to meet. Douglas knew why I preferred to travel in this way, and he thought he too would do it if he had to travel anywhere in the country. So that was why he decided to travel by land from Amman in Jordan to Jerusalem, because there was a lot of scenery and places along the way to see instead of just sky one sees when flying. He then realized how he had not traveled that much the whole time he had been in America and found out he had actually never been out of New York City since he first arrived here because he thought New York City was everything, but it was not; the City is really not America. The two of us had come from so far away to come to this country, he said, and the destination was not everything; but the journey was! I had never met so many who called themselves Americans, I said, which I found only when I traveled by land and taking the bus and stopping in the middle of anywhere and nowhere, and however brief the stops were, yet, and looked a some strangers, who also looked at me, without any of us saying anything. Some had to rush to resume their trips on another bus to go somewhere, while the others could take their own time, because their transit time was long and had to even sleep on the floor of the Greyhound station through the night like I had to do once when my luggage was 'stolen' in Davenport, Iowa, and it was delivered back to me in Chicago, Illinois two days later and during which time I managed to spend some time loitering around the station. And when my luggage was found and sent back to me I found that it was broken and a brand new camera I had in it, in the box that I had wanted to give as a present to a Malaysian friend of mine in New York City, was missing.

I could add just a bit more to my conscious attempt to also learn a bit more about myself and the others, especially even from the faint to the dark shadows that never failed to follow me wherever I went, because I was nothing, I told him; I am just the shadow to the one that mostly trailed me from behind, and sometimes at the side or in front, too, depending on where I was and at what time I was at then. There were night shadows and also day shadows but the strongest ones are those that appeared around noon! Sometimes at night there are a few shadows that clashed with each other and they were in different colors and intensity, too, with some being created by lights from the streetlights and others from advertisements in neon light. Douglas thought I had gone too far in my personal description of what I felt I had become and thought. But he never at anytime thought I was crazy, because all of us had come to this country, they called America for something, to offer and to get at the same time. He didn't know what he had offered to this country. But he knew he had taken quite a bit from it.

And why I still remember seeing an elderly American couple walking hand-in-hand in a playground in Coney Island; it was not an unusual sight, except for the fact that the man was Black and his wife was White; and they were in the fifties, so I unconsciously calculated that they might have known each other in the 1940s, if they were in their twenties and got to know each other better. That was when the racial conflict and biases were still very strong, and now I was seeing an example of a couple who managed to overcome all those prejudices that forced the Blacks to rise up to demand equal rights. We did not have such racial issues in Malaysia, and even before the 1940s, there were no real issues concerning race in the country except when politics crept in with the leaders from the respective race-based parties started to inflame their voters and more so when the Malayan Communist Party or MCP appeared to try and turn the country into a Communist one and aligned itself with China and fighting using arms supplied by Communist China then, that some of the racial sentiments were highlighted. But generally all the major races in Malaysia lived peacefully before the country gained Independence or 'Merdeka' from the British on 31 August, 1957 with the eventual collapse of the MCP which later disbanded after even China was not able to continue to support it anymore.

I was okay living in America, because no one knew who I was and where I had come from; most Americans thought I was from Japan and hardly knew I was a Muslim, because I did not appear to be like one to them, like an Arab, who had to be dark and had a turban around his head and wearing long flowing robes and also sporting hair on their faces, too, which I also did not have and I was clean-shaven. So when the American couple appeared before me, I did not see them as an interracial couple, with the man who was Black and his wife, who was White, but as a reflection of what America was in the past, although the racial issues in the late 1970s were not as bad as they were back in the 1940s, when the couple might have just met and got to know each other. All I saw and as I continued to stare at the couple walk past by me and on ahead towards the small ferries wheel, I kept asking myself if that part of America was being shown to me in the form of this couple!

I remembered the last time I went up to the observatory of the Empire State Building to look at the scenery around it of the whole City of New York City with the Twin Towers in South Manhattan and marveled at it. I had been to the observatory of one of the towers, the South Tower in August, 1981 with some Malaysian friends who were studying elsewhere in America and wanted to go there, so I took them there, and that was the last time I went to the observatory of the South Tower and also to the rooftop. And from the Empire State Building where I was in April, 1999, I took a photo of the view of South Manhattan with the Twin Towers in the foreground looking small and tiny, and with the palm of my left hand stretched out to cover much of the photo, thinking to myself if the towers would be there a long time. Yes, I did think about that, and it was two years and five months before they collapsed in a pile of dirt on 9 September, 2001.

Douglas wrote a long email on his nine-hour flight on El Al back from Tel Aviv in September, 1999 after I last met him in Amman, Jordan and told me how sad he was when he was back in Jerusalem where he traveled to other cities such as Hebron, Haifa and then to Tel Aviv how there were more than two hundred thousand Holocaust survivors all of whom were in advanced age, in their seventies and eighties, and how twenty percent of them, he said, lived in squalor and each year one thousand of them died. And the situation with the Jews in Jerusalem, especially was bleak with many of them living in poverty. He never saw any of them living in poverty when he was living in that city, he said. And people, especially the Arabs Muslims and Christians seemed to have moved on to live by themselves and the Jews in the city, too, live by themselves with no direct interaction with each other in their daily social and cultural and also religious activities. There were just so many Israel security personnel and some were perched on the top of the Walled City, looking at everything that moved and he feared the whole time he was there because he could be mistaken for an Arab by the Jews and for a Jew by the Arabs, from his looks and behavior. He felt like a stranger more than a tourist, despite being born there and growing up till his adulthood. There is also no joy for me, to live in Brooklyn, he added with a tinge of sadness and regret. But I am stuck here in Brooklyn and it will be here where I will live the last few years of my life. I will take you to the plot where I will lie eternally in the Jewish Cemetery in Brooklyn, the next time you come back to New York City, hopefully for you to finally complete your Masters of Fine Art in Film Directing at Columbia University, he added.

Yes, I did come back to the City of New York and visited Columbia and met with Douglas near the campus, and I did check to verify what he had written or said earlier concerning the poverty amongst Israelis in Jerusalem and Israel and found something on it in the internet, in the reports by the local Israeli newspaper called Haaretz which was also available online on their report dated 24 April, 2014 that confirmed it which was also published by another Israeli newspaper The Jerusalem Post.

Of course Douglas had died long ago, in September, 1999 after I last met him in Ramallah Park in Amman, Jordan and after he returned to the City of New York, but somehow each time I was back in the city, I remembered him and wanted to think that I had met him again, in person and hearing him speak in his own style of English, with a strong Jewish or Hebrew accent which made him embarrassed so he would speak in it and to me in low tones, almost 'soto voce' like in a whisper. But over the years his tone rose as he became more confident speaking in English now sounding like an American that he was as a citizen of the country where he would proudly show me his American passport that said he was indeed now a full-fledged American citizen. But in his hearts, he insisted that he was still a Palestinian citizen.

And as always, and the last time I sat on the wooden bench in the middle of Broadway beside the Columbia University campus was when I returned to New York City in 2017. It was in October, and not so cold or chilly; I had been to the flea market one Sunday and bought a GPS device there and did not know where else to go; so I decided to take the train and return to the campus just to sit there before I was to fly off from La Guardia Airport to return to Malaysia, with a transit the airport at Washington for the night and from there, to fly to Xiamen in South China for a few hours transit and then finally back at the Kuala Lumpur International Airport (KLIA). I remembered what Douglas had said about Poland and the Jews there in the 1930s and 1940s or so, when the Polish would scream at them by saying, 'Kauf nicht bei Juden' and 'Juden raus' which means 'Don't buy anything from the Jews!' and 'Jews out!' That was not a nice thing to say, I thought. He explained the situation there which his father never experienced the whole of his life living in Jerusalem or his father, who was Doughlas' grandfather; but the Jews in Poland had to endure it. I remember there were small communities of Jews in Malaysia then and there were synagogues in some cities especially in Pulau Pinang or Penang and in Singaore, too, where there was a small community of them, and one of them was even elected to become a chief minister of Singapore in the 1950s even though their numbers were small. David Saul Marshall was his name; he was a lawyer or attorney who served the people, all of them, regardless of who they were and what religion they professed so he endeared himself to all who later voted him to the highest office in the state then.

I told Douglas if he or his father, Moshe were in Poland during that time, they would not be recognized as Jews from their appearance. He did not think so. You look more like Arab, I said. Yes, he said; he agreed; and he spoke good Arabic and who could write in the language well. I admitted to him that I could not write or speak in Arabic that much. But no one could tell, I was a Muslim, I said. He agreed and added how he thought when he first met me that I was not the person who he was looking for and thought I was a Japanese student at Columbia or a tourist. I admitted that, and said the whole time I was in America as a student and even when I return to the country everybody here thought I was Japanese. And don't blame the Americans for not knowing better, I said; even in Japan the locals thought I was Japanese like them. I told him of a funny situation I experienced when I participated in the first or inaugural Yamagata International Documentry Film Festival (YIDFF) that was held in Yamagta. A film crew came to me when I was sitting in the lobby of a cinema while waiting for the next film in the festival to start and there was a Japanese man with a microphone who approached me and he asked me a very, very long question in Japanese, while the camera was running and the lights were shining on me. And when he was done with his question he put his microphone near my lips and probably asked, What do you think? I just said, No Japanese. The man and his crew were stunned and I felt embarrassed. He was recording interviews for a documentary on the festival he was producing.

But when my hair was very long, some people in New York City thought I was a Native American, which I am not.

Douglas said he would sometimes wear Arabian robes and the locals in Jerusalem thought he was Arab, but those who knew him knew he was not Arab but a Jew. You wear robes sometimes?, I asked. He nodded and said especially if he goes to his Arab friends' houses or functions.

I felt like he was there sitting beside me on the wooden bench. But he had long died and I felt a sense of loss despite not being related to him or who I had known all my life, but the brief period I knew him and had communicated with him made me feel a sense of loss, which was indescribable because he was just a few Americans who I knew the whole time I was studying at Columbia and living in New York City, who understood what I was thinking and feeling. I said to myself I would visit his grave in Brooklyn before I take the Greyhound bus to go westwards stopping at San Antonio in Texas and then on to Los Angeles, California to meet some Rohingya refugees who were resettled there from Malaysia where they had lived many years where I first met them, who I often visit and occasionally take them on rides in my car.

It was quiet on campus; but there was a bit of activity outside along the sidewalk beside it with temporary stalls selling a host of things. I bought an old book or novel for five American dollars called 'Garden of Allah' I promised to read when I am back in Malaysia. I then sat on the wooden bench and felt cold with the wood having been exposed to the cold winds that slowly became warm the more I sat on it. I tried to remember the late Douglas. I had not met his sons, Michael and Aaron; but I had only seen his photos their late father showed me on his phone. We had started to communicate more with the phone now that there is Wi-Fi and the internet and Whatsapp devices that were cheap to use. I did not want to think anymore; I just wanted to sit still and let the few people, strangers who passed in front of me think I was there as a street performer. I looked like one. A few turned to look at me as they walked past by me and I ignored them. I did not want them to enter my space and study what I might be thinking. I knew they could not go anywhere near them, other than to guess how I might be a tourist, because I looked like one with a digital camera I was holding and a camcorder whose strap was strung around my neck and also a sketch book sitting on the bench that was bare and not been written on. There was nothing for me to sketch. Broadway was almost bare with traffic and occasionally the buses would drive northwards or southwards; and there was a Halal cart at the junction where I said to myself I would go to later to have a kebab for lunch and soda or mineral water. The Bangladeshi man who operated the cart knew me because I had been there a few times on this trip to the city to get Halal food from.

16

Postscript

Did I have actually met Douglas a.k.a. Daghlas in person, and most of those I written about meeting them? I'm not quite sure. Maybe... maybe not! Does it matter?

Mahmud mentioned Tani Yataka who he said was shot by the British. He was wrong. Tani died because of malaria in Johor and was buried in the Japanese Cemetery in Singapore. And not long later a Japanese film company produced a film on him called, 'Tiger of Malaya' which I managed to watch on Youtube. And surprisingly, he was not a bandit and called 'Tiger' for no reason other than the fact that his sister was raped by some Chinese in Melayu Peninsula who took revenge against the Japanese in the country then when the Japanese forces invaded Mongolia and killed many Chinese there. Tani went out on a killing spree and managed to kill some Chinese as revenge for raping his sister. This was what I had of him thus far, and the true story may not be as what I knew then. But was fascinated me the most with this character was how he reverted to Islam and liked to wear Melayu clothes called 'baju Melayu' like what Mahmud also wore when he went on his pilgrimage to Mekkah and he even gave a set to Moath who wore it with pride and to thrill his fellow Palestinians who had not seen any Arab man wearing such clothes that also looked decent and 'shariah-complaint' too, that covered his body except that the 'baju Melayu' top was matched with loose pants that Moath did not wear, other than the top only.

But I had wanted to sit on the wooden benches in the middle of the road beside the Columbia University campus because it surely wouldn't look odd if I had done that, and besides the benches were there for anyone to use anyway. I also had never had any conversation with my own shadows, or knew anyone who had done so. The only thing that I had done and quite often was to watch my shadows following me on the pavement, sidewalks, or at the side or in front of me, or on the walls as I was walking; and I also took some shots of it. Sometimes they are short and other times, they are very long, depending on what time it is. Most of them are shot in the day but there are some shot in the night that are more dramatic because they are created by artificial streetlights and neon from the advertisements which change in color.

Did I also imagine I had gone to study at Columbia University, because it was not difficult for anyone to say so? And have I also gone to New York City or America before, or I had just seen photos of them in calendars my late father liked to hang on the walls of his house in Melaka Town, and I would stare at those photos of countries such as America that had winter; and winter to me would not be good or right if there was no snow and ice, and imagined I had been there and many times before?

I took out my cell phone to take a photo of the scene in front of me, the wide street called Broadway that stretched from all the way south of Manhattan to the north that was the only street that did not go straight but sideward reaching beyond the Columbia University campus, passing through the theater district in Midtown, and snapped a few shots, that showed nothing interesting except the street and nothing on it. I wanted to record not the street but what I might be thinking at that time. I then looked at my Gmail account and found an old email I had saved to the 'Personal' file and saw one I received from Douglas which I wanted to save to read when I felt like it; and now was such a time. It was on the 1884 Berlin Conference that I had not known of before. Douglas said he wanted me to check it out, a file he found in the internet. It was interesting the more I read it. It was also known as Congo Conference or 'Kongokonferenz' in German or West Africa Conference or 'Westafrika-Konferenz' in German and it was organized by Otto von Bismarck, first Chancellor of Germany. And to put it simply, it was the formalization of the Scramble for Africa. Scramble? I liked the word, like the whole of the Continent of Africa was useless and it was up for grabs with the people and their history of no significance to the Europeans who only looked at them at inferior beings and the natural resources the countries in the continent had were up for grab by anyone of the countries in Europe. Pitiful! Utterly disgusting! Remarked Douglas who I thought would be rolling in his grave in the Beth Olam Jewish Cemetery in Brooklyn right then, if he knew I was checking the last email he had sent me not quite moments before he died, but in the last hour or two before he did die. I could hear him shriek. He had taken me to this place the last time I was in the City and Borough and he showed me some graves of Jews like him who had come from Jerusalem and other cities in Palestine, some of them who were younger than he was. He was still agile then and was able to walk the long distance we had to walk in the wide cemetery. He then realized why I was limping and asked to stop for some rest while he checked more graves of other Jews who were not familiar to him because they had changed their names from Jewish ones to English ones, like he also did when he changed his name from Daghlas to Douglas. He had forgotten how I had three surgeries on my left knee due to the Giant Cell tumor of the Upper Left Tibia suffered from that I had explained to him once or twice before, except that now I was not on the two crutches I was on before for ambulation. And I did have a limp when I walked with the two crutches. Only then did I realize that he too had a limp when he walked but it was due to the sprain he experienced when he tripped to the side while walking on uneven ground that was partially covered with snow. But I never took it as another way to change the topic of our discussion. I am going on with age, he suddenly said, and added with a question that I did not least expect was when he asked why I had donated blood so many times. I had donated blood mostly when I was in Malaysia and at that time I had donated more than four hundred and fifty times! Really?, he asked. I just nodded and said I started to donate blood when I was in Form Six in Malaysia, or High School as they said it in America. But I was forced to stop for fifteen to sixteen years because of the surgery when I had to take antibiotic, and had forgotten to do it until 1994 when I started to resume doing that. I wished I had the courage to donate blood as frequently like you are doing, except that I feared being punctured by a needle in my arm, he added.

Hmmm…that's one hundred and five years before the fall of the Berlin Wall in 1989, he said. It was a year after I went to Germany to attend the Mannheim Short Film Festival where I also visited Frankfurt and Munich, but I didn't get any whiff on what was going to happen in Berlin, I added.

I did not know that, until so late in our relationship that he had an Arabic name or nickname that was given by his Arab friends when they were small. Want to know?, he asked. Naturally I was intrigued and started to guess but it was not easy. It could be anything. Majid, he said. Majid? And you know what Majid means? No. And you know what your name, Mansor means in Arabic? No. Majid means 'Glorious' or 'Magnificent' and Mansor means 'Glorious' too, or 'One who is glorious'. I was quite amazed. I had never attempted to translate my name from Arabic to know what it means in English. Now, I know. One of my elder brothers is called Majid, I said. You will be glorious, he added. You have a long road ahead of you, while I have arrived at my destination at my life's end, right here in Brooklyn and New York City, while you have been to forty countries and you are still searching and traveling and wanting to know more of yourself as much as the world. I admire you. But at the same time, I pity you, too, he added, sounding sorrowful which also made me quite guilty with myself for not having done much or anything significant since I returned to Malaysia from New York City after attending Columbia. I knew they were mighty proud of me when they first heard I was going to study at Columbia University in the City of New York. Why do I prefer to say City of New York instead of New York City because there is a nice ring to the former than the later that sounded not so right. I agree, added Douglas, er…Majid which I started to call him by this name. And I could see it also thrilled him. Why? Because the name in just two short syllables, could trigger in him a lot, especially the times when he was in Jerusalem and mixing with his buddies in the village outside of Jerusalem which included many Arab Muslims and Christians and also Jews who shared the same fate and future and common goals to be happy together. But fate was not on their side, when one by one they group became fractured and few of the Jews including him, started to leave Jerusalem and Palestine to come to New York City, er…the City of New York where they never made any attempt to gang up. They were grown-ups who had different vocations and goals and families of their own to look after, in a strange city and country they had scant knowledge on what to expect; and their only goals were too selfish to mention or discuss. You come to the city as a student then and now as a visitor; I am here by force, he said.

And he did not say it but I could guess how difficult it was for him to learn how to speak in English, a language he did not know of before he came to the city, and in the 1960s, he had to face discrimination and civil unrest and saw with his own eyes some ugly incidents that happened in Brooklyn. But the worst happened in Harlem, he said. He had never been there and he was warned not to go there or anywhere near there. So he perched over the hill beside the Columbia University campus, at Morningside Park to see the whole of the district of Harlem spread before him. Here everybody who lived here were Blacks. I told him I had gone there in 1978 and found it to be very quiet with not much economic activity and there was only one grocery store operated by a non-Black, a South Korean couple. But over the years, more and more white folks ventured into the area to buy properties so the last time I was there in 2017, I noticed tremendous changes to it with so many white folks coming and enjoying food in the restaurants and the sidewalks had a lot of stores and people of all shapes and colors milling on them. I also told Douglas, in fact, there were so few Black students at Columbia when I was studying there but there are so many of them now, which is good. Douglas admitted that he had problems communicating with the locals who mostly spoke in English, but with thick Italian or Spanish accents. So he only chose to speak in Hebrew with fellow Jews and sometimes in Arabic too. It took him a long while before he dared himself to start to speak in English and even till now he spoke it with a thick accent, with his vocabulary limited. But I told him, I could understand what he said. 'Shukran', he said, which means 'Thank you' in Arabic. His children, however, and the children of all his friends who came from Palestine and other countries in Europe and Russia, spoke good English in the American accent that they learnt since small, especially those who were born in the city and country. Unfortunately, many of them were not able to speak in Hebrew or Arabic like him and their parents who did.

And what made me feel very sad was when he said, I miss Jerusalem. I miss Palestine very much'. He would prefer to be buried in his family plot in Jerusalem but that would not be possible. He was born and grew up as a Palestinian Jew but would die as an American citizen, he said. He still keeps his Palestinian passport that he used to go to America with, and he only got his American passport much later when he wanted to return to Palestine or Israel by flying to Europe and traveling by land to Jerusalem and flying back from Ben Gurion Airport in Tel Aviv on El Al back to Kennedy Airport in Queens, New York City. He remembered when he fled from Jerusalem it was few years after the killing of sixty Jews in Hebron in 1928 by a group of Palestinian Arab-Muslim men whose emotions were fired by the fiery speeches by one Hajji Amin Al-Hussein who had returned from his studies at the Al-Azhar University in Cairo, Egypt. It was also before the heights of the Holocaust with the Nazis exterminating Jews as they saw fit. Hajji Amin had called for the curtailing of the immigration of Jews from Europe and Russia because he feared not only Jerusalem or Baitulmukaddis, as he called the city, but the whole of Palestine would be swamped by them.

Of course Douglas did not tell me in details on what happened in Hebron in 1928 and the Holocaust which I learnt on my won by reading books on them and also from the information I could get at the finger tips, in my phone, wherever I was especially when I was traveling in the Greyhound buses going from one city to the other in America, or when I was in the food stalls in Malaysia where I used to frequent, to have snacks at and to meet friends as it was very convenient for us to meet there.

Then there was silence; a long pause. I did not know what I was thinking. Douglas tried to find something else to talk about but there was nothing that came into his head. The two of us than sat on a bench in the cemetery and all around us were graves of many unknown people who had died over the years since the cemetery was opened many years ago. There are some vacant plots left for some others. It must be peaceful here, said Douglas. I like the neighborhood. Was he trying to crack a joke? I did not want to think so. I also did not want to think he had grown too old. I also did not want to think I was not that young anymore like I was when I first came to the City of New York in 1978 at the tender age of twenty-five!

Did I reply to the email that Douglas had sent me then? I must have done so and did not receive any reply and was later told he had died. So I could not say if he had received the reply I sent him, when I said how I was also shocked with the report on the Berlin Conference, too which was probably what he had expected me to say.

There are many other things I had wanted to write down, to remember Douglas by, but I had to choose which. I took him inside the Columbia University campus where he said he visited for the first time despite having been outside of it many times. He said he did not have the guts to go inside to step on the campus grounds where he thought he did not belong. I told him there were many people who were born outside of the campus and who grew up to become adults and died, but who never once entered the campus to step on the campus grounds. We stopped in the middle of the College Plaza, and to the south was the Butler Library building and to the north was the Low Library which was the administrative building and beside it was Dodge Hall, where the School of the Arts was and on the fifth floor is the Film Division where I studied at, I told him. I mentioned how on 14 May, 1981 I had come here to stand at almost the same spot as the two of us now were, to come to the Commencement ceremony but after it was done. I told him normally it was done on 13 May, but on this day in 1981, Pope John-Paul II was shot in the Vatican and Columbia decided to postpone the Commencement for that year to the next day. I also mentioned to

Douglas how I had seen a notable Palestinian intellectual and thinker, Edward Said, a Palestinian-Arab-Christian walking into the campus and on to the College Plaza to see the post-Commencement crowd thinning and the statue of the Alma Mater sitting on a chair frozen on the steps of the Low Library which was the main focus of many students or former students now alumni of the university posing photos with their friends or former classmates and relatives where other students and their relatives were sitting, to stare at the sight of the campus in its wide vista probably for the last time before the walk out of the university and never to return, if they lived or were going to find employment far away from it and the City of New York; more so for the foreign students who had to fly back to where they had come from. I also told Douglas I never failed to return to the campus each time I am back in the city, for leisure or some work that I had to do here in America.

Douglas did not say a word to respond or react to my commentary on the university and campus, and the design and also how this campus was in fact constructed in the 1920s at the height of the Great Depression being funded by money from the Mob! It was money being put to good use, I remarked. He nodded a bit. I wanted to feel how he was feeling at that time, being able to be inside of the campus. He then said something about how everybody can enter Columbia, but not many can actually graduate…because the gates are flung wide open in the day. I gave that statement or thought some thought of my own and found it to be profound and looked at the statue of the Alma Mater sitting behind him with her arms flung open.

I then took out three DVDs of my documentaries I worked on which caused me to return to America and hence, New York City and Columbia with the titles of 'A Crossed Amerika', 'Rohingya Kissa' or 'Rohingya Tales' and another one on the Tsunami of Aceh of December, 2004 called 'Aceh Does Not Believe in Tears' for him to watch at his own leisure or keep as a memento from me. It was in exchange for the DVD of Tel Aviv and Jerusalem he gave me, which he said he bought in one of the stalls in the Muslim Quarter in the Old City in Jerusalem.

Few days later, I returned to Columbia where I wanted to buy some Columbia University sweaters or tee-shirts, and bought some, where I saw some photos of distinguished alumni of the university hung on the walls and pillars one of which was of former American President Barack Hussein Obama and took a photo of myself standing in front of it with his photo in the background.

I then went out of the bookstore and sat on the steps near where Douglas and I were standing at few days ago, and looked at the photo of me with Barack in my cell phone and flicked to other photos and got to one of me with Douglas I shot with the Alma Mater in the background. But we never got to going to Astoria in the Borough of Queens in the City together after I told him I had stayed at an apartment there as a student for a few months, when I said it was a quiet place in 1981 to 1981 when I was there, but now it was busy and there were even two Islamic centers there with many restaurants offering Halal food operated by Pakistanis and Bangladeshis, and there were now more Muslims in this area than locals and non-Muslims, and the 'Five Corners Deli' near my former apartment in Astoria, too had changed hands, now operated by Arabs, the last time I was there and asked and the upholstery repair store at 21st Street at 26th Road that was once operated by a friend of mine, a fellow Malaysian who had come to the city in the 1960s and stayed on to open the store where there were few other Malaysians students some with their wives and children living in the same area with a family living in the apartment building as I was which I was sharing with another graduate or alum of Mara Institute of Technology (ITM) in Shahalam, Malaysia where I had graduated from with my degree in Advertising. I also knew of Jalid who was working with famed American architects such as Isamu Nogouchi and Buckminsterfuller who had their studio-office nearby which I visited when he was working with them. And after the two architects died, their studio-office was turned into the Isamu Nogouchi Museum that housed some of his pieces which I also visited when I was back in the city and neighborhood in April, 1990, when Haron Sihat was still there who took over our apartment in Astoria, where I would squat a few days. During the summer, all of the Malaysians living in our area in Astoria would go to the park to cook 'satay' or a dish or seasoned, skewed and grilled meat that is put in pieces a row in a thin stick, and fried, and we would eat some with peanut and sweet chilly sauce in the park. Some of our American friends came and sampled them and they were delighted to learn of its unique taste that also tingled their buds. I was not into cooking so I busied myself taking photos of the others. I wanted to take Douglas to an Indonesian restaurant in the city to get him to taste a bit of 'satay', but we never got to doing that.

But Wahab later sold it and it is now a convenience store with a restaurant in it when he finally decided after more than twenty years, to return back to Malaysia with his family. He was not surprised; he said there were also many Arabs and other Muslims in his area in Brooklyn, or everywhere in the city, he added. He thought it was lovely for such people to be there now, because they made him feel like he was back in Jerusalem when he was a small boy till he was a young man, before he fled from the city to come to Brooklyn. Most of the Arabs and other Muslims including the Rohingyas were forced to flee from their countries because of civil war and attacks launched against their countries by foreign forces which wanted their oil and which did not want to see those Arab countries prosper, he said. I was stunned by that statement, especially coming from him, and from someone who I did not think was critical of anything other than of himself, who he often said was 'a piece of humanity that did not deserve to live on this earth'. He said he did not mean to demean himself and all that he wanted to say was, he felt like a sand particle in the whole of the 'Sahawrah'. Sahawrah?, I asked. He used the Arab word and pronunciation for the Sahara Desert because it was how he knew it, and never knew its English version because he said he did not like the sound of it. I checked the internet and found out that the word 'Sahara' or 'Sahawrah' means 'Dawn' in Arabic. And not once did we discuss the Holocaust or the deaths of the many Armenian and the Al-Nakbah or 'Dispossession' of the Palestinians that happened in 1948 when seven hundred thousand of them were forced to flee from their country to go into exile in the neighboring Arab countries. Douglas only said he was lucky that he was not in Jerusalem or Palestine by then and he heard and read about it in Brooklyn, and felt sorry for them, some of who were his friends, too. But I could feel deep inside of him that he felt sad, very sad with the two tragedies and the others that happened in Europe and also in America with the Black slavery and the founding of America.

And the last time I returned to the City of New York, in 2017, I sat on the wooden bench outside of the Columbia campus near 114th Street along Broadway trying to free my mind and to remember Douglas who would be here sitting beside me, if he was healthy and able to come all the way from his home in Brooklyn. But he would be too old to even walk and was at least ninety years years! See, I never got to ask his age, as it was not me to ask anyone's personal questions; and he also never asked me personal questions. I also never knew his wife or children, except that perhaps or most likely he had married someone in Brooklyn who might be from Jerusalem like him, too, or a local-born Jew. How many children they had? I did not know. I had also never been to his house. We met outside in the streets and sometimes in a halal restaurant in Brooklyn or Manhattan or halal food we got from food carts there. And I would soon go to one at the junction near where I was to get some halal food they sold.

And I remembered the Hadith or Sayings of the Prophet Muhammad, (p.b.u.h.) liked to read, before and even when I met him the last time in Amman, Jordan in the late 1990s and the few times we sat on the same wooden bench I was sitting now, where we would talk and sometimes have food from the Halal cart at the junction, which he could read in the original Arabic style in such a perfect fashion that it never failed to stun me. He also said he had the calligraphy of the Sayings of the Prophet written by his own hand when he was a young boy and in Arabic and in a beautiful style, hung on the wall of his bedroom in his parents' house in Jerusalem and then in the living room of his rental house or apartment, as they said it here in the City of New York, which he later hung in his own house he bought for him and his family to live in, after saving enough money to buy it and in cash. He showed me the calligraphy that he had saved in his cell phone and I asked him to forward it to me.

So when I got back to Malaysia, I printed it in the A+3 size and had it framed in thick wood to hang in my bedroom so I could see it everyday to not only remember him, but also what it says. Did he say, if he died, he would like this Saying of the Prophet be inscribed in his tombstone and in Arabic and the Hebrew translation of it? No, it was not, as I would find out when I went to his grave to 'meet' him again. His relatives did not know what he had wanted; he only told me once and even that was done in passing. And I then thought he was just not serious although he was not joking.:

* * * * * * *

'Whoever among you sees an evil action,
let him change it with his hand (by taking action);
if he cannot, then with his tongue (by speaking out);
and if he cannot, then with his heart (by at least
hating it and believing that it is wrong), and that is
the weakest of faith.'
(Narrated by Muslim in his 'Saheeh'.)

* * * * * * *

Ends.

Made in the USA
Middletown, DE
18 December 2021

56460497R00235